STREET LAW

A COURSE IN PRACTICAL LAW

second edition

With
California State
Supplement

From The National Institute for Citizen Education in the Law
and West Publishing Company

STREET LAW

A COURSE IN PRACTICAL LAW

second edition

With California State Supplement

Lee P. Arbetman, M.Ed., J.D.
Adjunct Professor of Law
Georgetown University Law Center

Edward T. McMahon, M.Ed., J.D.
Adjunct Professor of Law
Georgetown University Law Center

Edward L. O'Brien, J.D.
Adjunct Professor of Law
Georgetown University Law Center

A Publication of the National Institute
for Citizen Education in the Law

West Publishing Company
St. Paul   New York   Los Angeles   San Francisco

Photo credits on p. 364.

Copyright © 1975 by WEST PUBLISHING CO.
Copyright © 1980 by WEST PUBLISHING CO. — Second Edition
Copyright © 1984 by WEST PUBLISHING COMPANY —
                    Second Edition With California State Supplement

WEST PUBLISHING CO.
50 W. Kellogg Blvd.
P.O. Box 64526
St. Paul, MN 55165-9979

Reprinted from *Street Law: A Course in Practical Law,* Second Edition

Printed in the United States of America

Library of Congress Cataloging in Publication Data

Nazario, Thomas A.
  Street law.

  SUMMARY: A textbook of California law for high school students, designed to give practical advice, knowledge, and skills in understanding state laws and how they affect daily life.
  1. Law—California—Popular works. [1. Law—California. 2. Life skills. 3. Consumer education] 1. Arbetman, Lee. Street law. 2nd ed. 11. Title.

KFC81.N39 1984	349.794'07'12	84-11914
ISBN 0-314-84398-1	347.9400712	

dedication

The writing of this book was in large measure supported and encouraged by the Robert F. Kennedy Memorial, an organization founded to challenge America's disadvantaged and its youth to affect the world in which they live, and to shape a better life for themselves and others. This book is dedicated to Robert Kennedy's ideals and to the people he served.

THE NATIONAL INSTITUTE FOR CITIZEN EDUCATION IN THE LAW

The National Institute for Citizen Education in the Law is an outgrowth of a Georgetown University program started in 1971 in which law students teach law courses in District of Columbia high schools, in juvenile and adult correctional institutions, and in a number of community based programs.

The Institute was created to promote increased opportunities for citizen education in law and is involved in course development, teacher training, and program replication. Other activities of the Institute include the provision of technical assistance and curriculum materials to law schools, school systems, departments of corrections, juvenile justice agencies, bar associations, legal service organizations, community groups, state and local governmental units, and others interested in establishing law-education programs.

The Institute is under the direction of a National Advisory Committee comprised of prominent individuals from the fields of law, education and public affairs. The Institute staff includes individuals with experience in both law and education.

For further information or assistance, please contact

The National Institute for Citizen Education in the Law
605 G Street, N.W.
Washington, D.C. 20001
(202) 624-8217

CONTENTS

one

INTRODUCTION TO LAW AND THE LEGAL SYSTEM · 2

CRIMINAL AND JUVENILE JUSTICE · 32

CONSUMER LAW · 102

FAMILY LAW · 166

HOUSING LAW · 218

INDIVIDUAL RIGHTS AND LIBERTIES · 270

PREFACE

This second edition of *Street Law: A Course in Practical Law* builds upon the success and popularity of the first edition. Incorporating the best features of the original text, this second edition provides new information, practical advice, and competency building activities designed to provide students with the ability to analyze, evaluate, and in some situations resolve legal disputes. The text reflects the changes in law and legal procedure that have taken place at the national level, since the appearance of the first edition. However, it should be noted that law varies, in some instances significantly, from state to state. Thus it should be emphasized that this is a textbook and not a substitute for the legal advice that can only be provided by a member of the Bar.

Street Law's approach to law-related education is to provide practical information and problem-solving opportunities which develop in students the knowledge and skills necessary for survival in our law-saturated society. The curriculum includes activities such as case studies, mock trials, roleplays, small group exercises, opinion polls and visual analysis activities. For optimal use, Street Law also requires the use of community resource persons (e.g., lawyers and police) and community experiences (e.g., court tours and police ride-alongs). This educational methodology requires that students be active participants in their own learning. In this way we hope to promote in students a willingness and capability to participate effectively in the legal and political system.

The text can be used as the basis of a separate elective course. In addition, selected chapters can be used in one-semester courses or short mini-courses, or materials can be selectively infused into existing government, civics, history, or economics courses. This student text is accompanied by a comprehensive teacher's manual.

ACKNOWLEDGMENTS

Development of this second edition of Street Law was assisted through the financial support of the Law Enforcement Assistance Administration's Office of Juvenile Justice and Delinquency Prevention and the Robert F. Kennedy Memorial.

Over the years many organizations have helped make the work of The National Institute for Citizen Education in the Law possible. We gratefully acknowledge their support here:

Cummins Engine Foundation
District of Columbia Department of Corrections
Eugene and Agnes Meyer Foundation
Federal Bureau of Prisons
Field Foundation
General Mills Foundation
Georgetown University Law Center
Hattie M. Strong Foundation
Law Enforcement Assistance Administration
Lawyers' Wives of the District of Columbia
National Home Library Foundation
National Institute of Corrections
New World Foundation
Public Schools of the District of Columbia
Robert F. Kennedy Memorial
Weyerhaeuser Foundation, Inc.

Many law students, attorneys, and educators have made significant contributions to the development of this book. They have provided valuable research, editorial suggestions, encouragement, inspiration, and criticism. We would like to thank the following persons who have worked closely with us in this effort:

Elizabeth Allendorfer, David Austern, Johnny Barnes, Lenore Cameron, Elisabeth Dreyfuss, Milly Durovic, David Esber, Robert Fallon, Louis Fischer, Larry Fox, Ron Gerlach, Grayfred Gray (and his colleagues at the University of Tennessee School of Law), James H. Heller, Pamela Hershinson, Sandra Johnson, Joel Joseph, Cindy Kelly, Richard Kobliner, Suzanne Kobliner, John Kramer, Adrienne Lever, Joanne Levine, Eleanor Roberts Lewis, Tony Magnon, Margo McKay, James McKenna, Rick Miller, Wallace Mlyniec, Wayne Moore, Phillip S. Morgan, Ira Nerken (and his colleagues at the Federal Trade Commission), Peggy O'Brien, Lee Reno, Jack Sheuermann, Francis Smith, Gail Sorenson, Dean Thomson, and David Wilmot.

In particular we would like to thank David Harris from the Oakland County, Michigan, Schools whose wit and wisdom helped keep us on the track, and Isidore Starr, often called the "father of law-related education," who read every word we wrote with attention to all of our shortcomings, from commas to concepts.

We are also grateful for the assistance provided to us by our colleagues and friends at The National Institute for Citizen Education in the Law: Mary Curd, Margaret Fisher, Pat McGuire, and Richard Roe. Their legal, educational, and editorial advice was invaluable. A special thanks to Loretta Moss who typed and retyped endless drafts with remarkable skill, patience, and understanding. We also wish to extend our gratitude to Angela Brown, Annie Cole, and Hattie Johnson for their typing of the Institute's work and doing all the other things that keep us above water.

While this list does not include the hundreds of law students and teachers who evaluated the first edition and helped field-test portions of the second edition, we very much appreciate their input and encouragement. To the extent that that this edition is an improved tool for teaching about the law, much credit must go to these imaginative, inspiring instructors.

We also feel a special debt to law-related education project personnel throughout the country who have given us much guidance and direction and who have encouraged and facilitated the use of the Street Law curriculum. We hope this edition continues to merit their support.

Jason Newman, Director
Edward O'Brien, Co-Director
Lee Arbetman
Edward McMahon

Washington, D.C.
May, 1980

STREET LAW

A COURSE IN PRACTICAL LAW

second edition

**With
California State
Supplement**

one
INTRODUCTION
TO LAW
AND THE
LEGAL SYSTEM

Street law is the concept of educating people about law that will be of practical use to them in their everyday lives (on the streets). Every purchase, lease, contract, marriage, divorce, crime, or traffic violation places the citizen face to face with the law. Thus, *Street Law* is designed to provide you with an understanding of your legal rights and responsibilities, a knowledge of everyday legal problems, and the ability to analyze, evaluate, and, in some situations, resolve legal disputes.

Many people believe that only those with power and money can win in our legal system. They see the law as a body of confusing, abstract, and technical rules that work against them. Some people would never believe, for example, that a tenant could get a court to make a landlord fix up a rundown apartment, or that a consumer could force a merchant to repair, replace, or give a refund for poor quality merchandise. It is true that these things do not always happen, but they are possible, especially when tenants or consumers are aware of their rights and take action to exercise those rights.

Besides addressing general problems in the areas of criminal, consumer, family, housing, and individual rights law, the text will

3

discuss many specific situations: what to do if you are arrested; when and how to select an attorney; what the legal rights and responsibilities between parents and children are; how to register to vote; and what to do about discrimination or any other violation of your constitutional rights. These and all of the topics covered in *Street Law* are designed to help you survive on the street.

WHAT IS LAW?

The answer to the question "What is law?" has troubled people for many years. In fact, an entire field of study known as **jurisprudence** is devoted to answering this question. Many definitions of law exist, but for our purposes, law can be defined as that set of rules or regulations by which a government regulates the conduct of people within a given society. Even with this explanation, many other questions arise. Where do laws come from? Do we need laws? Are all laws written? Can laws change? If so, how? Are all laws fair? What is the difference between law and morals?

In studying about the law, we often consider the relationship of law to morals. Our legal system is influenced by traditional ideas of right and wrong. Thus, most people would condemn murder, regardless of what the law said. However, everything that is considered immoral is not necessarily illegal. For example, lying to a friend may be immoral but would rarely be illegal.

One thing that is certain is that every society that has ever existed has recognized the need for some law. These laws may not have been written, but even primitive people had rules to regulate the conduct of the group. Without laws, there would be confusion, fear, and disorder. This is not to say that all of our existing laws are fair or even good; but imagine how people might take advantage of one another without some set of rules.

PROBLEM 1

Make a list of all your daily activities (e.g., waking up, eating, going to school). Next to each item in the list indicate whether there are any laws affecting that activity. Are these laws federal laws, state laws, or local laws? What are the purposes or functions of the laws that you have identified? Would you change any of these laws? Why?

KINDS OF LAWS

Laws fall into two major groups, criminal and civil. Criminal laws regulate public conduct and set out duties owed to society. A

THE CASE OF THE SHIPWRECKED SAILORS

While working as sailors on an ocean-going freighter, three young men were cast adrift in a life raft after their ship sank during a storm in the Atlantic Ocean. The ship went down so suddenly that there was no time to send out an S.O.S. As far as the three sailors knew, they were the only survivors. In the raft they had no food or water, and they had no fishing gear or other equipment which they might use to get food from the ocean.

After recovering from the initial shock of the shipwreck, the three sailors began to discuss their situation. Dudley, who had been the navigator of the ship, figured that they were at least 1,000 miles from land and that the storm had blown them far from where any ships would normally pass. Stephens, who had been the ship's doctor, indicated that without food they could not live longer than thirty days. The only nourishment they could be assured of was from any rain that might fall from time to time. He noted, however, that if one of the three died before the others, the other two could live for awhile longer by eating the body of the third.

On the twenty-fifth day, the third sailor, Brooks, who by this time was extremely weak, suggested that the three of them draw lots and that the loser be killed and eaten by the other two. Both Dudley and Stephens agreed. The next day lots were drawn and Brooks lost. At this point, Brooks objected and refused to consent. However, Dudley and Stephens decided that Brooks would die soon anyway, so they might as well get it over with. After thus agreeing, they killed and ate Brooks.

Five days later, Dudley and Stephens were rescued by a passing ship and brought to port. After recovering from their ordeal, they were placed on trial for murder.

The state in which they were tried had the following law: Any person who deliberately takes the life of another is guilty of murder.

PROBLEM 2

a. Should Dudley and Stephens be tried for murder?
b. As an attorney for Dudley and Stephens, what arguments would you make on their behalf? As an attorney for the state, what arguments would you make on the state's behalf?
c. If they are convicted, what should their punishment be?
d. What purpose would be served by convicting Dudley and Stephens?
e. What is the relationship between law and morality in this case? Was it morally wrong for Dudley and Stephens to kill Brooks? Explain your answer.
f. Can someone act legally but immorally? Can an act be morally right but unlawful?

criminal case is a legal action by a state or federal government against a person charged with committing a crime. Criminal laws have penalties requiring that offenders be imprisoned, fined, placed under supervision, or punished in some other way. Criminal offenses are divided into **felonies,** for which the maximum penalty is a term of more than one year in prison, and **misdemeanors,** for which the penalty is a prison term of one year or less.

Civil laws regulate relations between individuals or groups of individuals. A **civil action** (lawsuit) can be brought when one person feels wronged or injured by another person. Courts may award the injured person money to make up for his or her loss or it may order the person who committed the wrong to make other amends (to do or not to do a specific act). An example of a civil action is a lawsuit for recovery of damages suffered as the result of an automobile accident. Civil law attempts to resolve many other problems as well, such as disputes arising out of marriage or divorce, the sale of goods and services, the rental or sale of homes and apartments, the use of energy or the environment, and interpretations of the constitution.

Sometimes one action can violate both civil and criminal law. For example, if Joe beats up Bob, he may have to pay Bob's medical bills under civil law and may be charged with the crime of assault under criminal law.

PROBLEM 3

Matt and Luther decide to skip school. They take Luther's brother's car without telling him and drive to a local shopping center. Ignoring the sign "Parking for Handicapped Persons Only," they leave the car and enter a radio and TV shop.

After looking around they buy a portable AM–FM radio. Then they buy some sandwiches from a street vendor and walk to a nearby park. While eating they discover that the radio does not work. In their hurry to return it, they leave their trash on the park bench.

When Matt and Luther get back to the shopping center, they cut through the parking lot, where they notice a large dent in one side of their car. The dent appeared to be the result of a driver carelessly backing out of the next space. They also notice that the car has been broken into and that the tape deck has been removed.

They call the police to report the accident and theft. When the police arrive to investigate, they seize a small clear bag containing illegal drugs from behind the car's back seat. Matt and Luther are arrested.

a. What laws are involved in this story?

b. Which of these are criminal laws? Which are civil laws?

WHO MAKES LAWS?

Three different lawmaking groups exist in the United States: (1) legislatures, (2) agencies, and (3) courts. Legislatures pass laws directly, agencies develop laws that help put legislative rulings into effect, and courts establish laws as a result of case decisions.

Legislatures

The U.S. Constitution divides the power for making laws between the national government and the governments of the individual

states. Thus, the government of the United States has the power to pass laws called federal laws that are binding on the citizens of every state. In addition, every state has the power to pass laws that apply within that particular state.

The lawmaking authority of Congress is exercised by the passing of laws called federal **statutes**. Federal statutes affect every citizen and concern such issues as national defense, environmental quality, labor relations, veterans' affairs, public health, civil rights, economic development, postal services, and federal taxes.

America is also a nation of states. Every state has a constitution, which spells out the basic structure of state government, including an executive, legislative, and judicial branch. The lawmaking powers of the state are vested in the state legislature, which can pass state statutes. Except for Nebraska, every state has a two-house legislature. In most states the legislature meets on an annual basis to pass laws affecting the state. In the remaining states, the legislatures meet every two years.

Besides the U.S. Congress and the state legislatures, there are other legislative or lawmaking bodies, which are found on the local level in cities, towns, and counties. Local governments pass laws that may be called **ordinances** or **regulations** that apply only within a particular city or town.

Although these different legislatures have the power to pass laws affecting many aspects of our daily lives, all lawmaking—federal, state, and local—is limited by the U.S. Constitution. The Constitution sets out the structure of our government and establishes the basic rights of all Americans. If a legislature passed a law that violated one of these basic rights, such as the freedom of speech, citizens could go to court and ask that that law be overruled. The process by which courts decide whether the laws passed by Congress or state or local legislatures are constitutional is known as **judicial review**.

PROBLEM 4

Consider each of the following laws. Is it a federal, state, or local law?

a. "No parking on the east side of Main Street between 4:00 and 6:00 p.m."

b. "All persons between the ages of six and sixteen must attend school."

c. "Whoever enters a bank for purposes of taking by force or violence the property or money in custody of such bank shall be fined not more than $5,000 or imprisoned not more than twenty years or both."

d. "In order to sell any product on a public street, the seller must first apply for and receive a vendor's permit."

e. "No employer of more than fifteen persons may discriminate on the basis of race, color, religion, sex, or national origin."

f. "All persons traveling on interstate airline carriers are subject to search before entering the airplane departure area."

Give an example, not listed above, of a federal law, a state law, and a local law.

In addition to judicial review, citizens have other ways in which they can influence the lawmaking process. These methods include voting and lobbying.

> **WHERE YOU LIVE**
>
> Where and how do you register to vote in your community? Is there a residency requirement for state and local elections? If so, how long? Where do people in your area go to vote?

Voting   Voting is a basic right provided by the U.S. Constitution. Citizens of the United States may vote for candidates at all levels of government, including the president, vice-president, members of the U.S. Senate and House of Representatives, and numerous state and local government officials. Eligible voters may also cast their ballots on **referenda,** which deal with issues affecting a community. For example, many states have asked voters to decide whether the drinking age should be changed.

To qualify to vote a person must be a U.S. citizen and at least eighteen years old on or before the date of the election. In addition, all states require that voters be residents of the place in which they vote. At one time many states required voters to live in a state for a year or more before being eligible to register. The Voting Rights Act of 1970 changed this, and eligible persons are now able to vote in all federal elections after living in a state for only thirty days. Residency requirements for state and local elections, however, vary from place to place and may be longer than thirty days.

For persons who meet the above requirements, voter registration is relatively simple. Applicants can usually register by completing an application form, either in person or by mail. Registering to vote has not always been that easy. Until 1965 some states had literacy and character tests, which excluded millions of people from the voting process. These laws are no longer in effect, but almost all states still bar mentally ill persons and prison inmates from voting. In addition, in almost every state persons convicted of certain types of crime lose their right to vote.

PROBLEM 5

In recent years the percentage of eligible voters choosing to vote has gone down. If you are eligible to vote but have not registered,

Why is it important for citizens to register to vote?

explain why. If you are registered but just don't vote, explain why. What reasons can you suggest for the decline in voter participation? Should anything be done to change the situation?

Lobbying   There are other ways to affect the lawmaking process besides voting. One of the most common methods for influencing government and expressing public opinion is **lobbying**. Lobbying includes all those activities directed at public officials and designed to influence government policies and laws.

Today, interest groups and organizations lobby on behalf of every imaginable cause and issue. Many of these groups hire professional lobbyists, who maintain offices in the District of Columbia or the various state capitals. While not everyone goes to Washington or stands in the hallways of their state legislature, anyone who wants to express an opinion can be a lobbyist.

Elected representatives are influenced by pressure from their constituents. People, either in groups or as individuals can sometimes affect the way an official votes by expressing their opinion in either a letter or a phone call.

PROBLEM 6

Select a current issue that concerns you. Write a letter about it to your state legislator, federal representative, or Senator.

Agencies

Many of the laws that affect you are made by government agencies. Once Congress or a state legislature passes a law, they often au-

ADVICE ON WRITING A PUBLIC OFFICIAL

Write in your own words. Personal letters are far more effective than form letters or petitions. Tell how the issue will affect you, your friends, family, or job.

Keep your letter short and to the point. Deal with only one issue per letter. If you are writing about some proposed bill or legislation, identify it by name (e.g., the National Consumer Protection Act) and by number, if you know it (e.g., H.R. 343 or S. 675).

Begin by telling the official why you are writing. Ask the official to state his or her own position on the issue. Always request a reply and ask the official to take some kind of definite action (e.g., vote for or against the bill).

Always put your return address on the letter, sign and date it, and keep a copy, if possible. Your letter doesn't have to be typed, but it should be legible. Perhaps most importantly, it should reach the official before the issue is voted on.

WHERE YOU LIVE

What special interest, pressure, or lobbying groups exist in your state? On behalf of what issues or causes do these groups lobby? What techniques do they use?

thorize an administrative agency to develop regulations (rules) implementing the law. These regulations influence almost every aspect of our daily lives and are, in effect, laws. For example, Congress passed a law requiring that working conditions in places of employment be safe. To implement this law, Congress established the Occupational Safety and Health Administration, which has the power to develop specific regulations governing safety and health standards for places of employment. The regulations for this agency fill many volumes and cover such specifics as fire exits, employee clothing, and the height of guard rails in factories. Other federal agencies make laws in a similar manner. For example, the Internal Revenue Service (IRS) issues regulations and enforces federal tax laws, and the Federal Trade Commission (FTC) issues regulations that, among other things, control advertising across the nation.

State and local governments also have agencies that administer and implement the laws passed by legislatures and other governmental bodies. For example, city zoning commissions have the power to decide in what parts of a city different types of buildings, such as factories, homes, or office buildings, can be built. Many states have Alcoholic Beverage Control (ABC) boards, which make rules and regulations regarding the sale and drinking of alcoholic beverages in restaurants, liquor stores, night clubs, and other public places. In addition to their regulatory (lawmaking) function, agencies also administer government programs and provide many services.

WHERE
YOU
LIVE

What are the major de-
partments or agencies
of your state govern-
ment? How are they or-
ganized and what do
they do?

Courts

Law is also made by courts. This law is called case law or **common
law.** There are two distinct types of courts in the United States, trial
and appeals.

   Trial courts listen to testimony, consider evidence, and decide
the facts in disputed situations. Once a trial court has made a
decision, the losing party may be able to **appeal** the decision in an
appellate court.

THE CASE OF TAKING A CAR BY MISTAKE

*Joe Harper left his key in his 1972 blue Camaro. When he came back an hour
later, he got into someone else's 1972 blue Camaro by mistake. This car also
had the key in it but Harper, who did not notice it was a different car, started
it and drove away. He was arrested for auto theft.*

*At the trial, the judge told the jury it was not necessary for them to consider
whether or not Harper intended to steal the car. Instead, the judge instructed
the jury that to find Harper guilty of auto theft they only had to decide
whether he was caught driving a car that was not his. The jury found Joe
Harper guilty.*

FIGURE 1 The Government of the United States

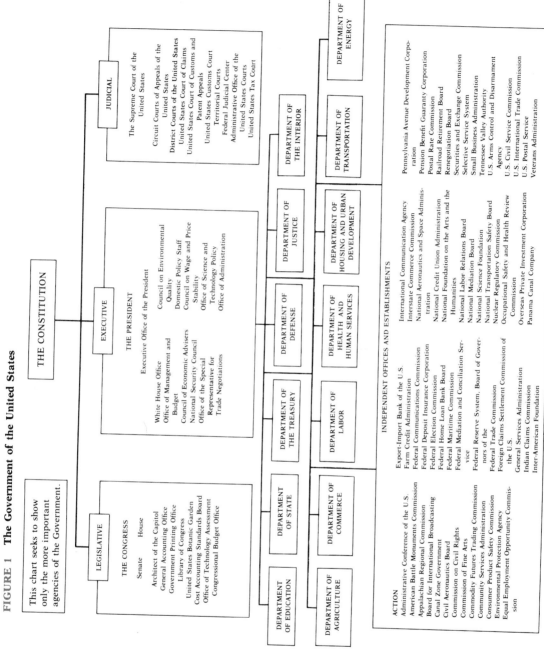

Source: United States Government Manual 1978/79.

In an **appeals court,** one party presents arguments asking the court to change the decision of the trial court and the other party presents arguments supporting the decision of the trial court. Not everyone who loses a trial can appeal. Usually an appeal is possible only when there is a claim that the trial court has committed an **error of law.** An error of law occurs when the judge makes a mistake as to the law applicable in the case (e.g., gives the wrong instructions to the jury or permits evidence that should not have been allowed).

The Case of Taking a Car by Mistake illustrates an error of law and could be appealed. The law regarding auto theft requires that the accused person must have intended to steal the car. Harper did not intend to steal the car, so the guilty verdict could be reversed.

When an appeals court decides a case, it will issue a written opinion or ruling. This opinion sets a **precedent** for similar cases in the future. When an appellate court gives an opinion on a matter, all lower courts in the place where the decision is made must follow the precedent stated in the opinion. This is what is meant by courts "making law." However, a higher court or a court in another area can disagree with this precedent. The most important precedents are those established by the U.S. Supreme Court, where nine judges hear each case and a majority rules. All courts in the United States must follow U.S. Supreme Court decisions.

Unlike other appellate courts, the Supreme Court does not consider all appeals that are brought to it but instead rules on only the most important cases. Of more than 4,000 cases appealed to the

The Supreme Court in 1979. Front row, from left: Byron R. White, William J. Brennan, Jr., Chief Justice Warren E. Burger, Potter Stewart, and Thurgood Marshall. Back row: William H. Rehnquist, Harry A. Blackmun, Lewis F. Powell, Jr., and John P. Stevens.

Supreme Court each year, the justices usually issue opinions on only about 200. Examples of laws changed through Supreme Court ruling include abolishing the death penalty under certain broad criminal statutes; restricting government intrusion into the privacy of citizens on matters such as abortion and wiretapping; and putting an end to the policy of school segregation.

These appellate precedents are very important to our whole system of law. Other courts follow the law announced in these cases, and prior decisions are looked to when courts decide subsequent cases.

THE CASE OF GIDEON v. WAINWRIGHT

In 1963 a case called Gideon v. Wainwright *came before the U.S. Supreme Court. In this case a Florida man named Gideon was charged with unlawfully breaking and entering into a pool-room. Gideon asked the trial court to provide him with a free lawyer because he was too poor to hire one himself. The state court refused to provide him with an attorney, saying that state law only provided free attorneys to those defendants charged with capital offenses (i.e., those crimes that carried the death penalty or life imprisonment).*

The Fourteenth Amendment to the Constitution says that no state may deprive a person of life, liberty, or property without **due process of law.** *Gideon argued that to try a* **defendant** *for a felony without providing him with a lawyer violated his right to due process of law. The Supreme Court agreed with Gideon.*

PROBLEM 7
a. In the case of *Gideon* v. *Wainwright,* what was the precedent that the Supreme Court set? Who has to follow this precedent?
b. Who would have to follow the precedent if the case had been decided by a judge in a state appeals court?
c. Does the *Gideon* case apply if you are charged with a misdemeanor? Does it apply if you are sued in a civil case?
d. Do you know of other precedents established by the U.S. Supreme Court? What are they?

Court Systems Figure 2 on page 16 illustrates the two separate court systems in the United States, federal and state. Federal courts hear both criminal and civil cases involving federal law, as well as cases involving **parties** from different states when the amount in dispute is more than $10,000. Federal trial courts are known as the U.S. District Courts. If you lose a trial in the U.S. District Court, you may be able to appeal to the U.S. Circuit Court of Appeals in your region. The United States has eleven of these courts throughout the country. The court of final appeal is the U.S. Supreme Court.

**WHERE
YOU
LIVE**

What courts exist in
your community? What
kind of cases do they
handle? How are ap-
peals handled in your
state? What is the high-
est state court and
where is it located?

FIGURE 2   **Federal and State Court Systems**

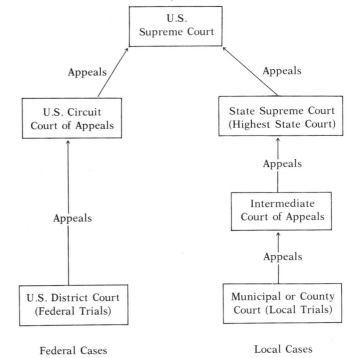

Federal Cases   Local Cases

Most state court systems resemble the federal courts in structure and procedure. All states have trial courts, which may be
called superior courts, county courts, district courts, or municipal
courts, depending on the state. In many areas these courts are
separated to deal with specific areas of law, such as family or
domestic relations, traffic, criminal, probate, and small claims.

The family or domestic relations courts hear all actions involving divorce, separation, and the custody of children. Juvenile cases
and intrafamily offenses (fights within families) are also heard.
Sometimes cases involving juveniles are heard in a special juvenile
court. The traffic courts hear all actions involving violations while
driving a motor vehicle. The criminal courts hear all actions involving violations of laws for which a person could go to jail.
Frequently the criminal court is divided between felony and misdemeanor cases. The probate courts handle all cases involving the
probate, or proving, of a will and of claims against the estates of
persons who die with or without a will. The small claims courts hear
all cases involving small amounts of money (e.g., $200, $500, or
$1,000, depending on the state). Individuals may bring cases here
without lawyers—though it is sometimes advised that lawyers be
present—and the court fees are low.

If you lose your case in the trial court, you may appeal to an
intermediate court of appeals or, in smaller states, directly to the
state supreme court. If a state supreme court decision involves

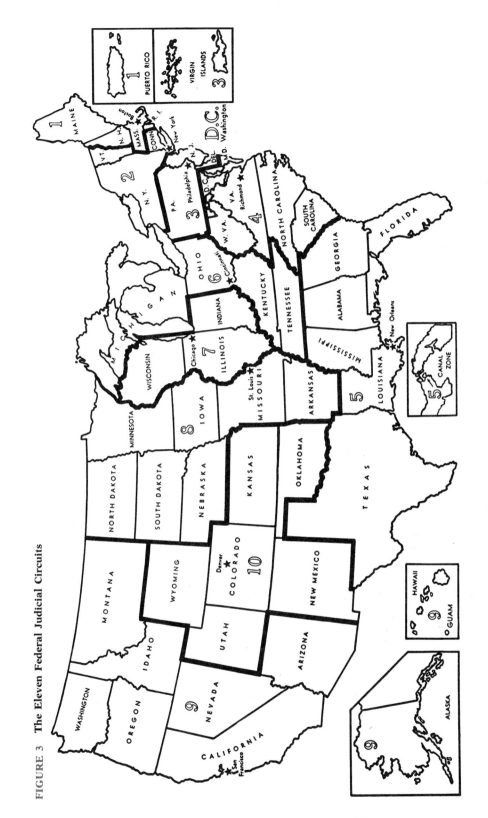

FIGURE 3 The Eleven Federal Judicial Circuits

17

only state law, it can be appealed no further; but if it also involves some federal law or constitutional issues, it can then be appealed to the U.S. Supreme Court.

PROBLEM 8

Consider the following cases. In each situation decide whether it will be tried in a federal or state court. To what court could each case be appealed?

a. A state sues a neighboring state for dumping waste in a river that borders the two states.

b. A wife sues her husband for divorce.

c. A person is prosecuted for assaulting a neighbor.

d. Two cars collide. One driver sues the other for hospital bills and auto repairs.

e. A group of parents sues the local school board, asking that their school be desegregated.

Give an example, not listed above, of a case that could be heard in a state court; in a federal court.

SAMPLE CIVIL CASE

Mike goes to Frank's house for a party. Mike has too much to drink and falls on top of Frank's $500 stereo. It costs Frank $150 to fix the stereo. Mike breaks his arm in the fall.

Frank files a complaint in the small claims branch of the civil court for $150 in **damages** against Mike. Mike files an an *answer*, denying it was his fault, and **counterclaims** against Frank for $300, claiming he fell because Frank's floor was slippery and that he suffered damages, including medical bills, loss of a week's wages, and pain and suffering.

Both attorneys make motions for *pretrial discovery*, which includes written and oral questions of the other person's witnesses. A trial is held six weeks after the complaint is filed.

The judge finds that the accident was Mike's fault since he had too much to drink and was clumsy in falling. The damages are set at $150 and the judge orders Mike to pay this to Frank. If Mike doesn't pay, Frank can go to court and file a writ of **garnishment** against Mike's wages. This means that Mike's employer will have to pay Frank twenty-five percent of Mike's wages until the $150 is paid off.

Criminal and Civil Process The following lists are a simplified version of the general steps taken in criminal and civil cases. You should note that criminal and civil cases are tried separately and can never be combined.

Criminal

1. Arrest—Police take person into custody. **Booking** (information recorded about person) and fingerprinting takes place.

2. Initial appearance: misdemeanor case—Defendant is given a copy of the complaint and asked to enter a plea. A trial date is set and the judge either imposes bail or releases the defendant. Initial appearance: felony case—Defendant is informed of the charge, advised of his or her rights to a preliminary examination and/or presentation of the case to a grand jury. No plea is entered.

3. Indictment or **information— Prosecutor** (government's attorney) either takes evidence before **grand jury** to get an indictment or has sufficient evidence from police that an information may be filed.

4. Pretrial proceedings—Hearings may be held on motions to dismiss the case, to have evidence ruled inadmissible, or to permit discovery. Defendant may enter a plea of guilty with the hope of receiving a lesser sentence.

5. Trial—Presentation of evidence by **prosecution** and defense.

6. Decision—Verdict is made by trier of fact, which may be jury or judge.

Civil

1. Complaint filed by **plaintiff**—Plaintiff files papers claiming a civil wrong done by the defendant.

2. Answer by defendant— Defendant files papers denying plaintiff's claim and stating the defenses in the case.

3. Pretrial proceedings—**Motions** (requests by the parties to the court) are filed requesting **discovery** (an exchange of information between the parties).

4. Trial—Presentation of evidence by plaintiff and defendant.

5. Decision—**Verdict** by trier of fact, which may be jury or judge.

6. Judgment—Pronounced by the judge in favor of plaintiff or defendant.

Criminal	Civil
7. Sentence—Imposition of a penalty, which may be a prison term, probation, fine, or other punishment.	**7.** Enforcement of judgment—Court forces the person against whom a judgment was pronounced to pay or do something.

SETTLING DISPUTES OUTSIDE OF COURT

Many problems that arise in everyday life can be settled without going to court. In fact, there are sometimes disadvantages in taking a case to court. Because of backlogged cases and complicated rules and procedures, courts are often quite slow. Furthermore, the total cost of an attorney, pretrial discovery, witness fees, and other court expenses may be more than the case is worth.

Most people solve both simple and complicated problems on their own without going to court. If a person's dog barks all night and disturbs a neighbor, the neighbor will probably complain to the dog owner before considering going to an attorney. It would be difficult for society to function if people had to hire attorneys and go to court every time they had a problem or a dispute.

Despite the important role of courts in our legal system, there are a number of other ways in which people can settle disputes. Among the most common methods for solving disputes outside of court are **negotiation, arbitration,** and **mediation.**

Negotiation simply means that the parties to a dispute talk to each other about their problem and try to reach a solution acceptable to all. Sometimes people cannot settle a dispute on their own and hire attorneys to negotiate for them. For example, people involved in auto accidents sometimes hire attorneys to negotiate with the insurance company over payments for injuries or damages to their car. People who hire attorneys to negotiate for them must approve any agreement before it becomes final. In some situations, attorneys will file a case in court and then attempt to work out a **settlement** so that the case never actually goes to trial. A large number of civil cases are settled this way, saving both time and money.

Another method for resolving disputes, mediation, takes place when a third person acts as a go-between who tries to persuade both parties to settle their problem. For example, a parent who sees two children arguing over which TV show to watch acts as a mediator by persuading the children to agree on a program.

In many places mediators help people solve legal problems or disputes. For example, consumer agencies often help settle disputes between consumers and store owners by acting as a mediator or go-between.

Do you know of any groups in your community that settle disputes outside of court?

A third method for settling disputes outside of court is called arbitration. This takes place when both parties to a dispute agree to have a third party listen to their arguments and make a decision. Arbitration differs from mediation because a mediator helps the parties to reach their own decision while an arbitrator makes a decision for the parties.

PROBLEM 9

Consider each of the situations below and decide the best method for settling the dispute. In each case decide whether the problem would be best handled by an informal discussion between the parties, negotiation, mediation, arbitration, by going to court, or by some other method. Discuss the reasons for your answer.

a. A parent agrees to pay all of his daughter's college expenses but later changes his mind.

b. A stereo you bought broke after two weeks and the salesperson refuses to fix it.

c. A landlord will not make needed repairs because he believes the tenant caused them.

d. A labor union and an employer disagree over the wages and conditions of employment.

e. A married couple wants a divorce.

f. The Internal Revenue Service sends you a letter stating that you owe another $200 in taxes. You disagree.

THE ADVERSARY SYSTEM

The trial system in the United States is an adversary process, which means it is a contest between opposing sides. The theory of this process is that trier of fact (judge or jury) will best be able to determine the truth if the opposing parties present their best arguments and attempt to discredit or to show the weaknesses in the other side's case.

If a criminal case goes to trial, the prosecution has the burden or responsibility of proving the defendant guilty **beyond a reasonable doubt.** In a civil case the burden is on the plaintiff to prove his or her case by a **preponderance of the evidence** (greater weight of evidence). The standard of proof is more difficult in a criminal case because of a belief that more evidence should be required to take away a person's freedom.

The adversary process is not the only method for handling legal disputes, and, in fact, many countries have systems differing from our own. Moreover, the adversary process is sometimes criticized as not providing the best setting for the discovery of truth with respect to the facts of a specific case. Critics believe that the adversary process is no more than a battle in which lawyers behave as enemies, making every effort *not* to present *all* the evidence they know. In this view the goal of trial is "victory, not truth or justice."

On the other hand, the adversary process has long served as the cornerstone of the American legal system, and most attorneys believe that approaching the same set of facts from totally different perspectives and objectives will uncover more truth than would other methods.

PROBLEM 10

a. Which of the viewpoints concerning the adversary process do you favor? Why?

b. Do you agree or disagree with the following statement: "It is better that ten guilty persons go free than that one innocent person suffer conviction." Explain your answer.

c. In a criminal case, should a lawyer defend a client whom he or she knows to be guilty? Discuss.

Steps in a Trial

The following is a short explanation of what occurs at a trial, whether in a criminal or a civil case.

1. Opening Statement by Plaintiff or Prosecutor—Plaintiff's attorney (in civil cases) or prosecutor (in criminal cases) explains to the trier of fact the evidence to be presented as proof of the **allegations** (unproven statements) in the indictment or complaint.

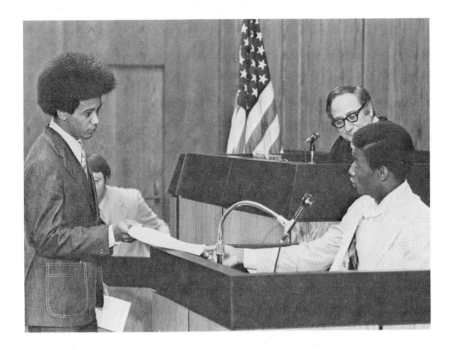

2. Opening Statement by Defense—Defendant's attorney explains evidence to be presented to deny the allegations made by the plaintiff or prosecutor.

3. Direct Examination by Plaintiff or Prosecutor—Each witness for the plaintiff or prosecution is questioned. Other evidence (e.g., documents, physical evidence) in favor of the plaintiff or prosecution is presented.

4. Cross-examination by Defense—The defense has the opportunity to question all witnesses. Questioning is designed to break down the story or to discredit the witness in the eyes of the jury.

5. Motions—If the prosecution/plaintiff's basic case has not been established from the evidence introduced, the judge can end the case by granting the defendant's motion to dismiss (in civil cases) or by entering a directed verdict (in criminal cases).

6. Direct Examination by Defense—Each defense witness is questioned.

7. Cross-examination by Plaintiff—Each defense witness is cross-examined.

8. Closing Statement by Plaintiff—Prosecutor or plaintiff's attorney reviews all the evidence presented (noting uncontradicted facts), states how the evidence has satisfied the elements of the charge, and asks for a finding of guilty (in criminal cases) or for plaintiff (in civil cases).

9. Closing Statement by Defense—Same as closing statement by prosecution/plaintiff. The defense asks for a finding of not guilty (in criminal cases) or for defendant (in civil cases).

10. Rebuttal Argument—Prosecutor or plaintiff has the right to make additional closing arguments.

11. Jury Instructions—Judge instructs jury as to the law that applies in the case.

12. Verdict—In most states, a unanimous decision is required one way or the other. If the jury cannot reach a unanimous decision, it is said to be a **hung jury,** and the case may be tried again.

Judges and Juries

Essential to an appreciation of the trial system is a basic understanding of the roles and functions of judges and juries. The judge is the person who presides over the trial and has the duty of protecting the rights of those involved and making sure that attorneys follow the rules of evidence and trial procedure. If the trial is held without a jury, the judge also has the function of determining the facts of the case and rendering a judgment. If the trial is held before a jury, the judge is required to instruct the jury as to the law involved in the case. Finally, if it is a criminal trial, judges are usually required to sentence individuals convicted of committing a crime.

The right to trial by jury is guaranteed by the Sixth and Seventh Amendments of the Constitution and applies in both federal and state courts. However, a jury is not required in every case, and, in fact, juries are not used as often as one might think. Generally, in a civil case either the plaintiff or defendant may request a jury trial. In a criminal case it is the defendant who decides whether or not there will be a jury. Many civil cases result in out-of-court settlements or trials by a judge. In criminal cases most cases are never brought to trial but are disposed of by **plea bargaining.**

Nevertheless, if a jury trial is requested, a jury is selected and charged with the task of determining the facts and applying the law in the particular case. In all states prospective jury members must be citizens of the United States, at least eighteen years of age, and residents of the state for a certain period of time. Persons commonly excused from jury duty include: clergy, attorneys, physicians, police officers, fire fighters, convicted felons, and persons who are physically or mentally ill.

Once selected, jurors are assigned to specific cases only after being screened through a process known as **voir dire** examination. This is the process in which opposing lawyers question each prospective juror to discover any prejudices or preconceived opinions concerning the case. After questioning each juror, the opposing attorneys are permitted to request the removal of any juror who does not appear capable of rendering a fair and impartial verdict. This is called **removal for cause.** In addition, each attorney is allowed a limited number of **peremptory challenges** in which they can have prospective jurors removed without stating a cause.

WHERE YOU LIVE

How are jurors selected by the courts in your community? How many persons are on the jury in a civil trial? In a criminal trial? Is a unanimous verdict required in a civil trial? In a criminal trial?

PROBLEM 11

a. Why would someone choose not to have a jury trial in a civil case? In a criminal case?

b. What reasons can you give for the exclusion from jury duty of attorneys, physicians, police officers, and convicted felons? Can you think of any other group that should be exempt from jury duty?

c. If you were a defense attorney questioning jurors at the voir dire in a murder trial, what basic questions would you ask to determine whether the jurors could render a fair and impartial verdict?

d. Can you think of any reasons why an attorney might use a peremptory challenge?

To be a juror, you must meet your state's qualifications of age, citizenship, and good character.

LAWYERS

There are over 450,000 lawyers in the United States and almost 325,000 attorneys in active practice. Law firms and lawyers in private practice account for about sixty-five percent of the lawyers in the United States. Around fifteen percent are government lawyers who work for the various federal, state or local agencies. Another fifteen percent work for various corporations, unions, or trade associations. A small number of lawyers work for public interest or legal aid organizations. An even smaller number are law professors, judges, or elected officials.

Contrary to popular belief, most lawyers rarely go to court. The practice of law usually involves giving advice, drafting legal opinions, negotiating settlements, or otherwise providing out-of-court legal assistance.

Some lawyers do, however, go to court. In a civil case the lawyers stand in place of their clients and act as advocates for their clients' positions. Likewise, in a criminal case the lawyer for the defendant has a duty to do anything possible (without violating a code of professional ethics) to secure the release and acquittal of his or her client.

Some lawyers work alone. Others work together as partners in a law firm.

When Do You Need A Lawyer?

One of the most important things a person needs to know is when to get a lawyer. Many people think of seeing an attorney only after they get into trouble, but perhaps the best time to consult an attorney is before the problem arises.

Preventive advice is one of the most important services a lawyer can provide. You should consider consulting an attorney about a number of common situations, including the following:

■ Buying or selling a home or other real estate

■ Organizing a business or making a major purchase

■ Changing your family status (e.g., by divorce or adoption)

■ Making a will or planning an estate

■ Signing a large or important contract

■ Handling accidents involving personal injury or property damage

■ Defending a criminal charge or bringing a civil suit

Of course, there are limits to the services a lawyer can provide. If your problem is one that requires a business or economic decision, a good businessperson may be a better adviser than a lawyer. For many other problems a teacher, doctor, or friend may be a better source of advice.

PROBLEM 12

Each of the following examples involve situations in which an attorney may or may not be needed. For each situation discuss the reasons why you may or may not need an attorney.

a. You run into another car in a parking lot. Your insurance agent indicates the company will pay costs for bodily injuries and property damages.

b. You borrow your brother's car without his knowledge and he reports it to the police as stolen.

c. You buy a new stereo for $300. At a party one month later the receiver and speakers blow out. You return to the store and they tell you they are sorry but their stereos only have a two-week guarantee.

d. You decide to trade in your old car and buy a new one.

e. Your friends are caught robbing a local store, and they name you as one who helped plan the robbery.

f. The principal suspends you from school for two days because of an article you wrote for the student paper criticizing the school dress codes.

g. You apply for a job and are turned down. You think you are rejected because of your sex.

h. You do not want your family to inherit the $10,000 you have saved. Told you will die within a year, you want the money to be used for cancer research.

i. You and your mate find that you can no longer get along. You want a divorce.

j. You earn $5,000 working in a restaurant during the year. You want to file your federal income tax return.

How Do You Find A Lawyer?

If you think you need a lawyer, how do you find one who is right for you and your particular problem? Perhaps the best way to find an experienced lawyer is through the recommendation of someone who has had a similar legal problem and whose lawyer resolved it to his or her satisfaction. You might also ask your employer, members of the clergy, businesspeople, or other professionals for the name of a lawyer they know and trust.

You can always find a lawyer by looking under "Lawyers" in the Yellow Pages of your phone book. In addition, *Martindale-Hubbell Law Directory*, available in your public library, lists most lawyers in the United States and provides some general information about their education, professional honors, and the type of cases they handle. As a result of a recent U.S. Supreme Court ruling, lawyers are now permitted to advertise their services. Depending upon where you live, advertisements for lawyers may be found in newspapers, magazines, or on radio or television.

Another way to find a lawyer is to contact a lawyer referral service in your community. Local attorneys often organize into **bar associations** and maintain a list of lawyers who specialize in certain areas. Many of these lawyers are willing to consult and advise clients at a special rate. Anyone who calls the referral service will be told the amount of the initial consultation fee and will be given the name of a lawyer for an appointment. If additional legal service is needed, the fee is subject to agreement between the lawyer and the client.

A person who is unable to afford the services of a lawyer may be eligible for free legal assistance at a legal aid, legal service, or public defender office. These offices are usually listed in the Yellow Pages under "Legal Services." You may also contact the Legal Services Corporation (address in Appendix A) or a local bar association or law school for the address of the legal aid office nearest you.

To get legal advice, poor people can go to a legal aid office.

ADVICE ON WHAT TO ASK YOUR LAWYER

Once you have found a lawyer who seems interested in your problem, you should get the answers to the following questions:

1. What is the lawyer's fee? Is the client required to pay a flat fee or by the hour? Is a *retainer* (down payment) required? What about a contingent fee in which the lawyer gets paid only if he or she wins your case?
2. Has the lawyer ever handled cases like this before? If so, with what results?
3. Will the lawyer provide you with copies of all correspondence and documents prepared on your behalf?
4. Will the lawyer keep you informed of any new developments in your case, and talk to you in "plain English?"
5. How much personal attention will you get? If the lawyer is a member of a law firm, is he or she the person who will actually do your legal work?

If you are not satisfied with the answers you get, don't hesitate to shop around.

Another thing to consider before choosing a lawyer is whether your problem is one that may be of interest to such organizations as the American Civil Liberties Union (ACLU), Environmental Defense Fund (EDF), National Association for the Advancement of Colored People (NAACP), American Conservative Union (ACU), or other public interest groups. These organizations are usually listed in the phone book and may provide free representation.

Problems With Your Attorney

Even if you take all of the above steps before hiring a lawyer, you still may be dissatisfied with the way he or she handles your case. A client has the right to discharge an attorney at any time, although once the case is in court, a judge may not permit this change except for a very good reason. A client who has a serious complaint that can't be worked out with the attorney can usually report this either to the local court or to the bar association, which has the power to reprimand, suspend, or even disbar an attorney for serious misconduct.

THE CAR CRASH CASE

On April 1, Al Sundance and his friend Marie Davis were driving along Sixth Street, returning home from a party. Al had stopped at a red light at the corner of Sixth Street and Florida Avenue, when a 1973 Buick hit his car in the rear.

Al's 1978 Volvo was smashed in as far as the back seat. Al suffered a severe neck injury, four broken ribs, and many cuts and bruises. As a result, Al spent three weeks in the hospital. Al's passenger, Marie, was also severely injured. She suffered a fractured skull, facial cuts, a broken right arm and hip, numerous cuts, and internal bleeding. Marie, an accountant making $15,000 a year, spent six weeks in the hospital and returned to work after twelve weeks.

The driver of the Buick, Fred Ortego, suffered minor cuts on his face and arm and was released from the hospital after twenty-four hours. As a result of the accident, Fred was given a ticket for speeding and reckless driving.

Fred's insurance company called Marie and offered her a $4,500 settlement. Marie is uncertain whether she should accept and decides to consult an attorney. After checking with a lawyer referral service, she is referred to a local attorney.

PROBLEM 13
Roleplay the initial attorney-client interview between Marie and the attorney. Persons roleplaying the attorney should attempt to ask all the questions an attorney should ask at this point. Persons roleplaying the client should provide the attorney with all necessary information and ask all those questions that are relevant to Marie's case and that relate to whether she should retain the attorney.

two
CRIMINAL
AND
JUVENILE
JUSTICE

A crime is something one does or fails to do in violation of a law. It can also be defined as behavior for which the state has set a penalty.

Criminal law designates certain conduct "criminal" and other conduct "noncriminal." Decisions as to what constitutes a crime are made by legislatures and courts, who try to protect the public based on what most people believe is right and necessary for the orderly conduct of our society. Certain acts are prohibited or commanded in order to protect life and property, to preserve individual freedoms, to maintain our system of government, and to uphold the morality of society. Ideally, the goal of law is to regulate human conduct so that people can live in harmony.

PROBLEM 1

A commission is established to evaluate laws. You are a member. Consider the following acts and in each case decide whether the act should be treated as a crime. Rank the offenses in order from most serious to least serious. Give reasons for your decisions.

a. Robert is a narcotics addict who pushes heroin to anyone who will buy.

b. John and Tom are homosexuals who live together as if they were married.

c. Liz pickpockets an individual's wallet containing fifty dollars.

d. Reuben refuses to pay his income tax because he does not support government policies.

e. Susan is caught with a pound of marijuana.

f. Ted robs a liquor store at gunpoint.

g. Ellen leaves a store with change for a ten-dollar bill after she realizes that she gave the cashier a five-dollar bill.

h. Lilly approaches a man for purposes of prostitution.

i. Ming refuses to wear a helmet while riding a motorcycle.

j. A company pollutes a river with wastes from its auto-making factory.

k. Marge gets drunk and hits a child while speeding through a school zone.

l. Burt observes his best friend shoplifting an item but does not turn him in.

Crime wears many faces. It may be the teenager snatching a woman's purse or the career criminal planning and executing a kidnapping. It may be the youth who steals a car for a joyride or the car theft ring that takes it for later sale. It may be the professional criminal who reaps huge profits from organized gambling, extortion, or narcotics traffic or the politician who takes a bribe in exchange for a favor. Crime may be committed by the professional person who cheats on his tax return, the businessperson who secretly agrees to fix prices, or the burglar who ransacks homes while the owners are at work.

PROBLEM 2

a. According to Table 1, what is the most commonly committed crime?

b. Make a list of crimes that are not included in the table.

c. Which of the crimes listed in the table has increased most since 1969? How might you explain this increase?

TABLE 1 National Crime, Rate, and Percent Change

CRIME INDEX OFFENSES	ESTIMATED CRIME 1978		PERCENT CHANGE OVER 1977		PERCENT CHANGE OVER 1974		PERCENT CHANGE OVER 1969	
	Number	Rate per 100,000 inhabitants	Number	Rate per 100,000 inhabitants	Number	Rate per 100,000 inhabitants	Number	Rate per 100,000 inhabitants
Total[1]	11,141,300	5,109.3	+1.9	+1.1	+8.7	+5.3	+50.3	+38.8
Violent	1,061,830	486.9	+5.2	+4.4	+8.9	+5.6	+60.4	+48.1
Property	10,079,500	4,622.4	+1.5	+.7	+8.6	+5.3	+49.3	+37.9
Murder	19,560	9.0	+2.3	+2.3	−5.6	−8.2	+32.5	+23.3
Forcible rape	67,130	30.8	+6.5	+5.8	+21.2	+17.6	+80.6	+66.5
Robbery	417,040	191.3	+3.0	+2.2	−5.7	−8.6	+39.5	+28.9
Aggravated assault	558,100	255.9	+6.8	+6.0	+22.3	+18.6	+79.4	+65.6
Burglary	3,104,500	1,423.7	+1.7	+.9	+2.1	−1.0	+56.6	+44.7
Larceny—Theft	5,983,400	2,743.9	+1.3	+.5	+13.7	+10.2	+53.9	+42.1
Motor vehicle theft	991,600	454.7	+2.4	+1.6	+1.5	−1.6	+12.9	+4.2

[1]Due to rounding, offenses may not add to Crime Index totals.

35

NATURE AND CAUSES OF CRIME

WHERE YOU LIVE

What is the major crime problem in your community? What crimes have increased most over the last three years? Have any crime rates decreased during this period? Where can you get this information?

Unfortunately, regulating human conduct is not an easy goal. Crime has long been a major problem in the United States. In 1978 more than eleven million serious crimes were reported to the police. This is an increase of over fifty percent since 1969. Recent reports suggest that the increase in crime is starting to level off, and in some areas the crime rate has slightly declined. Nevertheless, in 1980 there was more crime in the United States than there was five years earlier.

Crime rates are generally higher in large cities and urban areas, but in the last few years the crime rate has grown fastest in suburbs and rural areas. Crime is not confined to any particular group, but youths between the ages of fifteen and twenty-four commit more violent crimes than persons in any other age group. Males commit six times as many crimes as females, but in recent years the crime rate has grown fastest among women.

One way in which crime affects us all is that it costs everyone money. The costs of lost or damaged lives, or of fear and suffering, cannot be measured solely in dollars and cents, but the total cost of crime in this country has been estimated at close to $100 billion dollars per year.

Perhaps the most forgotten aspect of crime is its effect on its victims. Crime hurts people, and those who suffer are often a community's most vulnerable members. Victims of crime can be found among all segments of society—among young persons, the poor, and members of minority groups.

PROBLEM 3

According to Table 2, which has the highest crime rate, big cities, small cities, or rural areas? The lowest crime rate? Can you think of any reason for the difference?

In recent years there has been a growing public interest in aiding the victim. Many states are establishing victim assistance programs and are initiating victim compensation plans. These plans would allow the victim to receive money from the government to make up for his or her injury. In addition, courts sometimes order **restitution**, which means that convicted individuals are required to pay back or otherwise compensate the victim for their crime.

PROBLEM 4

a. Do you know anyone who has been the victim of a crime? What was the crime? How did it affect the person?

TABLE 2   **Crime Rate by Area, 1978 [Rate per 100,000 inhabitants]**

CRIME INDEX OFFENSES	TOTAL UNITED STATES	METRO-POLITAN AREA	RURAL	SMALL CITIES
Total	5,109.3	5,870.2	1,997.9	4,363.9
Violent	486.9	583.9	174.8	285.4
Property	4,622.4	5,286.3	1,823.1	4,078.6
Murder	9.0	9.9	7.5	5.2
Forcible rape	30.8	36.7	14.0	15.7
Robbery	191.3	249.2	20.9	50.1
Aggravated assault ..	255.9	288.1	132.3	214.4
Burglary	1,423.7	1,626.7	746.3	1,031.7
Larceny–theft	2,743.9	3,101.1	953.3	2,812.4
Motor vehicle theft ..	454.7	558.6	123.5	234.5

b. What steps can a community take to protect itself from crime? How can you minimize your chances of being a victim?

While most authorities agree that crime is a major domestic problem, there is much disagreement over the causes of crime and what can be done about it. Among the reasons suggested for the high rate of crime in America are poverty, permissive courts, unemployment, lack of education, abuse of alcohol and other drugs, inadequate police protection, rising population, lack of parental guidance, a breakdown in morals, an ineffective correctional system, little chance of being caught or punished, and the influence of television.

PROBLEM 5

a. Can you suggest causes of crime not mentioned in the text?

b. Rank each of the causes from the most important to the least important. Discuss your ranking.

The lack of agreement on the causes of crime indicates that they are many and complex. There is evidence that suggests that poor social and economic circumstances are somehow related to crime. However, crime cannot be totally explained in terms of poverty, particularly if one considers that crime rose fastest in this country at a time when the number of persons living in poverty was declining. And in recent years, crime rates have risen fastest in suburbs and other affluent areas. Furthermore, if poverty were the sole cause of crime, how does one explain why countries much poorer than the United States have far less crime?

What qualities should a good police officer have?

Some people explain increasing crime simply in terms of rising population. They say there are more people, particularly young people, so there is more crime. While this is true to a degree, the crime rate has risen much faster than the population rate.

Many people argue that tougher penalties will curb crime. However, the United States already has, on the whole, the most severe set of criminal laws of any advanced Western nation. Tough penalties may deter some people from crime, but, compared to the number of crimes, only a small number of people ever go to prison. Thus some experts say that longer prison terms are not the answer. Rather, they argue in favor of changing our laws and courts to insure that those who are arrested and convicted receive some punishment, no matter how slight. Adequate police protection obviously has something to do with the crime rate, but studies have shown that simply increasing the number of police officers does not necessarily reduce the overall crime rate. Finally, some experts point to peer group influence, family upbringing, and a decline in morality as the cause of crime. Still others blame the increase in crime on the use of hard drugs, such as heroin. Undoubtedly, family influences, a decline in moral standards, and drugs play a role in crime, but these factors probably aren't a total cause either.

Thinking about crime requires one to go beyond slogans and stereotypes and consider carefully each of the suggested causes and the possible solutions to the problem. Perhaps the best that can be said is that there is disagreement over the causes of crime and that the solution to the crime problem is not simple.

GENERAL CONSIDERATIONS

A single act can be both a criminal and a civil wrong. For example, Paul purposely sets fire to Floyd's store. The state may file criminal charges against Paul for arson. Floyd may also bring a civil action against Paul to recover for the damage to his store.

The U.S. Constitution forbids states from passing any **ex post facto laws.** This means that an act is not a crime unless, at the time it was committed, there was a law in effect stating the offense was a crime.

PROBLEM 6

Joe enjoys tormenting persons weaker than himself. One night while dining at a local drive-in he noticed Derek selecting a tune on the jukebox. To impress his girl friend, Joe ordered Derek to sing along with the record. When Derek refused, Joe punched him in the face, breaking Derek's jaw. As a result of the injury, Derek missed several weeks of work and had to pay both medical and dental bills.

a. Has Joe violated civil laws, criminal laws, or both?

b. Who would decide whether Joe would be charged criminally? Sued in a civil action?

c. If Joe were charged for a crime and sued in a civil action, would these actions be tried in one case? Why or why not?

d. Would procedures in a criminal trial be the same as those in a civil trial? Why or why not?

State and Federal Crimes

There are both state and federal criminal laws. Some acts, such as simple assault, disorderly conduct, drunken driving, or shoplifting in a local store, can only be prosecuted in a state court. Other acts, such as not paying federal taxes, mail fraud, espionage, or smuggling illegal goods into the country, can be prosecuted only in a federal court. Certain crimes, such as illegal possession of dangerous drugs and bank robbery, can be in violation of both state and federal law and can be prosecuted either in a state or federal court.

Classes of Crimes

A **felony** is a crime for which the maximum penalty is imprisonment for more than one year. Felonies are usually the more serious crimes. A **misdemeanor** is any crime for which the penalty is imprisonment for one year or less. Minor offenses, including such things as minor traffic violations, are not considered crimes although they are punishable by law. This chapter deals primarily with felonies and major misdemeanors.

Parties to Crimes

The person who actually commits a crime is called the **principal** (e.g., the person who fires the gun in a murder). An **accomplice** who helps another person commit a crime (e.g., the person who drives the getaway car during a bank robbery) may also be considered a principal to the crime. A person who orders a crime or who helps the principal commit the crime but who is not present (e.g., the underworld leader who hires a professional killer) is known as an **accessory before the fact,** and can usually be charged with the same crime, and can receive the same punishment as the principal. An **accessory after the fact** is a person who, knowing a crime has been

Shoplifting can be either a felony or a misdemeanor depending on the value of the article stolen.

committed, helps the principal avoid capture or escape. This person is not charged with the original crime but may be charged with a separate crime, such as harboring a fugitive, aiding the principal's escape, or obstructing justice (sometimes called aiding and abetting).

PROBLEM 7

Joe and Mary decide to rob Superior Jewelers. Their friend Carl, an employee at Superior, helps by telling them the location of the store vault. Mary drives a van to the store and keeps a lookout while Joe goes inside and cracks the safe. Joe later meets a friend, Fred, who was not involved beforehand, but who helps Joe get a train out of town after being told about the robbery. David, a former classmate of Joe and Mary's, witnesses the crime but doesn't tell the police, even though he recognizes both Joe and Mary. How will each be charged?

Crimes of Omission

Most crimes occur when a person does something or performs some act in violation of a law. However, in a few cases a person may be criminally liable for an omission or a failure to act. For example, there are laws making it a crime for a taxpayer to fail to file a tax return or for a motorist to fail to stop after involvement in an automobile accident. A person is guilty of a crime of omission if there is a failure to act when there is a legal duty to do so, and if that person is physically able to perform the required act.

THE CASE OF THE DROWNING GIRL

Allen, Betty, Chin, and Doris see a child drowning in a lake, but none of them takes steps to save her. Allen is her father. Betty had deliberately pushed her into the lake by shoving Chin against her. Doris, a medal-winning swimmer, just stands and watches. Would any of the four be criminally liable for her drowning? Explain your answer.

PRELIMINARY CRIMES

There are certain types of behavior that take place before the commission of a crime but which are nevertheless complete crimes in themselves. These offenses—**solicitation, attempt,** and **conspiracy** are aimed at giving the police the opportunity to prevent the intended crime. Each offense can be punished even if the harm intended never occurred.

Solicitation

A number of states make it a crime for a person to solicit (i.e., ask, command, urge, advise) another person to commit a crime. For example, Danny wishes to kill his wife Jean. Lacking the nerve to do the job himself, he asks Wally to kill her. Even if Wally refuses, Danny has committed the crime of solicitation.

Attempt

In most states an attempt to commit a crime is in itself a crime. In order to be guilty of the crime of attempt the accused must have both intended to commit a crime and taken some substantial step toward committing the crime. Mere preparation to commit a crime is not enough. The difficult problem with the crime of attempt is determining whether the actions of the accused were a step toward the actual attempt of committing a crime or mere acts of preparation. A common example of attempt is the situation where a person decides to shoot and kill someone but, being a poor shot, misses the intended victim. The person doing the shooting would be liable for attempted murder.

PROBLEM 8

Read the following situations and decide whether any of the individuals involved would be liable for the crime of attempt.

a. Howard, a bank teller, has figured out a foolproof method of stealing money from his cash drawer at the bank. It has taken him some time to get up the nerve to steal any money. Finally, he makes up his mind and tells his girl friend Donna that starting tomorrow he will steal the money. Donna goes to the police and Howard is arrested an hour later.

b. Gilbert, an accomplished thief, is caught while trying to pickpocket Lewis. He pleads not guilty and says he can't possibly be convicted because Lewis was broke and didn't have a penny on him.

c. Stuart and Johnson decide to rob a liquor store. They meet at a pub and talk over their plans. Stuart leaves to buy a revolver and Johnson leaves to steal a car for use in their getaway. Stuart is arrested as he walks out of the gun shop with his new revolver. Johnson is arrested while trying to hot-wire a car.

d. Amy decides to burn down her store in order to collect on the insurance money. She spreads gasoline around the building. She is arrested while leaving the store to get a book of matches.

Conspiracy

A **conspiracy** is an agreement between two or more persons to commit a crime. While the crime of conspiracy is designed as a means of preventing other crimes and striking against criminal activity by groups, it is sometimes criticized as posing a threat to a person's freedom of speech and association. When the government charged several people with conspiracy for speaking publicly to young men on how to avoid the draft during the Vietnam War, many critics of conspiracy said the accused were being denied the freedom of speech.

An example of conspiracy as a crime is the situation where Danny wants his wife Jean killed and asks Wally to commit the murder. If Wally agrees to Danny's request, both are guilty of conspiracy to commit murder, even if the murder is never attempted or accomplished.

In most states and in federal law an *"overt* act" is required for conviction on a conspiracy charge. In the example of the draft card cases, speeches made at an antidraft rally were cited as the overt acts on which conspiracy charges were based.

CRIMES AGAINST THE PERSON

Crimes against the person include **homicide, assault, battery,** and **rape.** All of those crimes are serious offenses, and a defendant found guilty of one or more of them may receive a harsh sentence. However, the law also protects the defendant by defining the various levels of these crimes and by considering the circumstances of each offense.

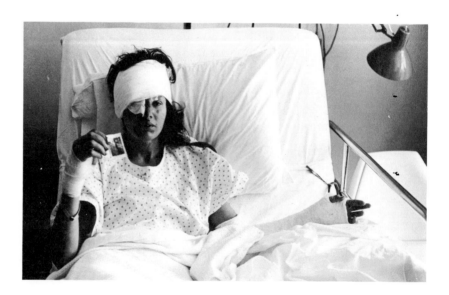

Homicide

Our society regards homicide—the killing of one human being by another—as the most serious of all crimes. The major categories of homicide are noncriminal homicide, criminal homicide (which is either murder or manslaughter), and negligent homicide.

Noncriminal Homicide Some homicides are not crimes at all. Noncriminal homicides are those in which the killing is justifiable or excusable and the killer is deemed faultless. Examples of noncriminal homicide include the following: killing an enemy soldier in wartime; the killing of a condemned criminal by an executioner; the killing by a police officer of a person who is committing a serious crime and who is resisting arrest; and killing in self-defense.

Criminal Homicide Murder, the most serious form of criminal homicide, is a killing that is deliberate and done with *malice.* Malice means having the intent to kill or seriously harm. At one time there were no degrees of murder. Any homicide done with malice was considered to be murder and punishable by death. To reduce the punishment for the less grievous homicides, most states now have statutes that classify murder according to the killer's state of mind or the circumstances surrounding the crime.

First degree murder is a killing that is premeditated (thought about beforehand), deliberate, and done with malice (i.e., with intent to kill).

Second degree murder is a killing that is deliberate and done with malice but without premeditation (i.e., the intent to kill did not exist until just before the murder itself).

Felony murder is a killing that takes place during the commission of certain felonies, such as arson, rape, robbery, or burglary. It is not necessary to prove intent to kill because felony murder includes most killing committed during a felony, even if accidental.

Voluntary manslaughter is an intentional killing committed under circumstances that mitigate (lessen), but do not justify or excuse, the killing. Manslaughter is based on the idea that even "the reasonable person" will lose self-control and act rashly if sufficiently provoked.

Involuntary manslaughter is an unintentional killing that results from conduct that is so reckless that it involves extreme danger of death or bodily injury. An example would be a killing that results from playing with a gun known to be loaded.

Negligent Homicide Negligent homicide is the causing of death through criminal negligence. Some states classify death by gross negligence as involuntary manslaughter. Vehicular, or automobile, homicide, a common form of negligent homicide, is killing that results from operating a motor vehicle in a reckless and grossly negligent manner. Any death that results from careless driving may lead to a civil suit for damages, but it is usually not considered a crime unless the death resulted from gross or extreme negligence.

PROBLEM 9

Candy is a member of a religious group that passes poisonous snakes around during church services. The group believes that the Lord will protect all true believers from harm, and they handle the snakes as a test of their faith.

One day Candy convinced her friend Gary to attend a service. Gary agreed to go, assuming he would be a mere observer. However, when they arrived at the church, Candy told Gary that everyone must take part in the service. Gary tried to back out but agreed to stay when Candy assured him the snakes had never bitten anyone and were harmless anyway. Candy knew this was untrue but believed that those bitten in the past were unbelievers. The first snake passed around bit Gary and he died before reaching the hospital.

a. Is Candy guilty of any crime? If so, what and for what reason?

b. Would it make a difference if no church member had ever been bitten?

c. Would it make a difference if Candy knew Gary was an unbeliever?

PROBLEM 10

Walt decided to shoot Clifford, whom he blamed for all his troubles. As he was driving to Clifford's home to carry out the murder, Walt hit a jogger who darted out from behind a tree. Stopping immediately, Walt rushed to help the jogger, who was already dead. Walt was upset until he discovered that the dead jogger was Clifford. Assuming Walt was driving at a safe speed and that the collision was unavoidable, is Walt guilty of murder?

PROBLEM 11

Belva was cheated when she bought a car from Fast Eddie's Car Mart. She attempted to return the car, but Eddie just laughed and told her to go away. Every time Belva had to make a repair on the car, she got more and more angry. Finally she decided to wreck Eddie's car to get even. Following Eddie home from work one evening, Belva tried to ram his car, hoping to bend the axle or frame. Instead of bending the frame, the collision smashed Eddie's gas tank, caused an explosion, and killed Eddie.

a. Is Belva guilty of any degree of homicide? If so, which degree and for what reason?

b. What was Belva's motive in acting as she did? Should the motive be considered at any stage in the criminal justice process? Why or why not?

Assault and Battery

Assault is any attempt or threat to carry out a physical attack upon another person. To constitute a crime the threatened person must reasonably believe that he or she is in real danger. For example, if John points an unloaded gun at Martha, this would be an assault if Martha believed the gun were loaded. Battery is any unlawful, unconsented to physical contact by one person upon another. Actual injury is not necessary. The only requirement is that the person intended to do bodily harm.

Just as there are "degrees" of murder, there are also different classifications for assault and battery. Aggravated assault and battery is an assault or battery with intent to murder, rob, rape, or do serious bodily harm. For example, if John knocks Martha down while trying to snatch her purse, he is guilty of aggravated assault. Many states impose greater punishment when the assault is made with a deadly weapon, a weapon that could cause death as used in the particular case. Many states also impose greater punishment for assaults on police, prison guards, or other law enforcement officers.

A typical assault results from an argument between persons who know or are related to each other in which rage—often stimulated by alcohol or jealousy—leads to violence. Whether the violence leads to serious injury or death often depends on whether or not a weapon is present. In a recent year sixty-four percent of all homicides were committed with firearms: almost eighty percent of these killings were committed with handguns. The ease with which firearms can be acquired has resulted in a number of proposals to regulate the sale and possession of guns. Some groups have opposed these proposals, citing the Second Amendment to the U.S. Constitution: "A well regulated militia, being necessary to the security of a free state, the right of the people to keep and bear arms, shall not be infringed."

Are there any laws in your community that regulate the sale or possession of firearms?

PROBLEM 12

a. Should the government require the registration of all handguns, rifles, and shotguns? Why or why not?

b. Should the government prohibit the sale and possession of all handguns? What about rifles?

c. Should the government prohibit certain persons, such as drug addicts, persons with a history of mental disturbance, and persons convicted of felonies, from buying, owning, or possessing firearms? Why or why not?

Rape

Traditionally there are two types of rape. Forceable rape is the act of unlawful sexual intercourse committed by a man with a woman by force and without her consent. Statutory rape is sexual intercourse by a male with a female who has not yet reached the age of consent (generally sixteen or eighteen).

Under the common law definition, to constitute rape there must have been sexual penetration of the female by the male. To constitute forceable rape the intercourse must have occurred without the consent of the female. There is no real consent if a woman submits as a result of force or threats of bodily harm. Likewise there is no consent if a woman is unconscious, mentally incompetent, or insensible from drugs or liquor.

A number of states have recently rewritten their rape laws. The newer laws classify the offense as "sexual assault" and make it applicable to both men and women. States that have not adopted new sexual assault laws continue to follow the common law definition.

In the case of statutory rape consent is not an issue. Sexual intercourse with a female under a designated age is rape, *whether she consents or not.* A mistake by a male as to the female's age is not a defense even if the male reasonably believed her to be over the age of consent.

Some states in their sexual assault laws have replaced statutory rape with the category of "sexual conduct with a minor." These laws do not limit the sex of the victim to females.

Nonchastity of a woman is *not* a defense to rape (i.e., a prostitute can be raped), but some states allow evidence of prior unchastity to be considered on the issue of consent. Moreover, in order to convict a person of rape, some states require independent proof that the act took place. This means confirmation or support for the story of the victim, including testimony of a witness, a doctor's report that there has been sexual intercourse, or a prompt report to the police.

PROBLEM 13

a. Statistics reveal that only a small proportion of rape cases are reported to the police. Why is this so? What can be done to encourage legitimate prosecutions?

b. Should the defense in a rape case be allowed to question the victim about past sexual relations with other people? Why or why not?

c. Why is statutory rape a crime? Should it be?

CRIMES AGAINST PROPERTY

This category includes crimes in which property is destroyed (such as **arson** and **vandalism**) and crimes by which property is stolen or otherwise taken against the will of the owner (such as **robbery** and **embezzlement**).

Arson

Arson is the willful and malicious burning of another person's property. Laws in most states make it a crime to burn any building or structure, whether owned by the accused or not. Moreover, any property that is burned with the intent to defraud an insurance company is usually a separate crime, regardless of the type of property burned and regardless of who the property belonged to.

Vandalism

Vandalism, also known as "malicious mischief," is the willful destruction of or causing of damage to the property of another. Vandalism causes millions of dollars in damage each year and includes such things as breaking windows, ripping down fences, flooding basements, and breaking off car aerials. Depending on the extent of the damage, vandalism can be either a felony or a misdemeanor.

PROBLEM 14

a. What, if anything, could be done to reduce vandalism?

b. Should parents be held liable for willful damage caused by their children? Why or why not?

c. If you saw two youths throwing rocks through the windows of a school at night, would you report the youths to the police? Why or why not? Suppose you saw two friends throwing rocks through the windows of a neighbor's home. Would you report your friends to the police? Why or why not? Did you answer both questions the same way? If not, explain why.

Larceny

Larceny is the unlawful taking and carrying away of the property of another with intent to steal it. In most states larceny is divided into two classes, grand and petty, depending on the value of the stolen item. Grand larceny involves the theft of anything above a certain value (often $100) and is a felony. Petty larceny is the theft of anything of small value (usually less than $100) and is a misdemeanor.

The crime of larceny also includes keeping lost property when there is a reasonable method of finding the owner. For example, if you find a wallet with the identification of its owner but nevertheless decide to keep it, you have committed larceny. Likewise, you may be guilty of larceny if you keep property delivered to you by mistake.

Embezzlement

Embezzlement is the unlawful taking of property by someone to whom it was entrusted. For example, the bank teller who takes money from the cash drawer or the stockbroker who takes money that should have been invested are both guilty of embezzlement. In recent years a number of states have merged the crimes of larceny, false pretenses, and embezzlement into the statutory crime of *theft*.

Robbery

Robbery is the unlawful taking of property from a person's immediate possession by force or intimidation. Robbery, unlike other theft offenses, involves two harms—theft of property and actual or potential physical harm to the person. In many states the element of force is the difference between robbery and larceny. Hence a pickpocket who, unnoticed, takes your wallet is liable for the crime of larceny. A mugger who knocks you down and takes your wallet by force is liable for the crime of robbery. Robbery is almost always a felony, but many states impose stricter penalties for armed robberies—that is, thefts committed with a gun or other weapon.

These four photos are not in any special order. Place them in any order you want and make up a story to go along with the photos.

Extortion

Extortion, popularly called "blackmail," is the use of threats to obtain the property of another. Extortion statutes generally cover threats to do future physical harm; threats to destroy property (e.g., "I'll burn down your barn unless you pay me $500"); or threats to injure someone's character or reputation.

Burglary

Burglary was originally defined as the breaking and entering of the dwelling house of another during the night with intent to commit a felony. Modern laws have broadened the definition to include the unauthorized entry into any structure with the intent to commit a crime, regardless of the time of day. Many states have stiffer penalties for burglaries committed at night, burglaries of inhabited dwellings, or burglaries committed with weapons.

Forgery

Forgery is a crime in which a person alters a writing or document with intent to defraud. This usually means signing, without permission, the name of another person to a check or some other document. It can also mean altering or erasing part of a previously signed document. **Uttering,** which in many states is a separate crime, is offering to someone as genuine a document (such as a check) known to be a fake.

Undercover "sting" operations are one method police use to recover stolen merchandise.

Receiving Stolen Property

A person who receives or buys property that he or she knows or has reason to believe is stolen has committed the crime of **receiving stolen property.** Knowledge that the property is stolen may be implied by the circumstances. In most states this is a felony if the value of the property received is more than $100 and a misdemeanor if the value is $100 or less.

Unauthorized Use of a Motor Vehicle

This crime is committed when a person takes, operates, or removes a motor vehicle without consent of the owner. This would include joyriding. A passenger in a stolen car may also be guilty if he or she had reason to know the car was stolen.

PROBLEM 15

Fred found an expensive looking Afghan hound wandering in the park near his home. The dog's collar included an address and indicated that the hound was registered. After keeping the dog for several days, Fred approached Phil and offered to sell the dog for twenty dollars. A dog lover, Phil was eager to buy the hound but was short of cash. He decided to write Fred a check even though he knew that the check was drawn on a bank where he did not have an account. When the bank later refused to honor the check, Fred returned to Phil and threatened to go to the police unless Phil gave him twenty dollars plus another fifty dollars in cash. Has Fred or Phil committed any crimes?

PROBLEM 16

Sue steals a watch from Jason and later sells the watch to Wally, who has no reason to believe the watch is stolen. Sue leaves town, but later Jason claims his watch when he sees Wally wearing it. Wally refuses to give the watch to Jason, claiming it belongs to him because he paid for it.

a. Who would settle the dispute between Wally and Jason, a civil court or a criminal court? In what ways might this dispute be settled without going to court?

b. What additional information would help to settle this dispute? How should the dispute be resolved?

CONTROVERSIAL CRIMES

This third category of crimes is made up of offenses that are considered to be crimes against society in general and that often involve issues of personal conduct, public health, or social welfare. Some of these offenses are referred to as "victimless" crimes, although there is considerable controversy over whether they are truly victimless.

Drug Offenses

Possession, distribution, or sale of certain drugs is a crime that may be in violation of federal law, state law, or both. The federal drug law known as the Controlled Substance Act classifies drugs into five groups, depending on medical use (if any), potential for abuse, and capability to create physical or psychological dependence. The penalties and criminal sanctions are different for each of the five groups.

Penalties are heaviest for individuals who manufacture, distribute, or sell controlled drugs—up to fifteen years in prison and fines up to $25,000. For second and subsequent offenses, penalties are double the original penalty. Simple possession of any controlled substance is a misdemeanor for the first offense under the federal law, but some states still treat simple possession as a felony.

Legislation has been proposed in Congress that would decriminalize but not legalize possession of small amounts of

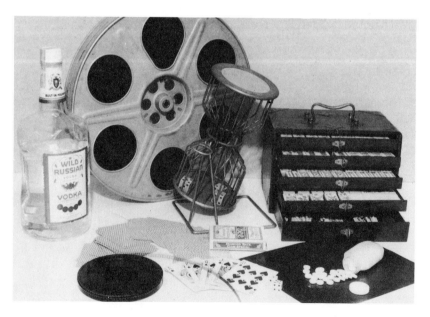

What laws could be violated using each of these?

marijuana. Violators of this proposed law would receive tickets and pay fines in much the same way that traffic violators are treated.

PROBLEM 17

a. What would be the difference between decriminalization and outright legalization of marijuana? What effect, if any, would each of these measures have on the use of marijuana?

b. Mike knows that he can be arrested for drunken driving but says that he can't be arrested for driving while under the influence of drugs. Is he right or wrong?

c. A presidential commission on crime and law enforcement concluded that it does no good to put drunks in jail. What would you recommend be done for those who abuse alcohol? Cocaine? Marijuana? Heroin?

d. Do you think there is any relationship between the abuse of drugs, including alcohol, and crime and juvenile delinquency? Explain your answer.

WHERE YOU LIVE

In your community, what are the penalties for possession and/or sale of marijuana, amphetamines, cocaine, and heroin?

Sex Offenses

Certain sex crimes, such as rape or child molestation, are regarded primarily as offenses against another person. There are other sex crimes, however, that are deemed illegal as offenses against public morality or decency. These offenses, which include **bigamy, adultery, homosexuality,** and **prostitution,** most often occur in private between consulting adults and are said to be largely unenforceable.

Bigamy is the offense of marrying a person while still validly married to someone else. Statutes making this a crime are based on the belief that the family is the basic unit of society. Bigamy is punishable as a felony in almost every state.

Adultery is the act of sexual intercourse between a married person and someone other than his or her own spouse. It is a ground for divorce in almost every state; it is also punishable as a crime in many states, although this law is almost never enforced.

Homosexuality is the condition of being sexually and emotionally oriented toward persons of the same sex. It is a status or condition of being and is not a crime. However, despite changing standards, many states consider specific sexual acts engaged in by persons of the same sex to be crimes.

Prostitution, the performance of sexual acts for money, is a crime in every state except for a few counties in Nevada. Prostitu-

tion almost always takes place between consenting individuals, but it is nevertheless outlawed as a violation of cultural norms and an offense against public decency.

PROBLEM 18

a. Although the acts are generally done in private, what would be the public consequences, if any, if society repealed laws against adulterous or homosexual conduct?

b. In the case of prostitution, the police often arrest and charge the prostitute but let the customer go free. Should prostitution laws be enforced equally against both the customer and the prostitute? Why or why not?

c. Can you think of any arguments in favor of or against legalized prostitution?

d. Why do you think we have laws, which are generally unenforced, regulating sexual conduct?

Suicide and Euthanasia

Suicide is the deliberate taking of one's own life. In earlier times suicide was treated as a felony punishable by burial in an unmarked grave and forfeiture of the dead person's belongings to the state. Today, criminal penalties for successful suicides have been abolished, but there are still criminal laws against attempted suicide and criminal penalties for aiding another in a successful suicide. However, as a practical matter these laws are rarely enforced. Instead, persons who have attempted suicide are generally referred for counseling or other appropriate treatment.

Euthanasia, often referred to as "mercy killing," is an act or method of putting to death persons who are terminally ill. Some people advocate euthanasia as a humane way of dealing with victims of incurable diseases, but many people feel it is a highly controversial moral and religious issue. Euthanasia is illegal in every state and may be prosecuted as a homicide.

PROBLEM 19

Richard loved his wife Dale. In fact, they were so close that Richard agreed to help Dale commit suicide when she became depressed because of poor health. According to the police Dale died from inhaling carbon monoxide fumes while sitting in a car in the couple's closed garage. Richard admitted helping her get into the car and closing the garage door but insisted that Dale wanted to commit suicide and that he could not talk her out of it. A suicide note left by Dale backed up this claim.

a. Can Richard be charged with any crime? If so, what crime and for what reason?

b. If Richard is charged, should he be convicted? Why or why not? If he is convicted, what should his sentence be?

c. Should society try to prevent suicides? Why or why not?

DEFENSES

For a conviction to occur in a criminal case, the prosecutor must establish beyond a reasonable doubt that the defendant committed the act in question. The defendant is not required to present a defense but can instead simply force the government to prove its case. There are, however, a number of possible defenses in a criminal case.

No Crime Has Been Committed

In this category the defendant establishes innocence by showing that either no crime has been committed (e.g., the defendant was carrying a gun but had a valid license; the defendant did not commit rape because the woman was of legal age and consented) or that there was no criminal intent (e.g., the defendant mistakenly took another person's coat when leaving a restaurant). The defendant is innocent of a charge of larceny if it was an honest and reasonable mistake.

Defendant Did Not Commit the Crime

Often times there is no doubt that a crime has been committed, in which case the question is, who committed it? In this situation the defendant could establish innocence by showing a mistake in identity or by an **alibi,** which is evidence that the defendant was somewhere else at the time the crime was committed.

Defendant Committed a Criminal Act but the Act Was Excusable or Justified

Defenses in this category include self-defense, defense of property and others, and **duress** or **necessity.**

Self-Defense and Defense of Property and Others   The law recognizes the right of a person unlawfully attacked to use reasonable force in self-defense. It also recognizes the right of one person to use reasonable force to defend another person from imminent attack. There are, however, a number of limitations to these defenses.

A person who *reasonably* believes there is imminent danger of bodily harm can use a reasonable amount of force in self-defense. A person cannot use more force than necessary, however. If after stopping an attacker, the defender continues to use force, the roles reverse and the defender can no longer claim self-defense. Deadly force can be used only if one reasonably believes that there is imminent danger of death or serious bodily harm. A person is allowed to use nondeadly force in defense of any third person if the person defended is entitled to claim self-defense. Reasonable nondeadly force may also be used to protect property.

PROBLEM 20

a. Mr. Roe kept a pistol in his home as protection against intruders. One evening he heard a noise in his den and went to investigate. Upon entering the room he saw a man stealing his television. The burglar, seeing the gun, ran for the window, but Mr. Roe fired and killed him before he could escape. In a trial for manslaughter Mr. Roe pleads self-defense. Would you find him guilty? Why or why not?

b. Suppose you see two men struggling with a casual friend. Thinking they are muggers, you rush to the rescue. It turns out that your friend is wanted for a crime and the men are plainclothes police officers attempting to make an arrest. You are charged with assault. Do you have a defense?

c. The owner of a jewelry store spots a shoplifter stealing an expensive necklace. Can the owner use force to prevent the crime? If so, how much?

Duress and Necessity   This category of defense involves situations where an individual violates a criminal law to avoid a greater harm. In the case of duress, a criminal act may be excused by showing that the accused was not acting of his or her own free will. To be a successful defense it must be shown that the accused or some member of his immediate family was threatened with death or seriously bodily harm. For example, Joe kidnaps Bill's child and threatens to kill her unless Bill steals money from his employer. Bill may claim the defense of duress.

Necessity may be a defense to a crime where the defendant acts in the reasonable belief that there is no alternative. For example, Sally steals a boat to escape an onrushing flood. This defense is only available where there is no other way to avoid the threatened harm. Mere economic necessity (need for money) is not sufficient to excuse a criminal act. Also, neither duress nor necessity is a defense to a crime of homicide.

Defendant Committed a Criminal Act but Is Not Criminally Responsible for His or Her Actions

In this category are the defenses of infancy, intoxication, insanity, and **entrapment.**

Infancy Traditionally, children of a very young age, usually under seven, were considered legally incapable of committing a crime. Children between the ages of seven and fourteen were generally presumed incapable of committing a crime, but this presumption could be shown to be wrong. Under modern laws, most states simply provide that children under a specified age shall not be tried for their crimes but shall be turned over to the juvenile court.

Intoxication Defendants sometimes claim that at the time of a crime they were so drunk on alcohol or high on drugs that they didn't know what they were doing. As a general rule, voluntary intoxication is *not* a defense to a crime. However, some crimes require proof of a specific mental state. For example, when Grady is charged with assault with intent to kill, he claims he was drunk. If he can prove this, intoxication is a valid defense because it negates the specific mental state (i.e., intent to kill) required to prove the crime. Grady can still be charged with assault, however, because specific intent is not required to prove that crime. If Grady decided to kill someone before he got drunk, or if he got drunk to get up enough nerve to commit the crime, then intoxication would not be a defense because the required mental state (i.e., intent to kill) existed before the drunkenness.

Insanity During criminal proceedings, insanity becomes an issue in determining the following: whether the defendant is *competent* to stand trial; whether the defendant was *sane at the time of the criminal act;* and whether the defendant is *sane after the trial.* In proving insanity as a defense to a crime, however, courts are only concerned with the accused's sanity at the time of the criminal act. Insanity or incompetence at the time of trial may delay the proceedings until the accused can understand what is taking place, but insanity during or after the trial does not affect criminal liability.

To prove insanity, the defense must produce evidence of a mental disease or defect. Psychiatrists are usually brought in to give testimony in this regard. Both the defense and the prosecution may have psychiatrists examine the defendant, and their testimony is often in conflict. The decision as to whether insanity is a valid defense rests with whoever—judge or jury—decides the facts of the case.

Courts agree that a person who, at the time of committing a criminal act, was so mentally ill or defective as to be deemed legally insane is not responsible for the act. However, courts in different states disagree over what constitutes insanity. Most courts say that defendants are not responsible for a crime if at the time of the act they didn't know what they were doing or they lacked the ability to distinguish between right and wrong. In other courts, insanity is a good defense if the criminal act was the result of an "irresistible impulse"—that is, as a result of a mental disease or defect, the accused was unable to control his or her actions. For example, Joan, a kleptomaniac, is constantly stealing things. If she is on trial for theft, she would have a valid insanity defense if she could show that as a result of a mental disorder—kleptomania—she could not keep herself from stealing.

Entrapment The defense of entrapment applies when the defendant admits committing a criminal act but claims that he or she was induced or persuaded to commit the crime by a law enforcement officer. However, it is not entrapment merely because a police officer provided the defendant with an opportunity to commit a crime; rather, it must be shown that the defendant would not have committed the crime *but for* the inducement of the police. Entrapment is difficult to prove and cannot be claimed as a defense to crimes involving serious physical injury, such as rape or murder.

PROBLEM 21

Can entrapment be claimed as a valid defense in either of the following cases? Explain your answer.

a. Mary, an undercover police officer masquerading as a prostitute, approaches John and tells him that she'll have sex with him in exchange for fifty dollars. John hands over the money.

b. Marvin, a drug dealer, offers to sell drugs to Walter, a police officer disguised as a drug addict. Walter buys the drugs and Marvin is arrested.

THE CRIMINAL JUSTICE PROCESS

WHERE
YOU
LIVE

How does the criminal justice system in your state compare to the system shown in Figure 4?

The criminal justice process consists of everything that happens to a person from the time of arrest until that person is free from the control of the state. That freedom may be gained almost immediately—at the stationhouse—or after serving time in a correctional institution. Freedom may also come at any stage in between. Figure 4 on pages 60 and 61 shows a typical state criminal justice system through which an adult must pass when charged with a felony. Note that there are various places in which a person can exit the system without completing it. The juvenile justice process discussed at the end of this chapter is somewhat different. You may find it useful to refer back to Figure 4 as we study each step of the process.

ARREST

An **arrest** means that a person suspected of a crime is taken into custody. A person can be taken into custody in one of two ways: by an arrest **warrant** or by a warrantless arrest based on probable cause. A person, once taken into custody and not free to leave, is considered to be under arrest, whether told that or not.

An arrest warrant is a court order that commands that the person named in it be taken into custody. A warrant is obtained by filing a complaint before a judge or magistrate. The person filing the complaint is generally a police officer but may also be a victim or a witness. The person making the complaint must set out and swear to the facts and circumstances of the alleged crime. If, on the basis of the information provided, the judge finds **probable cause** to believe that an offense has been committed and that the accused committed it, a warrant will be issued.

There are many occasions when the police don't have time to get a warrant and so may make a warrantless arrest based on probable cause. Probable cause is defined as a reasonable belief that a person has committed a crime. This reasonable belief may be based on less evidence than that necessary to prove a person guilty at trial. As an example, suppose the police receive a radio report of a bank robbery. An officer sees a man, matching the description of the bank robber, waving a gun and running away from the bank. The officer would have probable cause to stop and arrest the man.

There is no exact formula for determining probable cause. Police must use their own judgment as to what is reasonable under the circumstances of each case. In all cases probable cause requires more than mere suspicion or a hunch. There must be some facts that indicate that the person arrested has committed a crime.

FIGURE 4 A General View of the Criminal Justice System

This chart seeks to present a simple yet comprehensive view of the movement of cases through the criminal justice system. Procedures in individual jurisdictions may vary from the pattern shown here. The differing weights of line indicate the relative volumes of cases disposed of at various points in the system, but this is only suggestive since no nationwide data of this sort exists.

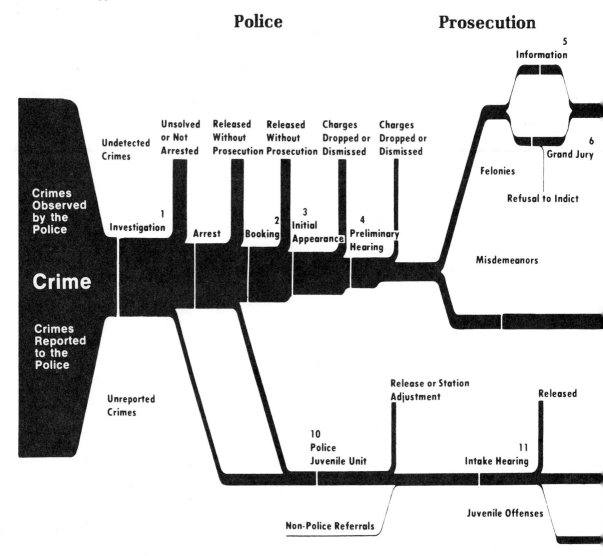

1. May continue until trial.

2. Administrative record of arrest. First step at which temporary release on bail may be available.

3. Before magistrate, commissioner, or justice of peace. Formal notice of charge, advice of rights. Bail set. Summary trials for petty offenses usually conducted here without further processing.

4. Preliminary testing of evidence against defendant. Charge may be reduced. No separate preliminary hearing for misdemeanors in some systems.

5. Charge filed by prosecutor on basis of information submitted by police or citizens. Alternative to grand jury indictment.

6. Reviews whether Government evidence sufficient to justify trial. Some States have no grand jury system; others seldom use it.

Courts

Corrections

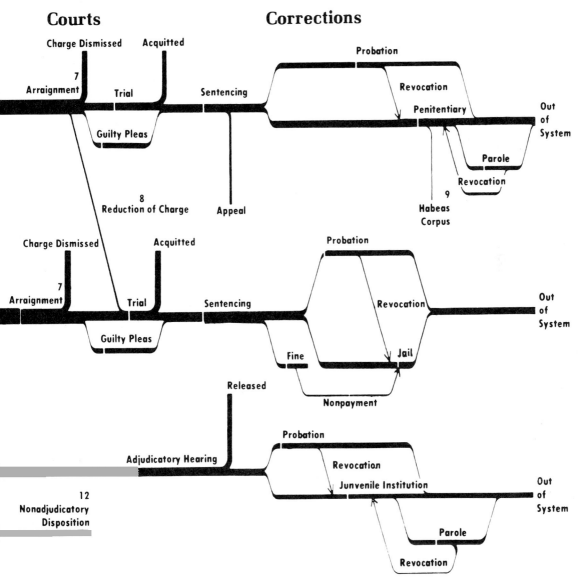

7. Appearance for plea; defendant elects trial by judge or jury (if available).

8. Charge may be reduced at any time prior to trial in return for plea of guilty or for other reasons.

9. Challenge on constitutional grounds to legality of detention. May be sought at any point in process.

10. Police often hold informal hearings, dismiss or adjust many cases without further processing.

11. Probation officer decides desirability of further court action.

12. Welfare agency, social services, counseling, medical care, etc., for cases where adjudicatory handling not needed.

This is a modified version of a chart published in the President's Commission Report, *The Challenge of Crime in a Free Society*, note 11, p. 39 *supra*, at pp. 8–9. Modification from *Introduction to the Criminal Justice System*, Second Edition, by Hazel B. Kerper as revised by Jerold H. Israel, West Publishing Company, © 1979. Reprinted by permission of the publisher.

What is the best thing to do if stopped by the police?

PROBLEM 22

Witnesses see two masked men flee from a holdup in an unidentified light-colored car. Later that day, in a neighboring town, police alerted to the crime see two men traveling a little too slowly in a light-colored car.

a. Based on what you know, do you think the police have probable cause to arrest the occupants of the car?

b. If the police stop the car for a traffic violation, can they question the men about the holdup? Can they order the men out of the car?

PROBLEM 23

The police receive a tip that a drug pusher named Richie will be flying from New York to Washington sometime on the morning of September 8. The informer describes Richie as being a tall man with reddish hair and a beard. He also tells police that Richie has a habit of walking real fast and that he will be carrying illegal drugs in a brown leather bag.

On the morning of September 8, the police watch all passengers arriving from New York. When they see a man who fits the description—carrying a brown leather bag and walking fast—they arrest him. A search of the bag reveals a large quantity of heroin.

a. Based on what you know, do you think the police had probable cause to arrest Richie? Why or why not?

b. Should the police have obtained a warrant before arresting Richie? Why or why not?

Even without probable cause, a police officer may stop and question an individual if the officer reasonably suspects the person of being involved in some criminal activity. In such a case, the police officer may ask for some identification and for an explanation of the suspicious behavior. If asked specific questions about a crime with which he or she may be involved, the individual does not have to answer. However, a refusal to cooperate may result in further detention. In some cases it may provide sufficient additional evidence to result in a valid arrest. For example, suppose a police officer has reason to suspect someone of a crime and the person refuses to answer the police officer's questions or attempts to flee when being approached by the officer. This conduct, when considered together with other factors, might provide the probable cause necessary to arrest. In addition, if a police officer, based on his or her experience, thinks a person is behaving suspiciously and is likely to be armed, the officer may **stop and frisk** (pat down) the suspect for weapons.

Police officers may search a suspect incident to (at the time of making) a lawful arrest.

A police officer may use as much physical force as is reasonably necessary to make an arrest. If a police officer uses too much force or makes an unlawful arrest, the accused may bring a civil action for damages or possibly a criminal action for violation of civil rights. In addition, many police departments have established procedures for handling citizen complaints about police misconduct. It should be noted, however, that a police officer is never liable for false arrest simply becuse the person arrested did not commit the crime. Rather, it must be shown that the officer acted maliciously or had no reasonable grounds for suspicion of guilt.

THE CASE OF THE UNLUCKY COUPLE

After an evening at the movies, Lonnie Howard and his girl friend Susan decide to park in the empty lot behind Briarwood Elementary School. Several beers and two marijuana cigarettes later, they are startled by the sound of breaking glass from the rear of the school.

Unnoticed in their darkened car, Lonnie and Susan observe two men loading office equipment from the school into the back of a van. Quickly concluding that the men must be burglars, Lonnie revs up his engine and roars out of the parking lot onto Main Street.

Meanwhile, unknown to Lonnie and Susan, a silent alarm has also alerted the police to the break-in at the school. Responding to the alarm, Officer Ramos heads for the school and turns onto Main Street just in time to see Lonnie's car speeding away.

PROBLEM 24
a. If you were Officer Ramos, what would you do in this situation? If you were Lonnie, what would you do?
b. If Officer Ramos chases after Lonnie, would he have probable cause to stop and arrest him?
c. How do you think Officer Ramos would act once he stopped Lonnie? How do you think Lonnie and Susan would act?
d. Roleplay this situation. As Officer Ramos, decide what you would say and how you would act toward the occupants of the car. As Lonnie and Susan, decide what you would say and how you would act toward the police.
e. What could Lonnie and Susan do if they were mistakenly arrested for the burglary? What could they do if they were abused or mistreated by Officer Ramos?

SEARCH AND SEIZURE

The right of the people to be secure in their persons, houses, papers, and effects, against unreasonable searches and seizures, shall not be violated, and no warrants shall issue, but upon probable cause, supported by oath or affirmation, and particularly describing the place to be searched, and the persons or things to be seized.

—Fourth Amendment to the U.S. Constitution

Americans have always valued their privacy. They expect to be left alone, to be free from unwarranted snooping or spying, and to be secure in their own homes. These expectations of privacy are important and are protected by the the U.S. Constitution. The Fourth Amendment sets out the right to be free from "unreasonable searches and seizures" and establishes conditions under which search warrants may be issued.

Balanced against the individual's right to privacy is the government's need to gather information. In the case of the police, this is the need to collect evidence against criminals and to protect society against crime.

ADVICE ON WHAT TO DO IF ARRESTED

1. *Don't struggle with the police.* Avoid fighting or swearing, even if you know the police have made a mistake. Resisting arrest and assaulting a police officer are usually separate crimes that you can be charged with even when you've done nothing else wrong.

2. Give your name, address, and phone number to the police. Otherwise, *keep quiet.* Don't discuss your case with anyone at this point and don't sign any statements about your case.

3. You may be searched, photographed, and fingerprinted. Notice carefully what is done but don't resist. If any personal property is taken from you, ask for a written receipt.

4. As soon as possible after you get to the police station, *call a trusted relative or friend.* Tell this person where you are, what you've been charged with, and what your bail or bond is (if you know).

5. *When you're arrested on a minor offense,* you may, in some places, be released without having to put up any money (this is called an unsecured bond or a citation release). If you don't qualify for a citation release, you may have to put up some money before release (this is called posting a cash bond or collateral). Ask for a receipt for the money.

6. *When you're arrested for a serious misdemeanor or felony,* you won't be released immediately. Ask the friend or relative you have called to get a lawyer for you. If you can't afford a lawyer, the court will appoint one for you at the initial appearance.

7. Before you leave the police station, be sure to find out when you're due in court. *Never be late or miss a court appearance.* If you don't show up in court at the assigned time, a warrant will be issued for your rearrest.

8. *Don't talk about your case with anyone except your lawyer.* Be honest with your lawyer or he/she will have trouble helping you. Ask that your lawyer be present at *all* lineups and interrogation sessions.

The Fourth Amendment is not an absolute right to privacy, and it does not prohibit all searches—only those which are unreasonable. In deciding if a search is reasonable, the courts look to the facts and circumstances of each case. As a general rule, courts have held that searches and seizures are usually unreasonable unless authorized by a valid warrant.

Searches with a Warrant

A search warrant is a court order obtained from a judge who is convinced that there is a real need to search a person or place. Before a judge issues a warrant, someone—usually a police officer—must appear in court and testify under oath concerning the facts and information that provide the probable cause or good reason to believe that a search is justified. This sworn statement of facts and circumstances is known as an **affidavit.** If a judge decides to issue a search warrant, the warrant must specifically describe the person or place to be searched and the particular things to be seized.

Once a search warrant is issued, the search must be executed within a limited period of time, such as ten days. Also, in many states a search warrant must be executed only in the daytime, unless the warrant expressly states otherwise. Finally, a search warrant does not necessarily authorize a general search of everything in the specified place. For example, if the police have a warrant to search a house for stolen televisions or other large items, it would be unreasonable for them to look in desk drawers, envelopes, or other small places where a television could not possibly be hidden.

PROBLEM 25

a. Examine Figure 5, an affidavit for a search warrant. Who is requesting the warrant? What are the searchers looking for? What persons or places are sought to be searched? What facts and circumstances are given to justify the search?

b. Examine Figure 6, a search warrant. Who authorized the search? When may the search be conducted? Considering the affidavit, do you think the judge had sufficient grounds to authorize the warrant? Is there anything missing from the warrant?

c. As a general rule, why do you think the Fourth Amendment requires police to obtain a warrant before conducting a search? Why do you think there is a general requirement that searches be conducted during daylight hours?

d. Under what conditions do you think police should be allowed to search without a warrant?

Searches without a Warrant

While the police are generally required to get a search warrant, the courts have recognized that there are also a number of situations when searches may be legally conducted without a warrant.

■ Search Incident to a Lawful Arrest. This is the most common exception to the warrant requirement, and it allows the police to search a lawfully arrested person and the area immediately around that person for hidden weapons or for evidence that might be destroyed.

■ Stop and Frisk. A police officer who reasonably thinks a person is behaving suspiciously and is likely to be armed may stop and frisk the suspect for weapons. This exception to the warrant requirement was created to protect the safety of officers and bystanders who might be injured by a person carrying a concealed weapon.

■ Consent. When a person voluntarily agrees, the police may conduct a search without a warrant and without probable cause. Normally a person may only grant permission to search his or her own belongings or property. There are some situations, however, in which one person may legally allow the police to conduct a search of another person's property (e.g., parent-child, teacher-student).

FIGURE 5 Affidavit for Search Warrant

**Affidavit for
Search Warrant**

United States District Court
FOR THE
Eastern District of Missouri

UNITED STATES OF AMERICA

vs.

John Doe

Docket No. A

Case No. 11246

**AFFIDAVIT FOR
SEARCH WARRANT**

BEFORE Michael J. Thiel, Federal Courthouse, St. Louis, Missouri
Name of Judge¹ or Federal Magistrate   Address of Judge¹ or Federal Magistrate

The undersigned being duly sworn deposes and says:

That he has reason to believe that (on the person of) Occupants, and
(on the premises known as) 935 Bay Street, St. Louis,
Missouri, described as a two story, residential dwelling, white in
color and of wood frame construction.....

in the   Eastern   District of Missouri

there is now being concealed certain property, namely

here describe property

Counterfeit bank notes, money orders, and securities, and
plates, stones, and other paraphernalia used in counterfeiting
and forgery,

which are
here give alleged grounds for search and seizure²
in violation of 18 U.S. Code ¶471-474

And that the facts tending to establish the foregoing grounds for issuance of a Search Warrant
are as follows:³ (1) Pursuant to my employment with the Federal Bureau of Investigation, I
received information from a reliable informant that a group of persons were conducting
an illegal counterfeiting operation out of a house at 935 Bay Street, St. Louis, Missouri.
(2) Acting on this information agents of the FBI placed the house at 935 Bay Street under
around the clock surveillance. During the course of this surveillance officers observed
a number of facts tending to establsh the existence of an illegal counterfeiting operation.
These include: observation of torn & defective counterfeit notes discarded in the trash
in the alley behind the house at 935 Bay Street, and pick-up & delivery of parcels at
irregular hours of the night by persons known to the FBI as having records for distribution
of counterfeit money.

Barry I. Cunningham Special Agent
Signature of Affiant.

Federal Bureau of Investigation
Official Title, if any.

Sworn to before me, and subscribed in my presence, *December 3rd* , 19 78

Michael J. Thiel
Judge¹ or Federal Magistrate.

FIGURE 6 Search Warrant

Form A. O. 93 (Rev. Nov. 1972)   Search Warrant

United States District Court

FOR THE

Eastern District of Missouri

UNITED STATES OF AMERICA   Docket No.   A

vs.   Case No.   11246

John Doe   SEARCH WARRANT

To Any sheriff, constable, marshall, police officer, or investigative
   officer of the United States of America.
   Affidavit (s) having been made before me by
   Special Agent, Barry I. Cunningham

that he has reason to believe that { on the person of
                                     on the premises known as }

   on the occupants of, and
   on the premises known as 935 Bay Street, St. Louis, Missouri
       described as a two story, residential dwelling, white in
       color and of wood frame construction .....

                       in the   Eastern   District of Missouri

there is now being concealed certain property, namely
   Counterfeit bank notes, money orders, and securities, and
   Plates, stones, **and other paraphernalia** used in counterfeiting and
       forgery

and as I am satisfied that **there is probable cause to believe** that the property so described is being
concealed on the person or premises above described and that the foregoing grounds for application for
issuance of the search warrant exist.

   You are hereby commanded to search within a period of ___10_____ (not to exceed 10
days) the person or place named for the property specified, serving this warrant and making the
search { ~~in the daytime (6:00 a.m. to 10:00 p.m.)~~
         at anytime in the day or night[1] } and if the property be found there to seize it,
leaving a copy of this warrant and a receipt for the property taken, and prepare a written inventory of
the property seized and promptly return this warrant and bring the property before me as required
by law.

Dated this 3rd   day of December   , 19 78   *Michael J. Thiel*
                                                      ---------------------------------,
                                                        Judge or Federal Magistrate.

---
[1] The Federal Rules of Criminal Procedure provide: "The warrant shall be served in the daytime, unless the issuing authority, by appropriate
provision in the warrant, and for reasonable cause shown, authorizes its execution at times other than daytime." (Rule 41(C))

Is an airport luggage search a violation of the Fourth Amendment?

■ Plain View. If an object connected with a crime is in plain view and can be seen by an officer from a place where he or she has a right to be, it can be seized without a warrant. For example, if a police officer issuing a routine traffic ticket observes a gun on the seat of the car, the officer may seize the gun without a warrant.

■ Hot Pursuit. Police in hot pursuit of a suspect are not required to get a search warrant before entering a building that they have seen the suspect enter. It is also lawful to seize evidence found during a search conducted while in hot pursuit of a felon.

■ Vehicle Searches. A police officer who has reasonable cause to believe that a vehicle contains **contraband** may conduct a search of the vehicle without a warrant. This does not mean that the police have a right to stop and search any vehicle on the streets. The right to stop and search must be based on probable cause.

■ Emergency Situations. In certain emergencies, the police are not required to get a search warrant. These situations include searching a building after a telephoned bomb threat, entering a house after smelling smoke or hearing screams, and other situations where the police don't have time to get a warrant.

■ Border and Airport Searches. Customs agents are authorized to search without warrants and without probable cause. They may examine the baggage, vehicle, purse, wallet, or similar belongings of persons entering the country. Body searches or searches conducted away from the border are allowed only on reasonable suspicion. In view of the danger of airplane hijacking, courts have also held it reasonable for airlines to search all carryon luggage and to search all passengers by means of a metal detector.

PROBLEM 26

Examine each of the situations below. Decide whether the search and seizure is lawful or unlawful and explain your reasons.

a. Jill's former boyfriend breaks into her apartment and looks through her desk for love letters. Instead he finds drugs, which he turns over to the police.

b. After Joe spends the night at a hotel, the police ask the maids to turn over the contents of the waste basket and they find notes planning a murder.

c. A student informs the principal that Bob, another student, is selling drugs on school grounds. The principal opens Bob's locker with a master key, finds drugs, and calls the police.

d. The police see Dell—a known drug pusher—standing at a bus stop on a downtown street. They stop and search him and find drugs in his pocket.

e. Susan is arrested for reckless driving. After stopping her, the police search her purse and find a pistol.

f. Larry is observed shoplifting items in a store. Police chase Larry into his apartment building and arrest him outside the door of his apartment. A search of the apartment reveals a large quantity of stolen merchandise.

g. The police receive a tip from a reliable informant that Rudy has counterfeit money in his office. Acting on this information, they get a search warrant and find the money just where the informant told them it would be.

h. Sandy is suspected of receiving stolen goods. The police go to her apartment and ask Claire, her roommate, if they can search the apartment. Claire says it's OK, and the police find stolen items in Sandy's dresser.

Do school authorities have the right to search student lockers?

yes.

While the language of the Fourth Amendment is relatively simple, search and seizure law is quite complex. Courts tend to look at the law on a case-by-case basis, and there are many exceptions to the basic concepts. Once an individual is arrested, it is up to the courts to decide whether any evidence found in a search was legally obtained. If the courts find that the search in question was unreasonable, any evidence found in the search cannot be used at

---

THE CASE OF FINGERS McGEE

Officers Smith and Jones receive a radio report of a robbery at the Dixie Liquor Store. The report indicates only that the suspect is male, about six feet tall, and wearing old clothes. Some five minutes earlier Fingers McGee saw the owner of the Dixie Liquor Store chasing a man carrying a sack and what appeared to be a knife down the street. McGee "thinks" the man looks like Bill Johnson, a drug addict who lives in a house a few blocks away. Officers Smith and Jones encounter McGee on a street corner.

PROBLEM 27
a. Roleplay this encounter. As the officers, decide what questions to ask McGee. As McGee, decide what to tell the officers.
b. Assuming McGee tells the police what he knows, what should the police do then?
c. Should the police get a search warrant before going to Johnson's house? If they go to Johnson's house without a warrant, do they have probable cause to arrest him? Why or why not?
d. If the police decide to enter Johnson's house, what should they do? Should they knock and announce themselves or should they break in unannounced?
e. If the police enter the house, decide whether Johnson can be arrested, where the police can search, and what, if anything, can be seized.

the trial against the defendant. This principle, called the **exclusionary rule**, does not mean that a defendant cannot be tried or convicted, but it does mean that the particular evidence that was seized in an unlawful search cannot be used at trial. (For a further discussion of the exclusionary rule, see the section "Pretrial Motions and the Exclusionary Rule.")

INTERROGATIONS AND CONFESSIONS

After an arrest has been made, it is standard police practice to question or interrogate the accused. These interrogations have often resulted in confessions or admissions, which were later used as evidence at trial.

Balanced against the police's need to question suspects are the constitutional rights of persons accused of a crime. The Fifth Amendment to the U.S. Constitution provides citizens with a

---

THE CASE OF MIRANDA v. ARIZONA

Ernesto Miranda was accused of kidnapping and raping an eighteen-year-old girl near Phoenix, Arizona. The girl claimed she was on her way home from work when a man grabbed her, threw her into the back seat of a car, and raped her. Ten days later Miranda was arrested, placed in a lineup, and identified by the girl as her attacker. The police then took Miranda into an interrogation room and questioned him for two hours. At the end of the two hours, the officers emerged with a written and signed confession. This confession was used as evidence at trial, and Miranda was found guilty.

Miranda later appealed his case to the U.S. Supreme Court, arguing that he had not been warned of his right to remain silent and that he had been deprived of his right to counsel. Miranda did not suggest that his confession was false or brought about by coercion, but rather that he would not have confessed if he had been advised of his right to remain silent or of his right to an attorney.

PROBLEM 28
a. Do you think Miranda's confession should have been used as evidence against him at trial? Why or why not?
b. Do you think police should be required to tell suspects their rights before questioning them?
c. Do you think anyone would confess after being warned of their rights?

privilege against self-incrimination. This means that a suspect has a right to remain silent and cannot be forced to testify against him or herself. Under the Sixth Amendment a person accused of a crime has the right to the assistance of an attorney.

For many years the Supreme Court held that a confession was not admissible as evidence if it was not voluntary and trustworthy. This meant that the use of physical force, torture, threats, or other techniques that could force an innocent person to confess was prohibited. Later, in the case of *Escobedo* v. *Illinois*, the Supreme Court said that even a voluntary confession was inadmissable as evidence if it was obtained after denying the defendant's request to talk with an attorney. While some defendants might ask for an attorney, other people might not be aware of their right to remain silent or of their right to have a lawyer present during questioning. In 1966, the Supreme Court was presented with such a situation in the case of *Miranda* v. *Arizona*.

After considering all the arguments, the Supreme Court ruled that Miranda's confession could not be used at trial because it was obtained without informing Miranda of his constitutional rights. As a result of this case, police are now required to inform persons accused of a crime of the following Miranda rights *before questioning begins.*

MIRANDA WARNINGS

That they have the right to remain silent. That anything they say can be used against them in court.

That they have the right to a lawyer and to have one present while they are being questioned.

That if they cannot afford a lawyer, one will be appointed for them before any questioning begins.

Suspects sometimes complain that they were not read their Miranda rights and that the entire case should therefore be dropped and charges dismissed. Failure to give Miranda warnings, however, does not affect the validity of an arrest. The police only have to give Miranda warnings if they want to use statements from the accused. In fact, in his second trial Miranda was convicted on other evidence.

The *Miranda* case has been very controversial. It illustrates the delicate balance between the protection guaranteed the accused and the protection provided society from crime. This balance is constantly changing, and the effect of the *Miranda* case has been somewhat altered by more recent cases, such as *Harris* v. *New York*.

THE CASE OF HARRIS v. NEW YORK

Fred Harris was arrested and charged with selling drugs to an undercover officer. At the time of his arrest, Harris made several statements indicating that he was indeed selling heroin. These statements, however, were made before he was warned of his right to remain silent.

During his trial, Harris took the stand and denied selling drugs to the officer. At this point the prosecutor introduced Harris's earlier statements to contradict his testimony at trial. The defense attorney objected, but the judge allowed the use of the earlier statements, and Harris was convicted.

Harris appealed his case to the U.S. Supreme Court, arguing that according to the Miranda rule no confession or statements of a defendant made prior to being warned of his rights could be used at trial.

PROBLEM 29
a. If you were the judge at Harris's trial, would you have allowed his earlier statements to be used as evidence? If so, how do you justify this in view of the Supreme Court's ruling in the *Miranda* case?
b. Which statements do you consider more reliable, those made at trial or those made immediately after arrest?
c. *Harris* v. *New York* was decided by the U.S. Supreme Court in October, 1971. Paraphrased below are the opinions of two of the justices on the Court. Which of these opinions do you agree with and why?

Opinion #1
> *Any* evidence obtained before giving the Miranda warnings should not be used at trial. It would be wrong for the courts to aid lawbreaking police officers. Allowing the use of illegally obtained statements to impeach or contradict testimony at trial would discourage defendants from taking the stand in their own defense.

Opinion #2
> Defendants cannot be forced to testify, but if they do, they give up their right against self-incrimination and can be cross-examined like any other witness. Since Harris took the stand and told a story different from the one he had given the police, the prosecutor was entitled to introduce the earlier statement for the sole purpose of cross-examining the defendant and impeaching his testimony.

PROCEEDINGS BEFORE TRIAL

Before a case ever reaches the courtroom, several preliminary proceedings take place. Some of these proceedings are standard for every case, while others may result in the charges being dropped or in a plea of guilty by the defendant.

Booking and Initial Appearance

After an arrest the accused is normally taken to a police station for booking—the formal process of making a police record of the arrest. Following this, the accused will usually be fingerprinted and photographed. In certain circumstances the police are allowed to take fingernail clippings, handwriting specimens, or blood samples.

Within a limited period of time following the arrest and booking, the accused must appear before a judicial officer. At this initial appearance the judge or magistrate will explain the defendant's rights and advise him or her of the exact nature of the charges. The defendant will also be appointed an attorney or given the opportunity to obtain one. In a misdemeanor case, the defendant will be asked to enter a plea of guilty or not guilty. The judge may also set **bail** at this time. In a felony case the initial appearance is known as the **presentment**. As in a misdemeanor case the defendant will be informed of the charges and advised of his or her rights, but a plea is not entered until a later stage in the criminal process, known as the felony **arraignment.**

The most important thing decided at this initial appearance is whether the defendant will be released from custody, and, if so, under what conditions.

After an arrest the accused may be fingerprinted, photographed, and required to participate in a lineup.

Bail and Pretrial Release

An arrested person can usually be released after putting up a certain amount of money known as bail. The purpose of bail is to assure the court that the defendant will return for trial. The right to bail has been recognized in all but the most serious cases, such as murder.

BAIL HEARING

Below are five persons who have been arrested and charged with a variety of crimes. In each case decide whether the person should be released and, if so, under what conditions. Choose from one of the following options and discuss your decision: (1) money bond—set an amount; (2) personal recognizance—no money required; (3) conditional release—set the conditions; and (4) pretrial detention.

Case 1

Name: Jerry Davis   Age: 26
Charge: Possession of Narcotics
Residence: 619 30th Street, lives alone, no family or references
Employment: Unemployed
Education: Eleventh grade
Criminal Record: As a juvenile had five arrests, mostly misdemeanors. As an adult had two arrests for petty larceny and a conviction for possession of dangerous drugs (probation was successfully completed).
Comment: Defendant arrested while leaving a pharmacy carrying a large quantity of morphine. Urine test indicates defendant presently using narcotics.

Case 2

Name: Gloria Hardy   Age: 23
Charge: Prostitution
Residence: 130 Riverside Drive, Apt. 10
Employment: Royal Massage Parlor; reportedly earns $1,500 per week
Education: Completed high school
Criminal Record: Five arrests for prostitution, two convictions; currently on probation.
Comment: Vice detective alleges defendant involved in prostitution catering to wealthy clients.

Case 3

Name: Stanley A. Wexler   Age: 42
Charge: Possession and Sale of Narcotics
Residence: 3814 Sunset Drive, lives with wife and two children
Employment: Self-employed owner of a drugstore chain, net worth $250,000

Bail may be paid directly to the court. Either the entire amount will be required or, in some places, the defendant will be released after paying a portion of the total amount (e.g., ten percent). If the defendant doesn't have the money, a bonding company may put up the cash in exchange for a fee. For example, a defendant with a bond of $2,000 might be released after paying $200 (ten percent of the total) to the bonding company. If a person released

Education: Completed college, advanced degrees in Pharmacy and Business Administration

Criminal Record: None

Comment: Arrested at his store by undercover police after attempting to sell a large quantity of unregistered morphine. Alleged to be a bigtime dealer. No indication of drug usage.

Case 4

Name: Michael D. McKenna   Age: 19

Charge: Armed Robbery

Residence: 412 Pine Street, lives with parents

Employment: Waiter, Vanguard Restaurant; earns $100 per week

Education: Tenth grade

Criminal Record: Eight juvenile arrests, runaway, possession of marijuana, illegal possession of firearms, and four burglaries; convicted of firearms charge and two burglaries; spent two years in juvenile facility.

Comment: Arrested after being identified as assailant in a street hold-up. Alleged leader of a street gang. Police consider dangerous. No indication of drug usage.

Case 5

Name: Walter Lollar   Age: 34

Charge: Possession of Stolen Mail and Forgery

Residence: 5361 Texas Street, lives with common-law wife and two children by a prior marriage

Employment: Works thirty hours per week at a service station; earns minimum wage

Education: Quit school after eighth grade; no vocational skills

Criminal Record: Nine arrests—mostly drunk and disorderly and vagrancy. Two convictions: (1) driving while intoxicated (fined and lost license); (2) forgery (completed two years probation).

Comment: Arrested attempting to cash a stolen social security check. Probation officer indicates defendant has a drinking problem.

What's your opinion of the bail system? Should it be easier or harder to get out of jail prior to trial? Discuss your reasons.

on bail fails to return, the court will keep the money.

The Eighth Amendment to the U.S. Constitution states, "excessive bail may not be required." However, a poor person unable to raise any money could be detained in jail before trial and without conviction. Many persons consider this unfair, and in recent years courts have started programs to release defendants without requiring any money at all.

To be eligible for these programs, known as **personal recognizance,** or personal bond, the defendant must promise to return and has to be considered a good risk to show up for trial. In determining the likelihood of the defendant's return, judges consider a number of factors, including the nature and circumstances of the offense; and the accused's family and community ties, financial resources, employment background, and prior criminal record.

In addition to personal recognizance programs, many courts are now allowed to set a variety of conditions designed to insure the return of the defendant. These conditions include third-party custody; and requiring the defendant to maintain or get a job, to reside at a certain address, or to report his or her whereabouts on a regular basis.

Despite the advantages of these programs, many people point to statistics that show that a large number of defendants commit crimes while out on bail and argue that it should be harder, not easier, to get out on bond. On the other hand, supporters of pretrial release say that it prevents punishment prior to conviction and gives defendants the freedom to help prepare their case.

Preliminary Hearing

A **preliminary hearing** serves as a screening device to determine if there is enough evidence to require the defendant to stand trial. The prosecutor is required to establish the commission of a crime and the probable guilt of the defendant.

In most states the defendant has the right to be represented by an attorney, to cross-examine prosecution witnesses, and to call witnesses in his or her favor. If the judge finds no probable cause, the defendant will be released. However, dismissal of a case at the preliminary hearing does not always mean the case is over because the prosecution may still submit the case to a grand jury.

Grand Jury

A grand jury is a group of between sixteen and twenty-three persons charged with responsibility for determining whether there is sufficient cause to believe that a person has committed a crime and should be made to stand trial. The Fifth Amendment to the U.S. Constitution requires that before anyone can be tried for a serious crime in federal court, there must be a grand jury indictment.

To secure an indictment a prosecutor will present evidence designed to establish that a crime has been committed and that there is probable cause to believe the defendant committed it. Neither the defendant nor his attorney has a right to be present, and the prosecutor is not required to present all the evidence or call all the witnesses, as long as the grand jury is satisfied with the merits of proceeding to trial.

Although grand jury indictments are only required in federal court, many states also use a grand jury indictment process. Other states bring defendants to trial following a preliminary hearing or based on a criminal information—a formal accusation detailing the nature and circumstances of the charge—filed with the court by the prosecutor.

Felony Arraignment and Pleas

After an indictment is issued, the defendant will be required to appear in court and enter an initial plea. If the defendant pleads guilty, the judge will set a date for sentencing. If the defendant pleads not guilty, the judge will set a date for trial and ask the defendant if he or she wants a jury trial or a trial before a judge alone.

Nolo Contendere is a plea by the defendant that does not admit guilt but also does not contest the charges. It is equivalent to pleading guilty, and the only advantage of this plea is that it cannot be used as evidence in a later civil trial for damages based on the same set of facts.

Pretrial Motions and the Exclusionary Rule

One of the most important preliminary proceedings is the pretrial motion. After the indictment or information is filed, a defendant may file a number of formal requests or motions seeking to have the case dismissed, or to obtain some advantage or assistance in preparing the case. Among the more common pretrial motions are the following: *motion for discovery of evidence*, which is a request by the defendant to examine, before trial, certain evidence in the possession of the prosecutor; *motion for a continuance*, which seeks more time to prepare the case; and *motion for change of venue*, which is a request to change the location of the trial to avoid community hostility, for the convenience of witnesses, or for other reasons.

Pretrial motions are an important part of the criminal justice process.

THE CASE OF BREWER v. WILLIAMS

On an afternoon in 1968 a ten-year-old girl disappeared from the YMCA in Des Moines, Iowa. Soon after the girl's disappearance, Robert Williams, a resident of the YMCA, was seen in the lobby carrying a large bundle. A witness later told police that he saw two legs sticking out of the bundle. Before anyone could stop him, Williams drove off. His car was found the next day in Davenport, Iowa, some 160 miles away. A warrant was issued for his arrest and Williams later turned himself in. Williams was warned of his right to remain silent and was allowed to talk to his attorney, who advised him not to say anything to the police. In return, the police agreed not to question him until he returned to Des Moines to meet with his lawyer.

On the ride back to Des Moines Williams expressed no desire to talk about the case but did carry on a discussion with the officers. One of the detectives, knowing Williams was a religious man, stated that they should stop and locate the girl's body "because her parents were entitled to give her a Christian burial." After apparently thinking this over, Williams made several incriminating statements and then directed the police to the girl's body.

Williams was later convicted of murder but appealed the decision, claiming that the evidence obtained during the trip was in violation of his constitutional right to assistance of counsel. The Iowa Supreme Court ruled that the evidence was admissable in court because Williams volunteered it. Arguing that this decision was in violation of

Perhaps the most important and controversial of these motions is the *motion to suppress evidence*, which alleges that certain evidence the government plans to use at trial was obtained illegally and should be thrown out. Most commonly, the defense attorney tries to exclude evidence obtained as the result of a police search or a confession obtained as a result of police interrogation. Motions to suppress evidence have been used in federal courts since 1914, but it was not until 1961, in the now famous case of *Mapp* v. *Ohio*, that the Supreme Court required their use in state court. The Court decided that any evidence obtained by the police in an unreasonable search (as defined by the courts) must be excluded from use at trial.

Since the *Mapp* decision, courts have been flooded with motions to suppress evidence, and the decision on the motion has become one of great importance. As a practical matter, if the judge rules that the evidence was unlawfully obtained, the case is often dismissed because the state has insufficient evidence to present. If the judge rules against the motion and says the evidence can be used, the defendant often pleads guilty.

the U.S. Constitution, he took the case to the federal courts. The U.S. District Court disagreed with the Iowa Supreme Court. The district court said that the evidence should have been excluded because the police had used a subtle form of interrogation in violation of their agreement not to question him and because they had failed to prove that Williams knowingly and intentionally waived his right against self-incrimination.

PROBLEM 30

a. What's the purpose of excluding illegally obtained evidence? What are some advantages and disadvantages of the exclusionary rule? What's your opinion of the rule?

b. How does the exclusionary rule apply to the case of *Brewer* v. *Williams*? If you were the judge, would you allow the incriminating statements made by Williams and the fact that these statements led police to the body of the murdered girl to be used as evidence? Why or why not?

c. Do you think the police violated Williams's constitutional right to assistance of counsel? Do you think Williams waived those rights by talking to the police?

d. How would you feel about excluding the evidence if you were Williams? If you were his defense attorney? If you were the parents of the murdered girl? If you were the police?

e. The case of *Brewer* v. *Williams* was finally appealed to the U.S. Supreme Court. How do you think the Court ruled on this matter ?

The rationale behind the exclusionary rule is that the police should not be allowed to benefit from the violation of a constitutional right and that excluding evidence at trial will deter police misconduct. On the other hand, some people argue that the exclusionary rule allows criminals to go free (i.e., guilt though acknowledged may not be proved), destroys respect for the courts, and punishes society rather than police.

Plea Bargaining

Contrary to popular belief, the great majority of criminal cases never go to trial. Rather, most defendants who are convicted plead guilty before trial. In many minor cases, such as traffic violations, the procedure for pleading guilty is simply to sign a form waiving the right to appear and to mail the court a check for the amount of the ticket or fine. In major cases guilty pleas result from a process of negotiation between the accused, the defense attorney, and the prosecutor. This process, known as plea bargaining, involves granting certain concessions to the defendant in exchange for a plea of guilty. Typically, the prosecution will either allow the defendant to plead guilty to a less serious charge or recommend a lighter sentence on the original charge.

Plea bargaining allows the government to avoid the time and expense of a public trial, and the defendant often receives a lighter sentence than if the case had resulted in a conviction at trial. When accepting a guilty plea, the judge is responsible for deciding if the plea was made freely, voluntarily, and with knowledge of all the facts. Thus, once a defendant pleads guilty, it is very hard to withdraw it.

Plea bargaining is very controversial. Some critics charge that plea bargaining allows dangerous criminals to get off with light sentences. Others, more concerned with the plight of the defendant, argue that the government should be forced to prove guilt beyond a reasonable doubt at trial and further charge that the system is unfair to the accused, particularly if the prosecution has a weak case.

PROBLEM 31

a. Should plea bargaining be allowed? Do you think plea bargaining offers greater advantages to the prosecutor or the defendant? Explain your answer.

b. Marty, who is twenty-two years old, is arrested and charged with burglarizing a warehouse. He has a criminal record, including a previous conviction for shoplifting and two arrests for auto theft. The prosecution has evidence placing him at the scene of the crime. The defense attorney tells him the prosecution will reduce the charge to petty larceny in exchange for a guilty plea. If you were Marty, would you plead guilty to the lesser charge? Why or why not?

c. Suppose Marty pleads guilty after being promised probation by the prosecutor, but instead he receives a long prison term. Is there anything he can do about this?

d. Do you think anyone accused of a crime would plead guilty if he or she were really innocent? Explain your answer.

THE TRIAL

In all criminal prosecutions, the accused shall enjoy the right to a speedy and public trial, by an impartial jury of the State and district wherein the crime shall have been committed, which district shall have been previously ascertained by law, and to be informed of the nature and cause of the accusation; to be confronted with the witnesses against him; to have compulsory process for obtaining witnesses in his favor, and to have the Assistance of Counsel for his defense.
—Sixth Amendment to the U.S. Constitution

Due process of law means little to the average citizen unless and until he or she is arrested and charged with a crime. This is because many of the most basic rights set out in the U.S. Constitution apply to persons accused of a crime. Accused persons are entitled to have a jury trial, to be prosecuted in public and without undue delay, to be informed of their rights and of the charges against them, to confront and cross-examine witnesses, to refuse to testify against themselves, and to be represented by an attorney. These rights are the essence of due process of law and, taken together, they make up the overall right to a fair trial.

Right to Trial by Jury

The right to a jury trial is guaranteed by the Sixth Amendment to the U.S. Constitution and is applicable in both federal and state courts. However, a jury is not required in every case and, in fact, juries are not used very much. As we have already seen, most criminal cases are resolved by guilty pleas before ever reaching trial. Jury trials are not required for certain minor offenses— generally those punishable by less than six months in prison. Defendants can *waive* (give up) their right to a jury trial; in some states, waivers may occur in the majority of cases.

Jury panels are selected from voter registration or tax lists and are supposed to be generally representative of the community. Federal law requires that juries consist of twelve persons who must reach a unanimous verdict before finding a person guilty. State courts are not required to use twelve jurors nor are they required to reach a unanimous verdict. However, the U.S. Supreme Court has held that juries in state courts must have at least six jurors.

PROBLEM 32

a. Why is the right to a jury trial guaranteed by the Bill of Rights? Why would someone choose not to have a jury trial?

b. Do you think jury verdicts should be unanimous? Why or why not?

Right to a Speedy and Public Trial

The Sixth Amendment to the U.S. Constitution provides a right to a speedy trial in all criminal cases. The Constitution does not define "speedy" exactly, and courts have often had trouble deciding what this term meant. To remedy this problem, the federal government and some states have set specific time limits within which a case must be brought to trial.

Public defenders represent persons who cannot afford to hire a lawyer.

If a person does not receive a speedy trial, the case may be dismissed. However, defendants often waive the speedy trial requirements because of unavailability or illness of an important witness, or because of the need for more time to prepare the case. Before dismissing a case, courts will consider the cause and reasons for the delay and whether the defendant was free or in jail during the pretrial period.

The Constitution also sets out a right to a public trial. In most cases the general public is freely admitted, although judges may limit the number of spectators and, in certain cases, may exclude the public completely, such as in juvenile cases and cases involving crimes against small children. In 1979 the Supreme Court held that if the prosecution and defense agreed, the judge could bar the public from pretrial proceedings.

PROBLEM 33

a. Why is the right to a speedy trial important? How soon after arrest should a person be brought to trial? What are the reasons for and against bringing a defendant to trial in a short time after arrest?

b. Do you think it would be a good idea to televise criminal trials? Why or why not?

Right to Confront Witnesses

The Sixth Amendment provides persons accused of a crime with the right to confront (face-to-face) the witnesses against them and to ask them questions by way of cross-examination. Although a defendant has the right to be present in the courtroom during all stages of the trial, the U.S. Supreme Court has said that this right may be restricted if the defendant becomes disorderly or disruptive. In such instances judges have the power to remove the defendant from the courtroom, to cite him for *contempt of court*, or, in extreme circumstances, to have the defendant bound and gagged.

Freedom from Self-incrimination

Freedom from self-incrimination means that the defendant cannot be forced to testify against him or herself. This right comes from the Fifth Amendment and can be exercised in all criminal cases. In addition, the prosecutor is forbidden to make any statement drawing the jury's attention to the defendant's failure to testify.

While a defendant has a right not to testify, this right can be waived. Moreover, a defendant who takes the witness stand in his or her own criminal trial must answer all questions.

Related to the right against self-incrimination is the concept of **immunity**. Immunity laws force a witness to answer all questions, even those which are incriminating. In exchange for the testimony, the witness is granted freedom from prosecution. Prosecutors often use these laws to force persons to testify against codefendants or others involved in the crime.

PROBLEM 34

a. If you were a defense attorney, what would be the advantages and disadvantages of placing a criminal defendant on the stand?

b. If you were a member of the jury in a criminal trial, what would you think if the defendant failed to testify? Would you be affected by the judge's instruction not to draw any conclusion from the defendant's failure to testify?

c. If a defendant is forced to stand in a lineup, give a handwriting sample, or take an alcohol breath test, does this violate the privilege against self-incrimination?

Right to an Attorney

The Sixth Amendment provides that "in all criminal prosecutions, the accused shall enjoy the right to have the assistance of counsel for his defense." Until 1938 this meant that, except in capital cases, a defendant only had the right to an attorney if he or she could afford one. However, in that year the Supreme Court required the federal courts to appoint attorneys for indigent defendants in all federal felony cases. Twenty-five years later, in the case of *Gideon* v. *Wainright*, the Supreme Court extended the right to appointed counsel to *all* felony defendants, whether in state or federal court. In 1972 the Supreme Court further extended this ruling by requiring that no imprisonment may occur, even in misdemeanor cases, unless the accused is represented by an attorney.

As a result of these decisions, criminal defendants who cannot afford an attorney are appointed one free of charge by the government. These attorneys may be either public defenders or private attorneys.

PROBLEM 35

a. Do you think court-appointed attorneys will be as good as those who are privately paid? Why or why not?

b. Assume a defendant wanted to handle his or her own defense. Would this be allowed? Do you think this is a good idea?

c. Assume a lawyer knows that his or her client is guilty. Would it be right for the lawyer to try to convince the jury that the person is innocent? Why or why not?

SENTENCING

The final phase of the criminal justice process begins with the sentence. Once found guilty, the defendant will be sentenced by the judge or, in a few states, by the jury. The sentence is perhaps the most critical decision in the criminal justice system because it can determine a defendant's fate for years or, in some cases, for life.

Most criminal statutes set out a basic sentence structure, but judges generally have considerable freedom with respect to actual sentence, including the type, length, and conditions of the sentence. Depending upon the state, judges may choose from one or a combination of the following options:

■ *Suspended Sentence* A sentence is given, but the convicted person is not required to serve it and is released with no conditions attached.

■ *Probation* The defendant is released to the supervision of a probation officer after agreeing to follow certain conditions, such as maintaining a job, avoiding drugs, and not traveling outside of the area.

■ *Fine* The defendant must pay an amount of money set by the court.

■ *Restitution* The defendant is required to pay back or make up for whatever loss or injury was incurred by the victim of the crime.

■ *Work Release* The defendant is allowed to work in the community but is required to return to prison at night or on weekends.

■ *Imprisonment* The defendant is sentenced to a term in prison. Some states require that a *definite* sentence be given, in which case the judge would specify the exact number of years to be served (e.g., two years). Some states provide for an *indeterminate* term, in which case the sentence is not stated in a specific number of years but as a minimum and maximum term (e.g., not less than three years nor more than ten years).

Many factors go into the sentencing decision. These include the judge's theory of corrections and what he or she thinks is in the best interests of society and of the individual. In addition, most states authorize the judge to ask for a **presentence report,** which is prepared by the probation department. The report contains a description of the offense and the circumstances surrounding it, the defendant's past criminal record, data on the defendant's social, medical, educational, and employment background, and a recommendation as to sentence. After studying the report and listening to recommendations from the defense attorney and the prosecutor, the judge will impose sentence.

Purposes of the Sentence

Over the years, the criminal sentence has served a number of different purposes, including **retribution, deterrence, rehabilitation,** and **incapacitation.**

At one time the primary purpose for punishing a criminal was retribution. This was based on the idea of "an eye for an eye and a tooth for a tooth." Punishment was given as a kind of revenge to pay back the criminal for his or her wrongdoing.

Another reason for sentencing criminals is deterrence. Many people believe that punishment will discourage the offender from committing another crime in the future. In addition, the punishment will serve as an example to deter other people from committing crimes.

In recent years one of the primary goals of sentencing has been rehabilitation. The idea of rehabilitation is based on the assumption that criminals can be helped to overcome the social, educational, or psychological problems that caused them to commit a crime and to become responsible members of society.

Persons convicted of a crime may be sent to a correctional institution. Where are offenders from your community incarcerated?

A fourth reason for sentencing is incapacitation, which means that society will be protected by physically separating the criminal in a jail or prison from the community. While locked up, the offender will not pose a threat to the safety of the community.

Today there is no single purpose behind the criminal sentence, and many people disagree over how to handle persons convicted of a crime. When sentencing a criminal, the court may have one or more of these purposes in mind.

PROBLEM 36

a. Refer back to the bail hearing for the five separate cases. Assume that all five of the defendants in this hearing were tried and found guilty. Consider the information provided and impose a sentence in each case.

b. Be prepared to explain your decision and discuss those factors which you considered most important in each case. Which of the purposes of punishment would you hope to achieve in each sentence?

c. Should all people convicted of the same crime receive the same sentence, or should the judge look at each case and determine each sentence on an individual basis? Explain your answer.

Capital Punishment

The most severe and controversial form of sentencing is the death penalty. The death penalty has a long history in American law. During the colonial years capital punishment was imposed for a number of different crimes, although in later years it was generally reserved for murder, rape, and kidnapping. Crimes for which capital punishment is imposed are called **capital offenses.** Since the 1930s the use of the death penalty has gradually declined. For example, in 1935 there were 199 executions in the United States, in 1960 there were 56, and by 1967 there was only 1. Finally, in the 1972 case of *Furman* v. *Georgia*, the U.S. Supreme Court ruled that the death penalty, as then administered, was in violation of the Constitution.

The Court did not rule out the use of the death penalty as a punishment but rather held that capital punishment was being arbitrarily applied and left too much discretion to the judge or jury in each case. After the *Furman* case, many states changed their laws to comply with the Supreme Court decision. In 1976 the Court held that the death penalty was not necessarily "cruel and unusual punishment" in violation of the U.S. Constitution.

What is your state's law regarding capital punishment?

More than thirty-five states now have laws that authorize the use of the death penalty in certain cases. In line with the Supreme Court ruling on this issue, most of these laws forbid the state from automatically imposing the death penalty in murder cases. Rather, they require that the judge and jury consider any factors that might raise or lower the seriousness of the offense. These are known as **aggravating and mitigating factors.**

Opponents of capital punishment argue that it is morally wrong to take the life of anyone convicted of a crime. They also contend that the death penalty does not deter crime. In support of this contention, they cite studies which show that most murders result from fear, passion, mental disorder, or anger of the moment. Thus, they say the death penalty is no more of a deterrent than the possibility of a long prison term. Opponents also point to the possibility of executing an innocent person. Unlike lesser sentences, the death penalty cannot be reversed if new evidence is found.

Those favoring the use of capital punishment point to opinion polls, which indicate that most Americans favor the death penalty and say that it is morally justifiable to take the life of a convicted murderer. They also argue that it does serve as a deterrent to crime and that it will save the government the cost of keeping convicted murderers in prison for long periods of time.

PROBLEM 37

a. Do you favor or oppose use of the death penalty? Explain your answer. If you favor it, to what crimes should it apply?

b. If you oppose the death penalty, what do you think is the strongest argument in favor of it? If you favor the death penalty, what do you think is the strongest argument against it?

JUVENILE JUSTICE

In the United States, juveniles involved with the law are treated differently from adults. This has not always been the case, however. In earlier times children were thrown into jails with adults. Long prison terms and corporal punishment were common, and some children were even sentenced to death for their crimes.

Reformers concerned over the harsh treatment of children urged the establishment of a separate court system for juveniles. The idea behind this separate court system was that children in trouble with the law should be helped rather than punished. Central to the concept of juvenile court was the principle of **parens patriae**. This meant that instead of lawyers fighting to decide the guilt or innocence of the defendant, the court would act as a parent or guardian interested in protecting and helping the child. Hearings would be closed to the public, proceedings would be informal, and, if convicted, children would be separated from adult criminals.

In 1899 Illinois set up the country's first juvenile court. Today, every state has a separate court system for juveniles. These courts generally handle two different groups of juveniles, the delinquent offender and the status offender. A **delinquent** child is one who has committed an act that is a crime under federal, state, or local law. **Status offenders,** on the other hand, are youths who are considered unruly or beyond the control of their legal guardians, or who have committed acts that would not be crimes if done by adults, such as violating a curfew or being truant from school. In different states status offenders are called PINS, CHINS, or MINS—*p*ersons, *c*hildren, or *m*inors *i*n *n*eed of *s*upervision.

In addition to dealing with youthful offenders, juvenile courts usually have the power to hear cases involving the abuse or mistreatment of children. This includes handling cases of parental *neglect, child abuse,* or **abandonment.**

PROBLEM 38

a. Explain the concept of 'parens patriae'. Do you agree with this idea?

b. Should juveniles and adults accused of the same crime be treated the same or differently? Should they have the same rights? The same punishment? Explain your answer.

JUVENILE LAW TERMS

The vocabulary used in the juvenile justice system is quite different from that used in the adult criminal justice system. The major terms used in the adult and juvenile systems are compared below.

Adult	Juvenile
Crime	Delinquent act
Arrest	Contact or take into custody
File charges	Petition
Not guilty plea	Denial
Guilty plea	Admission
Trial	Hearing
Verdict of guilty	Found to be involved
Sentence	Disposition or placement

WHERE
YOU
LIVE

In your state, what is
the maximum age
jurisdiction of juvenile
court?

Can juveniles be trans-
ferred to adult court in
your state? If so, at what
age and under what cir-
cumstances?

Who Is a Juvenile?

Before the establishment of a separate juvenile court system, children under the age of seven were never held responsible for a
criminal act because the law did not consider them capable of
forming the necessary criminal intent. Children between the ages
of seven and fourteen were generally thought to be incapable of
committing a criminal act; but this belief could be disproved by
showing that the youth knew that the act was a crime or would
cause harm to another and committed it anyway. Children over
the age of fourteen could be charged with a crime and handled in
the same manner as an adult.

Today, all states set an age limit that determines whether a
person accused of a crime is treated as an adult or a juvenile. In
most states young people are considered to be juveniles until age
eighteen. However, some states set the limit at sixteen or seventeen.

In many states juveniles charged with a serious crime, such as
robbery or murder, can be transferred to criminal court and tried
as an adult. States that allow such a transfer require a hearing at
which the court considers the age and record of the juvenile, the
type of crime, and the likelihood that the youth can be helped by
the juvenile court. As a result of a "get-tough" attitude involving
juvenile crime, many states have revised their juvenile codes to
make it easier to transfer youthful offenders to adult court.

PROBLEM 39

In each of the following situations decide whether the person
should be tried as a juvenile or transferred to criminal court and
tried as an adult. Explain the reasons for your decisions.

a. Eric, age fifteen, is accused of robbing an eighty-six-year-old
woman at gunpoint. Eric, who has a long juvenile record, including acts of burglary, brags about the robbery.

b. Marcia, age seventeen, is accused of killing a pedestrian while
driving a stolen car. She has never been in trouble before, is
remorseful about the killing, and claims that she planned to return
the car after a short joyride.

Juvenile Court Today

The juvenile court system was founded with high goals. In theory,
the system was supposed to help and rehabilitate young offenders
and to act as a guardian looking out for the best interests of
children. In practice, juvenile court often failed to rehabilitate,

Today, juveniles are given many of the same rights as adults.

while at the same time denying young persons the protection and rights guaranteed to adults. In many cases juveniles were processed through a system with few safeguards and little hope of treatment. Then, beginning in 1966, the U.S. Supreme Court began to change the theory and operation of the juvenile justice system.

THE CASE OF GERALD GAULT

Gerald Gault, age fifteen, was taken into custody and accused of making an obscene phone call to a neighbor. At the time Gerald was taken into custody, his parents were at work, and the police did not notify them of what had happened to their son. Gerald was placed in a detention center. When his parents finally learned that he was in custody, they were told that there would be a hearing on the next day, but they were not told the nature of the complaint against him.

Mrs. Cook, the woman who had complained about the phone call, did not show up at the hearing. Instead, a police officer testified to what he had been told by Mrs. Cook. Gerald blamed the call on a friend and denied making the obscene remarks. No lawyers were present and no record was made of what was said at the hearing.

Since juries were not allowed in juvenile court, the hearing was held before a judge who found by a preponderance of the evidence that Gerald was delinquent and ordered him sent to a state reform school until age twenty-one. An adult found guilty of the same crime could be sent to county jail for no longer than sixty days.

PROBLEM 40
a. Make a list of anything that happened to Gerald Gault that you consider unfair. Explain your reasoning for each item on the list.
b. How would you change any of the things you thought were unfair?

In deciding the Gault case, the U.S. Supreme Court held that juveniles being tried as delinquents and in danger of losing their freedom were entitled to many of the same rights as adult defendants. Specifically, the Court ruled that juveniles charged with a delinquent act were entitled to be notified of the charges against them; to be represented by an attorney; to confront and cross-examine witnesses; and to remain silent.

PROBLEM 41
a. What rights that adults have were not granted in the *Gault* decision?
b. Do you agree with the *Gault* decision? Why or why not? Should adults and minors have the same legal rights? Why or why not?
c. Do you think Gerald Gault's hearing would have turned out differently if he had been given the rights the Supreme Court later ruled he was entitled to?

The *Gault* decision guaranteed young people accused of a crime many of the same protections available to adults, but it also left many unanswered questions. In the case in *In re Winship* (1970), the Supreme Court decided that juveniles charged with a criminal act must be found "delinquent by proof beyond a reasonable doubt"—the same standard required in adult court. However, in *McKeiver* v. *Pennsylvania* (1971), the Supreme Court decided that jury trials were not required in juvenile cases. In reaching this decision the Supreme Court restated the protective philosophy of juvenile court (*parens patriae*) and expressed concern that jury trials could hurt juveniles by destroying the privacy of juvenile hearings. Thus, while juveniles now receive many of the procedural rights available to adults, the Supreme Court has made it clear that not all of the procedures used in an adult criminal trial apply in a juvenile proceeding.

Status Offenders   When a juvenile court is confronted with a status offender, special problems arise. Youths who fall into this category are charged with the status of being "beyond control" or "habitually disobedient", or with truancy from school or other acts which would not be crimes if committed by an adult.

Often status offenders are emotionally troubled youths who need help. Many status offenders are runaways or young people with drinking and drug problems. It has been estimated that over 500,000 minors run away from home each year. Of this number over 80 percent are between the ages of fifteen and seventeen. While most runaways simply return home of their own accord, others are picked up by the police and referred to the juvenile court.

In recent years, a number of programs have been set up to help runaway youths. These include counseling centers, shelter homes, and a nationwide toll-free phone number which runaways can call for assistance (see Appendix A).

As a general rule a single act of unruly behavior is not enough to support a finding that a youth is in need of supervision. Rather, most states require a showing that the youth is "habitually" disobedient or has "repeatedly" run away, skipped school, or been out of control.

Because of problems at home, it is often the parents who ask the court to file a PINS petition against their own child. Youths charged with status offenses are entitled to have an attorney, and they may defend their conduct by showing that it was justified or that it was really the parent who was unreasonable and who is in need of supervision. In such a case, the PINS petition might be withdrawn and replaced by a neglect petition against the parents.

PROBLEM 42

a. Who are PINS, CHINS, and MINS? Explain how such persons differ from delinquents.

b. Do you think courts should interfere in disputes between parents and children? If not, why not? If so, why and under what circumstances?

c. Should attendance at school be mandatory? Why or why not? What should be done about students who are chronically absent from school?

Procedures in Juvenile Court

Suppose a young person is accused of a delinquent act. What happens to this person from the time he or she is taken into custody until he or she is freed from the juvenile justice system? The exact procedures vary from state to state, but the general process that follows is the same throughout the country.

Taking into Custody   On the whole, young people may be taken into custody for all the same reasons the police might arrest an adult. In addition, juveniles can be taken into custody for so-called status offenses. These are acts that would not be considered criminal if committed by an adult. These offenses include running away from home, truancy, promiscuity, disobeying one's parents, or other actions suggesting the need for court supervision.

After taking a juvenile into custody, the police have broad authority to release or detain the juvenile. If the offense is minor, the police may give the juvenile a warning, release the juvenile to

FIGURE 7 Typical Juvenile Court Process

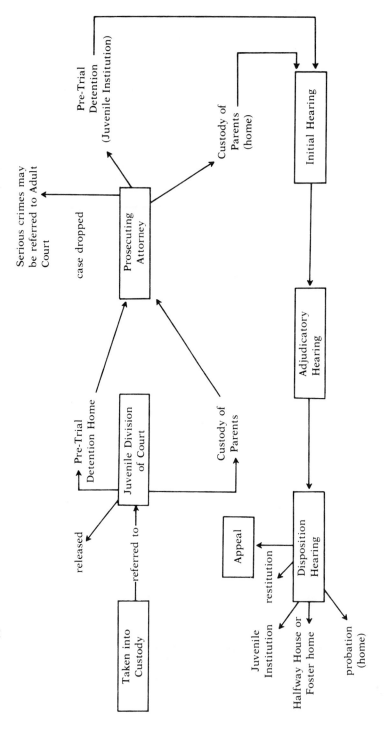

his or her parents, or refer the case to a social service agency. If the offense is more serious or the youth has a prior record, the police may detain the youth and refer him or her to juvenile court.

Intake refers to the informal process by which court officials or social workers decide if a complaint against a youth should be referred to juvenile court. This decision is usually made after interviewing the child and considering the seriousness of the offense, the past record of the accused, the child's family situation, and other factors.

It is estimated that as many as one-half of all complaints received by juvenile courts are disposed of during the intake process. While some of these cases result in outright dismissal, other cases are referred to social service agencies or otherwise diverted from the juvenile justice system.

Initial Hearing   Youths who are taken into custody and formally referred to juvenile court are entitled to an initial hearing on the validity of their arrest and detention. At this initial hearing, the

After juveniles are taken into custody a decision is made to either release the youths to their parents or guardians or detain them pending trial.

state must generally prove two things: that an offense was committed and that there is reasonable cause to believe that the youth
committed it; and that—if the state wants to further detain the
youth—the juvenile is a danger to himself or others or that he is
likely to run away if released. If the youth does not have an attorney, the court will usually assign one at this time and set a date for
a hearing on the facts.

Adjudicatory Hearing   Instead of a trial, a juvenile charged with
a delinquent act is given a hearing. Generally known as an adjudicatory hearing, the purpose is the same as an adult trial—to
determine the facts of the case. Unlike an adult trial, a juvenile
hearing is generally closed to the public, and the names of the
accused and the details of the offense are withheld from the press.

At the adjudicatory hearing, the juvenile is entitled to be
represented by an attorney, who can offer evidence, cross-examine
witnesses, and force the prosecution to prove its case beyond a
reasonable doubt. If the judge finds the juvenile nondelinquent
(not guilty), he or she is free to go. If the judge decides that the
facts, as set out in the petition, are true, the court will enter a
finding of delinquent, which is similar to a conviction.

Dispositional Hearing   The dispositional hearing is perhaps the
most important stage in the juvenile justice system for juveniles
who have been found to be delinquent. At this hearing the judge
decides what sentence or **disposition** the juvenile offender should
receive. The judge's sentence is usually based on the presentence
report prepared by the probation department. This report is the
result of an investigation of the juvenile's social, psychological,
family, and school background.

In theory, the court tries to provide individualized treatment
for the youth. In practice, the alternatives are usually probation,
placement in a group home or community treatment program, or
commitment to a state institution for juveniles.

Probation is the most common disposition. The judge can
impose a number of conditions on the juvenile. For example, the
juvenile might be ordered to attend school regularly, to hold a
steady job, to obtain counseling at a treatment center, to be home
by 8:00 p.m. at night, or to stay away from certain persons. Once
on probation, a juvenile will probably have to meet with a probation officer on a regular basis. Violation of the conditions set by the
court can result in revocation of the probation.

For serious offenses, the juvenile can be committed to a
juvenile institution. Most courts have the power to place a youth
for an indeterminate length of time. This means that no matter
what the offense, the youth can be committed for up to the
maximum period allowed by state law. This generally varies from
one to three years or, in some cases, lasts until the youth reaches

the **age of majority.** Although most youths never serve the maximum sentence, the exact time of release is usually up to the agency that operates the institution.

What happens to status offenders after disposition presents special problems. Should they be taken out of the home? Should they be committed to institutions? Should they be mixed with delinquents or adult offenders? In response to these concerns many states have taken steps to remove status offenders from large institutions and place them in foster homes, halfway houses, or other community facilities.

PROBLEM 43

a. Do you think juvenile offenders should be treated and rehabilitated or punished? Explain your answer.

b. Do you think there should be a set penalty for each juvenile offense or should the judge have the discretion to set a different sentence for each offender?

Post Disposition Most states give young people the right to appeal decisions of a juvenile court. However, because the U.S. Supreme Court has never ruled on this issue the provisions for appeal vary greatly from state to state.

Once released from an institution a juvenile may be placed on **aftercare,** or parole, as it is known in the adult system. This usually involves supervision by a parole officer who can counsel the juvenile on job referral, vocational training, or other services.

WHERE
YOU
LIVE

What are the provisions for the appeal of a juvenile case in your state? Does your state allow juveniles to have their records sealed or destroyed? Who is allowed to inspect juvenile records?

Unlike an adult, a young person found to be delinquent or in need of supervision does not lose any of his or her civil rights. Upon reaching adulthood, for example, the juvenile can still register to vote. In addition, all states make juvenile court records confidential and limit public access to them. Despite this confidentiality, a juvenile record can still cause problems. Only certain states have juvenile records permanently sealed or destroyed, and even though juvenile court records are confidential, a number of persons and agencies may gain access to them.

PROBLEM 44

Assume that a parent has gone to the county prosecutor and asked that a PINS petition be filed to have his son taken out of the home and placed in the county institution because he is beyond control and needs the state's supervision. An attorney is appointed and defends the youth, saying that his father is guilty of neglect.

The PINS STATUTE Reads: A child may be declared a person in need of supervision (PINS) for continually refusing to obey the lawful orders of his or her parents, being beyond the control of the parents, running away from home on a repeated basis, or being a habitual truant from school.

The NEGLECT STATUTE Reads: A child may be declared neglected if the child's parents fail to provide necessary support or education required by law, abandon or abuse the child, or fail to provide the supervision and care necessary for the child's well being.

Mock Hearing on a PINS Petition

Statement of Mr. Jones (father): I give up. There is nothing more I can do with my fifteen-year-old son. He won't do what I say, which is just to come home and be with his sisters and me. He stays out all night with friends who are constantly getting into trouble. He has been in custody at least three times—once for possession of drugs and twice for burglary. Two times he was released, but he got six-months probation for the second burglary when he was fourteen. He has run away twice. He is failing in school. His mother died three years ago and things haven't been the same since. I need him to be home to take care of his two sisters when I'm not there. They are ten and twelve years old. I may sometimes go out after work for a drink and not be home for dinner but I'm not an alcoholic. Now he refuses to be home at dinner time and I know he's out using drugs and committing crimes.

Statement of Billy Jones (age 15): I've gotten into some trouble. There is never any food in our house and my father won't give me any money to go out to eat. I had to get money somehow. Dad is almost never home at dinner time. He comes home drunk almost every night of the week and gives me a bad time. Sometimes he hits me across the face when he has been drinking. We are always arguing and he often yells at me. He's been weird since mom died and I can't take it. So, I run away or stay out all night.

Play the roles of Mr. Jones and his attorney (the county prosecutor), Billy Jones and his attorney, and the judge, following these steps:

1. The judge should announce the case and ask the county attorney to call his or her witness. The father should be questioned by the county attorney as to his reasons for wanting the PINS petition.

2. The father should be cross-examined by Billy's attorney (the judge may interrupt with questions at any time).

3. Billy should be called to the stand and is questioned by his attorney.

4. Billy then should be cross-examined by the county prosecutor.

5. At this point the judge may ask additional questions of anyone involved and should ask the attorneys to make summations if they desire.

6. Finally, the judge should decide whether Billy is a PINS or whether he is neglected. Depending upon what the judge decides, an order may be issued to remove him from the home either temporarily or permanently and place him in a juvenile institution, youth group home, or foster home; leave him in the home; have a social worker or court psychiatrist provide some follow-up treatment; or place other conditions on the father or the son that the judge believes are appropriate.

three
CONSUMER
LAW

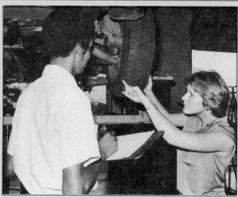

On an average day John buys a hamburger in the school cafeteria, rides the bus to school or work, and goes to the movies. When John does these things he is a consumer of food, transportation, and entertainment. A **consumer** is a person who buys goods or services from another. Since everyone buys goods and uses services, we are all consumers.

When a seller agrees to provide, and a consumer agrees to pay for, goods or services, the parties have entered into a legal relationship. The agreement they make is called a **contract.** Every time John buys a hamburger, he promises to pay for it and the seller promises to give John a hamburger that is fit to eat. If the seller and the consumer have a dispute they can't settle themselves, the law will be important in determining how the dispute should be decided.

For many years, consumer law was symbolized by the legal expression **caveat emptor** which means "let the buyer beware." In other words, consumers had to look for unfair and misleading sales practices before buying or else be prepared to suffer the consequences. Once consumers agreed to buy something, they were stuck with the purchase, even if they got less than they had bargained for, such as goods of poor quality or products that were unsafe or defective.

Recently the law has begun to change in favor of the consumer. Consumers now have a right to be correctly informed of certain important information, such as quality, price, and credit terms. The seller must avoid selling and advertising practices that mislead, deceive, or are otherwise unfair to the consumer; and sellers may only market products that will not harm the consumer in normal use. This increased concern for the consumer is based on the fact that the seller is better informed about the product or service being offered, and is usually in control of the sales transaction.

Even though the law is beginning to favor the consumer, the best protection is still a careful purchase. Many consumers do not realize that being knowledgeable about the product or service they are buying and being informed of their rights as consumers may be the best way to avoid a problem. Consumers should also recognize that if they receive poor quality merchandise or fall victim to a deceptive practice, all is not lost. They can often solve the problem themselves. And when they can't, the law may provide a remedy. This chapter will help you become a more informed consumer, better able to recognize, avoid, and, where necessary, resolve consumer problems.

PROBLEM 1

Make a list of five goods or services that you have purchased in the last week. For each item explain how you decided to purchase that particular good or service.

a. Do you think you were a wise consumer?

b. Have you ever had a problem with these or any other goods or services you've purchased?

PROBLEM 2

Read each of the statements below. Decide whether you strongly agree (SA), agree (A), are undecided (U), disagree (D), or strongly disagree (SD) with each statement. There are no right or wrong answers.

a. Minors (persons under eighteen) should not be allowed to make contracts.

b. Contracts should always be in writing.

c. Consumers should not purchase items, except a house or car, unless they can pay the full price at the time of the purchase.

FIGURE 8   Where Consumers' Dollars Go

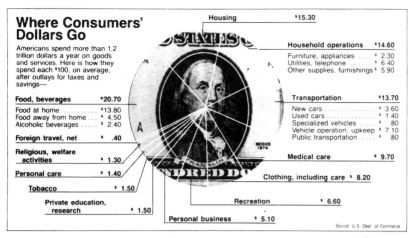

Reprinted from *U.S. News & World Report*, May 1, 1978. Copyright 1978 U.S. News & World Report.

d. Merchants who trick consumers into making purchases should be sent to jail.

e. Most consumers are not affected by television advertising.

f. A car dealer providing financing should be able to take back the car if a consumer misses a payment.

g. The government should forbid the sale of any item harmful to consumers.

HOW LAWS PROTECT THE CONSUMER

The federal government and many state and local governments have a variety of laws that protect the consumer. As you go through this chapter, and whenever you are thinking about consumer protection problems, ask yourself: What are my rights under federal law? Under state law? Under local law?

Federal Law

Congress has passed many laws dealing with the rights of consumers and the responsibilities of sellers. These laws protect consumers in three ways. First, they prohibit unfair or misleading trade

**WHERE
YOU
LIVE**

What governmental or-
ganizations within your
state and community
make or enforce laws af-
fecting consumers?

practices, such as false advertising, unfair pricing, or mislabeling. The Federal Food, Drug, and Cosmetic Act, for example, requires that certain important information be listed on most products offered for sale.

Second, federal laws set standards for the quality, safety, reliability, and sale of many goods and services. Failure to comply with these standards can result in legal action against the seller. For example, the Consumer Product Safety Act allows the government to ban, seize, or prevent the sale of harmful products.

Third, the federal government has established many procedures and agencies that enforce consumer laws and that provide help and redress for the consumer. For example, among the major agencies is the Federal Trade Commission (FTC), which has the power to prohibit unfair trade practices (such as false advertising) and take legal action to stop such practices.

State Law

Most states also have laws protecting consumers. These laws often copy the Federal Trade Commission Act and make unfair and deceptive trade practices a violation of state law. These state laws allow the consumer to bring complaints into state court and before state agencies. They also enable agencies, such as the state attorney general or the state Office of Consumer Affairs, to halt illegal practices.

Like federal consumer protection laws, state laws give the government power to stop unfair and deceptive practices and provide consumers with a variety of remedies. For example, some laws make consumer fraud a crime and subject the offender to fine or imprisonment. Other remedies include: **cease and desist orders,** by which an agency can require a business to stop a forbidden practice; **consent orders,** which are voluntary agreements to end a practice that is claimed to be illegal; and **restitution,** which is an order to refund or repay any money illegally obtained. In some cases consumers can join together to bring **class actions,** which allow one or more persons to bring suit on behalf of a larger group.

Local Law

Some cities and counties also have laws protecting consumers. Most of these laws have been passed quite recently, and they range from requiring the inspection of restaurants for health hazards to declaring certain trade practices illegal.

HOW YOU CAN PROTECT
YOUR RIGHTS AS A CONSUMER

As we will see throughout this chapter, consumers can have a wide variety of problems. The following section will help you avoid some of these problems and explain how to deal with difficulties that may arise.

PROBLEM 3

Responding to a radio ad, Harriet purchased a ten-speed bicycle from Ron's Speed Shop. She paid $135 in cash for the bicycle but was told that she'd have to wait a week for the bicycle because it was presently out of stock. The bicycle arrived a week later, but when Harriet unpacked it she found a three-speed bicycle instead of the one she ordered.

a. Is there anything Harriet could have done differently at or before the time of purchase?

b. What steps should Harriet take after discovering this error?

c. If this happened in your community and the seller refused to exchange bicycles, who could Harriet contact for help?

What To Do Before Buying

Generally it is not wise to make large purchases "on impulse." When shopping for a particular product or service, consumers should learn as much as possible about it. Careful consumers always comparison shop before making an important purchase. They choose the item to be purchased only after considering other products that could also meet their needs. They select the seller from among merchants in their area offering the same product or service.

PROBLEM 4

Select either a good or a service that you would like to buy (e.g., sports equipment, clothes, vacation). After you have selected the item, answer the following questions.

a. Is the item you have chosen something you need or something you want? What is the difference between a need and a want?

b. List all the various places the item could be purchased. What factors would be important to you in deciding where to buy the item?

c. Are there different brands or models for the same item (e.g., different model cars)? If so, what factors do you consider important in deciding which brand to purchase?

d. How can you learn more about products and services and the firms that provide them?

When you go shopping, information is your most important resource. Informed consumers need information on the product or service, the seller or manufacturer, and the terms or conditions of the sale.

Become Informed About the Product or Service   Shoppers naturally consider the price when seeking a product or service, but they need other information as well. If you are buying a product, you need to know how to operate or use it, how long it will last, how to take care of it, whether there are any hazards or safety features involved in its use, and, if it needs service or repair, where to take it and what it will cost.

If you are buying a service, you need to know who will be performing it and what their qualifications are. You should also find out if there are any guarantees, or what happens if you are not satisfied. Finally, you should find out when the service will be started and completed.

Becoming an informed consumer may involve reading publications such as these.

To help you find out the information you'll need, there are many reliable trade and consumer publications that discuss the price, quality, and reliability of everything from food to furniture. *Consumer Reports* and *Consumer Bulletin* can be found on newsstands and in most public libraries. Consumers can often get information on a particular product by contacting the dealer or manufacturer. In addition, federal, state, and local governments provide information on a wide variety of goods and services. Perhaps most importantly, the consumer should ask friends or neighbors about their experiences with particular products or services.

Check Out the Seller   Whether you are buying wholesale or retail, from another person or from a huge store, it is always wise to check out the seller's reputation for honesty and reliability. Find out about the seller's policy with respect to returns and refunds. Will you get a cash refund on defective merchandise, a credit toward future purchases, or a replacement at no extra cost? What is the seller's attitude toward service and repair? Will you get prompt, courteous service, or will you get the runaround?

To find out about sellers, ask your friends and any other people who have dealt with the particular store or business. In addition, there are many groups and organizations that can provide information and assistance. These include consumer groups and organizations of business persons. In particular, you might contact the local Chamber of Commerce or Better Business Bureau.

Buying on impulse can cost you money. Before buying an expensive product such as a camera, you should shop around.

Be Sure You Understand the Terms of the Sale   While many purchases require no special knowledge, understanding the terms and conditions of the sales transaction can prevent problems and save money. Consumers need to know the *total* price of a purchase. Are there any hidden costs or conditions? Is delivery free or is there a charge? If you are charging the item or buying on time, what is the **interest** rate and what will you pay? Is there a guarantee? If so, what does it cover and how long will it last? Finally, ask yourself if the price is reasonable and whether this is the best time to buy.

After gathering information, shop around. Watch for genuine sales and specials. Prices often vary from day to day and from store to store. Comparison shopping not only saves money but helps the consumer to make the best possible purchase.

What To Do After Buying

Sometimes even a careful shopper will encounter a problem after buying a product or a service. When this happens, it is important to remain cool and be persistent. Consumers who follow the suggestions below can usually solve their problem. If they can't, there may be an agency or organization that can help them.

First, the consumer should always try to contact the seller. Reputable businesspersons are interested in a customer's future business, and many problems and misunderstandings can be cleared up with a face-to-face discussion or a telephone call.

Provide the seller with all the necessary information—identification of the item, date of purchase, a description of when and how the problem arose, and a statement of what you want done. Be sure to bring along any pertinent papers or documents, such as the sales receipt or estimate of repair. Be polite but firm. If the seller refuses to help or gives you the runaround, follow up with a written request to the owner or manager of the store. You might mention in this letter that you will take other measures if you do not receive satisfaction. Be sure to date the letter and keep a copy for your records.

If the seller still refuses to help you, consider contacting the manufacturer of the product. If the seller is part of a chain of stores, consider writing to the corporate headquarters of the store. If you don't know the address of the manufacturer or the corporate headquarters, go to your local library and look it up in *Standard and Poor's Register of Corporations.* Many companies have consumer affairs departments, but you may get faster action by writing directly to the company president. State the facts clearly and send photocopies of any important documents (e.g., canceled checks, past letters to the seller). Include a description of the problem, what you've already tried to do about it, and what you want the company to do. Consider sending copies of your letter to local and state consumer protection organizations and to your local Better Business Bureau.

If you are still dissatisfied, it may be time to seek outside help. There are a number of agencies and organizations that may be able to help you. These groups are discussed in the next section. Above all, don't give up if you feel you have a valid complaint.

PROBLEM 5

Terry and Martha Tubman saw an ad in the newspaper for major brand color TV sets on sale at Tally's Radio & TV Shop. They rushed down to Tally's, where they bought a twenty-one-inch model for $435. Several weeks after they bought the TV it completely lost its picture. A TV service mechanic who came to their home told them the picture tube had blown and that it would cost $200 to repair. The next morning Terry and Martha returned to the store and asked to speak to Mr. Foxx, the salesman who had sold them the TV.

a. Roleplay the meeting between the Tubmans and Mr. Foxx. What should the Tubmans say and what should Mr. Foxx say?

b. If Foxx refuses to help, what should the Tubmans do then? If they decide to write a letter of complaint, to whom should it be sent? Make a check list of information needed in the letter. Write a letter for the Tubmans.

c. What should the Tubmans do if they get no response to their letter?

ADVICE ON COMPLAINING

1. Get together all of the key facts. Save all important documents (e.g., bills, canceled checks, repair estimates).
2. Give the seller a chance to correct the problem.
3. If this doesn't work, contact the manufacturer of the product or the store's headquarters (if it's a chain).
4. If you still do not receive satisfaction, take your complaint to a consumer protection agency or organization, a media action line, or a small claims court. You may also wish to contact an attorney at this point.

Consumer Protection
Agencies and Organizations

While consumers can solve most disputes on their own, there may be occasions when they will need to enlist the help of one or several of the various agencies and organizations that have been set up to aid consumers.

Consumer Groups There are many private organizations that help consumers. National organizations, such as the Consumer Federation of America and the Consumer's Union, concentrate on educating consumers and lobbying for passage of consumer protection legislation. However, there are many state and local consumer groups that give advice, investigate complaints, contact sellers, try to arrange settlements, and make legal referrals. To find these organizations, contact a local university, your state attorney general's office, or a member of your city council. You should also check the phone book under both "Consumer" and "Public Interest Organizations."

Business and Trade Associations One of the best known consumer-help organizations is the Better Business Bureau (BBB). The BBB is made up of reputable local businesspersons who will advise consumers who contact them before making a purchase. In many places the BBB will investigate consumer complaints, contact the company involved, and try to arrange a settlement. Reasonable complaints can often be settled with the help of the BBB, but the BBB can only act as a negotiator and cannot force a business to settle.

In communities that do not have a BBB, you may want to contact the local Chamber of Commerce. If it's an appliance that's causing the problem and neither the dealer nor the manufacturer has been helpful, consider contacting the Major Appliance Consumer Action Panel (MACAP)—the address is lised in Appendix A—which can help with complaints.

Professional Associations and Unions Many business and professional persons belong to professional groups or associations that act on behalf of the entire profession or occupation. While such associations may have no legal enforcement powers over its members, a consumer complaint may result in pressure or dismissal of the offending member. For example, if you had a complaint against a local attorney, you might contact the American Bar Association or the bar association for your state or locality.

State and Local Government All states and many local governments have special agencies or departments that protect consumers. These agencies deal with everything from public utility regulation to making sure you get a fair deal when having your car repaired. These departments are often located within the state attorney general's office or may be called the Consumer Affairs Bureau, Consumer Protection Agency, Public Advocates Office, or Public Utilities Commission.

In addition, most states and cities have boards or agencies that set minimum standards for health and safety. For example, local public health inspectors routinely inspect restaurants to insure that they are clean and free of health hazards.

Finally, state and local licensing boards regulate a wide variety of occupations and businesses by setting standards and issuing permits. Businesses that violate these standards can have their licenses taken away. Among commonly regulated occupations are architects, attorneys, barbers, bill collectors, engineers, funeral directors, and real estate agents.

Federal Government   As already mentioned, the federal government has numerous laws and agencies that protect consumers. It is usually best to try to solve your problem on a local level, but for certain problems, the federal government may provide the only remedy. Even if a federal agency can't help, it can often suggest another way to solve your problem. Some of the major federal agencies providing consumer protection are listed below. The address for each of these agencies appears in Appendix A.

The Office of Consumer Affairs (OCA) conducts consumer education and is concerned with all kinds of consumer problems. If you are not sure which agency to turn to, or if you just want advice, OCA will refer you to the specific agency, state or federal, that may be able to help you.

The Federal Trade Commission (FTC) is the federal government's main consumer protection agency. The FTC acts to prevent

What consumer protection agencies exist in your community?

unfair trade practices, such as false or misleading advertising, unfair pricing, false or mislabeled goods, and problems with bills, credit, or warranties. The FTC, which has regional offices throughout the country, has the power to order a business to stop an unlawful activity.

The Food and Drug Administration (FDA) is responsible for maintaining and regulating the safety of food, drugs, cosmetics, and medical devices. It conducts tests to assure the safety of these items and can order unsafe products off the market.

The Consumer Product Safety Commission (CPSC) has the authority to make and enforce safety standards for most consumer products, with the exception of food, drugs, automobiles, airplanes, boats, and firearms. It may ban or seize unsafe products and require that warnings be placed on hazardous substances and products.

The U.S. Postal Service (USPS) can investigate mail order companies and seek criminal prosecutions for mail fraud. If you receive unordered goods through the mail, or if you suspect mail fraud of any kind, USPS may be able to help.

The Occupational Safety and Health Administration (OSHA) regulates health in the workplace. If your complaint concerns dangerous conditions or hazardous substances on the job, OSHA can investigate and seek a solution.

The Civil Aeronautics Board (CAB) sets standards for the regulation of air travel. If you have a complaint against an airline for being overcharged, mistreated, illegally "bumped," or for losing or mishandling your baggage, the CAB may provide a remedy.

The Interstate Commerce Commission (ICC) regulates rates and services of interstate bus, railroad, truck, and moving companies.

The National Transportation Safety Board (NTSB) sets standards for vehicle safety and handles complaints related to auto dealer fraud or tampering with odometer (auto mileage) readings.

PROBLEM 6

How would you handle each of the following problems? If you think an agency or organization can help you, indicate which one and explain your answer.

a. You planned to fly from St. Louis to Chicago for your brother's graduation. You purchased a ticket in advance, but when you arrived at the airport you were told that the flight was overbooked and you would have to wait for the next plane. Four hours later you arrive in Chicago, but you miss the graduation and think the airline should compensate you.

b. You become ill after eating a can of sardines purchased from a local supermarket. You know several friends who have also gotten sick eating this particular brand of sardines. You protest to the supermarket, but they do nothing.

c. You apply for a charge account at a local department store. You are over twenty-one and have a good job but are turned down anyway. You are given no reason for the rejection and wonder what you can do.

d. You see an ad stating, "You'll have a glamorous career as a disc jockey after only twenty home lessons." You pay $100 and complete the correspondence course, but radio stations tell you your training is useless. None will hire you.

e. Your three-year-old sister was badly injured when a toy she was playing with shattered and cut her. You think the toy is too dangerous; your family wants compensation for her injuries.

f. Three weeks after you buy a set of new radial tires, one of them blows out and you run off the road, causing minor damage to your car. The dealer offers to replace the tire, but you are not satisfied.

g. You buy some furniture on a time payment plan. When you get your first bill, you discover the total cost of the payments to be over $1,000, while the price of the furniture was only $700. You call the store and they tell you that the interest amounts to twenty percent a year. You wouldn't have bought the furniture if you had known it cost so much.

Media   Many local newspapers and radio and television stations have special "action line" or "consumer affairs" programs. Even when they don't, they are often interested in publicizing legitimate stories regarding consumer problems. Publicity is a powerful weapon, and many consumers find that contacting, or even threatening to contact, the media can encourage settlement.

Taking Your Case To Court

If you can't settle your complaint and a consumer agency has been unable to help, you may wish to take your case to court. Minors can sue through their parents or guardians, and free or low-cost legal services may be available to consumers who cannot afford an attorney.

Trial Court   If the dispute involves a large amount of money, the case will be brought in your local civil trial court. Taking a case to court can be costly and time consuming, but a consumer in a civil case can ask for a number of different remedies.

First, you can ask for money to make up for any losses growing

How can a small claims court help a consumer?

out of the case. For example, if you were injured because of a defect in the power drill that you bought, you can ask for money for a new drill, medical expenses, time lost from work, and any other related damages. Second, the court can release you from any further obligations under the contract and order the other party to return any money you've already paid. Third, the court may order the seller to carry out the specific terms of the contract. For example, if a consumer ordered goods which were never delivered, the court could order the company to deliver the items. However, the consumer must still pay for the item.

MOCK TRIAL: JAMES PHILLIPS v. THE RADIO SHOP

FACTS

In this case James Phillips purchased an inexpensive radio from The Radio Shop and later attempted to exchange it because it did not work. The date of the sale was November 14; the return was made ten days later. The sales slip has the following language typed at the bottom: "This product is fully guaranteed for five days from the date of the purchase. If defective, return it in the original box for credit toward another purchase."

The store refused to make the exchange and James brings this action in small claims court.

EVIDENCE

James has (1) the sales slip for twenty-five dollars paid to The Radio Shop and (2) the broken radio. He claims to have thrown away the box the radio originally came in.

WITNESSES

For the Plaintiff
1. James Phillips
2. Ruby Phillips,
   James' sister

For the Defendant
1. Al Jackson, the salesman
2. Hattie Babcock, store
   manager

COURT

The judge should provide an opportunity for James to make his case and should give the representatives of the store a chance to tell the court why the money should not be returned. Both sides should call their witnesses.

At the end the judge should decide the case and provide reasons for the decision.

WITNESS STATEMENT: James Phillips

"I went into The Radio Shop to buy a transistor radio. I looked at a few different radios but the salesman talked me into buying the Super

In some cases, the actions of the seller may be a crime as well as a violation of civil law. For example, a builder who takes money to buy materials for a new porch on your house but has no intention of ever doing the job and skips town with your money has committed a crime. If you think you've been the victim of criminal fraud, contact your local prosecutor or district attorney.

Small Claims Court   Most states have **small claims courts,** in which consumers can sue for small amounts of money. The most money these courts can award varies from $100 to $3,000, depending on

---

Electro Model X-15. I paid him the twenty-five-dollar price and he gave me the radio in a cardboard box. When I got home to listen to the radio, I found that it didn't work. I went back to the store to get my money back, but the salesman wouldn't return it. He said I should have brought it back right away. I explained to him that my mother had been sick and I'd been busy. Here's the broken radio and the receipt as proof. I want my money back!"

WITNESS STATEMENT: Ruby Phillips
"All I know is that when James got home the other day he was all excited and wanted to show me something. He called me into the kitchen to show me his new radio. I said, 'Let's hear how it works.' He turned it on and nothing came out but static. He moved the dials around but couldn't get it to play. Was he ever mad! I told him that he ought to take it back to the store and demand his money back."

WITNESS STATEMENT: Al Jackson
"I sold the kid the radio, but as far as I know it worked OK. All the table models worked well enough, so why shouldn't the one boxed and straight from the factory? I'll bet what really happened is that he dropped the radio on his way home. Or maybe he broke it during the ten days he had it. That's not my fault, is it?"

WITNESS STATEMENT: Hattie Babcock
"As Jackson said, all the other X-15's have worked fine. We've never had a single complaint about them. We have a store policy not to make refunds unless the merchandise is returned within five days in the box we sold it in. Also, the guarantee on the radio says that the radio must be returned in the original box. That's the reason Jackson didn't give the kid his money back. Otherwise, we'd have been more than happy to give him credit toward a new purchase. After all, pleasing our customers is very important to us. Personally, I agree with Jackson. The kid probably didn't bring back the box because it was all messed up after he dropped it."

**WHERE
YOU
LIVE**

Is there a small claims court in your community? If so, where is it located? What is the filing fee? What is the largest amount of money that can be awarded? Are lawyers permitted in this court?

the state. The cost of filing a suit is generally low, attorneys are not required (in some states they are not even allowed), and there are few time-consuming delays. There are three steps to filing a suit in small claims court.

First, contact the clerk of the court to determine if the court can handle your type of claim. If so, you'll be required to fill out some forms and pay a small filing fee (from two to fifteen dollars). To fill out the forms, known as a complaint or statement of claim, you'll be asked to state the name and address of the party you are suing, the reason for your complaint, and the amount you are asking for.

Second, prepare for your case in advance. In most states the court will notify the defendant of the date and place of the hearing. In the meantime, you should gather all the evidence necessary to present your case. This includes receipts, letters, canceled checks, sales slips, and estimates of repair. If a defective product is involved, be sure to bring it along, if possible. Contact all witnesses to be sure they come to court. Uncooperative witnesses can be ordered to appear by a **subpoena.** If you have time, sit in on a session of court before your hearing date so you'll know what to expect. Also, practice presenting your case to a friend beforehand.

Third, be on time to present your case in court on the date scheduled for the hearing. If for any reason you can't make it, call the clerk of the court to ask for a postponement. Once your hearing begins, outline your story and present your facts, witnesses, and any evidence you may have. Don't get emotional. Be prepared for questions from the judge. After both sides have had an opportunity to present their stories, the judge will make a decision.

PROBLEM 7

a. Using the complaint form in Figure 9 (or a copy of the form used in your local small claims court), fill out the form with a complaint that you, a friend, or a family member may have had. Write a short description of the events giving rise to your claim.

b. What would you do if you received a notice that you were being sued in small claims court for failing to pay a bill? What would happen if you ignored the notice or did not show up in court?

DECEPTIVE SALES PRACTICES

Most sellers are honest and never use what are known as deceptive or unfair sales techniques. Some, however, do use such methods and consumers should be able to recognize and avoid them.

FIGURE 9   Complaint Form for Small Claims Court

SUPERIOR COURT OF THE DISTRICT OF COLUMBIA
CIVIL DIVISION
SMALL CLAIMS AND CONCILIATION BRANCH
613 G STREET, N.W.   THIRD FLOOR

WASHINGTON, D. C. 20001   Telephone 727-1760

_____
Plaintiff

_____   vs.

_____
Address   Zip Code

(1) _____

(2) _____

(3) _____
Defendant

No. SC _____

STATEMENT OF CLAIM

DISTRICT OF COLUMBIA, *ss:*

_____ being first duly sworn on oath says the foregoing is a just and true statement of the amount owing by the defendant to plaintiff, exclusive of all set-offs and just grounds of defense.

_____
Attorney for Plaintiff

_____   _____
Address   Zip Code   Plaintiff (or agent)

Subscribed and sworn to before me this _____ day of _____, 19___

_____
Deputy Clerk (or notary public)

NOTICE

To:

(1) _____
Defendant

_____
Home Address   Zip Code

☐ CHECK ADDRESS
TO BE USED FOR
MAILING

_____ ☐
Business Address   Zip Code

(2) _____
Defendant

_____ ☐
Home Address

_____ ☐
Business Address

You are hereby notified that _____

_____ has made a claim and is requesting judgment against you in the sum of _____ dollars

($_____),

as shown by the foregoing statement. The court will hold a hearing upon this claim on _____ at 9:00 a. m. in the Small Claims and Conciliation Branch located at 613 G Street, N. W., third floor.

SEE REVERSE SIDE FOR COMPLETE INSTRUCTIONS

Chief Deputy Clerk
Small Claims and Conciliation Branch

BRING THIS NOTICE WITH YOU AT ALL TIMES   [B6401]

119

THE CASE OF THE HOME FREEZER/FOOD PLAN

For Mr. and Mrs. Reichard feeding a family of four had always been a struggle, so they were especially interested when they saw an ad for a family food plan. The ad declared:

> *Veribest Family Foods will beat inflation and save you money. Top-quality meats, vegetables, and other foods delivered to your home for three years with no increase in price. Start the Veribest plan now and receive a freezer free of charge.*

The Reichards had their doubts, but they called the number on the ad. Sam Jones, a salesman for Veribest, came to their home the same evening. Jones explained that for only $30 a week over the next three years, Veribest would supply enough top quality food to feed their entire family. Since the food would be delivered once a month, the Reichards would need a freezer, which Jones would "throw in" for only $100 down and $25 a month for the next three years.

When the Reichards protested that they thought the freezer was free, Jones replied that it would last a lifetime and was really like a gift since the Reichards would save so much on food. To make the offer even more attractive, Jones said that for every person the Reichards referred as a possible customer, he would deduct $30 from the price of the freezer.

The Reichards still weren't sure, but Jones wouldn't take no for an answer. They soon signed the contract. The very next day the Reichards saw an identical freezer selling at a local store for only $390, but they had already signed the contract and figured they were stuck.

When the food started coming, it turned out to be of poor quality and in such small amounts that it ran out by the middle of the month. After several months the freezer no longer kept food frozen and the Reichards decided they had had enough. Mrs. Reichard called Veribest to tell them about the food and broken freezer and to demand the $150 they expected for giving Jones the names of five friends as possible customers. She was told that they could not cancel the plan and that there would be a small service charge to repair the freezer. Also, in order for the Reichards to get the $150 reduction, the referrals actually had to buy the plan. None had, so the Reichards weren't entitled to anything.

PROBLEM 8

a. Did any unfair or deceptive practices take place in the Reichards's story? If so, explain why they were unfair or deceptive.

b. Did the Reichards make any mistakes? What could they have done to prevent the problem from occurring?

c. What can the Reichards do now? Can any state or federal agencies help them? If so, which ones?

Door-to-Door Sales

Most door-to-door salespersons are honest and offer products and services consumers may need and want. Some, however, use high-pressure tactics and smooth talk to get consumers to buy things that they otherwise wouldn't buy. This type of salesperson, once in the door, just won't take no for an answer and will do anything to make the sale.

Mr. and Mrs. Reichard had the misfortune to meet such a high-pressure salesperson. They signed the contract and after Mr. Jones left they began to have doubts. What could they have done? *They could have canceled the contract.* A Federal Trade Commission rule (and the law in most states) now gives consumers a three-day "cooling off" period after they have signed a contract with a door-to-door salesperson for over twenty-five dollars. During this period the Reichards could have notified Veribest in writing that they wished to cancel the contract. The FTC rule also requires that door-to-door salespersons tell their customers about the right to cancel and put it in writing. If the seller does not do this, the consumer may be able to get out of the contract.

Referral Sales and Phony Contests

Jones tricked the Reichards with a referral sales technique when he misled them into thinking that they would save money on the contract by referring him to other customers. Jones used this technique to help make the sale and also to get the names of new

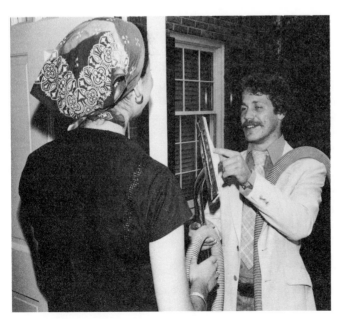

Federal law gives you three days after the sale to cancel any purchase made from a door-to-door salesperson.

victims. In many states referral sales are unlawful and the consumer is entitled to cancel the contract and demand a refund.

THE CASE OF THE FREE DINING ROOM TABLE

Ron Harris received a call telling him that he had won a contest at the Finkel Furniture Store. The caller announced that Mr. Harris had won a "free" dining room table. All he had to do was buy the chairs to go with it at their regular price of $160 per set. After investigation, it was discovered that the entire dining room set (table and chairs) was regularly sold for only $160. Has the store done anything wrong?

Ron Harris has been the victim of a phony contest. It is illegal to use the word "free" and then require the consumer to do something in order to get the free item. Mr. Harris can cancel the contract if he was lured into buying the chairs as a result of the phony contest.

PROBLEM 9
Assume that Ron Harris received the call in the case above but that he was suspicious about the contest and decided not to purchase the chairs.

a. Should Harris report the call even though he was not a victim of this practice? Why?
b. Would you report a deceptive consumer practice you knew about even if you were not harmed by it? Why?

Advertising and the Consumer

Advertising has an enormous impact on the behavior of consumers. Advertisements, designed both to inform and to influence, create in consumers a desire for the products advertised. Typical American consumers are bombarded by a variety of ads telling them hundreds of things, such as what to eat, how to dress, where to travel, when to shop, and how to look and feel better.

PROBLEM 10

Refer to the ad in the Case of the Home Freezer/Food Plan.

a. Why was the ad effective?

b. What was unfair, deceptive, or misleading about the ad?

c. Give an example of an ad you have read or heard that is particularly effective. Why is the ad effective?

d. Give an example of an ad you have read or heard that might be unfair, deceptive, or misleading. What is wrong with the ad?

Of course, advertising can be beneficial. For example, merchants use advertising to tell potential customers about their products. Ads can also help consumers by telling them about new goods and services and by providing other useful information. The primary purpose of ads, however, is to sell the product. While ads can be helpful, they can also mislead, deceive, and confuse.

Some ads mislead consumers by vague claims or, in a few cases, outright lies. Other ads try to create in consumers a desire for a product they don't really need or want. Many ads appeal to emotion rather than provide the kind of factual information needed to make a wise buying decision.

The federal government and most of the states have passed laws prohibiting false or deceptive advertising. Despite these laws, deception can take many forms, and these laws are difficult to enforce.

When the public has been widely exposed to a misleading ad, the FTC can not only order the seller to stop the false advertising, but they can also order **corrective advertising.** This requires that the seller admit the deception in all future ads for a specified period of time. For example, a well-known mouthwash company advertised for over thirty years that its product helped cure sore throats and colds. When an investigation proved this claim false, the FTC ordered that all new ads admit that the previous claims were untrue.

While the general rule is that false or misleading ads are illegal, there is one type of ad that appears to be an exception to

Have you ever bought anything because of advertising? Were you pleased or disappointed with your purchase? What are some places that ads can be found?

THE CASE OF THE PHONY SALE

The ad read, "Giant Sale. Top Quality Stereos formerly $220 now only $175". In fact, the stereos had never cost $220 and could be bought for $175 even when not on sale. Is this ad legal?

Ads that make false claims are clearly illegal. The FTC could order this stereo ad discontinued because it was untrue.

---

this rule. Ads based on the seller's opinion or personal taste, or on some obvious exaggeration, are called **puffing.** While perhaps not literally true, puffing is not illegal. For example, a used car dealer advertising the "World's Best Used Cars" is engaged in puffing because a reasonable person should know better than to rely on the truthfulness of such a statement.

The difference between illegal advertising and puffing is small and consumers should be on guard. If the statement tends to mislead about an important fact concerning the product, it is illegal; but, if an ad is merely an opinion, it is puffing and legal.

PROBLEM 11

Decide whether the italicized language from the following ads, if untrue, is false advertising or puffing. Explain your answer.

a. ". . . *handsewn* crepe sole shoes."

b. "You'll love Gerry's *famous* hamburgers."

c. ". . . *jump higher, run longer* with Sportsman Joggers."

d. "Lose three to ten pounds in *a week or less* with Body Toner."

For many consumers the biggest problem is not being conned by false and illegal advertising but being seduced or influenced by perfectly legal advertising to buy things they really don't want, need, or know much about. Many ads try to sell products by appealing to the buyer's emotions. For example, some ads *associate* the product with popular ideas or symbols, such as family, motherhood, wealth, and sex appeal. The object of these ads is to convince the consumer that purchasing these products will also associate him or her with the same ideas or symbol.

The *bandwagon approach* is another technique that promotes the idea that because everybody's using the product, you should too. Related to this is *celebrity appeal*, which involves having famous athletes or movie stars advertise the product. These people bring glamor and style to the ad, but this does not mean the product is of high quality.

Still other ads try to convince consumers by resorting to the *claims of authorities,* such as doctors, or by relating the results of a study, which appears to be scientific. A common television technique is based on the notion that *seeing is believing.* These ads often show everyday people successfully using certain household products.

Some ads simply try to make you laugh or feel good, hoping you'll think of their product whenever you want to feel good. Some advertisers don't care what information you have about their product as long as it is the only brand you consider. The people who make these ads know that many shoppers select nationally advertised brands even though local or store brands may cost less and be of the same quality. Whatever technique advertisers use, consumers should learn to separate the product from the characters and images in the ad.

PROBLEM 12

Read and analyze each of the ads below. What is the technique or appeal used in each ad? What important information is missing from each ad? To whom is this ad trying to appeal—children, adults, women, men, some other groups?

a. "Don't wait until your house burns down. Buy Homeowners *associate* Insurance now."

b. "Nine out of ten doctors recommend 'Super Strength' Pain *claims of auth* Reliever."

c. "If you want to get that special man in your life, use AvecMoi *associate* Perfume."

d. "Going out of Business! Bargains galore! Everything at the *bandwagon* Pants Palace is priced to sell, sell, sell."

e. "Be the first in your neighborhood to drive the new Super-Sport *associate* Sedan."

f. "Your mother used Stuart's Baby Powder; shouldn't you too?" *associate*

g. "For the time of your life drink Brewmeister Beer." *association*

h. "You've come a long way baby. Why not smoke a woman's *association* cigarette?"

i. "Try Crunch King cereal and you'll get a free surprise in every *association* box."

THE CASE OF THE APPLIANCE SWITCH

Ms. Moss saw an ad in the paper that read, "Beautiful Microwave Oven. Only $200." She then went to the A-1 Appliance Store that had run the ad and encountered Sam Shifty, who said to her "You don't want that oven. It doesn't have the latest features. But look over here at our other ovens."

Ms. Moss is about to fall victim to the sales technique known as **bait and switch.** This technique involves an offer to sell a product on what sounds like very good terms—an almost-too-good-to-be-true deal. The seller does not really want to sell the product or "bait" being offered. It is simply used to get the buyer into the store. Once the consumer is in the store, the product turns out to be much less appealing than expected, enabling the seller to "switch" the consumer to a more expensive item.

Bait and Switch

Salespersons using the bait and switch technique "talk down" the advertised product and then refer the consumer to another higher-priced item. As encouragement, salespersons may be given an increased commission if they sell the higher-priced item. On some occasions the product advertised as bait may not even be in stock.

Bait and switch gives sellers a strong advantage over the unwary consumer. Already in the store and anticipating a purchase but disappointed in the quality of the bait, the consumer is a captive audience unlikely to bother with comparison shopping. The Federal Trade Commission has rules against bait and switch and will take appropriate action when it receives complaints from consumers. Many state and local agencies also handle these complaints. If local law prohibits bait and switch, a consumer may be able to cancel the contract with a seller.

PROBLEM 13

Mr. and Mrs. Rose are looking for a new washing machine. They see an ad that says, "Come on down to Dyco Discount for the best deal in town on an inexpensive washer." The salesperson in the appliance department has been instructed to try selling a washer-dryer combination to every customer seeking a washer. If the combination can't be sold, the salesperson is to try selling a more expensive washing machine before showing the cheaper models.

a. Roleplay this encounter.

b. Have you ever encountered a situation like this? If so, how did you handle it? What are the advantages and disadvantages of aggressive selling for the customer? For the store?

THE CASE OF THE ELECTRIC MIXER

One day, Barry received a package in the mail containing an electric mixer from the Super-Mix Corporation. A letter was enclosed that said he was getting the appliance for a free ten-day trial. Barry used it once and then forgot about it. Three weeks later a bill came for $39.95. Must Barry pay?

Barry does not have to pay for the mixer, nor does he have to return it. Under federal law all unordered merchandise received by mail may be kept as a gift. Sending unordered merchandise is unlawful, and such activity should be reported to the U.S. Postal Service or the Federal Trade Commission. It is lawful to send free samples and to ask for charitable contributions, but the receiver of the goods cannot be forced to pay.

Mail Order Sales

Consumers should watch out for ads sent through the mail offering "free" items in exchange for subscriptions or memberships. These free items almost always require a commitment to purchase other items in the future (e.g., "four free books now if you purchase four more during the next year at the member's price"). These offers often include mailing a catalog to members on a monthly basis, with a preselected purchase item that will be sent unless the member takes some action (usually within ten days) to make another selection or to reject all selections. These plans are legal, but they can be inconvenient and possibly expensive if a consumer is not careful.

PROBLEM 14

Shannon received three unordered records in the mail. An enclosed letter stated that she could have the records for two dollars if she joined a record club and promised to buy ten more records within a year.

a. Was this mailing legal?

b. Does Shannon have to pay the two dollars? If she doesn't pay the two dollars, does she have to return the records?

**WHERE
YOU
LIVE**

Is there a repair and estimate law in your community? If so, how does it work?

c. If she does send in the two dollars, is she obligated to buy the other records?

THE CASE OF THE COSTLY ESTIMATE

Nichole took her car to Scott's Repair Shop. The mechanic told her the car needed a tune-up and estimated the cost at thirty dollars. Nichole told the mechanic to go ahead with the tune-up, but when she returned to pick up the car, the bill amounted to eighty-five dollars. Did Nichole do something wrong? What can happen if she refuses to pay?

Nichole has become a victim of the "open-ended estimate." Service mechanics often give an estimate of the cost of the repair but then have the consumer sign a repair agreement, which provides (usually in small print) that the owner authorizes all repairs deemed necessary. Consumers should always demand a written estimate and should insist that any repairs not listed on the repair agreement be made only after getting their specific approval.

Repairs and Estimates

In some places laws have been passed requiring repair shops to give written estimates. Frequently these laws also limit the percentage difference between the estimate and the final bill.

Consumers should watch out for "free estimates." Sometimes the estimate is free only if the consumer agrees to have the particular shop make the repairs.

A final protection when having repairs made on your car or appliance is to request that the repair shop save and return all used and replaced parts. This identifies you as a careful consumer. Also, if you suspect fraud, you will have the old parts as evidence to make it easier to prove your case.

Being careful ahead of time is particularly important because if you refuse to pay for repairs after they have been made, the repair shop or garage can place a **lien** on the repaired item. This means that the repair shop can keep your car or appliance until you agree to pay.

CONTRACTS

A contract is an agreement between two or more persons to exchange something of value. In a contract, each person is legally bound to do what is promised. For example, in the Case of the Home Freezer/Food Plan, a contract was signed in which Veribest promised to deliver the freezer and monthly supplies of food and

need to make contra
1) offer

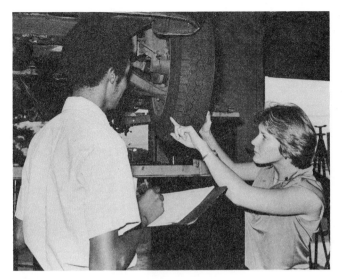

Consumers should check out repair shops for service, reliability, and honesty.

the Reichards promised to make their payments. The Reichards entered into a formal contract, but you also make a contract when you buy a hamburger in the school cafeteria. If one party to the contract does not carry out the promise, the other party can go to court for help. In order to protect yourself as a consumer, it is important to understand how a contract is formed and how a contract may affect your rights.

Elements of a Contract

In order to have a legally binding contract, certain elements must be present. There must be an **offer** by one party and an **acceptance** by the other. In addition, the two parties must agree exactly to the terms of the contract. This is called **mutual agreement.** The parties do not always have to say "we agree." The law infers the agreement from certain actions, such as signing a contract or beginning to carry out your end of the bargain.

In every valid contract there must be an exchange of **consideration,** which means something of value is given for something else of value. For example, when you buy an item at a store, your consideration is the money you agree to pay and the merchant's consideration is the item you are buying. *competent = insane age enough!*

Persons entering into a contract must be legally competent to make contracts. For example, they cannot be mentally ill or intoxicated. Also, agreements to do something illegal or against public policy are not enforceable in court.

When Kevin says to Sally, "I will sell you my motorcycle for $150," there is an offer. When Sally says "OK," or when she pays the $150 to Kevin, or when she signs an agreement to pay $150;

6 competent subject matter legal or illegal

A consumer should always read a contract before signing it.

there is an acceptance. They have agreed to the exact terms, and the motorcycle being exchanged for the money is the consideration. Also, both parties were competent, and the agreement was not illegal or against public policy. Therefore, a contract has been made.

The consumer should not be too quick to enter into a contract. Be sure you understand and agree with all the terms before you accept; otherwise it may be too late to back out of the deal.

PROBLEM 15

For each of the following situations, decide whether a contract has been made. Be prepared to give your reasons.

a. An auctioneer says, "What am I bid for this antique sofa?" Someone in the crowd says, "$300."

b. Adam says to Basil, "I'm going to sell my car for $500." Basil replies, "All right, here is the money. I'll take it."

c. The citizens of a small town collect $1,000 and offer it as a reward for catching a suspected criminal. The sheriff captures the suspect and seeks the reward.

d. Sara's father promises to pay her $1,000 when she turns eighteen. On her eighteenth birthday she seeks the money.

e. Standing at one end of a long bridge Shelly says to Lynn, "I'll give you five dollars if you walk across the bridge." Lynn says nothing, but starts walking across the bridge.

f. Liz offers Sharon $100 to steal four hubcaps for her sportscar. Sharon steals the hubcaps, brings them to Liz, and asks for the *no* money.

THE CASE OF THE REQUIRED COSIGNER

Keith, sixteen, a drummer in a popular rock band, goes to a local music store to purchase a new set of drums. The cost of the set is $750. He offers to put down $150 and make monthly payments on the remaining amount. Because an adult is not present to cosign the loan, the manager of the store refuses to sell him the drums. Is this fair?

Minors and Contracts

A minor is a person under the age of legal majority (twenty-one in some states, but eighteen in most). Although minors may make contracts, as a general rule they cannot be forced to carry out the promises made and may cancel or refuse to honor the contract. Minors who cancel contracts usually must return any goods or consideration still in their possession. The reason for this rule is to protect minors from being taken advantage of because of their age and lack of experience. However, because of this rule, minors have a tough time getting credit. Many stores require a minor to have a parent or other adult **cosign** any major contract entered into by the minor. The adult cosigner is responsible for making payments if the minor backs out of the deal.

A minor may, however, be held to contracts which involve necessities, such as food, clothing, shelter, or medical aid. The minor can be required to pay for the reasonable value of such goods and services.

In most states, a minor who signs a contract is held to it upon reaching the age of majority. For example, a minor who continues to make payments after reaching the age of majority cannot then decide to cancel the contract and return the goods.

Written and Oral Contracts

A contract may generally be either written or oral (spoken). However, certain kinds of contracts must be in writing to be enforceable in court. These contracts include the sale of land or real estate, the sale of goods priced at $500 or more, agreements to pay another person's debt, and agreements that cannot be performed within a year from the date of the agreement.

The law favors written contracts. For the protection of both parties, it is always better if a contract is in writing. Otherwise it is

ADVICE ON CONTRACTS

1. Never sign a contract with blank spaces.
2. Never sign a contract to get rid of an irritating salesperson.
3. Never sign a contract without getting a copy.
4. Never sign a contract unless all promises are included in writing and the total amount of money to be paid by you is clearly stated.
5. Don't sign a contract unless you read and understand everything. If necessary, take it to a lawyer or consumer help office and have it explained.

THE CASE OF THE BROKEN PROMISE

Ruth orally agreed to sell her car to Mike for $2,000. A few days later she got an offer of $2,300 from Paul. Thereafter she refused to sell her car to Mike. Can Mike hold her to her agreement? Should he be able to?

Because the car sold for more than $500, a court would not force Ruth to sell her car to Mike unless they had a written contract.

difficult to prove later that a party promised to do something. The usual rule is that if there is a written contract, a court will not even listen to evidence of promises made before the signing of a contract unless the written contract is unclear or one party was tricked by the other into entering the contract.

THE CASE OF THE DEAL TO STEAL

Gilbert made a written agreement with Lionel to pay him $200 if he would steal a valuable painting. Lionel stole the painting but Gilbert refused to pay him. Can Lionel take Gilbert to court to force him to pay?

No court would enforce this contract! It is an agreement to commit an illegal act (larceny) and is therefore void.

Illegal Contracts

There are many types of contracts that courts will not enforce because they are considered either illegal or against the interests of society. Also, courts sometimes find that a contract is so unfair, harsh, and oppressive that it should not be enforced. Such a contract is considered to be *unconscionable*. However, courts will usually require more than just a very high price before refusing to enforce a contract.

PROBLEM 16

In each of the following situations decide whether the contract could be enforced. Explain your answer in each case.

a. Mrs. Williams buys a stereo at a store where she has made many credit purchases in the past. Everytime she buys a new item the store makes her sign a contract which says that until she pays the full price on everything, the store still owns each item. The store knew that she was unemployed and receiving public assistance. She misses two payments on the stereo. Can the store take back all the merchandise?

b. Roe, a candidate for governor, promises to appoint Doe, also a candidate, to a high government office if he withdraws from the race. Doe withdraws. Roe wins. Can Doe force Roe to make the appointment?

c. Paolo rented a bike from Rainbow Rental Company. Before he could take out the bike he had to sign a form that said, "Rainbow will not be responsible for any damage or injury caused by any accident involving this bike." As a result of careless maintenance, the brakes failed on Paolo's bike and he was injured. Can Rainbow use the contract to defend against a lawsuit by Paolo?

WARRANTIES

A **warranty** or guarantee is a promise made by a seller concerning the quality or performance of goods offered for sale. There are two types of warranties; express and implied. Warranties give consum-

ers very important rights. You should always be aware of the warranties that exist when you make a purchase.

Express Warranties

An **express warranty** is a statement—written, oral, or by demonstration—concerning the quality or performance of goods offered for sale. For example, if a salesperson says to a customer, "this TV will not need any repairs for five years," this is an express warranty. Similarly, an express warranty would be created if a consumer purchased a vacuum cleaner from an appliance store after seeing a demonstration of the vacuum picking up small particles from a deep shag rug.

Express warranties are created by statements of fact, but not everything a seller says is a warranty. If the seller's statement is merely an opinion or an obvious exaggeration it is considered puffing or sales talk and cannot be relied on. For example, a used car lot advertising "Fantastic Used Cars" is engaged in puffing. No warranty is created and no customer should rely on such a statement.

When a product's warranty is violated or **breached,** the consumer can go to court to (1) cancel the contract, return the item, and have any money refunded; (2) sue for damages; or (3) demand a product that conforms to the warranty.

Sellers do not have to give written warranties, but if they do, the Federal Consumer Product Warranties Act requires that written warranties be in simple and easy-to-read language and be made available to the consumer before sale. The Warranties Act also requires that written warranties tell the buyer exactly what is included and what is not included. For example, if the product breaks and needs repair, the warranty must explain what repairs are covered and who will make them. The Warranties Act does not apply to products that cost five dollars or less.

Under the act, warranties are labeled either "Full" (for the period of the warranty) or "Limited." A full warranty means:

■ a defective product will be fixed or replaced free, including removal and reinstallation, if necessary;

■ the consumer will not have to do anything unreasonable to get the warranty service (such as shipping a piano to a factory);

■ the product will be fixed within a reasonable time after you complain;

■ if the item can't be fixed after a reasonable number of attempts, the consumer can get a refund or a replacement (this is called the Lemon Law).

Any protection less than this is called a limited warranty. Part of a product could have a full warranty and part could be limited. Read all of the warranty carefully.

PROBLEM 17

Read and evaluate the one-year limited warranty below and answer the following questions.

a. Who is making the warranty? Who will make any repairs—dealer, service center, manufacturer, or independent repairperson?

b. How long is the warranty in effect? Does the buyer have to do anything to make the warranty effective?

c. What is covered—the entire product or only certain parts? What is promised—repair, replacement, labor, postage? Are there any limitations or exclusions? Is this a full or limited warranty? Why?

ONE-YEAR LIMITED WARRANTY

Electro Toasters fully guarantees this entire product for one year from purchase date to owner against defects in material or workmanship.

Defective product may be brought to purchase place, authorized service center in phone book, or Service Department, Electro Toasters, Inc., 3rd & Maple Streets, Arlington, PA., freight prepaid, for free repair or replacement at our option.

Warranty does not include: cost of inconvenience, damage due to product failure, transportation damages, misuse, abuse, accident or the like, or commercial use.

For information, write Consumer Claims Manager, at above Arlington address. Send name, address, zip, store or service center involved, model, serial number, purchase date, problem.

This warranty gives specific legal rights. You may have other rights which vary from state to state.

This warranty becomes effective upon purchase. Mailing the enclosed registration card is one way of proving purchase date but is not required for warranty coverage.

Implied Warranties

In addition to express warranties, the law requires that a product be of a certain minimum quality and performance, even if no express promise is made. An **implied warranty** is the unwritten standard of quality required, by law, of a product offered for sale. There are three types of implied warranties: (1) warranty of merchantability; (2) warranty of fitness for a particular purpose; and (3) warranty of title.

A *warranty of merchantability* means that the item sold is of at least average quality for that type of item. For example, a radio must play, a saw must cut, and a freezer must keep food frozen. This warranty is always implied unless the seller expressly disclaims it. However, this warranty does not apply to goods sold by casual sellers (e.g., your friend sells you her bike).

A *warranty of fitness for a particular purpose* is read into a contract when the consumer tells the seller before buying that the item is needed for a specific purpose or will be used in a certain way. A salesperson selling an item with this knowledge makes an implied promise that the item will meet the purpose. For example, if Terry tells a salesperson she wants a waterproof watch and the second time she goes swimming water leaks into the watch, then this warranty has been breached (broken).

A *warranty of title* means simply that sellers are held to have promised that they own the item being offered for sale. Sellers must own the goods and be able to transfer title or ownership to the buyer. If a person knows an item is stolen but still sells it, the warranty of title has been broken.

What is the purpose of a warranty?

If any of these implied warranties or promises are broken, the consumer usually has the right to return the goods, cancel the contract, and demand a refund or replacement.

PROBLEM 18

Is there a warranty created in any of the following situations? If so, what type of warranty? Has the warranty been broken?

a. John sells Terri his used car. On the way home the car breaks down so completely that the cost of fixing the car is greater than the sale price.

b. Deitra buys a dress after telling the sales clerk that she plans to wash it in a washing machine. The clerk replied, "That's fine. This material is no trouble at all to clean." The dress shrinks after being washed in a washing machine.

c. The salesperson tells Sharon, "This is the finest camera on the market. It will last for years." Eighteen months later the lens breaks.

d. Mike steals a diamond ring from a jewelry store and sells it to Marie after telling her his mother had given it to him.

e. Sandy orders a baseball bat from a catalog. The catalog said, "31-inch baseball bat, $7.95," and included a picture of a wooden bat. Two weeks later Sandy receives an aluminum bat in the mail.

f. Ned buys a new sofa from a furniture store. One of the legs falls off two weeks after delivery.

THE CASE OF THE GUITAR THAT QUIT

Sherry bought a new guitar for $100. The contract she signed had a clause that read, "This writing is the exclusive statement of the terms of the agreement between the parties. Seller makes no warranties either express or implied with respect to this product." The third time Sherry played the guitar, one of the strings popped. Can she return the guitar?

Disclaimers

The clause quoted in the Case of the Guitar that Quit is a **disclaimer.** In other words, it is an attempt to limit the seller's liability should anything go wrong with the product. Implied warranties can usually be disclaimed by using such expressions as "with all faults" or "as is." Unless these or other easily understood words

ADVICE ON WARRANTIES

1. Not all warranties are the same. It's worth checking warranties when comparison shopping.
2. When you look at a warranty, consider the duration (how long does it last?); the scope (what parts or problems are covered or excluded?); and the remedy (what do you get under the warranty? what must you do to get the remedy?).
3. Check out your own state's law. Sometimes it gives you rights that are not in the warranty.

are used, the seller must actually use the word "merchantability" to disclaim the warranty of merchantability, and it must be written so as to be easily seen by the consumer. Although the seller in the above case did not make any express warranty to Sherry, the language in the contract would probably *not* be effective to disclaim the implied warranty of merchantability.

Consumers should also know that under the Consumer Product Warranties Act, discussed in the section on express warranties, sellers offering a written warranty may not disclaim or modify any implied warranty during the effective period of the written warranty.

Disclaimers are sometimes used by sellers to limit the consumer's remedy. For example, a contract may read, "It is expressly understood and agreed that the buyer's only remedy shall be repair or replacement of defective parts. The seller shall not be liable in damages for injury to person or property." Courts generally enforce these clauses. However, courts have sometimes found it to be unfair to limit a consumer's remedy for a personal injury arising out of a purchase. Therefore, a consumer who buys a television set and signs a contract containing the above clause could sue for medical expenses, despite the words in the contract, if the television exploded and caused personal harm.

You should remember that if you fully examine the goods (or had the opportunity to do this) before making a purchase, the implied warranty will not apply to those defects that should have been discovered during the inspection. Therefore, *inspect whatever goods you are buying carefully for any defects.* Be especially careful with used cars. It is wise to have a mechanic you trust examine the car before you purchase it.

Be sure to read all instructions which come with a product carefully. If you fail to use the product properly, or if you use it for an improper purpose, you may not be able to make a successful claim if the product does not work or if you are harmed by it.

UNSAFE OR DANGEROUS PRODUCTS

Sometimes a product is not only poor in quality but also so defective that it actually harms or even kills the person using it. The area of law that deals with the problem of injury to consumers is known as product liability law.

The U.S. government estimates that each year over twenty million Americans are injured as a result of home incidents involving consumer products. Of the total, 110,000 are permanently disabled, and almost 30,000 are killed. In addition, thousands of other Americans are killed or injured driving their cars or engaging in recreational activities, such as biking, skiing, skateboarding, and hunting.

THE CASE OF THE EXPLODING BOTTLE

John's mother realizes she doesn't have anything to serve her guests, so she asks John to run to the store and get her a bottle of soda. As John is on his way home, the bottle suddenly explodes, injuring his eye and cutting his hands. Who, if anyone, is responsible for the injury to John?

Almost everyone agrees that the consumer has a right to safety. But how safe do you have a right to be, and who is responsible if you are injured in your home or on the highway? Sellers are expected to make products safe for their intended purpose. If products are defective or dangerous, the maker may be liable for the resulting harm. This liability may be based on warranty, negligence, or a theory of *strict liability*.

In the Case of the Exploding Bottle, the bottle was not of ordinary quality. Thus, there is probably a breach of the warranty of merchantability. The results of the breach, however, are far more serious than usual. Another way to look at the case is in terms of **negligence**. Negligence law deals with a person's lack of care toward another to whom a duty is owed, ending in harm. Here it is possible that the soda company, the bottle manufacturer, the store, or all three failed to exercise sufficient care in designing, manufacturing, or handling the bottle that injured John.

Because it is hard to prove negligence, the trend in products liability law is to hold the manufacturer and others in the chain of supply (e.g., distributor, retailer) strictly liable if someone is injured because of a defect in the product. Using strict liability, the consumer must prove the purchase, defect, and injury but need not pinpoint who was at fault in causing the defect.

Sometimes manufacturers are required to put warnings on potentially dangerous products, such as drugs, cigarettes, machinery, and cleaning fluids. Consumers who ignore these warnings may not be able to recover damages if they are injured by the product. Also, there may be no liability if a consumer uses a product for an unintended purpose, or uses it in a careless manner.

The federal Consumer Product Safety Commission handles complaints and deals with the safety of most consumer products and product-related injuries. The commission has the power to force dangerous products off the market and will advise consumers on the safety of products.

Hazardous Products?
The Consumer Product Safety Commission has rated the following common items as the most hazardous around the home. This index is based on the seriousness and frequency of accidents, with greater weight for those involving young children.

Hazard Index	
1. Bicycles and equipment	40.6
2. Stairs, ramps and landings	23.5
3. Footballs and football gear	13.7
4. Baseballs and equipment	12.9
5. Playground equipment	12.5
6. Power lawn mowers	12.0
7. Skates, skateboards, scooters	11.1
8. Swimming pools and equipment	11.1
9. Nonglass tables	11.0
10. Beds and bunk beds	9.7
11. Chairs, sofas and sofa beds	8.3
12. Basketballs and equipment	7.8
13. Floors and flooring materials	7.4
14. Nails, carpet tacks, thumbtacks	7.2
15. Architectural glass	6.3

FIGURE 10 Hazardous Products?

PROBLEM 19

a. Make a list of five items that are or can be dangerous to use.

b. For each item decide whether the government should ban it, regulate it (e.g., provide warnings), or take no action at all.

Does your state have a "helmet law" for motorcycles? What are some other examples of laws affecting consumer safety?

c. Explain why you treated each item as you did. Consider in your explanation both the danger and the benefits of each item.

CREDIT

Credit means buying goods or services now in exchange for a promise to pay in the future. It also means borrowing money now in exchange for a promise to repay it in the future. The person who loans the money or provides the credit is called a **creditor**. The person who borrows the money or buys on credit is called the **debtor**. Creditors usually charge debtors additional money over the amount borrowed for the privilege of being given the credit. This additional money owed to the creditor is called **interest**.

Types of Credit

For most consumers there are two general types of credit available, unsecured and secured. **Unsecured credit** simply means using credit (buying goods or borrowing money) based only on a promise to repay in the future. Credit cards and store charge accounts are examples of this kind of credit. In the case of **secured credit,** the consumer must put up some kind of property as protection in the event the debt is not repaid. For example, a person buying a house must give the lender a security interest called a mortgage in the

mortgage security interest in large debts.

house until the debt is repaid. If the person buying the house fails to pay off the debt, the lender can sell the house and use the proceeds of this sale to pay off the debt.

Credit Cards and Charge Accounts   Today, many stores and companies issue credit cards and allow their customers to maintain charge accounts. As a consumer you can use credit cards to buy gasoline, to take a vacation, to go out to dinner, and to buy furniture, clothing, or hundreds of other things.

Credit cards, which are engraved with the holder's name and identification number, entitle the consumer to buy goods or services on credit. Some companies provide these cards free; some charge a yearly fee, typically fifteen to twenty dollars. The consumer is given a credit limit and can make purchases up to that limit.

Companies issuing credit cards send out monthly statements that show the consumer how much is owed. Most credit card companies allow the consumer to pay bills over time, making minimum monthly payments. If the consumer pays the entire bill on or before the due date, there is usually no extra charge. However, if the consumer pays only part of the amount owed, there is usually a finance or interest charge of one to one-and-a-half percent of the unpaid monthly balance, or twelve to eighteen percent a year.

While various companies use slightly different methods of computing interest, you can estimate the interest charge by multiplying the balance owed by .015 (i.e., if the interest is one to one-and-a-half percent per month). For example, if the balance owed is $500, the monthly interest charge will be about $7.50 ($500 × .015). The total amount owed for the month will be approximately $507.50 ($500 + $7.50 interest).

THE CASE OF THE LOST CREDIT CARDS

Sally lost her wallet containing a Master Charge card and a Sears credit card. By the time Sally realized her wallet was missing, someone had charged $800 on the Master Charge and $100 on the Sears account. Does Sally have to pay these bills?

The loss or theft of a credit card should be reported immediately to the company or store that issued the card. For protection, any person with credit cards should keep a list of the following information: (1) the name of the company issuing the card; (2) the account number on each card; and (3) the number to call if the card is lost or stolen.

FIGURE 11 Credit Card Application

Applicant's Information
Please read special instructions*

FIRST NAME	MIDDLE NAME	LAST NAME		BANK USE ONLY

STREET ADDRESS | CITY | STATE | ZIP

CL _____ NO CDS

SOURCE _____

SOCIAL SECURITY NUMBER | HOME PHONE NUMBER [ ] | APPLICANT'S AGE | NO OF DEPENDENTS

PRESENT ADDRESS YRS ___ MOS ___ | HOME W/RELATIVES BUYING ___ RENTING ___ OWN ___ | IF BUYING/OWN VALUE ___ BALANCE ___

DR _____

TO WHOM DO YOU PAY RENT/MORTGAGE | ADDRESS | MONTHLY PAYMENT

BANK AND BRANCH

FORMER ADDRESS | CITY | STATE | ZIP | FORMER ADDRESS YRS ___ MOS ___

NAME OF NEAREST RELATIVE (not living with you) | ADDRESS | RELATIONSHIP

FULL SIGNATURE

EMPLOYER | POSITION | HOW LONG YRS ___ MOS ___

BUSINESS ADDRESS | CITY | STATE | ZIP | BUSINESS PHONE NUMBER [ ]

PREVIOUS EMPLOYER | POSITION | ADDRESS | HOW LONG YRS ___ MOS ___

GROSS MONTHLY INCOME | AMOUNT AND SOURCE OF ADDITIONAL INCOME (See special instructions)* | IF OBLIGATED TO PAY ALIMONY, CHILD SUPPORT LIST MONTHLY AMOUNT

IF ALIMONY/CHILD SUPPORT | NAME AND ADDRESS OF PAYER

BANK AND BRANCH | CHECKING ACCT NO | SAVINGS ACCT NO | LOAN ACCT NO

BANK AND BRANCH | CHECKING ACCT NO | SAVINGS ACCT NO | LOAN ACCT NO

AUTO MAKE | YEAR | FINANCED BY/ADDRESS | PRESENT BALANCE | MO PAYMENT

CREDITORS | ADDRESS | ACCT NO

TOTAL OF ALL DEBTS AND MONTHLY PAYMENTS (See special instructions)* _____

Under federal law, if a credit card is lost or stolen, the card-holder is not responsible for any unauthorized charges made after notifying the issuer that the card is missing. The law limits the consumer's liability for charges made before notification to fifty dollars per card. In the Case of the Lost Credit Cards, Sally would probably be liable for fifty dollars on each card. If she had notified Sears and Master Charge before any charges were made, she would have owed nothing.

Billing errors can be a real headache. It takes time and energy to sort them out, but they can also cost you money if you don't discover them. To avoid billing problems, check *all* sales slips carefully, save receipts and canceled checks, and go over each bill or monthly statement carefully.

If you still encounter a problem, the Fair Credit Billing Act provides you with a measure of protection. If you have a complaint about your bill, this law requires creditors to acknowledge and respond to your written complaint within ninety days. You may withhold payment of the amount in dispute pending the investigation; however, amounts not in dispute must be paid as normally required. Until your complaint is settled the law forbids the creditor from reporting the matter to a credit bureau.

In order to receive the protection of the Fair Credit Billing Act, your communication to the creditor must meet certain requirements. You must submit a written notice (phone calls do not protect a consumer's rights under this act). The notice must be received at the creditor's address for complaints as indicated on the statement within sixty days of when the statement was first sent to you. In the notice you must include your name and your account number (if any). Finally, you must indicate in the notice that you believe there is a billing error, stating your reasons for this belief and the amount of the error.

If the bill turns out to be correct, you may have to pay a finance charge on the unpaid amount in dispute. However, a creditor who does not follow the requirements of this law may not collect the first fifty dollars of the disputed amount, even if the bill turns out to be accurate. A consumer can sue such a creditor for damages and can also recover attorney fees.

THE CASE OF THE CHARGE ACCOUNT BILLING ERROR

You pay the bill on your monthly department store charge account. The next month, you are again charged for the amount already paid. You call the store to straighten out the mistake, but the next month you receive the same bill plus a letter threatening to close your account. What can you do?

PROBLEM 20

Examine the billing statement reproduced in the text and answer the following questions.

a. Who is the creditor?

b. Who is the debtor?

c. What is the new balance? How did the creditor arrive at the new balance?

d. How much credit is available? How did the creditor determine the credit available?

e. Assume the debtor had a store receipt from the camera shop for $77.67. Draft a letter to the creditor about this billing error.

FIGURE 12 Billing Statement

PAYMENTS SHOULD BE ADDRESSED TO:
UNITED VIRGINIA BANK CARD CENTER
7818 PARHAM RD . P. O. BOX 27182
RICHMOND. VIRGINIA 23270

UNITED VIRGINIA BANK CARD
STATEMENT

ACCOUNT NUMBER		STATEMENT CLOSING DATE
4366-040-878-010		03/12/80

CREDIT LIMIT	CREDIT AVAILABLE
1,000	810.50

CUSTOMER REPRESENTATIVE TELEPHONE NUMBER
(804) 270-8414

INQUIRIES SHOULD BE ADDRESSED TO:
UNITED VIRGINIA BANK CARD CENTER
7818 PARHAM RD . P. O. BOX 27172
RICHMOND. VIRGINIA 23261

JOHN .Q. CONSUMER
1000 MAIN STREET
ANYWHERE, USA

POSTING DATE	REFERENCE NUMBER	TRANSACTION DATE	TRANSACTION DESCRIPTION			AMOUNT
07 18	*76145324	07 07	DODGE STATE PARK	FT WAYNE	IN	30 03
07 25	*81983773	07 03	ECONOMY HOTEL, INC.	ASHVILLE	NC	19 71
08 02	21407856	08 02	PAYMENT - THANK YOU			100 00-
08 08	21575724	07 27	THRIFTY MOTEL	SOUTH HILL	VA	14 51
08 09	22161982	08 05	SNAP SHOT CAMERA	WASHINGTON	DC	87 67

VISA.   VISA.

TYPE OF CREDIT	PREVIOUS BALANCE	CREDITS	PAYMENTS	NEW TRANSACTIONS	PERIODIC RATES	CORRESPONDING ANNUAL PERCENTAGE RATES	BALANCE ON WHICH COMPUTED	FINANCE CHARGE	NEW BALANCE
ADVANCES	00	00	00	00	1.00%	12.0%	00	00	00
OTHER EXTENSIONS OF CREDIT	136 08	00	100 00	151 92	1.50%	18.0%	100 36	1 50	189 50
TOTALS	136 08	00	100 00	151 92	ANNUAL PERCENTAGE RATE 18.0 %		100 36	1 50	189 50

171870

PAST DUE	00
CURRENT DUE	10 00
MINIMUM PAYMENT DUE	10 00

TO PAY IN INSTALMENTS PAY THIS AMOUNT BY THE PAYMENT DUE DATE

DUE DATE
04/08/80

To avoid additional FINANCE CHARGE on other extensions of credit, pay this amount by the payment due date.

NOTICE: SEE REVERSE SIDE FOR IMPORTANT INFORMATION

Loans and Installment Sales Contracts   Probably the biggest difference for consumers between unsecured and secured credit transactions is the requirement that consumers post **collateral** in secured transactions. Collateral is property put up by the debtor that may be taken by the creditor if the loan is not repaid.

If Joan wants to buy a new car she can go to a bank to borrow money. The bank loans her the money (if her credit is good) in exchange for her promise to repay it. The bank may also require collateral. For example, they may ask that she put up the car or other valuable property as security for the loan. This means that the bank can take the car if she **defaults** (misses payments) on her loan.

Who Should Use Credit?

To make an informed decision about a credit purchase, a consumer must first answer this question: Is it worth having a car, television, vacation, or other item before you have saved the entire purchase price, even though you'll be paying more for the item in the long run?

Most American families have answered yes to this question. In a recent year consumer debt averaged approximately $1,000 for every man, woman, and child in the country! And this figure did not include money owed for home mortgages. Many American familes are seldom out of debt.

While extensive use of credit is here to stay, consumers should know that credit purchases cost more than cash purchases. In addition, studies have shown that consumers who use credit spend more and buy more often. This is the reason merchants often dangle the lure of "easy credit."

Consumers who buy on credit not only pay more but also run the risk of losing their products (and their payments) and harming their credit rating if they fail to make the required payments. As a rule of thumb consumers who spend more than twenty percent of their take-home salary to pay off debts (excluding mortages) have used too much credit. Consumers who must occasionally skip payments to cover living expenses or who take out new loans to cover old loans have already used too much credit.

PROBLEM 21

a. Make a list of situations in which you, your friends, or your family have made credit purchases.

b. What are the advantages and disadvantages of using credit to pay for clothing to be worn at a formal party? Tuition for college or vocational school? A car to get you to work? A vacation?

c. Write out some rules that will help you in deciding when to use credit.

The Cost of Credit

Consumers should comparison shop for credit just as they comparison shop for products and services. The cost of credit includes interest and other finance charges. Because there are a number of different methods for calculating interest rates, always ask lenders for the Annual Percentage Rate (APR) so that you can compare rates.

Interest Rates Each state sets limits on the amount of interest that can be charged for various types of credit. Any amount charged above that allowed by the state is called **usury**. Lenders who charge interest rates higher than the legal maximum may be liable for both civil and criminal penalties.

The interest rate ceiling varies from state to state. Generally, however, a loan of money from an individual, bank or finance company can carry an interest rate from five to fifteen percent per year. Credit cards and store charge accounts are usually one-and-a-half percent a month (eighteen percent a year). Installment contracts for consumer goods sometimes have finance charges amounting to over twenty percent a year.

Banks loan money to consumers. Where else can a consumer borrow money?

THE CASE OF THE 50/50 CREDIT PLAN

Sally Saleswoman told Linda, "This washing machine is a good buy—only $500. Now, if you don't have the cash, I can arrange easy credit for you. Only $50 down and $50 a month for twelve months. Just sign here." Linda signed and paid the $50. How much interest would she be paying if the contract called for twelve monthly payments?

Linda would have paid a total of $650 at the end of twelve months ($50 down and $600 in installment payments). Since the cash price of the washing machine was $500, she paid a $150 finance charge for the right to borrow $450 ($500 minus $50 down payment). According to a formula set up under federal law, the APR would be forty-nine percent!

Other Finance Charges Besides the regular finance charge of interest on an installment sale, there are sometimes other charges added onto the basic price. These include:

■ Credit Property Insurance, which insures the purchased item against theft or damage

■ Credit Life Insurance, which insures the life of the buyer and guarantees payment of the balance due if the buyer should die during the term of the contract

■ Service Charge, which covers the seller's bookkeeping, sending of bills, etc.

■ Penalty Charges, which cover the seller's inconvenience in the case of early or late payments, and may include court costs, repossession expenses, and attorney fees

PROBLEM 22

Choose an item you would like to have but could only purchase by using credit.

a. Where could you shop for this credit?

b. What interest rates do the different sources of credit charge for this item? What is the APR for each creditor? What other finance charges are required?

Costly Credit Arrangements   Low-income consumers and persons heavily in debt may fall prey to **loan sharking,** the lending of money at high, often usurious (illegal) rates of interest. Loan sharks usually promise "easy" credit and appeal to persons who have problems obtaining and keeping good credit standing.

Some creditors use **balloon payment** clauses in their agreements. In such an agreement, monthly payments are small but the last payment is much larger, causing the consumer to miss the payment or default. Consumers should look out for balloon payment clauses.

Another clause to avoid in financing agreements, if possible, is the **acceleration clause**. This clause permits the creditor to accelerate the loan, making all future payments due immediately in the event a consumer misses a single payment.

You should also watch out for the popular practice of **bill consolidation**. The lender claims to wipe out all those bills with one low easy monthly payment. This plan, in effect, gives the consumer a loan large enough to pay other current debts. However, the consolidation loan may require payments over a longer period of time and at a higher interest rate. In the long run the consumer may pay more.

Truth in Lending To prevent credit abuses, such as in the Case of the Hidden Charges, Congress passed a law commonly referred to as the Truth in Lending Act. This act requires credit sellers to tell consumers the total cost of their purchases and to express the total amount of interest both in dollars and cents and in the annual percentage rate (APR). Thus, if interest is one-and-a-half percent a month, the consumer must be told this amounts to eighteen percent a year.

The law also requires that consumers be given a copy of the contract and be told the rules and charges for any late payments. Violations of this law should be reported to the Federal Trade Commission. Violators are subject to both civil and criminal penalties, and consumers who sue creditors under this act may recover damages, court costs, and attorney's fees.

ADVICE ON USING CREDIT

1. Credit costs money. Don't buy things on credit you don't need or want. Resist high-pressure sales techniques.
2. Determine how much debt you can handle.
3. Comparison shop for credit. If you are suspicious, check to see if the lender is licensed and whether complaints have been filed.
4. Before making a credit purchase, read and understand the entire contract. Don't sign contracts with blank spaces. Don't sign contracts with large final payments.
5. Once you've signed a contract agreement, keep a copy in a safe place. Keep receipts for each payment.

FIGURE 13 **Retail Installment Contract**

Seller's Name: Lowell's Department Store
Pittsburgh, Pennsylvania

Contract # 32.83

RETAIL INSTALLMENT CONTRACT AND SECURITY AGREEMENT

The undersigned (herein called Purchaser, whether one or more) purchases from Lowell's Dept Store (seller) and grants to Lowell's Dept. Store a security interest in, subject to the terms and conditions hereof, the following described property.

QUANTITY	DESCRIPTION	AMOUNT	
1	Refrigerator	300	00
Description of Trade-in:			
	Sales Tax	15	00
	Total	315	00

PURCHASER'S NAME Mr. John Jones
PURCHASER'S ADDRESS 74 Woods Place
CITY Pittsburgh STATE Pa ZIP 15210

1. CASH PRICE $ 315.00
2. LESS: CASH DOWN PAYMENT $ 50.00
3. TRADE-IN —
4. TOTAL DOWN PAYMENT $ 50.00
5. UNPAID BALANCE OF CASH PRICE $ 265.00
6. OTHER CHARGES:
   Service Charge $ 8.00
   $
7. AMOUNT FINANCED $ 273.00
8. FINANCE CHARGE $ 49.14
9. TOTAL OF PAYMENTS $
10. DEFERRED PAYMENT PRICE (1+6+8) $ 372.14
11. ANNUAL PERCENTAGE RATE 18

Insurance Agreement

The purchaser of insurance coverage is voluntary and not required for credit. (Type of Ins.) insurance coverage is available at a cost of $ 10.00 for the terms of credit.

I desire insurance coverage

Signed ________ Date ______

I do not desire insurance coverage

Signed ________ Date ______

Purchaser hereby agrees to pay to Lowell's Department Store at their offices shown above the "TOTAL OF PAYMENTS" shown above in 12 monthly installments of $ 26.85 (final payment to be $ 26.85) the first installment being payable March 5, 1979, and all subsequent installments on the same day of each month until paid in full. The finance charge applies from (Date) Feb. 5, 1979

Signed ________

Notice to Buyer: You are entitled to a copy of the contract you sign. You have the right to pay in advance the unpaid balance of this contract and obtain a partial refund of the finance charge based on the "Actuarial Method."

THE CASE OF THE HIDDEN CHARGES

Art buys some new furniture on the installment plan. When he receives an itemized bill, he discovers that he owes a total of $745, while the price of the furniture was only $553. He calls the store and they tell him that he is paying twenty percent interest. He would never have bought the furniture if he'd known it would have cost this much. What mistakes did Art make? What can he do now?

PROBLEM 23

Carefully read the contract reprinted in the text.

a. What is the annual percentage rate in this contract?

b. Are there any balloon payments?

c. Must the consumer buy credit insurance?

d. What do you think "deferred payment price" means?

e. Are there any blank spaces that should be filled in? If there are, what goes in the spaces?

f. If Jones misses a payment, can the store take back the refrigerator?

Obtaining Credit

Any store, bank, or credit card company that extends credit to a consumer wants to know that the money will be repaid. To help in making a decision, the creditor will want to know several things about the consumer.

■ Is the consumer a reliable person (e.g., does he or she move or change jobs frequently)?

■ Does the consumer have a steady income that is likely to continue into the future?

■ Is the consumer's income high enough to enable the consumer to pay for the items likely to be purchased?

■ Does the consumer have a good record in paying off other previous bills and loans?

Because creditors are in business to make money rather than lose money, it is understandable that they would ask questions such as these. However, creditors have sometimes gone further and unfairly denied credit for such reasons as race, sex, or the source of a person's income (e.g., public assistance or alimony).

Since 1975 a federal law, the Equal Credit Opportunity Act, has protected consumers against credit discrimination based on sex or marital status. In 1977 this law was extended to include protection from discrimination based on race, color, religion, national origin, age (so long as the applicant is not a minor), and source of income. The Federal Trade Commission handles credit discrimination complaints against retail stores, oil companies, and travel and entertainment credit card companies. The Civil Aeronautics Board handles complaints relating to airline credit cards. Bank regulatory agencies, such as the Comptroller of the Currency, handle complaints against banks and bank credit cards. A consumer who thinks he or she has been discriminated against may complain to one of the agencies or sue the creditor in court.

Many states also have laws that forbid discrimination in the granting of credit. Complaints should be directed to the state or local consumer affairs office or human rights commission.

PROBLEM 24

You are a loan officer at a local bank. Each of the following persons is seeking a loan. Based on the information provided, evaluate each applicant and make a decision regarding each loan request. Discuss your reasons for granting or denying credit.

a. Alice Johnson is the mother of four children. Her only income consists of public assistance payments of $420 per month and $80 per month from the pension of her deceased husband. She wishes to buy a new stove and refrigerator totaling $700. She lives in a public housing development. Her rent and other expenses usually total about $375 a month.

Why should you shop for credit?

b. Jerry Levitt is a carpenter seeking work wherever he can find it. Depending on the weather and other factors he is subject to seasonal unemployment. He currently brings home about $650 per month and has car payments of $150 a month, stereo and TV payments of $105 a month, rent of $220 a month, and no money in the bank. He would like to borrow $2,500 to buy a motorcycle.

c. Sue Sullivan, twenty-two, is in her second year of college. She has excellent grades and plans to attend medical school after graduation. Until recently her parents paid her bills, but she is now on her own. She is seeking $2,000 for her college tuition and expenses. She has never borrowed money before, but she plans to repay all loans after finishing medical school.

FIGURE 14 Charge Account Application

Applicant's Signature: Sam K Richards
Identification: VA. Drivers License P831947 | Date: 3-23-79

Co-Applicant's Signature: Susan Lynn Richards
Identification: VA DRIVERS LICENSE C139246 | Date: 3-23-79

Office Use Only: Store Number | Date | Courtesy Card Amount | Approved By | Account Number
Taken By No. | Courtesy Card Authorized By | Date | FLC | CBC | RI

Account Previously Applied For?
Applicant: ☐ Yes ☒ No — Where — When
Co-Applicant: ☐ Yes ☒ No — Where — When

Charge Card(s) To Be In The Name Of
1. First: SAM | Initial: K. | Last: RICHARDS | Date of Birth Mo. Day Yr.: 10 06 48

Type of Account Requested: ☒ Joint ☐ Individual
Number of Charge Cards Requested: 2
Co-Applicant's Name (If Joint Account Requested)
2. First: SUSAN | Initial: L. | Last: RICHARDS | Relationship To Individual Named In Box 1.: wife

Present Residence (Mailing) Address-Street: 089 South Maple Street | Length of Time at This Address: 3 years
City, State: Alexandria, Virginia | Zip: 22314 | Area Code & Phone Number: (017) 342-8619

Social Security Number: 084-74-8574 | ☐ Own Home ☐ Own Mobile Home ☒ Rent ☐ Room ☐ Live With Parents | Monthly Mtge./Rent: $350 | No. of Dependents Including Self: 2 | Other(s) Authorized To Use This Account – Relationship(s):

Applicant's Information		Co-Applicant's Information (If Joint Account Requested)	
Former Address - Street: 012 West 14th Street	How Long: 3 yrs	Former Address - Street: 012 West 14th Street	How Long: 3 yrs
City, State: Washington, D.C.	Zip: 20036	City, State, Zip: Washington, D.C.	Social Security Number: 20036
Employer's Name (Give Firm's Full Name): Fix-It Plumbing Company	How Long: 3 yrs	Employer's Name (Give Firm's Full Name): West 12th St Elem. School	How Long: 2 years
Employer's Address: 389 "C" Street Wash. D.C.	Business Telephone: 861-4819	Employer's Address: 1201 12th St. Wash. D.C.	Business Telephone: 391-0842
Position: Plumber	Gross Salary (Monthly): $1500.	Position: Teacher's Aide	Gross Salary (Monthly): $500.00

You Need Not Furnish Alimony, Child Support Or Separate Maintenance Income Information If You Do Not Want Us To Consider It In Evaluating Your **Application.**

Other Income – Source(s):	Amount (Monthly):	Other Income – Source(s):	Amount (Monthly):
Former Employer – Address: Garry Plumbing & Heating	How Long: 4 yrs	Former Employer – Address: Franklin Elementary School	How Long: 2 years
Position: Plumber	Gross Salary (Monthly): $1000	Position: Teacher's Aide	Gross Salary (Monthly): $400
Bank – Branch: Security American Bank	☒ Checking ☒ Savings ☐ Checking & Savings ☐ Loan	Bank – Branch: Security Amer. Bank	☒ Checking ☒ Savings ☐ Checking & Savings ☐ Loan
Nearest Relative Not At Your Present Address: Robert Richards	Relationship: brother	Nearest Relative Not At Your Present Address: Sally M. Cook	Relationship: sister
Relative's Address: 1001 Market Street Lanham, MD.		Relative's Address: 813 Apple Lane Vienna, Virginia	

Credit Cards (Include Loan or Finance Companies)

Firm Name	Location	Account No.	Exact Name In Which Account Is Carried
American Oil	Richmond, VA.	M482-613	SAM K. RICHARDS
Hahns Dept Store	WASHINGTON DC	014-892	Susan L. RICHARDS

For Office Use Only
Credit Bureau Report: In File Since ______ Last Checked ______

PROBLEM 25

Susan and Sam Richards want to open a charge account at a local department store. Their application is reproduced in the text.

a. As a credit department officer, would you approve their application? Why or why not?

b. Is there information not on this form that would be helpful in making a decision? Is any of the information on the form unnecessary? Explain your answers.

What To Do If You Are Denied Credit

Whenever a consumer applies for credit, the creditor will evaluate the application according to certain standards. The creditor may either undertake his or her own investigation of the consumer or pay a credit bureau for a report on the consumer. There are thousands of credit bureaus across the country. Financial and personal information about consumers is often stored in computers and may be passed among the various bureaus.

If the credit report indicates that the buyer is a poor risk, the creditor will probably deny credit. Also, if a person is trying to get credit for the first time and has no record at all, the creditor may deny credit. Sometimes a creditor decides not to give credit simply on the basis of information on the application, without taking the time and paying the cost of ordering a credit report.

The Equal Credit Opportunity Act says that a creditor must tell a consumer why he or she was turned down. If a credit report was involved, another federal law helps protect the consumer from inaccurate credit bureau reporting. The Fair Credit Reporting Act, passed in 1971, says that a creditor who denies an application for credit based on information received from a credit bureau must inform the consumer of that fact and give the consumer the name and address of the credit bureau that supplied the report.

Any consumer has the right to learn the nature of information in his or her credit file. Although the credit bureau is not required to show the consumer a copy of the actual file, the bureau must disclose the nature and substance of the information contained in the file.

A consumer who discovers false, misleading, incomplete, irrelevant, or out-of-date information in his or her file can require the credit bureau to recheck its information and correct the errors. If the credit bureau does not cooperate in correcting the consumer's credit file, the consumer may complain to the Federal Trade Commission or sue the bureau in court. If after reinvestigating the information the bureau does not believe that it is incorrect, the consumer has the right to have his or her version of the dispute inserted in the file.

DEFAULT AND COLLECTION PRACTICES

Consumers who use credit sometimes have difficulty making all their payments. Problems can arise because the consumer is over-extended or too deeply in debt. Problems can also arise because of unexpected unemployment, family illness, or a variety of other reasons. A consumer who is unable or unwilling to pay off a debt goes into **default**.

How could a budget help this consumer?

What a Consumer Can Do in Case of Default

Consumers who have problems paying their bills should consider each of the following options.

1. Reassess their financial lifestyle to determine where the problem arose. If they are not already on a budget, they should consider starting one.

2. Notify each creditor of the problem and ask to have the term of the debt extended (leading to smaller monthly payments) or to have the amount of the debt reduced or refinanced. Keep in mind that refinancing over a longer period usually results in increased finance charges.

3. Contact a Consumer Credit Counseling Service or a Family Service Agency that offers financial counseling (see Appendix A for addresses).

4. Seek assistance from friends or relatives to reduce the debt to a manageable level.

5. Consider debt reorganization under Chapter XIII of the Federal Bankruptcy Law. Under this plan the wage earner, the creditors, and a court-appointed referee work out a plan to repay debts on an installment basis. The entire process is supervised by a federal court.

6. Declare voluntary bankruptcy. This is usually the least desirable option and should be considered only as a last resort. All assets (except items such as one's home and necessary clothing, which are exempted under your state's law) are assembled and sold. The proceeds are distributed among the creditors.

Creditor Collection Practices

Creditors have a variety of means for collecting money from consumers who are unwilling or unable to pay their debts. It is understandable that creditors take action to recover money or property

WHERE YOU LIVE

What agencies and organizations in your community provide financial counseling services? Do they charge a fee for their services?

owed them. However, in the past, some bill collectors have engaged in unsavory practices resulting in family problems, loss of jobs, and invasions of privacy for debtors.

These practices prompted Congress to pass the Fair Debt Collection Practices Act in 1978. This act protects consumers from abusive and unfair collection practices by professional debt collectors (however, not by creditors collecting their own bills). Under the act, the debt collector's communications are limited to reasonable times and places. False or misleading statements as well as acts of harassment or abuse are strictly prohibited.

Calls and Letters If phone calls or letters are unreasonable and become harrassing, consumers should report the collection practice to the Federal Trade Commission or to their local consumer protection agency. The consumer should also consider contacting the phone company, which has the power to remove telephones from anyone using them for harrassment.

Repossession As mentioned earlier, consumers sometimes post collateral when they take out a loan or sign installment sales contracts. The creditor can usually **repossess,** or take back, the collateral if the consumer defaults on the loan or obligation. Most states do not permit creditors to repossess if it involves violence or a breach of the peace.

The creditor can sell the collateral and then apply the proceeds of the sale to the amount the debtor owes. The debtor is also charged for any costs incurred in the repossession and sale. After the sale, the consumer is entitled to get back any amount received

---

THE CASE OF THE MISSED PAYMENT

Orlando bought a used car from Top Value Cars for $1,200 and signed a contract calling for monthly payments for three years. After paying $800 he missed a payment because of large doctor bills. Leaving home one morning, he found that the car was gone. Top Value had hired someone to come and take the car in the middle of the night.

PROBLEM 26
a. Assume that Top Value sold the car for $500 and incurred expenses of $200 in the repossession and sale. Will Orlando get money back or will he still owe money to Top Value (even though he no longer has the car)? How much is owed and to whom?
b. The action taken by Top Value is legal in most states. Do you think the repossession laws are fair? What arguments could creditors make on behalf of these laws? What arguments could debtors make against them?

by the seller that is in excess of the amount owed (plus expenses). However, if the sale brings in less than what the consumer owes (plus expenses), the consumer still owes the difference. In some states a creditor who repossesses gives up the right to collect any amount remaining after the sale.

Court Action A creditor, usually as a last resort, may sue a debtor in court for the exact amount owed on the debt. At times the trouble and expense of suing in court will make creditors avoid this method. However, a creditor may avoid high court costs and long delays by filing the case in small claims court (so long as the suit is limited to the maximum amount that that court can award).

A consumer receiving a summons to go to court should contact a lawyer immediately. If unable to afford one, the consumer may call the local Legal Services or Legal Aid Office or ask the court to appoint a free attorney. However, a consumer does not have a constitutional right to an attorney in a civil case.

The main thing to avoid when being sued is a *default judgment*. This is a judgment entered for the plaintiff (creditor) and against the defendant (debtor) because the defendant simply did not show up in court. A consumer who cannot appear in court on the date set in the summons should contact the clerk of the court in advance to arrange for a postponement of the trial.

Garnishment and Attachment A creditor who wins a court judgment against a consumer may still have trouble collecting if the consumer does not pay voluntarily. It was once common practice to have people imprisoned for not paying debts; however, this is no longer allowed.

One solution for the creditor is to get a court order that forces the consumer's employer to withhold part of the consumer's wages and pay it directly to the creditor. This is called **garnishment**. The federal Consumer Credit Protection Act limits the amount that can be garnished to twenty-five percent of the consumer's take-home pay (i.e., after taxes and social security deductions). Persons employed by the federal government or otherwise receiving federal money, such as welfare or unemployment compensation, cannot have their income garnished (unless the money is used to meet court-ordered child support payments). The act also prohibits employers from firing employees who have their wages garnished for a single debt. State law may further limit and sometimes completely prohibit garnishment.

A creditor can also get possession of a debtor's money or property by **attachment**. This is a court order that forces a bank to pay the creditor out of a consumer's bank account or allows the court to seize the consumer's property and sell it to satisfy the debt.

While garnishment and attachment are usually used by creditors after a court judgment has been rendered, some states permit creditors to use these remedies *before* suing the consumer in order to guarantee that funds will later be available. The U.S. Supreme Court has ruled that in most such instances a consumer's wages cannot be garnished, nor can his or her property be attached, without first giving the consumer notice and an opportunity to be heard in court.

CARS AND THE CONSUMER

The most important consumer purchase made by many persons is an automobile. The purchase, ownership, maintenance, and sale of an automobile involves many legal issues. Earlier in this chapter you looked at how the law affects car owners in cases of repair fraud and repossession. Now you will apply some other concepts you have already studied (comparison shopping, contracts, warranties, and credit) to automobiles. You will also look briefly at the sometimes confusing but important topic of insurance.

Buying a Car

In comparison shopping for a new car or used car, a consumer should consider at least three general characteristics: (1) safety, (2) price, and (3) warranties. Many consumers fail to take safety features into account in shopping for a car. Safety features are important because in an average year, one in three motorists can expect to have an automobile accident! Federal law requires that car dealers provide a pamphlet that details safety aspects of new cars,

including acceleration and passing ability, stopping distance, and tire load. In addition, buyers should always check visibility from the driver's seat (i.e., check for blind spots, windshield glare in strong sunlight, positioning of inside and outside mirrors); ability to reach all controls while sitting in the driver's seat with the seat belts fastened; and protection afforded by bumpers and safety belts.

When shopping for a car within a certain price range, remember that virtually no one pays the list price for a new or used car. Discounts of hundreds of dollars are quite common, depending upon when during the model year the purchase is made, whether a

WHERE YOU LIVE

When buying a car in your community, what procedures must you follow to register the car and obtain license plates?

THE CASE OF THE USED CAR PURCHASE

Having saved $500 from her summer job, Sharon responded to an ad for "like-new, one-owner used cars." A salesperson for A-1 Used Cars watched Sharon wander around the lot until she was attracted to a sharp-looking, late-model compact car. Sharon told the salesperson that this car looked just right for her. He replied, "You've made a good choice. This is an excellent car. It will give you many years of good service."

Although the sticker price was $1550, the salesperson thought that he might be able to get her a $50 discount because she was "a nice young kid getting her first car." After conferring with the sales manager, he told her that she could have the car for $1500 and that the dealer could arrange to finance the car and sell her all necessary insurance.

Sharon knew that she'd need a loan and her parents had warned her that insurance was required by law. Her excitement increased as it appeared that all her problems could be solved in one stop.

The salesperson told her that A-1 would make any repairs to the engine, not caused by her misuse, for thirty days or 10,000 miles, whichever came first. Now she even felt confident about using all of her savings as a down payment. After all, what repair bills could she have with such a nice car accompanied by a terrific warranty?

PROBLEM 27
a. Make a list of things Sharon should have done or thought about before going to A-1.
b. Make a list of things she should have done at A-1 before agreeing to buy the car.
c. Did the seller make any promises to her? Did he say anything that could be considered puffing?
d. What are the advantages and disadvantages of having the dealer provide Sharon with financing and insurance?
e. Taking into account the lists you've made, roleplay Sharon's encounter with the salesperson.

special sale is in effect with manufacturer's bonuses for dealers, and other factors.

PROBLEM 28

In addition to the purchase price, what other costs should a consumer consider in making a decision to purchase a car? Where is information available about each of these costs?

Consumers should compare warranties and the dealer's capability to make repairs just as they compare safety features and price. Many new cars have a warranty covering most parts, except batteries and tires, against defects for 12,000 miles or twelve months, whichever comes first. Some manufacturers warrant the engine and drive train for a longer period. Still other manufacturers offer a warranty as part of the purchase price but also make available an extended warranty (actually a service contract) for an additional price. Because of the variations in available warranties, consumers must be certain that they read and fully understand exactly what protections the warranty provides.

Used cars may also come with warranties. In some instances, even where a warranty is not offered a smart shopper may be able to bargain for a warranty as part of the sales agreement. Used car warranties usually last for thirty or sixty days from the date of purchase, and some require the buyer to pay half the cost of warranty repairs.

The U.S. Environmental Protection Agency requires dealers to provide car buyers with information on gas mileage.

Although car warranties have been made easier to read in recent years and protections have been expanded, there are still time and/or mileage limits to the warranties. Also, a warranty may become ineffective if the owner has failed to perform proper maintenance.

Always be sure the warranty and any additional promises are in writing. Keep these papers in a safe place.

Financing a Car

Two out of three new car buyers and half of the used car buyers make their purchases on time. Buyers may select the length of the repayment period which, in the case of new cars, may be as long as four years. The longer the repayment period, the lower the monthly payments will be (but a larger sum will have to be paid in interest). Table 3 shows the total interest charges on a $4,000 loan, depending on the interest rate and the length of the repayment period. In some places, interest rates can be lower than eleven percent or higher than twelve.

PROBLEM 29

Sam is buying a $5,000 car. He can put down $1,000 and needs to borrow the remaining $4,000. Assume that credit is available only from the four sources listed in Table 3.

a. What is the total cost of the $5,000 car using each of the loans?

b. If Sam decides to borrow, which credit arrangement will be least expensive? Which would be most desirable? Explain your answer.

Automobile financing is usually available from several sources —the car dealer, a bank, a credit union, or a finance company. Generally credit unions and banks offer financing on better terms than the dealer or finance company. When comparing finance charges among the lenders, make certain that the same

TABLE 3 **Interest on a $4,000 Loan**

	APR	LENGTH OF LOAN	MONTHLY PAYMENT	TOTAL FINANCE CHARGE
Creditor A	11%	3 years	$131	$ 716
Creditor B	11%	4 years	$103	$ 962
Creditor C	12%	3 years	$133	$ 783
Creditor D	12%	4 years	$105	$1,056

down payment and repayment periods are used for each loan. In comparing terms, you'll mostly be concerned with the Annual Percentage Rate. However, you should also read all of the terms carefully so that you can answer such questions as:

1. Will there be a refund of finance charges if the loan is repaid ahead of schedule?

2. Will there be fair warning in the event of a repossession?

3. Is there a penalty for late payments? If so, how much?

4. Will all payments immediately become due if a payment is missed?

Insuring a Car

The major reason for having insurance is to protect against a possible loss you can't afford. Although insurance cannot prevent losses, it can provide some compensation. Insurance can pay for such losses as the cost of repairing the car, medical bills, lost wages, and pain and suffering of those injured in an accident.

When you buy an insurance policy, you can choose from various combinations of *coverage*, depending on what kind of protection you want and how much you can afford to pay. Common coverages include liability, medical, collision, comprehensive, uninsured motorist, and no-fault.

Liability insurance will pay for injuries to other people and property if you are liable or responsible for the accident. Policies pay for damages up to, but no more than, the limits of the policy. If

---

THE CASE OF THE NONSTOP CAR

Pulling left into the outside lane to pass a slow-moving truck, Larry saw the traffic light ahead turn yellow. "If I step on it I'll make this light," he thought. Just then an oncoming car made a left-hand turn in front of him. Larry pushed hard on the brakes. Nothing happened. Two seconds later, pinned against the steering wheel, he saw the other driver, Charles, stagger out of the car, bleeding and holding his shoulder in pain.

The kind of insurance policies each driver had, or didn't have, will determine the insurance benefits, if any, they will receive.

PROBLEM 30
Who should be responsible for paying for the medical bills and car repairs resulting from this accident? In most cases, who pays for repairs resulting from auto accidents?

injuries and property damages are greater than the policy limits, the person at fault will have to pay the difference. Policies generally have three limits: (1) on bodily injury per person, (2) on bodily injury per accident, and (3) on property damage per accident. For example, a "10/20/5" policy would pay up to $10,000 per person for personal injury, $20,000 per accident for personal injury, and $5,000 per accident for property damage. Accidents sometimes result in lawsuits where injured persons are awarded damages of $100,000 or more. Therefore, careful consideration should be given to how much insurance a person carries. Also, the insurance company usually promises to defend any lawsuit resulting from an accident.

Medical coverage will pay for your own medical expenses resulting from an accident involving your car or the car you're driving. It will also pay the medical expenses of any passengers in your car, no matter who is at fault. The amount of medical benefits, and the kind of medical costs (e.g., hospital bills, office visits), are limited in the policy. For example, medical coverage usually pays up to $500 or $1,000 per person injured.

Collision coverage pays for accident damage to your own car in an accident, even if the collision was your fault. Policy benefits usually cover up to the actual value of the car (not its replacement by a new car). The cost of collision insurance can be lowered by including a *deductible*—that is, an amount which you pay toward repairs before the insurance pays anything. For example, $100 deductible means that if there are $250 damages the insurance company will pay $150 and you will pay $100. The greater the deductible, the less costly the insurance.

Comprehensive coverage protects you against damage or loss to your car from a cause other than by collision. For example, damages due to vandalism, fire, or theft are covered under the comprehensive section of your policy. Read your policy carefully to determine whether valuables in your car, such as a tape deck, are covered in case of theft. Insurance policies may also include, usually at an extra charge, coverage for towing costs or car rental costs. These coverages may be subject to certain limits and conditions, so read your policy carefully.

Uninsured motorist coverage will protect you from drivers who don't have insurance by paying for the personal injuries or damage they cause. Be sure to find out how much your policy will pay for personal injuries caused by an uninsured motorist, and, in the event you don't have collision coverage, whether it will pay for damages to your car. This feature is usually an inexpensive addition to your policy and well worth the cost.

No-fault insurance, now required in some states, pays you (up to a certain amount) for injuries you receive in an accident, regardless of fault. With liability insurance your company pays others for their injuries if you were at fault. No-fault laws allow settlement of

ADVICE ON BUYING AUTO INSURANCE

1. Learn about the various types of insurance and comparison shop before making a decision.

2. Ask insurance agents several questions about the coverage (e.g., what is the company policy about raising rates if you are at fault in an accident?) Insist on clear answers.

3. Find out if there are any special discounts for persons who've had driver's training or a good safety record. Young people are often required to pay higher insurance premiums.

4. Check to see which company charges less if young persons are insured under the parents' policy and not issued a separate policy.

**WHERE
YOU
LIVE**

Does your state require insurance coverage on all registered cars? If so, how much insurance must be carried? How much is insurance likely to cost a seventeen-year-old youth in your area?

these claims without the delay and expense of determining fault in a court case. No-fault benefits are limited (e.g., $5,000 or $10,000) and are usually only for personal injuries. When injuries are greater than the no-fault limits, the injured person can still sue the other party.

PROBLEM 31

Reread the Case of the Nonstop Car. Assume that the accident happened in a state without no-fault insurance and that both Larry and Charles had full insurance coverage. Also assume that Larry was at fault.

a. Whose insurance company pays for Charles's hospital and car repair bills?

b. Whose insurance company pays for Larry's hospital and car repair bills?

c. What do you think would happen if the damages to Charles were greater than the limits of Larry's policy (i.e., Charles has personal injury damages of $200,000 and Larry's policy limit is $100,000)?

PROBLEM 32

Assume that the insurance policy you have on your new car includes collision insurance with a $250 deductible. Answer the following questions:

a. Skidding off an icy road into a guard rail you dent your bumper. The repair cost is $200. Who has to pay for this damage?

b. Your fender is smashed and the repair cost is $1,000. Who has to pay in this situation?

c. After you have had your car six years its market value is only $600. If the state doesn't require collision insurance, should you continue to take it out? Why?

What To Do in Case of an Accident

If involved in an accident, there are certain important things to do and not to do. While many of these tasks are based on common sense, accidents can be emotionally upsetting (as well as physically dangerous), so it is best to think about how to handle these problems ahead of time.

At the scene of the accident, check to see if there are injuries, call the police, and set up a system for routing the traffic around the automobiles. Then all drivers involved in the accident should exchange name, address and phone number; driver's license number and registration number; make, model, and year of the car; name, address, and phone number of insurance agents; and name and phone numbers of any witnesses (or at least their license plate numbers so you can locate them later if needed).

Do not tell people the extent of your insurance; *do not* confess guilt; *do not* say your insurance company will take care of everything; *do not* sign any paper that says you were not injured because some auto accident injuries are not noticeable for several days.

Keep a record of the name and badge number of the police officer responding to the accident. Even though the officer makes notes as to the circumstances surrounding the accident, you should also keep a record of this information. Write down all important information as soon as possible after the accident while your memory is still fresh, but don't give this to anyone except your insurance agent or attorney.

After an accident, contact your insurance agent as soon as possible. Keep a copy of your agent's name and phone number (also the phone number of branch offices in the event you're out of town) in your glove compartment. After speaking with your agent, you should also send a registered letter, including your policy number, fully describing the accident to your insurance company. Failure to notify your company within a certain limited period of time may allow the company to deny all financial responsibility.

Let your insurance agent handle calls and letters from other parties involved. If the accident is a serious one in which there is a

What should you do if you're involved in an auto accident?

personal injury, it may be wise to have a lawyer handle all calls and letters.

PROBLEM 33

On a winter's evening after dinner, your car is hit in the rear right fender. The accident occurred as you proceeded through an intersection on a yellow light. There appears to be no personal injuries. In speaking with the driver of the other car, you notice that his eyes were bloodshot.

a. Make a list of the kinds of information about this accident that you would need to write a thorough report.

b. Roleplay a meeting between the two drivers at the scene of the accident.

c. Making reasonable assumptions about information you need but that has not been given, draft a letter to your insurance company.

four
FAMILY
LAW

In the same way that we are all affected by consumer law, each of us is in some way a member of a family and, therefore, affected by family law. This area of law includes such topics as marriage, divorce, the rights and duties of parents and children, inheritance of family property, and government support for families, through such programs as welfare and social security. You have already seen how some criminal and consumer laws have changed in recent years. As you study this chapter, think about how recent changes in family law reflect the way society has come to view the family.

Before beginning the study of family law, it is important to consider the question "What is a family?" Although the family is the basic unit of our society, the underlying role of family life often goes unnoticed. Statistics show that ninety-eight percent of all children are raised in families, that the vast majority of Americans will get married, that nearly two-thirds will remain married until death, and that of those who get divorced, most will remarry.

Nevertheless, the nature of family relationships is changing, and today the image of the nuclear family—a working father, a homemaking mother, and dependent children—is no longer always accurate. More than half of all married women now hold jobs outside of the home. Couples are having fewer children or no children at all. Increases in divorce and illegitimate births have created millions of single-parent families. At the same time, unmarried couples, trial marriages, communal living arrangements, and other alternative life-styles have become more common. Thus, while the family remains the basic unit of society, there is great diversity in family life, and it is now difficult, if not impossible, to define the typical American family.

PROBLEM 1

Examine the photos at the beginning of the chapter. For each photo, answer the following questions:

a. Is this a family? Why or why not?

b. Is this a common living arrangement?

c. Is there such a thing as an "ideal family?" If so, what are its characteristics?

MARRIAGE

Marriage has many dimensions: personal, religious, social, economic, and legal. This section of the chapter will concentrate on the legal aspects of marriage. You will learn the steps one must follow in order to get married, the requirements for a legal marriage, and the difference between formal and common law marriage.

PROBLEM 2

a. Marriage involves many considerations. How important do you regard each of the following to a successful marriage: happiness, children, money, sexual relations, religious factors, common interests, romance, relationships with in-laws, faithfulness, age differences, and other factors? Rank these considerations in order of importance.

b. Make a list of all the questions you would ask yourself before deciding to get married. Do any of these questions involve the law?

c. If you were getting married within the next six months, what social, religious, and legal arrangements would you have to make?

A traditional wedding ceremony.

In the eyes of the law, marriage is a contract between two persons who agree to live together as husband and wife. Like other contracts, marriage creates certain rights and duties for each partner. However, unlike other contracts, the marriage contract cannot be changed or ended without court approval. This is because the state considers marriage to be a relationship in which it has an interest. For that reason, every person who gets married must meet certain legal requirements. For example, a person who is married to someone else cannot marry again until the first spouse (husband or wife) dies or until a court order ends the first marriage. A person who marries while an earlier marriage is still going on is guilty of the crime of **bigamy**.

The law also forbids marriage between close relatives. For instance, in most states people who marry or have sexual relations with their children, parents, grandparents, brothers, sisters, aunts, uncles, nieces, or nephews are guilty of the crime of **incest**. Some states forbid marriage between first cousins, and, in a few places, marriages are not allowed between people related by marriage, such as stepparents and stepchildren or half brothers and sisters.

For most young people, age requirements are the biggest legal barrier to getting married. Every state has two different minimum age requirements. The first requirement establishes an age under which no one may legally marry. The second requirement establishes a higher age under which a person must have parental permission.

FIGURE 15 Marriage License Application

APPLICATION FOR A MARRIAGE LICENSE

TO THE CLERK OF THE CIRCUIT COURT:

I hereby make application for Marriage License, to be issued in accordance with the Laws of this state, under penalties of perjury, the following statement, to wit:

Male's Name
William Halder

Female's Name
Myra Gambrell

Age 16

Age 15

Date of Birth 9/17/64

Date of Birth 5/8/65

Birthplace Colorado
State

Birthplace Louisiana
State

Residence
6220 Clay Street

Residence
311 Mountain View Drive

Denver, Colorado

Boulder, Colorado

Marital Status:
Single ✓

Marital Status
Single ✓

Widowed _____

Widowed _____

Divorced _____

Divorced _____

(If previously married list exact date of death and place or exact date of divorce decree and where granted for all previous marriages)

Relationship, if any NONE

Signature of person consenting if male is a minor

_____
(Parent or Guardian)

Signature of person consenting if female is a minor

_____
(Parent or Guardian)

_____
(Applicant)

Sworn to and subscribed before me this ___ day of _____, A.D., 19__.

Check here if License is to be mailed:
  To one of the contracting parties
  To Minister of the Gospel

_____

_____

_____

(Give name and mailing address)

_____
Clerk of the Court or other Comparable Official

County of _____

State of _____

_____

_____

(Give complete address and affix Court Seal)

PROBLEM 3

a. Refer to the marriage license application reprinted in the text. Can William and Myra be legally married in Colorado? Why or why not? Could they be legally married if they lived in your state?

b. Why do you think states have minimum ages for getting married? Should there be age requirements, and, if so, what should they be?

c. Some states allow females to get married at a younger age than males. For example, one state has a law that males under eighteen years of age must have parental permission to get married, but females only need parental permission until age sixteen. Why do you think the age requirement is different for males and females? Is this fair? Explain.

In the application for a marriage license, William and Myra cannot legally marry in their state before Myra's sixteenth birthday. At that time, they can be legally married only if they obtain the written permission of their parents. Their situation shows the two different age requirements that exist in all states: (1) the age under which no one can marry (sixteen in this case and fourteen or fifteen in some other states); and (2) the age under which permission is required (eighteen in most states but nineteen or twenty-one in others).

> **WHERE YOU LIVE**
>
> What is the minimum age for getting married in your state? What is the age under which a couple must have their parent's permission to marry? Which relatives are not allowed to marry in your state?

Before getting married the couple must fulfill the legal requirements set by the state.

WHERE YOU LIVE

Where does a person go to obtain a marriage license in your state? Is a physical exam or blood test required? Is there a waiting period before one can get married? If so, how long is it?

When two people go through a wedding ceremony without meeting the requirements for a legal marriage, the marriage may be annulled or declared invalid. An **annulment** is a court order that sets aside the marriage as if it never existed. The grounds for annulment vary from state to state and are somewhat confusing. Under certain circumstances a marriage can be annulled or ended without a formal divorce. Reasons why this might occur include the following:

■ Age—the couple was under the required age or did not have their parent's permission

■ Incest—the persons were related to each other

■ **Coercion**—one spouse forced the other to marry against his or her will

■ **Fraud**—one spouse lied to the other about an important matter, such as his or her desire to have children

■ **Physical incapacity**—one spouse was incapable of engaging in sexual intercourse

Formal Marriage

A couple who wants a valid, fully legal marriage must follow certain steps before they can get married. Usually they must first

---

THE CASE OF THE ELOPING COUPLE

Marie, age twenty-five, and Jose, age twenty-seven, live in a state that requires a three-day waiting period for a marriage license. A neighboring state allows marriages without any waiting period at all. Marie and Jose drive to the neighboring state and get married. Is this marriage valid in the state where they live?

Marie and Jose's marriage will probably be legal in their home state. The general rule is that if a marriage was legal in the state or country where it was performed, it will be upheld as legal in any other state or country. However, note that some states may not uphold marriages where their residents go to neighboring states specifically to get around important marriage requirements. It is doubtful that any state would consider a waiting period so important as to later rule the marriage invalid. But if Marie and Jose were underage and went to the other state to get around their state's parental permission requirement, some states would not recognize their marriage.

have a brief physical examination. In most states this includes a blood test for venereal disease, given by either a private doctor or a public clinic. Tests must be performed close to the time the couple intends to apply for the marriage license.

Once they have the results of the blood test, the couple can go to the clerk of the court or the marriage license bureau to apply for a license. The clerk will ask the couple a number of questions, such as their names and ages, whether there is a blood relationship between them, the names of their parents or guardians, and whether either of them has been previously married.

The couple must swear to the truth of all of the information and then pay a small license fee. There is often a short waiting period, usually a few days, before the couple can return to the clerk's office to pick up the license. Some states also have a waiting period between the time the couple pick up the license and the date of the marriage. A few states require the couple, especially if they are young, to take part in premarital counseling before the license is granted.

Depending upon state law, any of the following persons may perform the marriage ceremony: a judge or justice of the peace; a minister, priest, or rabbi; a clerk of the court; or an elected public official. The law does not require the ceremony to follow any particular form.

> **REQUIREMENTS FOR A VALID MARRIAGE**
>
> Each spouse must:
>
> **1.** be above the minimum age for marriage
> **2.** be single or legally divorced
> **3.** not be a close relative of the other
> **4.** have required physical exams or tests
> **5.** have carried out the requirements involved in applying, paying for, and waiting for the marriage license
> **6.** have the marriage ceremony performed by a person authorized by law

---

THE CASE OF LOVING v. VIRGINIA

In 1958, Harvey Loving, a white man, and Diana Jeter, a black woman, decided to get married. Both legal residents of Virginia, they traveled to Washington, D.C., to get around the Virginia state law forbidding marriage between persons of different races. After they were married, they returned to Virginia, where they were arrested and charged with violating the ban on interracial marriages. The Lovings pleaded guilty and were sentenced to one year in jail. The judge, however, suspended the sentence on the condition that the Lovings leave Virginia and not return for twenty-five years. The Lovings moved to Washington, D.C., but appealed their case to the U.S. Supreme Court, asking that the law against interracial marriages be declared unconstitutional.

PROBLEM 4
a. How would you decide this case and why?
b. Should the right to marry be regulated in any way by the state? If so, how?
c. Which, if any, of the following should be concerns of the state in licensing marriage: age, sexual preference, mental capacity, health, blood relationships, religion, race? Why?

THE CASE OF THE COMMON LAW MARRIAGE

Kim Johnson and Arthur Little move in together and live as husband and wife. They never obtain a marriage license or have a formal marriage ceremony, but Kim signs her name as Mrs. Kim Little. Are Kim and Arthur legally married? Could either of them legally marry someone else without first getting a divorce?

Common Law Marriage

The answer to the questions raised in the Case of the Common Law Marriage depends on the state where Arthur and Kim live. The District of Columbia and thirteen states—Alabama, Colorado, Georgia, Idaho, Iowa, Kansas, Montana, Ohio, Oklahoma, Pennsylvania, Rhode Island, South Carolina, Texas—allow what is known as **common law marriage.** Common law marriages are established without blood tests, licenses, or a formal ceremony.

To have a valid common law marriage a couple must meet the following requirements:

1. They must consider themselves to be husband and wife.

2. They must hold themselves out to the public as husband and wife.

3. They must act like a husband and wife by living together and having sexual relations.

4. They must meet the minimum age requirements for a legal marriage.

If Kim and Arthur meet these four requirements and live in one of the states recognizing common law marriage, they would be legally married and would need to obtain a divorce from a court before they could marry someone else. If they live in a state that does not recognize common law marriage, they are not legally married and are free to move out and marry someone else whenever they desire.

The time required to create a valid common law marriage varies from state to state. In some states, a couple may be considered married after a short period of time (maybe only a day). Other states require a longer period of time, such as a year or more.

Most states that don't allow common law marriage, will nevertheless recognize such a marriage if it was legal where it took place. Persons who have a valid common law marriage have the same obligations and rights as persons married in a formal wedding ceremony.

PROBLEM 5

Patrick Lee lives with Ann Jones in Georgia in 1975. They tell people they are married. They open a joint savings account and several joint charge accounts. Ann uses the name of Mrs. Lee. In 1978 Patrick meets DeDe Young in Illinois and falls in love with her. He and DeDe are married in a ceremony in Illinois that same year. In 1979 Ann asks an Illinois court to declare the marriage of DeDe and Patrick invalid since Patrick was, and still is, married to her.

a. Did Patrick and Ann have a valid common law marriage in Georgia before 1978?

b. Does Illinois recognize common law marriage? What is the difference between a state's recognizing and allowing a common law marriage?

c. How should the Illinois court rule? Explain.

d. Do you think common law marriage should be legal? Why or why not?

WHERE YOU LIVE

Does the law in your state allow common law marriages? If so, how long must a couple live together to make the common law marriage valid?

HUSBANDS AND WIVES

The traditional model of marriage viewed the husband as the provider and the wife as the homemaker. The husband was considered the head of the household and had a duty to support and provide for his wife and children. In return for this support, he was entitled to the household services and companionship of his wife.

The law reflected this traditional view by giving the husband the legal right to make the ultimate decision on such matters as where the family would live, how money would be spent, the names of children, and other important matters.

Over the last twenty years, the traditional marriage model has been challenged by a variety of economic and social changes in our society. Today the image of the husband as the sole breadwinner and wife as the sole homemaker is no longer accurate. Married women now play a large role in the ranks of the employed, and there is a more equal division of responsibilities within the family. The law is also changing to reflect the idea that marriage is a partnership between equals.

Financial Responsibilities

More and more the law requires husbands and wives to support one another in accordance with their respective needs and abilities. As a result, many states now require both spouses to pay for necessary family items purchased by either of them. However, a number of states retain the traditional rule that the husband has a legal duty to provide his wife with food, clothing, shelter, medical care, and other **neccessaries** of family life. If the husband fails to provide such essentials, the wife can purchase the necessary items and make her husband pay for them. At the same time, the wife has no legal duty to pay her husband's bills.

In addition to the basic necessities, some courts have required the husband to maintain the family in accordance with his economic position. In general, however, a woman could not obligate her husband to pay for luxury items bought without his knowledge.

THE CASE OF THE UNPAID BILLS

Bryan and Kelly have been married for five years. Both work and each earns about $12,000 per year. They are having problems paying their bills and often fight over money. Kelly goes shopping and charges groceries, clothes for the children, and a stereo costing over $400. Bryan gets angry and tells Kelly he is not paying for anything.

PROBLEM 6
a. Is Bryan responsible for the debts of his wife?
b. Suppose Bryan was out of work and charged the above mentioned items without telling his wife. Would she have to pay?
c. Do you agree or disagree with the following statement? "Husbands should be required to support their wives, but wives should not have to support their husbands." Explain your answer.

The law regarding ownership of marital property has also changed. At one time the law considered a husband and wife as one person. Under this theory the wife had no property rights. Any money or other belongings a woman owned before marriage or acquired during marriage became the property of her husband. This is no longer true.

Today, any property owned by either spouse before the marriage remains the property of that person throughout the marriage. In most states, any property acquired during the marriage belongs to the person who acquired it. Under this **separate property** system, whoever earns it, pays for it, is given it, or has title to it is considered to own it. Husbands and wives are of course free to make gifts to each other or to place property, such as bank accounts, real estate, or automobiles, in both names. When they do this, the property is considered to be the **joint property** of both spouses.

Eight states—Arizona, California, Idaho, Louisiana, Nevada, New Mexico, Texas, and Washington—have a **community property** system derived from French and Spanish law. Under this system all property acquired during the marriage belongs equally to the husband and wife. If the marriage breaks up, either by death or divorce, each spouse is entitled to one-half of all the property acquired during the marriage.

Contrast the community property system to the separate property system by considering the case of a married woman who does not work outside the home. In a community property state the wife is considered to own half of the combined wealth of the couple, including the income of her husband. In a separate property state the wife is considered to own only that property which she herself acquires or which is acquired in the name of both the husband and wife.

PROBLEM 7

a. Lloyd and Gloria were married four months ago. Before they were married, Gloria inherited a piece of land from her grandfather. Now that they are married, who does the land belong to?

b. Frances and Leon are married and have two children. Frances is an architect making $30,000 a year. Leon is an artist who earns very little. Frances uses some of her income to buy a vacation home. If Frances and Leon split up, who owns the vacation home in a community property state? In a separate property state?

c. Which is fairer, a separate property or community property system? Why?

Decisions in a Marriage

Married life involves many decisions and responsibilities. It calls for cooperation, sharing, and a division of labor. Just how marital responsibilities are divided depends upon the individual couple. In most marriages husbands and wives make important decisions based on what they work out between themselves. Historically, however, the law gave the husband most of the decision making authority within the family.

Today, the roles of women and men are changing both in and out of marriage. There is now a greater sharing of marital roles and responsibilities. Employment outside of the home has given many women new status and independence. Likewise, men are now more likely to share household duties and child care. Despite the changes, many laws and social customs remain that can have a legal and practical impact on marriage.

THE CASE OF THE NAME CHANGE

Rose Palermo and Walter Dunn are getting married. A successful businesswoman, Rose would like to continue to use her maiden name, but someone tells her this is against the law. What does the law require?

Because women have traditionally used their husband's name as a matter of social custom, most people believe that a name change is a legal requirement. However, no state requires such a name change by statute. Despite this fact, the tradition of changing one's name upon marriage is so ingrained in our society that a woman who does not adopt her husband's name may have trouble convincing other people that this is legally permitted.

A woman like Rose Palermo, who wishes to keep her own name after marriage, may do so. To avoid problems, she may want to go through a state's formal name change procedure or, at the very least, formally notify all friends and business aquaintances that she is retaining her birth-given name or whatever other name she desires.

PROBLEM 8

Consider each of the following statements and decide whether you agree or disagree with it. In each case discuss your answer.

a. Wives should take care of the house and children, and husbands should provide the family income.

b. When a woman gets married, she should keep her own name and not change it to that of her husband.

How are the roles of women and men changing in our society?

c. Married women should work only if they have no young children.

d. As the head of the household, the husband should have the sole right to choose where the family will live.

e. Husbands and wives should own everything equally, regardless of who earns it or pays for it.

Spouse Abuse

Spouse abuse is a serious problem. It is estimated that throughout the United States at least three million families experience domestic violence each year. Studies show that this violence occurs among couples of all ages, races, and economic levels. Though cases exist where wives physically assault their husbands, the vast number of cases involve husbands abusing their wives. The seriousness of the problem is illustrated by the fact that domestic violence has frequently resulted in serious injury or death.

Opinions differ as to how spouse abuse should be handled. Some people believe that the law should not interfere in family life because interference can make things worse. They say that police, prosecutors, and judges can't force people to love each other, and that even if charges are filed against a husband, the wife is not likely to testify when it comes time for trial. Thus, they argue, most arrests are a waste of time since they do not result in convictions.

On the other hand, critics of the way the legal system has operated in the past say that police often fail to respond to spouse abuse calls. When they do respond, they say that the police often refuse to arrest, file charges, or even take the victim out of the

Spouse abuse often goes unreported.

home to a safer place. Finally, these critics charge that prosecutors and judges are too lenient on those accused of spouse abuse.

Presently, spouse abuse cases are handled differently from area to area. Many states try to keep abuse cases out of the courts by training police in crisis intervention, by setting up complaint centers to handle domestic disputes, or by treating it as a noncriminal matter in the family court. When a case is handled in family court, the judge has several options. The court can issue a **protective order** or **cease and desist order,** which notifies the husband that he can be held in contempt of court and sent to jail if he continues to abuse his wife. Another option is a **peace bond,** an order requiring the husband to deposit a sum of money with the court. If the husband continues to mistreat his wife, he will lose the money. In some places judges can also order the husband out of the home or refer the case for criminal prosecution.

Finally, an abused spouse has the option of filing for a divorce or bringing suit against the assaulting spouse for money damages. Suing for damages can be a problem when the spouses are still living together or if the offending spouse has little or no money. In

---

A CASE OF SPOUSE ABUSE

Late one night you hear screams and the sounds of crashing furniture coming from the apartment next door. You look out in the hall and see your neighbor, Mrs. Darwin, being slapped and punched by her husband as she tried to get out the door. Before she can get away Mr. Darwin pulls her back in and slams the door. You hear breaking glass, more screams, and running around. You know that Mr. Darwin has a drinking problem and that this isn't the first time he has beaten his wife.

PROBLEM 9

a. If you were the neighbor in the Case of Spouse Abuse, what would you do? Would you call the police? If you would, what would you tell them? If you wouldn't call the police, explain why not?

b. Suppose you are a police officer and you receive a call that a man is beating his wife. When you and your partner arrive at the Darwin's, you find that Mrs. Darwin is cut, bruised, and obviously beaten up. Role-play the encounter between the Darwins and the police.

c. As the police, decide what you would do in this situation. Would you question the couple? Would you arrest the husband? Would you take the wife out of the house?

d. As the husband, decide how you would react to the police in this situation. As the wife, decide how you would react. Would you press charges against your husband? Would you stay in the home? Would you do something else?

e. Suppose you are a judge confronted with the Darwin case. Would you send Mr. Darwin to jail? Would you take some other action?

addition, some states have **family immunity laws,** which make it impossible for husbands and wives to sue one another for damages.

A number of groups, have proposed changes to help abused spouses. These proposals include training police to be sensitive to the special needs of abused women, establishing temporary shelters for abused women and their children, and requiring criminal prosecution of husbands who assault their wives.

WHERE YOU LIVE

What programs are available in your community to help abused women? Are there facilities where abused women can go if they decide to leave home?

PROBLEM 10

In most states the law says that a husband may not be criminally prosecuted for raping his own wife.

a. What do you think are the reasons behind this law? Should the law be changed or kept as it is?

b. Assume you are a prosecutor in one of the states where a husband can be prosecuted for raping his wife. A woman comes to you and states that she and her husband have been having marital problems and violent arguments for years. She says that during one of these arguments her husband forced her to have sexual intercourse. Assuming that a rape conviction carries a possible penalty of twenty years in prison, would you file a rape charge against the husband? Explain. Is there anything else you could do?

PARENTS AND CHILDREN

Until recently, most married couples chose to have children. In fact, parenthood ranked as one of the few topics on which Americans could favorably agree. Today, however, many couples are choosing to have fewer children or no children at all. Influenced by the availability of **contraceptives**, the high cost of living, concerns over the growth of world population, and changing attitudes toward marriage, careers, and childbearing, the national birth rate has moved slowly but steadily downward. The number of children per family has fallen from 3.5 at the end of World War II to a low of 1.8 in 1977.

Family Planning, Birth Control, and Abortion

Family planning allows couples to say "whether" and "when" to have a baby. Some couples oppose certain methods of family planning for religious or other reasons, but most agree that planning of some sort is desirable. Among the best sources of family planning

FIGURE 16   The U.S. Birth Rate Drops

Births per 1,000 women 15-44 years old

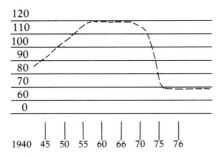

| | 1940 | 45 | 50 | 55 | 60 | 66 | 70 | 75 | 76 |

Why do you think the U.S. birthrate has gone down?

Do you think family planning is a good idea? Why or why not?

information are the family doctor, neighborhood health center, public health department, or family planning clinic.

In past years abortion was considered a crime and information about birth control and contraceptive devices was generally available only to married couples. In 1965 the U.S. Supreme Court struck down a state law that prohibited the use of contraceptives by married couples. In a later case the Supreme Court declared

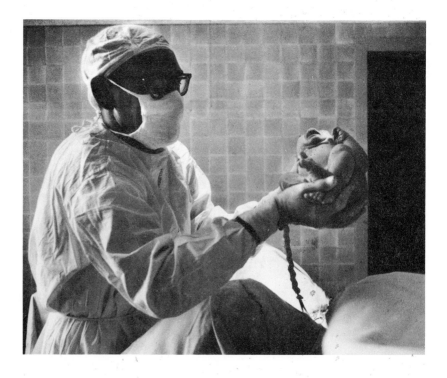

that a law prohibiting the sale of birth control devices to unmarried people was also unconstitutional because it violated the right to privacy. Today states allow the sale of birth control devices to any adult, whether married or single. However, some states restrict sale of contraceptives to minors.

THE CASES CHALLENGING ABORTION LAW

Before 1973, Texas and Georgia had laws making **abortion** *a crime except when performed to save the life or health of the mother. Citizens in these states filed suits asking that the laws be declared in violation of the U.S. Constitution. The plaintiffs argued that a woman has a constitutional right to control her body. Texas defended by saying that the law was necessary to safeguard the life of unborn children and to preserve and protect the health of pregnant women. If you were a justice on the Supreme Court, how would you decide this case and why?*

In the cases of *Roe* v. *Wade* and *Doe* v. *Bolton*, the U.S. Supreme Court decided that women, married or single, have a right to an abortion. Basing its decision on the constitutional right to privacy, the Court defined the right to abortion in three stages:

1. First trimester (first twelve weeks of pregnancy)—a woman can have an abortion upon demand without interference by the state.
2. Second trimester (thirteenth week until viability, somewhere between the twenty-fourth and twenty-eighth week)—the state can establish regulations to make abortions safe but cannot prohibit them.
3. Third trimester (the child may be capable of living outside of the woman's body)—the state can regulate or forbid all abortions except to save the life of the mother.

Abortions are now available in every state. The 1973 Supreme Court decision did not, however, end the debate over abortions, nor did it settle all the issues: Does a woman need her husband's consent to have an abortion? Can a minor have an abortion without her parents' permission? Can the government be required to use Medicaid funds to pay for abortions?

In 1976 on the first two issues the Supreme Court reached a decision when it struck down two Missouri laws. The first law required a woman to get her husband's written consent for an abortion during the first trimester of her pregnancy. The second law gave parents an absolute veto right over abortions sought by their minor children. The Court held both laws unconstitutional as a violation of the right to privacy.

On the final issue the Supreme Court upheld three state laws that prohibited states from having to pay for elective abortions. The Court reasoned that the right to have an abortion does not mean that states must use Medicaid funds to pay for abortions or that hospitals are required to provide free abortions for women who can't pay for them.

Thus, since 1973, controversy over the Supreme Court decision on abortion has continued. Opponents of abortion have proposed measures at the local, state, and federal level designed to restrict the availability of abortion. On the other hand, people who feel

Public opinions about abortion are strongly divided.

that abortion is a woman's decision have worked equally hard to make abortions freely available.

PROBLEM 11

a. Whose rights are involved in the abortion controversy? What are some of the legal, moral, and social arguments for and against abortions? What do you think of these arguments?

b. If you support legalized abortion, under what circumstances, if any, would you find abortion least acceptable? If you oppose legalized abortion, under what circumstances, if any, would you find abortion most acceptable?

c. Do you agree with the Supreme Court decision that a woman does not need her husband's consent to have an abortion? Explain your answer.

d. If given a choice, would you support or oppose a constitutional amendment designed to prevent or regulate the availability of abortions? Why?

Responsibilities Between Parents and Children

Once people become parents, they have certain legal duties toward their children. Parents must provide the amount of support necessary for minor children to survive. This support includes such items as food, clothing, housing, and medical care. It may include more, depending on the parents' wealth and the needs of each child. Financial support has usually been the principal responsibility of the father, but some states have changed their laws to impose an equal obligation on both mother and father.

THE CASE OF THE UNWED FATHER

Martha, age sixteen, becomes pregnant. She claims that Michael, age seventeen, is the father, but Michael denies it and refuses to marry her or support the child. Should the law require Michael to marry Martha or to provide support for the child?

No one can be legally forced to marry someone else. If this did occur, the marriage could be annulled. Michael, however, may be required to support the child if he is the father. To prove this, Martha might have to file what is called a **paternity suit.** The court would then hear evidence and decide if he is the father. In some places, an attorney for the city or county where the woman lives may help her file a lawsuit to force the father to pay support.

THE CASE OF THE RICH SON

Ira, forty-two, is the owner of a successful business. His mother, sixty-five, will retire from her job at the end of the year. Her meager savings and social security payments will not be enough for her to continue paying rent where she lives. She can move to a publicly supported home for the elderly but would prefer to stay in her own apartment. Does Ira have a legal obligation to support his mother? Should the law require adult children to support their parents when they are in need?

There is a long tradition of law and social custom that has called upon adult children to support their parents when in need. Some states have **family responsibility laws,** which require children to care for their parents in their old age. Other states have abolished these laws and almost all limit the support obligation to what a relative can fairly afford.

Just as the law requires parents to support their children, children must obey the reasonable commands of their parents. They also may be required to turn over any of their earnings from jobs to their parents. However, parents often let their children keep whatever they earn, and some states even require this once children reach a certain age.

What is a reasonable parental demand? Certainly children do not have to obey parents who order them to commit an illegal act, such as robbing a grocery store. Nor must they obey parents who order them to do something that seriously endangers their physical and mental health such as staying in a locked room for a week without food. But parents are entitled to ask their children to do such things as chores around the house and yard.

As long as parents don't abuse or neglect their children, the law gives them considerable power over the decisions of their minor children. For example, parents may decide where their children live, what religion they practice, what school they attend, what time they come home at night, and whether they work or date.

Courts are usually reluctant to interfere in disputes between parents and children, though in extreme cases a child may be declared a PINS or CHINS—a person or child in need of supervision. In these cases the youth may be removed from the home if the court finds that he or she has been continually disobedient or is otherwise beyond the control of the parents. (For a further discussion of PINS and CHINS, refer to the section in Chapter 2 on juvenile justice.)

The duty of parents to support their children and of children to obey their parents continues until **emancipation**. This occurs when a youth reaches the age of majority. It may also occur before this time if the youth gets married or becomes (with parental consent) self-supporting. A few states recognize **partial emancipation,** which allows youths to keep and spend their own earnings. As one court said, "This is because there is a point at which minors must have some right to their own views and needs for their independent transition from minority to adulthood."

PROBLEM 12

Consider the following situations. In each case decide whether the parents have the legal authority to make the decision involved.

What rights do you think the children should have in each situation? What arguments can you make in support of the parents? In support of the children?

a. Mr. McBride disapproved of the lifestyle of his eighteen-year-old son, Larry, a minor. When Larry, who was attending college, moved out of the dorm into a commune, Mr. McBride cut off his support, including tuition.

b. Monica, age seventeen, is pregnant and, on the advice of a friend, decides to seek an abortion. Her parents absolutely forbid it.

c. Murray, a high-school senior, does not want to move to a new city with his parents. He wants to finish high school with his friends. His parents insist that he live with them.

d. Mr. and Mrs. Parham think their sixteen-year-old daughter is mentally ill and needs psychiatric treatment. The daughter objects but her parents decide to commit her to a mental institution.

Child Abuse and Neglect

Although the legal system tries to stay out of most disputes within families, all states have laws that protect children against parental neglect and abuse. The legal definition of child abuse includes physical abuse, abandonment, and failure to provide adequate support or care. Despite the legal definition, it is sometimes difficult to determine exactly what is child abuse.

PROBLEM 13

Consider each of the following situations and decide whether the action of the parent or parents should be considered child neglect or abuse. Explain your answer.

a. An unmarried parent goes to work and leaves her two children, ages seven and three, at home unattended.

b. A parent beats his twelve-year-old son until he is black and blue.

c. A father tells his fourteen-year-old daughter she can stay out all night or do anything else she wants, as long as she doesn't bother him.

d. A mother spanks her four-year-old son until he cries.

e. A married couple refuses to allow their teenage son to date or go anywhere without them.

Parents have a right and a duty to discipline their children. However, they may be prosecuted for use of excessive force, and a child who is injured or mistreated can be taken from the parents. It has been estimated that one million cases of child abuse occur each year in the United States. Some experts claim that child abuse is a leading cause of death among children. One of the problems with neglect and child abuse is that many cases are not reported. Understandably most people are reluctant to interfere in the family affairs of others. To help solve this problem, most states have passed laws requiring that doctors, nurses, teachers, social workers, or the general public report suspected cases of child abuse.

After a child abuse case is reported, several questions arise. What should the police do when faced with such cases? What should courts do? Should the child be returned home or removed from the parents' care? Should parents found guilty of neglect or child abuse be fined, sent to jail, or provided with some other services?

WHERE YOU LIVE

Does your state have a neglect or child abuse law? Who is required to report evidence of child abuse in your state?

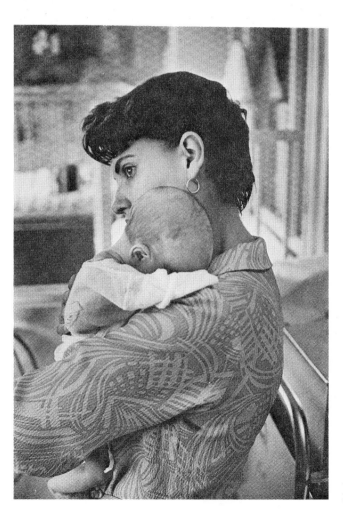

How are suspected cases of child abuse handled in your community?

PROBLEM 14

Assume that you are looking through a window and see the father of the family next door beating his ten-year-old son. The boy is screaming in obvious pain.

a. What would you do?

b. Roleplay a visit by the police to this family's home. What should the police say and do?

c. If the father is taken to court for continually beating and injuring his son, what should the court do? Do you think child abuse should be a crime that subjects a parent to a possible jail term?

d. Some say that a child learns to be violent when he or she is a victim of violence. Do you agree?

FOSTER CARE AND ADOPTION

When neglect or child abuse is proven against a parent, a court may order a child removed from the family home, placed in a foster home, or made available for adoption. Other times, parents may simply decide to give up their children for adoption.

Foster parents are people who take on the care of a minor who is not their natural child. Foster parents are usually not the legal guardians of the child. Full legal guardianship and custody rights are still held by the natural parents or a government agency. Foster parents are usually paid to care for the child, and the child can often be taken out of the foster home at any time with the agency's permission. Though foster parents usually have little or no legal rights regarding the child, they often form close attachments and sometimes apply to adopt the child.

Adoption is the legal process by which an adult or adults become the legal parents of another person. Though adults usually adopt a minor, most states permit adults to adopt another adult. There are usually no legal restrictions on who can adopt another. Therefore, people—whether single or married and regardless of race, religion, or age—are eligible to adopt anyone else. In practice, however, some adoption agencies and courts try to make the child's new family as much like that of the natural parents as possible and may be reluctant to place a child with parents of a different race or religion.

Most adoptions are set up through public or private adoption agencies, which must be licensed by the state. People wishing to adopt apply to these agencies and are investigated as to whether they will be suitable parents. Public agencies usually charge little or no fee for this service, while private agencies may charge much more. Because there is a shortage of children available for adoption, some people apply to adopt children living in other countries. Other people turn to **black market adoptions,** in which go-betweens arrange for women to have their babies and turn them over to adopting parents without going through licensed adoption agencies. This practice is illegal in most states.

After contacting an adoption agency, people who wish to adopt must then apply to a court to have the adoption legally approved. An attorney is often necessary to take the legal steps to make the adoption final. An adoption agency will submit its report on the parents and an attempt will be made to obtain written consent from the natural parents. In some states this consent is required, but in most places, even if the natural parents refuse consent or cannot be found, courts may still grant adoptions that they decide are in the best interests of the child. A child who has reached a certain age (often twelve or fourteen) must also consent to the adoption.

In most states, when the court approves an adoption, a temporary order is issued and the agency or natural parents remain the

Adopted children have all the legal rights and responsibilities of natural children.

legal guardian for a specified waiting period, such as six months or one year. After this, a new birth certificate is issued showing the adopting parents as the parents of the child. The adopted child and the adopted parents then assume the same rights and responsibilities of natural born children and their parents.

Another controversy regarding adoption is whether adopted children have a right to know who their natural parents are. Traditionally, adoption records have been sealed and adopted children were not allowed to find out the names or whereabouts of their natural parents. However, many adoptive children become

---

THE CASE OF SCARPETTA v. SPENCE-CHAPIN ADOPTION SERVICE

Olga Scarpetta, thirty-two, comes from a wealthy, California family. During an affair with a married man, she becomes pregnant. Rather than embarrass her family, Olga goes to New York to have the baby. The child, born May 18, is turned over to the Spence-Chapin Adoption Service four days later. On June 1, Olga signs a document giving the agency full authority to find new parents for the child.

The agency has no trouble finding interested couples. They place the child with the DeMartino family on June 18. Mr. DeMartino, a doctor, and his wife have already adopted a four-year-old boy from the same agency and everything worked out very well.

Within two months following the baby's birth, Olga changes her mind and asks for the return of her baby. The agency refuses to help her and will not tell her who has the child. After several weeks of arguing with the agency, Olga goes to court. She tells the judge that she was physically and emotionally upset following childbirth. She is sure that she now wants to keep the child. Her family in California has learned the truth and also wants Olga to get the baby back.

PROBLEM 15

Read the following two opinions and decide with which you most agree. Be prepared to give reasons for your choice. Note that the adoption agency is the defendant in this case because the DeMartinos had not yet received final legal custody of the child. The court must decide whether to return the child to the natural parent or leave the child with the adoptive parents.

Opinion #1

There are a number of reasons why this court believes it is in the best interests of the child to leave her with her adoptive parents, the DeMartinos.

First, Olga waited six weeks after putting the child up for adoption before requesting the child's return. During this period the DeMar-

interested in learning about and meeting their natural parents. Some adoptees even spend a great amount of time searching to discover their family history. Today, only a few states allow them to look at adoption records. However, many states are now considering changing these laws to provide adopted children, when they reach the age of majority (eighteen in most states), with the right to obtain the names of their natural parents. Other states are opposed to changing these laws because they believe the natural parents have a right to privacy and a right not to see children they put up for adoption unless they desire to do so.

---

tinos formed a strong attachment to the child and made many sacrifices because they had every reason to believe the child would be their own.

Secondly, the background of the DeMartinos is greatly superior to that of Olga. Olga is thirty-two, unmarried, and, from the evidence before us, appears emotionally unstable. As for the adoptive parents, the agency selected them because they had already adopted a four-year-old boy and proved themselves well able to provide for the child's moral and physical well-being. They can give the attention of two parents to the child. To take the baby away at this point would cause a great deal of suffering to them.

Finally, the mother freely gave up the child and the agency acted in a proper manner in obtaining her consent.

Opinion #2

There is a presumption in the law that unless proven unfit the natural mother is best suited to provide adequate support and care for the child. This court believes Olga Scarpetta is such a natural parent.

First, Olga was under a great deal of pressure when she placed the child up for adoption. She had just gone through an unwanted pregnancy, labor, and delivery. She was very worried over the reaction of her highly religious family. I believe this decision could not have been freely given under these circumstances.

Second, she now clearly wants the child and is very able to provide for the child's welfare. Her wealthy family also supports her in this decision and will help her out if she needs financial assistance.

Finally, there is no evidence that Olga will be an unfit parent, and even though the DeMartinos may be good or even better parents, this does not mean they should be given rights ahead of the natural mother.

PROBLEM 16

Assume the following law has been proposed in your state: "All adopted persons over the age of twenty-one shall have the right to obtain a copy of their original birth certificate and shall be given the name and last known address of their natural parents." At a hearing on the proposed law, two people testify.

Mrs. Margaret Jones says, "When I was sixteen I became pregnant. The father, a soldier at a nearby army base, was transferred and I never saw him again. My parents did not have the money to support another child in our family and I didn't want to leave high school. I also was embarrassed, so I went to visit my aunt in another town, had the baby, and then placed him for adoption. I returned to my home town and finished school. I am now happily married and the mother of two children, ages eleven and fourteen. My husband does not know about my earlier affair or the child I put up for adoption. I was promised by the adoption agency that they would never tell anyone my name. I do not wish to see the child I put up for adoption and I believe it best that we live our own separate lives."

Michael Franklin says, "I am nineteen years old and only last year my adoptive parents told me that I was adopted at birth. I love my adopted parents but I feel a strong need to find out who my natural parents are and to meet them. I want to know where I came from and a little more about why I am the way I am. Everyone needs to belong somewhere. It's inhuman not to let me know who my real parents are."

What is your state's law regarding whether adopted children can find out who their natural parents are?

a. If you were a member of the legislature and heard the testimony of the two witnesses above, how would you vote on the adoption records law? Explain your answer. Would the law be better if it allowed adopted children to look at records only when the natural parents were first asked and gave their consent?

b. Would fewer people place their children for adoption if they knew the children would later find out their names? Would opening adoption records result in more abortions or more black market adoptions?

c. What problems do you think may arise if the proposed law is passed? Can you rewrite the law to improve it?

d. Do you think Michael's adopted parents should have told him sooner that he was adopted? If they know, should they tell him who his natural mother is and why he was placed up for adoption?

ENDING MARRIAGE

This section deals with the procedures that can be used to end a valid marriage, namely separation and divorce. It also discusses some of the problems that arise when a marriage breaks up. These include child custody and support, and alimony and property division.

PROBLEM 17

a. What do you think are the five most common marital problems that lead to separation or divorce?

b. Before a person marries, can that person anticipate those problems and decide whether or not they are likely to occur? Explain.

c. Once these problems occur, what can the couple do to try to work them out?

Separation

If serious problems arise in a marriage, couples sometimes decide to separate. Separations may be mutually agreed upon, or the husband or wife may simply leave home. When one spouse leaves against the other's wishes, this is known as **desertion** and is generally a ground for divorce.

Couples who separate don't always want a divorce. They may meet to discuss their problems or they may receive marriage counseling from someone, such as a therapist, psychiatrist, social

WHERE
YOU
LIVE

What marriage or family counseling agencies exist in your community? Are these privately or publicly operated? How much do they charge?

worker, or member of the clergy. Other couples may talk with a friend or relative. Marriage counseling services vary in cost from expensive to free, depending on the income of the couple and who is doing the counseling. Most states do not require marriage counselors to be licensed, and some counselors may be poorly trained. Thus, persons in need of marriage counseling would be wise to investigate the qualifications of whoever they are considering as a counselor.

When a married couple separates, financial and other responsibilities between them and toward their children continue. For this reason it is usually necessary for them to have some kind of agreement. This agreement may be informal, or it may be a formal document drawn up by lawyers representing each person. If the couple later decides to seek a divorce, the terms of the agreement will usually be made part of the divorce decree.

A separation agreement is a legal contract. It will be enforced in court unless the judge decides it was unfair or did not provide for the children. If the couple wishes, they can go to court and make this agreement part of what may be called a **legal separation or limited divorce.** This may be useful because it will make it easier to require a spouse to pay money promised under the separation agreement.

Whether or not a couple needs to have lawyers involved depends on the circumstances. In a simple situation with little or no property or with no children involved, lawyers might not be needed. But if the separation is more complicated involving children or division of property, such as a house, cars, or joint bank accounts, each spouse should be represented by an attorney.

Problems sometimes arise when one spouse fails to provide the agreed-upon financial support. It this happens, the other spouse may go to court and seek an order requiring payment. Many states provide free legal aid to needy spouses trying to collect such payments. In addition, the federal government has a Nationwide Locator Service, which helps find spouses who are behind in their support payments.

PROBLEM 18

Bill and Rachel were married at age twenty-one. One year later they had a baby. After two years of marriage they find themselves constantly fighting and are generally miserable. They are not sure they want a divorce, but both think it might be better to live apart for a while. Bill works as an auto mechanic and brings home $1,000 a month. Rachel used to work as a teller in a local bank, making $800 a month, but has not worked since having a child. They rent an apartment for $300 a month, and they own the following property: $500 in a savings account; a car worth $1,500; and furniture and appliances.

a. Do you think it is necessary for Bill and Rachel to have a written separation agreement? Explain.

b. Do they need a lawyer to help them? Should they each have their own lawyer or can they use the same one?

c. List all the things Bill and Rachel must decide before separating and then roleplay a meeting between the two of them in which they try to work out a separation agreement. Draft an agreement.

d. What can Rachel do if Bill fails to pay any support agreed upon?

During the past fifteen years, the number of unmarried couples living together has greatly increased. Such nonmarital relationships can lead to legal controversy when one partner dies or the couple splits up. Consider the case of *Marvin* v. *Marvin* and

FIGURE 17 Singles Living Together in the U.S.A.* Unmarried Persons Living with Someone of the Opposite Sex

Year	
1970	654,000
1977	1,508,000

*U.S. Census Bureau Report, 1977

Why do you think the number of unmarried persons of different sexes living together has changed between 1970 and 1977?

THE CASE OF MARVIN v. MARVIN

Lee Marvin, a movie actor, and Michelle Triola lived together for seven years. As residents of California, a state which does not recognize common law marriage, they were never formally married, although Michelle did have her name changed to Marvin. After they split up, Michelle filed suit asking for support payments and half of all property acquired by Lee during the time they lived together. She claimed that they had an unwritten agreement to combine earnings and share equally all property acquired by either of them during the time they lived together. Lee denied that they had an agreement and contended that even if they did it was unenforceable because of the "immoral" character of their relationship. Should Michelle be awarded support payments and given half of Lee's property? Why or why not?

The California Supreme Court held that adults who voluntarily live together and engage in sexual relations can nevertheless make contracts regarding their earnings and property rights. Thus, if Michelle could prove that she and Lee made an express agreement or if an agreement could be inferred from their conduct, then a court could award her support payments and part of the property. Most states, however, still do not recognize such implied contracts in nonmarital living arrangements.

PROBLEM 19
a. As a result of the *Marvin* decision what consequences do you see for the future of marriage? Do you think the precedent set by the *Marvin* case undermines marriage? Explain your answer.
b. Because of the *Marvin* case, will unmarried couples have to make some sort of written agreement before they move in together? If so, what might this agreement include?

WHERE
YOU
LIVE

What are the grounds
for divorce in your
state? Does your state
allow no fault divorce or
divorce by consent?
How long does it take to
obtain a divorce in your
state?

decide whether individuals who live together without getting married should be given the same legal rights and responsibilities as those who are married.

Divorce

A couple who goes through a wedding ceremony without meeting the legal requirements for a valid marriage may be able to obtain an annulment. The effect of the annulment is to declare that the marriage never existed and was not recognized by the law.

If a valid marriage breaks down, a couple may legally dissolve their relationship by obtaining a **divorce.** Within the last fifteen years the divorce rate has doubled, and it is now estimated that one in every three marriages ends in a divorce.

At one time most states would grant divorces only if one spouse could prove that the other spouse had been at "fault." The grounds for fault included such things as adultery, desertion, physical or mental cruelty, and insanity. Proving one of these fault grounds could be both difficult and embarrassing, so many estranged couples found themselves unable or unwilling to get a divorce. Because of the difficulty in obtaining a divorce, many couples would travel to foreign countries or move to a state with more liberal divorce laws.

In recent years, most states have revised their laws to allow for divorce without regard to fault. Known as **no fault divorce** or divorce by consent, these laws only require a couple to show that there are "unreconcilable differences" or an "irretrievable breakdown" in the marriage. In addition, many states now automatically grant divorces when a couple can show that they have voluntarily lived apart for a specified period of time. Depending on the state, this period varies from six months to two years. Despite the

Over one million couples are divorced each year.
Why do you think there are so many divorces?

trend toward more liberal divorce laws, some states still require that one of the fault grounds be proven before granting a divorce.

PROBLEM 20

a. Why do you think the divorce rate has doubled over the last fifteen years?

b. Do you think states should make it harder or easier to get a divorce? Why?

Divorce may be **contested** or **uncontested.** Most divorces are informally agreed to by the husband and wife who then go through the formality of appearing in court to finalize their breakup. In a small percentage of cases the parties actually go to court and battle over such issues as who gets custody of the children, the amount of alimony to be awarded, or whether a divorce should be granted at all. In either contested or uncontested divorces, the emotional and financial costs can be high. If the divorce is at all complicated, both the husband and wife should seek separate legal help.

In cases where the divorce is uncontested and the issues are simple and straightforward, the couple can avoid the legal expense by seeking a **pro se** or "do-it-yourself" divorce. To find out the procedure for a pro se divorce, the parties can check with the clerk of their local court, call the nearest law school or legal aid office, or consult one of the recently published books on do-it-yourself divorce. This procedure is not permitted in every state and should probably not be tried if the couple has children, substantial property, or any disagreement concerning the divorce.

PROBLEM 21

a. Some courts require a couple to see a marriage counselor before granting a divorce. Do you think this is a good idea?

b. Why do you think it is important for a husband and a wife to each have their own attorney in a divorce situation?

There are five basic steps in a typical divorce case.

1. A complaint or petition is filed in the state court where one of the spouses lives (most states have residency requirements, which vary from six months to three years).

2. The defendant spouse is given a copy of the complaint and then files an answer stating whether the divorce is uncontested or contested. (Note: spouses might agree on divorce but disagree on such issues as child custody, alimony, or property settlement.)

3. During the period between filing the case and the divorce hearing or trial, a judge can require one spouse to pay support money or grant temporary custody until the case is completed.

4. A date is set for a court hearing. If the divorce or property settlement is contested, the spouses or their attorneys will usually try to reach an out of court settlement. (It is estimated that over ninety percent of contested cases are settled and never go to trial.)

5. If the divorce is granted, there is usually a waiting period, such as sixty days, during which time either spouse can appeal and neither can marry.

Child Custody

In the event of a divorce or separation, one of the most important questions to be decided is with whom the children will live. In legal terms the question is, Who will have **custody** of the children? The importance of the custody issue is illustrated by the fact that in 1980, there were over eight million minor children in the United States living with divorced or separated parents.

The parent who receives custody of a minor child has the right to decide most aspects of the child's life, such as where the child will live and go to school. Custody may be temporary or it may be permanently awarded to one parent. Once custody is awarded, it is

Until recent years, divorced fathers rarely received custody of their children.

rarely changed. However, the court has the power to do so if there is a change in circumstances. For example, if the parent with custody became addicted to drugs, the court might order a change of custody. The parent who does not have custody is usually given visitation rights. This means that he or she can spend time with the child on certain days and times of the year. This parent is also usually required to contribute money for the child's support.

There also may be joint custody, which gives both parents an equal say concerning the child. In such cases, the child might live with one parent during the school year and with the other during the summer. It is becoming more common for children of divorced parents to split up their time of living with each parent. People differ in their opinions as to whether joint custody or custody in one parent with visitation rights is best for the child.

PROBLEM 22

What are the advantages and disadvantages of each of the custody arrangements? Which custody arrangement do you think children would prefer?

When the parents cannot agree on custody, the decision is made by the court. For many years, the law presumed that young children would be better off with their mother. This is called the *tender years doctrine*. Today, many states either have changed or are considering changing their laws to treat men and women equally in custody disputes.

In determining who should be given custody most courts ask the question, "What is in the best interests of the child?" This is sometimes difficult. Different courts look to different factors, such as the youth's actions in the home, school, and community, the emotional and economic stability of the parents, and the religion of each parent. Many courts also listen to the child's desires, especially if he or she is over a certain age (e.g., twelve). To help with this decision, judges often order a social service agency to do a study of the parents and children. The results of this study are then used as the basis for a custody recommendation. One court issued the Bill of Rights for Children shown on page 202.

PROBLEM 23

a. Should a child's wishes be considered in making the custody decision? Does it make a difference if the youth is four, twelve, or sixteen years old?

b. Should a child have his or her own attorney in a custody case? Assume that an attorney is appointed for Billy, a thirteen-year-old,

BILL OF RIGHTS FOR CHILDREN IN DIVORCE ACTIONS*

    I. The right to be treated as an interested person and not as a pawn, or possession of either or both parents.

   II. The right to grow up in that home environment which will best guarantee an opportunity for the child to grow to mature and responsible citizenship.

  III. The right to the day by day love, care, discipline, and protection of the parent having custody of the child.

  IV. The right to know the parent they don't live with and to have the benefit of that parent's love and guidance through adequate visitation.

   V. The right to a positive relationship with both parents, with neither parent being permitted to degrade or downgrade the other in the mind of the child.

  VI. The right to have moral and ethical values developed and to have limits set for behavior so that the child may develop self-discipline and self-control.

 VII. The right to the most adequate level of economic support that can be provided by the best efforts of both parents.

VIII. The right to the same opportunities for education that the child would have had if the family unit had not been broken.

  IX. The right to a regular review of living arrangements and child support orders as the circumstances of the parents and the benefit of the child may require.

   X. The right to recognition that children involved in a divorce are always disadvantaged parties and that the law must take steps to protect their welfare, including a social investigation and the appointment of an attorney to protect their interests.

* Adapted and printed with permission from "A Bill of Rights," developed by The Family Court of Milwaukee County, Wisconsin.

Do you think any changes should be made in this "bill of rights" for children? Explain any you propose. Do you think the protections in this document should be the law in your state? Why or why not?

in a custody case and the boy wishes to live with his father. However, the attorney believes the father is a criminal and thinks the boy would be better off with the mother. What should the attorney recommend to the court?

c. Should courts make decisions regarding child custody? If not, who might be better able to make such decisions?

    Custody disputes sometimes result in **childsnatching.** This occurs when the parent who does not have custody physically takes the child and moves to another state. The parent with legal custody is often unable to locate the child. Even if the child is located, many states will not necessarily order the child returned.

Therefore, parents who kidnap their own children may sometimes be able to go to court and obtain a new custody order. Estimates of childsnatching have risen to somewhere between 25,000 to 100,000 children a year. There are now proposals in a number of states to change the law and force the return of these children.

Child Support, Alimony, and Property Division

As mentioned above, financial questions may be resolved by a couple through a separation agreement. If they cannot agree, however, or if the agreement is unfair, the court will decide such issues as child support, **alimony,** and property division.

Most important to the court in a divorce case is establishing adequate support for any children involved. Since husbands often have higher-paying jobs and wives more often take custody (over seventy percent of the time), fathers usually pay child support. In most states the law places an equal obligation for child support on both parents, even though fathers usually are given the major responsibility for supporting the child. If the mother has a better paying job than the father, she may have to pay more. Child support usually continues even if one or both of the spouses remarries—unless the child is adopted by the new stepparent.

Alimony is a continuing support payment made after divorce, usually by the husband to the wife. Some states have changed their laws to allow for alimony payments by a wife to a husband. The U.S. Supreme Court recently decided that state laws which require only husbands to pay alimony violate the **equal protection** clause of the Constitution. Alimony payments are usually based on need. Nevertheless, the amount awarded will differ in each case according to the circumstances. This is because some courts believe the spouse has a right to be supported in the "manner to which he or she has become accustomed," or because of the feeling that if one spouse has stayed home for a period of years caring for the home and children, that spouse should be compensated for this work.

How to divide up the property owned by the couple is another issue to be settled in case of a divorce. In all states, property owned by one spouse prior to the marriage remains his or hers throughout the marriage. Unless this property is awarded as alimony, it remains with the same owner after the divorce. In all but eight states property acquired during a marriage belongs to the spouse who paid for it. Property that is owned in the names of both spouses will usually be divided equally in the event of a divorce. In community property states, all property acquired by either spouse during a marriage belongs equally to both spouses. So, if a husband buys a car and registers it in his name, it still belongs equally to his wife. Upon divorce in a community property state, the court will divide in half all the property acquired during the marriage.

PROBLEM 24

In each of the following situations, the couples are divorcing. Should either spouse pay alimony or child support? If so, which one should pay? How much should be paid and for how long?

a. Miguel, a successful plumbing contractor, earns $30,000 per year. His wife, Carmen, stays home and takes care of their four children. When they divorce, the two older children—a junior in high school and a freshman in college—wish to stay with Miguel; the two younger children prefer to stay with Carmen.

b. Alan and Ming married just after college. Ming took a $10,000-a-year job as a secretary while Alan went to medical school. In his last year of school they divorce.

c. Angela, a social worker for the city, divorced her husband Leroy, an occasionally employed writer. He had been staying home taking care of their two-year-old son. Her yearly salary was $14,000; he had earned $3,000 in the past twelve months.

GOVERNMENT SUPPORT FOR NEEDY FAMILIES AND OTHERS

Since the economic depression of the 1930s, the government has assumed a public responsibility to operate antipoverty and other social programs to provide for the general welfare. Who benefits from these programs, how much individuals should receive, and how these programs operate are questions debated by politicians and ordinary citizens alike.

The U.S. government estimates that there are twenty-eight million poor people in America. Others claim the number is even higher because government statistics define poor people as those who make less than a certain annual income. (In 1979 it was less than $5,850 per year for a nonfarm family of four.) In the mid-1970s federal, state, and local governments were spending close to $200 billion a year to assist with these programs. However, at least half of this money goes to the nonpoor through social insurance programs, such as social security, medicare, and unemployment compensation. These programs provide benefits to people who have worked in the past but are now retired, disabled, or otherwise unable to work.

About $100 billion a year goes to programs to aid the poor, such as Aid to Families with Dependent Children, food stamps, medicaid, and public housing. How much a person receives under these programs depends on individual state laws. The federal government pays a minimum amount to the states and asks them to increase this with state funds. The state contributions vary, and the result is that an unemployed person or someone receiving welfare in one state may receive two or three times as much as a similar person in another state.

PROBLEM 25

a. What do you think are the causes of poverty in America? Can government programs help solve these problems? If so, how?

b. Should people receiving money under these programs receive the same amount no matter what state they live in? Why or why not?

Social Insurance Programs

Some government aid programs provide protection for all Americans, regardless of income. Most of these programs act like insurance policies, whereby people receive benefits based on the amount of money they paid to the government when they were working.

Social Security Social security is officially called Old Age, Survivors, and Disability Insurance. It is like an insurance policy in that workers have money deducted from their paychecks by their employers. Those who are self-employed pay social security directly to the Internal Revenue Service. The percentage of a person's income that must be paid to the government changes periodically. (In 1979 employers and employees each paid 6.05% of earnings up to $17,700.)

Social security can provide the following benefits to those who have worked and paid social security taxes for a certain period of time:

1. Retirement benefits—workers age sixty-two, or older can usually retire and receive a monthly social security check. A worker's spouse and children may also be eligible. The amount a person receives is a percentage of earnings. In 1977 it ranged from $114.30 a month to $437.10 for those who had retired.

2. Disability benefits—workers who are blind, injured, or too ill to work can receive monthly checks if the disability is expected to last at least twelve months or result in death. Spouses and children are also eligible.

WHERE
YOU
LIVE

Where in your community does a person apply for medicare benefits? for social security benefits? What is the procedure for applying?

3. Survivor's benefits—when workers die, their families become eligible for payments. This is like a government life insurance policy.

To illustrate how social security works, take the case of Mary Smith, age twenty-eight, a single parent with two children. She has worked in a bakery for several years. Mary becomes very ill and must stop working. After a required waiting period, social security will pay Mary and her children a monthly check until she is able to return to work. If Mary died, social security would continue to pay each of her children until they reach the age of eighteen, or twenty-two if they are full-time students.

Medicare Nearly all persons in the United States over the age of sixty-five are eligible for medicare. This medical insurance coverage pays the cost of hospitalization and certain hospital-related expenses. It may also cover some doctor fees and other medical expenses. As with all insurance plans, not all medical expenses are covered.

Unemployment Compensation Each state has an unemployment compensation system to help workers if they lose their jobs. To receive benefits, a person must have worked for a certain period of time, prove they lost their job through no fault of their own (e.g., they were not fired for misconduct), and be willing to take a similar job if one becomes available.

A few states provide unemployment compensation even for those who are fired, though the law may lower the amount of benefits one can receive under the program. Benefits vary from state to state. In 1977 one state paid a maximum of $74 a week and

Medicare is a program to protect the aged and disabled against hospital and medical costs.

ADVICE ON HOW TO OBTAIN UNEMPLOYMENT COMPENSATION

1. Contact the state unemployment office in your area.
2. Visit the office and apply for compensation.
3. Be interviewed by a case worker, who will decide whether you are eligible.
4. Your former employer will be sent a letter asking why you are no longer employed.
5. If you are awarded benefits, you must report on a regular basis to pick up your check and report on where you looked for work and what happened.
6. If you are denied benefits or if they are reduced for some reason, you may request a written explanation of the reasons. If you are not satisfied, you may file an appeal and a hearing will be held to rule on your eligibility.

WHERE YOU LIVE

What are the maximum and minimum benefit levels per month that a person in your state can receive for unemployment compensation? Where does a person apply for this compensation?

one paid $140 a week. The amount of the benefit also depends on the worker's income before unemployment. Likewise, the number of weeks a person can receive unemployment ranges from twenty-six to sixty-five weeks, depending on the state.

Programs to Aid the Poor

Though social insurance sometimes aids poor people, there are also a number of programs specifically designed to assist low-income Americans. These programs include aid to families with dependent children, medicaid, food stamps, public housing, and job placement and training programs.

Aid to Families with Dependent Children (AFDC) and General Assistance Aid to Families with Dependent Children is designed to aid needy families. In most cases these are single-parent families, for example, a mother with small children. In all states the family must be making less than a certain income. This income varies widely (in a recent year, a family of four in one state had to make less than $187 a month to be eligible, while in other states the same family could be making up to $497 a month and still be eligible). In about half the states children can only receive money if the father is not living at home.

There are two other AFDC requirements in every state: (1) the mother must agree to work if she has no children under six, and (2) the mother must tell the state welfare agency the name of her children's father so that efforts can be made to get support payments from him. Government agencies sometimes attempt to locate fathers to reduce the number of families receiving welfare.

Welfare programs have been criticized for a number of reasons. Some critics say the programs discourage people from going to work because welfare payments are reduced based on income received from employment. Others argue that it breaks up the family because many states will not pay AFDC if the father is living in the home. Still others contend that the cost of the program is high because of welfare fraud. A few critics argue that the costs of the welfare system, including salaries of the many government workers needed to run it, are too high compared to the benefits. While nearly everyone agrees that the present system needs improvement, so-called welfare reform has been slow in coming, and controversy over welfare continues.

Some communities make direct payments of money, called general assistance, to poor people who are not covered by other programs or who receive inadequate assistance. Approximately twenty-seven states provide such money, but it is often limited to short-term emergencies.

PROBLEM 26

Discuss whether you approve of the aspects of AFDC listed below. Explain your answer.

a. That the father not be living in the home for the mother and children to receive payments

b. That families are usually given money under this program without working

c. That the amount one receives varies substantially from state to state

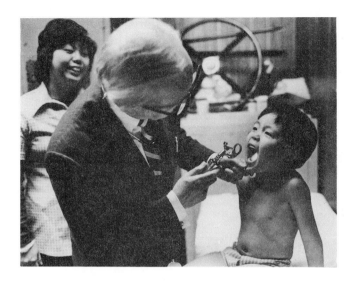

What public health facilities exist in your area?

d. That it is possible for parents to receive AFDC payments during the entire time they have a child under the age of eighteen

PROBLEM 27

Some people propose that the welfare system be abolished and replaced by a program whereby all Americans below a given income level be paid a certain amount of money that would raise their income to a guaranteed level. What are reasons for and against this proposal? Do you support it?

Medicaid   Medicaid is a government program that provides medical services to poor people. It does not cover all medical expenses, but it does pay for most common medical services including: hospital and outpatient care, nursing home services, hearing aids, eyeglasses, drugs, dental care, physician fees, medical supplies, and transportation to and from the hospital or doctor's office.

Anyone receiving welfare (AFDC) is automatically eligible for medicaid. In addition, persons over 65, or who are blind, or totally disabled, are eligible for medicaid, if they are U.S. citizens or legal aliens, live in the state where they apply, and have a low income.

Food Stamps   People who have incomes below a certain level may be eligible to receive food stamps. These people are given coupons they can use to buy food at grocery stores. The program is funded chiefly by federal money through the U.S. Department of Agriculture. It is administered under uniform national standards, so eligibility requirements and amounts a household can receive are the same in all states.

WHERE YOU LIVE

What government job programs exist in your community? Are there any government-operated housing projects in your area?

Housing Assistance and Employment Training   Federal, state, and local governments have programs designed to provide poor people with housing assistance. These programs include government-operated housing projects, direct payments of rent money, low-interest loans, and insurance to help people buy homes.

In addition, there are programs to train people in skills necessary to obtain a job. Some programs also provide full-time, part-time, or summer jobs. Interested persons should check with their state manpower, labor, or employment agency. The U.S. Department of Labor may also be able to provide information on government programs in your area (see Appendix A).

PROBLEM 28

The people in the following situations call a local government office and ask if they can receive aid. To what program or agency should each be referred?

a. Gerald retires at age seventy after fifty years as an employee of Banks & Company. He needs money for living and medical expenses.

b. Bertha is about to have a baby. She had to quit her job and the father has run off. She needs money for living and medical expenses now and after the baby is born.

c. Gertrude is laid off from work. Several weeks later, her husband (who had a good job) is killed in a construction accident. She needs money for living expenses for herself and their one child.

d. William and Mildred have four children and can't afford to pay their bills for food, housing, clothes, and medical expenses.

e. John, age seventeen, dropped out of high school. He has little money and is having trouble finding a job.

f. James, age sixty-five, is in very poor health but can't afford a nursing home.

DEATH AND THE LAW

Our society has traditionally held that suicide and euthanasia are both morally and legally wrong. However, advances in modern medicine have resulted in a number of situations where people who in the past would have died can now be kept alive for relatively long periods of time. Sometimes the person's condition is so poor,

the pain so strong, or the chance of recovery so remote that a question arises as to whether it would be merciful to keep the person alive.

THE CASE OF KAREN QUINLAN

One night, for no apparent reason, Karen Quinlan, age twenty-two, stopped breathing for two fifteen-minute periods. She was admitted to a local hospital, where she was placed on a respirator to assist her breathing. She went into a coma and doctors who examined her stated that she was in a "vegetative state" with no ability to reason or think. The doctors concluded that there was no chance of recovery and that she could not survive if she were removed from the respirator.

After Karen had been in this condition for three-and-a-half months, her father, believing her comalike condition would never change, asked the doctor and the hospital to "stop using all extraordinary measures, including the use of a respirator for Karen." The doctor refused, saying that her father had no legal right to make such a decision. Mr. Quinlan filed suit and asked the court to appoint him Karen's guardian for purposes of ordering her removed from the respirator.

PROBLEM 29
a. If you were Karen's father, would you have tried to have the respirator removed?
b. If you were the doctor, would you have removed the respirator if asked to do so by the father?
c. How do you think the judge should rule in this case?

The trial court in the *Quinlan* case appointed a lawyer to act as a guardian for Karen and heard the testimony of the family members, who said that if Karen could talk she would want the respirator removed, and that her religion supported this decision. Other testimony was given by doctors who believed she would never recover the ability to think, speak, or otherwise function, but that she did not exactly meet the medical definition of "brain death." The trial judge ruled against the father and refused to order the respirator removed.

The father appealed the case to the state court of appeals, which reversed the trial court's decision. The court of appeals stated that there was a right to privacy that allowed the respirator to be removed: (1) if the guardian and family desired; (2) if responsible doctors agreed that there was no reasonable possibility of her coming out of the coma; and (3) if the doctors had the support of a hospital ethics committee. As a result, the respirator was removed, and, to the surprise of many, Karen continued to live in her coma-like state.

The *Quinlan* case involved the issue of an unconscious person. But what if a conscious person wished to stop other types of medical care? In most cases, if the person understands what he or she is doing, the courts will allow a person to refuse medical treatment unless that person's death will cause serious harm to others. For example, in one case a court did not allow a woman, who was eight-months pregnant and who had been in an automobile accident, to refuse a blood transfusion. The court ruled that this would be unfair to the unborn child.

Some people worry that they may be severely injured in an accident or become very ill and consequently become a great burden to their family. These people say that if they ever lose their ability to think or to physically function, they would rather die than be maintained by artificial or extraordinary medical means.

To be prepared for the possibility that they may someday be in this condition, some people have written **living wills** (page 213). These documents state that, if the person ever reaches the stage where he or she is being kept alive only by artificial means, the means should be stopped. In most states these documents are not legally binding, but a few states have passed laws to make living wills binding. Some courts also might give consideration to a living will when faced with a decision in a case like that of Karen Quinlan.

PROBLEM 30

Would you consider signing a living will? What are the moral and legal reasons for and against living wills?

A LIVING WILL*

To my family, my physician, my lawyer, my clergyman to any medical facility in whose care I happen to be. To any individual who may become responsible for my health, welfare and affairs

Death is as much a reality as birth, growth, maturity and old age—it is the one certainty of life. If the time comes when I, ... can no longer take part in decisions for my own future, let this statement stand as an expression of my wishes, while I am still of sound mind.

If the situation should arise in which there is no reasonable hope of my recovery from physical or mental illness, I request that I be allowed to die and not be kept alive by artificial means or "heroic measures." I, therefore, ask that medication be mercifully given to me to end suffering even though this may hasten the moment of death.

This will is made after careful thought. I hope you who care for me will feel morally bound to follow my directions. I recognize that this appears to place a heavy responsibility upon you, but it is with the intention of relieving you of such responsibility and of placing it upon myself in accordance with my strong convictions, that this statement is made.

Signed_____

Date_____

Witness_____

Witness_____

_____

* Adapted from Model Living Will distributed by the Euthanasia Education Council.

The issue of whether a person has a right to live or die arises in a number of other situations. One such situation might involve a newborn baby who is severely retarded or physically handicapped. Another situation might involve elderly people who are senile or otherwise unable to decide for themselves whether they should receive certain types of medical treatment. In reality, family members in these situations often tell doctors to withhold treatment and the patient dies. However, if faced with the decision, courts may differ in the way they would decide the cases, depending on the specific circumstances and the judge's own feelings.

PROBLEM 31

In each of the following situations, decide whether the court should order treatment or not order treatment. Explain your decision.

a. A woman whose religion forbids blood transfusions is in an automobile accident. She needs a blood transfusion to live, but she refuses to consent to one.

b. A nine-year-old whose religion forbids blood transfusions is in a coma. He will die if he doesn't have a blood transfusion, but his mother refuses to allow one.

c. A mentally alert seventy-three-year-old man, suffering from an incurable form of cancer, wishes to stop treatment and leave the hospital.

d. A twenty-six-year-old professional athlete is permanently paralyzed from the neck down as a result of a motorcycle accident. Doctors say he may be able to live without a respirator after thirty days, but the athlete asks that the respirator be turned off now.

e. A child is born with brain damage and physical problems requiring an operation if she is to live. The father refuses to consent to surgery.

Wills and Inheritance

A **will** is a document in which a person tells how his or her property should be distributed after death. Everyone who has money or property, no matter how little, should consider making out a will. A will insures that anything you own goes to whom you wish in the amount you choose.

Why should someone make a will?

A person who dies without a will is said to die **intestate.** In this case any property or money the person owns will be distributed according to the law of the state where he or she lives. This could result in a distribution of property different from what the person would want.

Intestacy laws differ greatly from state to state. As a general rule, if the person who dies is married and has children, part of the property will go to the surviving spouse (usually one-third or one-half) and part to the children. If the person who dies is widowed but has children, the children will usually receive all the property. If an unmarried person dies, any property will go to the parents, brothers and sisters, or other relatives, depending on the state. If a person dies without a will and without any living relatives, all the property can go to the state. Dying without a will can sometimes cause real hardship for the survivors.

In most states a person cannot legally make out a will until reaching the age of majority. Usually wills must be in writing. However, in some states, an oral will is good if made during a person's final sickness before death. Approximately half the states allow wills to be in a person's own handwriting, but a typewritten will is best. Many states require that the will be witnessed by at least two, and sometimes three, witnesses.

Most states require a husband or wife to provide for the other in the will. If they do not, the law usually gives the living spouse a *share*—usually one-third or one-half of the property. So, if a married woman dies and leaves all her property to a brother, her husband can still claim and receive a share of her property. The law also requires parents to provide for minor children in a will. However, once children reach the age of majority, there is no requirement to include them.

There are many rules and technical details involved in writing a will. As a result, most people should consult an attorney. A good lawyer can usually draft a simple will and can advise on tax-saving ways to divide up a person's estate.

The following is an example of a simple will. *It should not be copied under any circumstances. It may be incorrect for your circumstances, or invalid under your state law.*

WHERE YOU LIVE

How old does a person have to be to write a will in your state? How many witnesses are required?

Last Will and Testament of Martha Yates Schwartz

I, Martha Yates Schwartz of 621 Marshall St., Jamestown, Virginia, being of sound mind, do declare this to be my last will and testament and hereby **revoke** all prior wills I have made.

1. I direct my **executor,** named below, to pay my just debts, taxes, and funeral expenses as soon after my death as possible.

2. I give and bequeath to my oldest friend, Jennifer Schmidt, my red sapphire ring, which is kept in my bureau in my bedroom.

3. All the rest, residue, and remainder of my estate, real and personal, of which I am now or may hereafter be possessed or to which I may be entitled, I give to my husband, Mark Schwartz, if he survives me. If he does not survive me, I give the rest to my children, Peter and Ellen.

4. I appoint my husband, Mark Schwartz, to be the executor of my last will and testament to serve without **bond or undertaking.** In the event he does not survive me or fails to serve for any reasons, I appoint my brother, Ken Yates, to serve as executor without bond or undertaking.

5. If my husband dies before me or at the same time, I nominate our good friends, Jacob and Wilma Stern, to be the guardians of our children. If they are unable or unwilling to serve, I nominate my brother, Ken Yates, and his wife, Elizabeth, to be the children's guardians.

In witness whereof I have hereunto set my hand this _____ day of _____, 19____.

_____

Martha Yates Schwartz

The foregoing instrument was signed, published, and declared by said Martha Yates Schwartz as her last will and testament in our presence, and we, at her request and in her presence and in the presence of each other, have hereunto fixed our signatures as witnesses thereto.

Date	Name	Address
_____	_____	_____
_____	_____	_____
_____	_____	_____

PROBLEM 32

Refer to Martha Schwartz's will and answer the following questions:

a. Who will get Martha's property if she dies the day after she makes the will?

b. Who will take care of her children if she and her husband die in an accident?

c. Most states require two witnesses. Why do you think there are three spaces for witnesses here?

d. Are wills really necessary? Couldn't Martha accomplish her wishes by just telling her husband what to do if she dies? Explain.

Wills may be simple, like Martha's, or they can contain very detailed instructions as to what is to happen to every item the person owns, exactly what is to happen at their funeral, and many other things. People with young children often include a clause naming someone to be guardian of their children. The courts are not required to follow this direction, but they usually do unless there is strong reason not to or the named guardian is unwilling to take the children.

Wills can usually be revoked by ripping them up. Wills can also be changed by adding a **codicil** or an amendment to the original will. However, any significant change should usually be accomplished by destroying the old will and writing a new one.

When someone dies, the executor or executrix named in the will becomes very important. If there is no will, this person is named by the court and is called an **administrator.** The executor or administrator usually does the following: arranges for the funeral and the burial or cremation of the body; locates the will and delivers it to the local Register of Wills or probate court, who will **probate** (verify and read) it; and takes charge of all property of the deceased, keeps records, files, and pays all income, estate, and inheritance taxes, and, with court approval, gives out the property to the persons named in the will, called **heirs.**

The executor will often hire a lawyer to assist with the above responsibilities. The attorney may charge an hourly fee or a fixed percentage of the value of the property left by the decedent (e.g., six percent). Some executors, depending on their own knowledge and the rules in the local probate court, may be able to handle the probate without an attorney. The executor is also eligible for a fee. This is usually a fixed percentage of the value of the property and must be approved by the probate court.

PROBLEM 33

a. If you died today, what would happen to what you own?

b. At what stage in your life would you consider drawing up a will?

c. If you were named as executor in a will, could you perform the duties listed in the text? Would you need to have a lawyer to carry out the duties? Would you want to pay the lawyer a percentage of the value of all the property or an hourly fee? Explain.

five
HOUSING
LAW

Whether we live in a farmhouse or a high-rise, a mobile home or a suburban split-level, a condominium or a walk-up flat, we all use and pay for housing. Many Americans own their own homes. Many others rent houses or apartments owned by someone else. Whether you and your family own or rent, you need to be aware of some of the practical issues and problems involving housing.

This chapter discusses the advantages and disadvantages of renting and buying, where and how to find a place to live, and how to calculate the amount you can afford for housing. It also discusses what to do if you are discriminated against in buying or renting a home, what to look for in an apartment, and what to look out for in a lease.

PROBLEM 1

Assume you and your family are moving.

a. Make a list of all the features you would like in a home (house or apartment, size, type, location, price, convenience, etc.)

b. Look in the classified section of your local newspaper to see what you find that meets your description. Could you and your family afford to live there?

c. Are there more listings for some locations than others? Does the cost of similar houses or apartments vary, depending on where they are located? Why? What advantages and disadvantages are claimed for the various neighborhoods and housing types? In choosing a place to live, what do you think is the most important consideration? Why?

CHOOSING A PLACE TO LIVE

Choosing where to live is an important decision. Every year over forty million Americans move into a new house or apartment. This change of residence often involves a move into a new neighborhood, a different city, or another part of the country. Before looking for a place to live, you should ask yourself three questions: Where do I want to live? What can I afford? Do I want to rent or buy?

Location

A key factor in finding a place to live is location. In considering location, you should decide whether you prefer a city, suburban, or rural setting. If you have to travel to work or school every day, you should consider the cost of commuting, including how long it will take and whether public transportation is available. If you have children, you should consider the quality and availability of schools and child care facilities. You should also consider community services and neighborhood character. Find out if stores and shopping areas are conveniently located, and if police, fire, and sanitation services are reliable. Try and determine whether the neighbors seem friendly. Before deciding on a location, walk and drive around the neighborhood or community you're considering. Talk to people who live there and give careful thought to whether you really want to live in the area.

PROBLEM 2

a. Would you rather live in a city, suburb, small town, or rural area? Why?

b. What are some advantages and disadvantages of each location?

Cost

People can't always live where they want. The choice of housing is often limited by what is available. Even more often our choice of

What are some advantages and disadvantages of living in the city?

housing is limited by price. You may find a house or apartment in the area you like but the price is just too high. How much people can afford to pay is often the key factor in determining where they live.

A person who rents a house or apartment is known as a **tenant**. Tenants have to pay a set amount of money every month to the **landlord**. Depending on the agreement that you have with your landlord, you may or may not have to pay utilities (electricity, gas, water, etc.). Remember that utility costs have been rising rapidly in recent years and must be considered along with the rent. *Before renting or buying, find out what the average monthly utilities were for the past year.*

If you are buying a home, you will probably be required to pay a cash amount called a **down payment** before you can move in. The amount can vary from no down payment, under certain government loan programs, to as much as twenty or thirty percent of the price of the house. (The remainder of the cost of the house, called a **mortgage** loan, must be paid by the buyer over time.) For example, if you buy a house for $60,000, you might be required to make a down payment of twenty-five percent, or $15,000. The remainder, $45,000, would be your mortgage loan, which you pay in monthly payments over a number of years (e.g., thirty years). Buyers are also responsible for paying other costs relating to the property.

The rule for either renting or buying used to be that you should not pay more than twenty-five percent of your monthly take-home income for housing. Using this formula, your rent or mortgage payment should not be more than $250 per month if you take home $1,000 a month. In some parts of the country the high cost of housing has forced many recent home buyers to spend more than twenty-five percent of their income for housing. As will be seen, this is not necessarily bad, especially if one is buying a house that is a good investment. However, people who are forced to spend a large portion of their income on housing will naturally have less money available for other things. In some cases, people are spending so much on housing that they are not able to pay their other bills.

PROBLEM 3

Mr. and Mrs. Furlong looked at an apartment for $275.00 per month. The cost of the rent does not include utilities. They have a monthly income of $1,500. Consider the information provided on the chart "Record of Housing Expenses 1979" and then answer the following questions:

a. Using the 25 percent formula, how much can the Furlongs afford to pay each month for housing?

When deciding whether to rent or buy, what things should you consider?

Record of Housing Expenses 1979

MONTH	FUEL OIL HEATING BILL	WATER BILL	ELECTRIC BILL
January	$ 80.00	$ 12.00	$ 21.05
February	83.40	13.00	22.60
March	64.60	12.46	21.55
April	50.02	12.52	18.00
May	36.78	13.80	18.43
June	—0—	18.00	23.90
July	—0—	19.67	25.40
August	—0—	22.40	26.92
September	34.60	19.01	20.23
October	50.90	14.06	19.27
November	69.41	12.36	20.34
December	78.50	12.38	21.70
	$548.21	$182.06	$239.39

b. What was the average cost per month of utilities?

c. Will the Furlongs be able to afford the apartment if the utilities stay the same? If they go up?

d. How can the Furlongs try to keep down the cost of utilities?

Renting vs. Buying

Should you buy or rent? Whatever you decide, there are obviously advantages and disadvantages for each choice. Cost is a key consideration. If you're thinking of buying, you will need a certain amount of cash for a down payment, and this prevents many people from buying. Mortgages often run for twenty or thirty years, and the homebuyer will be required to keep up monthly payments for the entire time. In addition, homeowners must pay for utilities, taxes, maintenance, repairs, insurance, and home improvements. Another disadvantage of buying is that the bank or other lender who gave the mortgage loan can take the house and sell it if you fail to make the mortgage payments.

While the cost of buying a home can be quite high, particularly in the beginning, there are also a number of advantages to buying. First, the monthly mortgage payment is a form of forced savings, which usually can be recovered when the house is sold. This means that each month part of your mortgage payment pays off part of the total loan. Second, buying a house is a good way to fight inflation. This is because the price of housing is continually going up while the monthly mortgage payment usually remains the same. Third, there are tax advantages to owning a home. The interest on a mortgage (usually a sizeable part of your payments in early years) and the amount of any property taxes can be deducted from your federal income tax each year. Fourth, owning a house is usually a good investment. In recent years housing values have increased faster than the rate of inflation. Finally, many people buy houses to enjoy the "pride of ownership." Homeowners can generally change or improve the house or yard in any way they see fit, and the fact of ownership often builds pride in and concern for the community.

Like buying, renting also has its pros and cons. Renters have fewer responsibilities. They can call the landlord to make major repairs and don't have to worry about property taxes or homeowner's insurance. Renting gives people more freedom to move on a short notice, and if you lose your source of income, your commitment to pay lasts only as long as the **lease**.

In the short run, renting probably costs less, although over a period of years a renter has little but receipts or canceled checks to show for his or her payments. Moreover, the monthly rent can go up periodically, while monthly mortgage payments usually remain the same. Renters may have more flexibility if they decide to move, but they generally also have more rules and less privacy than a homeowner. Deciding whether to buy or rent is a difficult decision. During a lifetime many people do both.

PROBLEM 4

Fred and Jill, both twenty-three years old, have decided to get married. They both have jobs paying about $12,000 a year. Each takes home $800 a month ($1,600 total). Between them they have

about $5,000 in savings. They are trying to decide if they should rent or buy. They visit a real estate agent who takes them to see a small two-bedroom house. The agent says the owner is willing to rent or sell it to them. If they rent, the owner wants $375 a month rent, plus utilities, which average $50 a month. The owner will give them a one-year lease and make the major repairs. If they buy, the price of the house is $40,000 and a cash down payment of $5,000 would be required. They would then have to get a mortgage loan of $35,000 from a local bank, which would require monthly loan payments of $400 a month, plus $1,000 a year in real estate taxes, $300 a year in insurance, and $1,200 in closing costs.

a. List all the reasons why Fred and Jill should buy the house.

b. List all the reasons why they should rent the house.

c. Roleplay a discussion between them in which they decide whether to rent or buy.

Discrimination in Housing

THE CASE OF THE UNWANTED TENANT

Since the death of her husband, Mrs. Amy Weaver had run a small five-unit apartment house. She lived in one unit and made a meager income by renting out the other four. She doesn't really dislike members of minority groups but knew that several of her regular tenants had threatened to move out if she rented to such people. Anyway, she felt she had the right to do what she wanted in her own building.

Nuy Van Tran, a refugee from Vietnam, was looking for an apartment to rent. When a friend at work told him about a vacancy at Mrs. Weaver's, he called and made an appointment to inspect the apartment. When Mr. Van Tran arrived for the appointment, Mrs. Weaver took one look at him and told him the apartment had been rented. "After all," she said to herself, "it's my property, and no one has the right to tell me whom I must allow to live here."

PROBLEM 5

a. What happened in this case? Why did Mrs. Weaver refuse to rent the apartment to Mr. Van Tran?
b. Do you think what Mrs. Weaver did was legal or illegal? Why?
c. Should the law allow landlords to rent to whoever they want?
d. Which do you think is more important, the right to control one's own property or the right to live where one chooses?
e. Is there anything Mr. Van Tran can do? Explain.

Choice of housing is sometimes limited by discrimination. For various reasons, some landlords, real estate agents, mortgage lenders, and owners prefer to sell or rent to certain types of people over others.

Usually a major consideration of those who sell or rent is whether the money owed them will be paid in full and on time. To help insure this, they usually want to know several things about potential tenants or buyers, including:

1. Does the person have a steady income that is likely to continue into the future?

2. Is the income high enough to enable the person to pay for the housing?

3. Does the person have a good record in paying off previous bills or loans?

4. Will the person take good care of the property?

The Federal Fair Housing Act of 1968 forbids discrimination because of a person's race, color, sex, national origin, or religion. This law covers the rental, sale, or financing of privately owned houses and apartments with four or more units. An executive order also prohibits discrimination in federally owned, operated, or assisted housing, including public housing.

Many states and cities have also passed antidiscrimination laws. Some of these laws provide more protection than the federal law by forbidding discrimination against unmarried persons, families with children, homosexuals, handicapped persons, and others.

Discrimination can take many forms. It may exist when owners say their homes are sold when they really are not, or when real estate agents practice **steering**. This means directing buyers or renters to particular areas because of their race or other reasons. Another type of discrimination related to the purchase of homes is called **redlining**, a practice whereby banks and others refuse to make loans to homebuyers in certain areas or neighborhoods. Redlining also violates federal law and the laws of many states.

Not all discrimination is illegal. For example, landlords and sellers may refuse to rent or sell to persons who have poor credit ratings.

It is not always easy to prove discrimination, and there are some valid reasons for turning down would-be tenants or homebuyers. Nevertheless, if you think you've been unfairly discriminated against, you may file a complaint with the U.S. Department of Housing and Urban Development's (HUD) Fair Housing Office (see Appendix A for the address). HUD has the power to investigate the complaint and can attempt to solve the problem.

EQUAL HOUSING OPPORTUNITY

We Do Business in Accordance With the Federal Fair Housing Law

(Title VIII of the Civil Rights Act of 1968, as Amended by the Housing and Community Development Act of 1974)

IT IS ILLEGAL TO DISCRIMINATE AGAINST ANY PERSON BECAUSE OF RACE, COLOR, RELIGION, SEX, OR NATIONAL ORIGIN

- In the sale or rental of housing or residential lots
- In advertising the sale or rental of housing
- In the financing of housing
- In the provision of real estate brokerage services

Blockbusting is also illegal

An aggrieved person may file a complaint of a housing discrimination act with the:

U.S. DEPARTMENT OF HOUSING AND URBAN DEVELOPMENT
Assistant Secretary for Fair Housing and Equal Opportunity
Washington, D.C. 20410

> **WHERE YOU LIVE**
>
> What laws prohibit housing discrimination in your state or community? What state or local agencies enforce these laws and investigate complaints?

You may also be able to file a complaint with a local or state antidiscrimination agency or take the case to court. U.S. district courts have the power to order an end to the discrimination and can award money to compensate the person discriminated against.

PROBLEM 6

Consider each of the following situations and decide whether you think the action of the landlord, homeowner, lender, or sales agent was legal or illegal under the Federal Fair Housing Act. If the action is legal under the act, do you think the law should be changed to prohibit the discrimination?

a. A real estate company has a policy of taking whites to white neighborhoods and blacks to black neighborhoods.

b. A woman seeking a two-bedroom apartment is turned down by the landlord, who thinks the apartment is too small for her and her three children.

c. A landlord turns down a man who collects unemployment benefits because the landlord is worried he won't be able to pay the rent.

d. A homeowner refuses to sell to a Hispanic couple because he thinks the neighbors won't approve.

e. A woman is rejected for a mortgage by a bank officer who believes her divorce makes her a financial risk.

f. A zoning change to allow a group home for the retarded is blocked by a neighborhood association.

g. A young lawyer is rejected as a tenant because the landlord is afraid he'll complain too much and stir up the other tenants.

h. A young musician is rejected by a landlord, who thinks he looks like a hippie and might make too much noise.

i. A credit union official discourages an elderly man from buying a house because the official thinks the man won't live long enough to pay off the mortgage.

RENTING A HOME

Many persons rent their homes. A renter pays the owner a certain amount of money in return for the right to live there for a period of time. The person who receives rent money is called the landlord, and the person who pays rent money is called the tenant.

The landlord-tenant relationship is usually created by a type of contract called a lease or rental agreement. A lease sets out the

If you were looking for a rental house or apartment, how would you find one?

amount of rent that must be paid and the length of time the apartment may be rented. It also states the rights and duties of both landlord and tenant.

Before you rent an apartment or a house, there are at least two things to do to protect your interests. First, completely inspect the dwelling to insure that it meets your needs. Second, because most leases are written to the advantage of the landlord, carefully read the lease. If you don't understand or can't read the lease, you should get help from someone else before signing.

PROBLEM 7

Assume that you are looking for a new apartment. You are married and have a two-year-old child and a small dog.

a. Make a checklist of all the things you would look for in an apartment.

b. What questions would you ask the landlord?

c. If you inspect an apartment, what things should you look out for?

The House or Apartment

Once you've decided to rent, your first job is to find a suitable house or apartment. Sometimes landlords put "For Rent" signs on their property. More often you'll find yourself looking in the classified section of the local newspaper or on community bulletin boards. Many landlords hire real estate agents or brokers to rent their property for them. These agents have the power to make promises on behalf of the owner and are paid a fee for finding tenants and managing the owner's property.

Before you look at an apartment, it is wise to make a list of your needs and wants. Ask yourself questions such as: Where do I want to live? How much rent can I afford? What facilities and services do I need? How much living and storage space do I require? What other costs such as utilities or maintenance may be involved?

Once you've found an apartment, you can avoid a lot of potential problems by giving it a thorough inspection *before* signing the lease to determine the condition of the place and to see that it meets your needs. It is also a good idea to talk with other tenants. Ask them about their experience with the building and the landlord. Most importantly, never rent an apartment you haven't seen, even if you're shown a model apartment and told yours will be just like it.

ADVICE ON WHAT TO INSPECT BEFORE RENTING

■ What is the condition of the building?
■ Are hallways, lobbies, and common areas clean and well lighted?
■ Does the building have laundry facilities?
■ Is there enough parking space?
■ Are there any signs of insects or rodents?
■ How is routine and emergency maintenance handled?
■ Is storage and closet space adequate?
■ Is the apartment soundproof?
■ Are the plumbing, heating, and electrical fixtures in working order?
■ Are kitchen appliances clean and in good condition?
■ Is there any evidence of water stains or peeling paint on walls and ceilings?
■ Are there at least two electrical outlets in each room?
■ Does the building provide protection against burglars or uninvited guests?
■ Is it likely to be too cold in winter or too hot in summer?
■ Is the apartment furnished or unfurnished?
■ Do windows and doors open easily?
■ Are there any broken windows or screens?
■ Are fire extinguishers and safety exits available?
■ Is the apartment big enough?

The Lease

Once you've inspected the rental house or apartment, you'll probably be asked to sign a lease. A lease is a legal agreement or contract in which both the landlord and tenant agree to do certain things and not to do other things. A lease usually includes the date you may

Tenants should always inspect the apartment before signing a lease.

move in, the amount of the rent, the dates on which the rent is to be paid, and the length or *term* of the lease. It also includes the amount of any **security deposit** that may be required, the conditions under which the rent may be raised, and rules governing repairs, maintenance and other conditions in the apartment.

Depending upon your particular situation, one type of lease may be better for you than another. For example, if you are planning to rent for only a short period, or if your job requires that you be ready to move on short notice, you might prefer a **month-to-month lease**. This type of lease usually enables you to leave after thirty days' notice. However, it has the disadvantage of allowing the landlord to raise the rent or evict you with just thirty days' notice as well.

Another type of lease allows a tenant to move in with the understanding that the lease is for an indefinite period. This arrangement, called a **tenancy at will**, allows the tenant to leave or be told to leave at any time.

A lease for a fixed period of time—such as six months or a year—is called a **tenancy for years**. This type of lease is very common and generally prevents the landlord from raising the rent or evicting the tenant during the period of the lease. If you are plan-

---

THE SUMMER RENTAL CASE

A college student goes to a resort town to work for the summer and rents an apartment for three months. After a month she moves to a cheaper apartment down the street. The landlord demands rent for the two remaining months, but the young woman claims she doesn't owe any money because the lease was not in writing.

PROBLEM 8
a. Is the student obligated to pay the additional two months rent? Would it make a difference if the landlord rented the apartment immediately after she moved out?
b. What should the woman have done when she found the cheaper apartment?
c. Roleplay a phone call between the woman and the landlord after she finds the cheaper apartment and wishes to get the landlord's permission to move.

Leases for less than one year do not have to be written to be legal. Because the lease in the Summer Rental Case was for only three months, the landlord was right. The oral agreement was binding and the tenant would still owe rent for two more months. To avoid problems, you are *always* better off getting a written lease, signed and dated by both you and the landlord. Leases that are for more than one year must always be in writing.

ning to rent for a long period of time, this may be the best type of lease for you.

RANDALL REAL ESTATE CO.
PROPERTY MANAGEMENT—INVESTMENT
PROPERTY—SALES—INSURANCE

THIS AGREEMENT, Made and executed this ____ day of _____ A.D., 19 ____, by and between **RANDALL REAL ESTATE COMPANY**, hereinafter called the Landlord, and _____ _____,
hereinafter called the Tenant.

WITNESSETH, That Landlord does hereby let unto Tenant the premises known as Apartment No. 301, at 12 Marshall Street in Johnstown, for the term commencing on the ____ day of _____, 19___, and fully ending at midnight on the day of ____, 19___, at and for the total rental of _____ Dollars, the first installment payable on the execution of this agreement and the remaining installments payable in advance on the ____ day of each ensuing month, to and at the office of **RANDALL REAL ESTATE COMPANY**, 1000 Columbia Road, in Johnstown.

On the ____ day of _____, 19___, a sum of _____ shall become due and payable. This sum shall cover the period up to the day of _____, 19___; thereafter, a sum of _____ shall be due and payable on the ____ day of each month.

AND TENANT, does hereby agree as follows:

1. Tenant will pay the rent at the time specified.
2. Tenant will pay all utility bills as they become due.
3. Tenant will use the premises for a dwelling and for no other purpose.
4. Tenant will not use said premises for any unlawful purpose, nor in any noisy or rowdy manner, or other way offensive to any other occupant of the building.
5. Tenant will not transfer or sublet the premises without the written consent of Landlord.
6. Landlord shall have access to the premises at any time for the purpose of inspection, to make repairs the Landlord considers necessary, or to show the apartment to tenant applicants.
7. Tenant will give Landlord prompt notice of any defects or breakage in the structure, equipment or fixtures of said premises.
8. Tenant will not make any alterations or additions to the structure, equipment, or fixtures of said premises without the written consent of the Landlord.
9. Tenant will pay a security deposit in the amount of $_____, which will be held by Landlord until expiration of this lease and refunded on the condition that said premises is returned in good condition, normal wear and tear excepted.

Written leases are generally difficult to read and understand. To protect yourself, be sure to read all clauses of the lease carefully

10. Tenant will not keep any pets, live animals, or birds of any description in said premises.

11. Landlord shall be under no liability to Tenant for any discontinuance of heat, hot water, or elevator service, and shall not be liable for damage to proerty of Tenant caused by rodents, rain, snow, defective plumbing, or any other source.

12. Should Tenant continue in possession after the end of the term herein with permission of Landlord, it is agreed that the tenancy thus created can be terminated by either party giving to the other party not less than Thirty (30) Days' Written Notice.

13. Tenant shall be required to give the Landlord at least thirty (30) days' notice, in writing, of his intention to vacate the premises at the expiration of his tenancy. If Tenant vacates the premises without first furnishing said notice, Tenant shall be liable to the Landlord for one month's rent.

14. Both Landlord and Tenant waive trial by jury in connection with any agreement contained in the rental agreement or any claim for damages arising out of the agreement or connected with this tenancy.

15. Landlord shall not be held liable for any injuries or damages to the Tenant or his guests, regardless of cause.

16. In the event of increases in real estate taxes, fuel charges, or sewer and water fees, Tenant agrees during the term of the lease to pay a proportionate share of such charges, fees, or increases.

17. Tenant confesses judgment and waives any and all rights to file a counterclaim, or a defense to any action filed by the Landlord against the Tenant and further agrees to pay attorney fees and all other costs incurred by the Landlord in an action against the Tenant.

18. Tenant agrees to observe all such rules and regulations which the Landlord or his agents will make concerning the apartment building.

IN TESTIMONY WHEREOF, Landlord and Tenant have signed this Agreement the day and year first hereinbefore written.

Signed in the presence of _____

_____

_____

_____

_____

_____

before signing it. Never sign a lease unless all blank spaces are filled in or crossed out. If you're unsure of any of the items in the lease, consult with a tenant organization, legal aid office, or private attorney. Moreover, any promises made by the landlord should be written into the lease. For example, if the landlord promises to make certain repairs before you move in, get the promise in writing.

In most places you'll probably be asked to sign a standard form lease. These leases are written to the landlord's advantage and may even contain illegal clauses that are not enforceable in court. The lease reprinted in the text contains many of the provisions included in a standard form lease. A few of the clauses contained in this lease are illegal in some states. However, before examining the lease, remember that landlord-tenant law differs from state to state. You should always inform yourself about the landlord-tenant laws in your own state.

PROBLEM 9

a. What are the key provisions of this lease? Who is the landlord? Who pays for utilities? Is the tenant allowed to have a pet?

b. As a tenant, would you object to any of the provisions in this lease?

Landlord-Tenant Negotiations

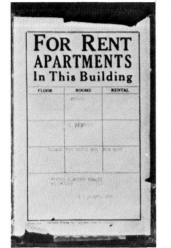

Tenants should know that in many places housing is in big demand and short supply. In this kind of market, landlords generally have the upper hand and can often tell tenant applicants to take it or leave it. Trying to negotiate with a landlord can be difficult, but it is worth a try, particularly if tenants know their rights and know what they want in an apartment. If a tenant does try negotiating with a landlord, it is best to be assertive, but tactful and polite. Tenants want the landlord to know they'll be good tenants but that they expect something in return—namely, fair treatment and a clean, well-maintained place to live.

To strike a section from a lease, both the tenant and the landlord or rental agent should cross out the particular clause and put their initials next to the change. If anything is added to the lease, be sure the addition is written on all copies of the lease and signed by both the landlord and the tenant.

PROBLEM 10

Read the following information and then have two persons role-play the landlords (the Randalls) and two other persons roleplay the tenants (the Monicos). Persons roleplaying the Monicos should inspect the apartment and ask the landlord all the questions a tenant should ask in deciding whether to rent the apartment. Persons roleplaying the Randalls should find out everything a landlord would need to know before renting to a tenant. The landlords should give a copy of the lease to the tenants, who should discuss it and reach a decision on whether or not to sign it.

Mr. and Mrs. Randall own an apartment building in the city of Johnstown. They have a nice two-bedroom apartment for rent. They require all their tenants to take a two-year lease, to pay a two-month security deposit, and to sign a lease (the same as the one printed in the text). They don't allow pets in the building. The rent is $250 per month plus utilities, which average about $30 a month. They are eager to rent the apartment right away because it has been empty for two weeks.

Mr. and Mrs. Monico have just moved to Johnstown because they have both obtained jobs there. Mr. Monico's job may only last one year, and they may then move back to Williamsport, a city 100 miles away. They have a three-year-old son and a dog. Based on their salaries they only wish to pay $225 a month in rent and utilities. They want a nice neighborhood and are a little worried about the crime in Johnstown. They want to rent an apartment right away because they start work in three days. They see a notice advertising the Randalls's apartment. They don't know much about the neighborhood, but they decide to look at the apartment.

The apartment has two bedrooms, a living room with attached dining area, and one bathroom with a tub but no shower. It is on the second floor and has a small balcony overlooking a parking lot. The paint is peeling in the larger bedroom, and a small window is broken in the bathroom. The kitchen has a fairly new refrigerator and sink, but the stove is old and worn and has a missing handle. The front door and the door to the balcony have locks that could easily be opened by an intruder.

After the role play, answer the following questions:

a. Did the Monicos ask any questions about the neighborhood or building as a whole? Should they have?

WHAT TO CONSIDER BEFORE RENTING

1. What kind of area do you wish to live in?
2. What are the costs, including rent, utilities, security deposit, maintenance fees, etc.?
3. What is the condition of the apartment or house? Will repairs be made by the landlord before you move in?
4. How long will the lease last and how can it be ended?
5. Will the landlord make or pay for repairs that occur after you move in?
6. What services (storage, trash removal, maintenance of yard, appliances) will the tenant receive?
7. Are there any special rules (no pets, no children, no parties)?
8. Do you understand all the clauses in the lease? Are any of them illegal or difficult for you to accept?

b. What was decided regarding the amount of rent and other costs of the apartment? In reality, can tenants ever convince landlords to take less than they are asking?

c. In discussing the conditions in the apartment, did the tenants get the landlords to agree to make repairs?

d. Did the Monicos ask about such services as laundry, parking, and playgrounds? Should they have?

e. Are there any special rules in the lease that the Monicos didn't like? Did they ask the landlords to discuss these, and, if so, what occurred? Could the Monicos have done a better job negotiating these rules?

f. Is it worthwhile for tenants to try to negotiate with landlords? Can tenants be hurt by doing this?

RIGHTS AND DUTIES OF LANDLORDS AND TENANTS

After a person signs a lease and moves into a rental home or apartment, both the landlord and the tenant assume certain rights and duties. Most of these rights and duties are set out in the lease. However, certain responsibilities exist even without being stated in the lease. In the following sections, several clauses from the lease reprinted in the text are discussed in detail. Each discussion is designed to give you some idea as to how to read a lease and to alert you to certain problems.

Paying the Rent

Tenant will pay the rent at the time specified. (Clause 1)

A tenant's most important duty is paying the rent. The lease will generally state the amount of rent to be paid and the date on which it is due. Most leases require payment on the first day of each month. If you and the landlord agree to a date other than the first, be sure that it is written into the lease.

Historically, courts have held that the tenant had to continue paying rent no matter what happened to the house or apartment. For example, if the apartment was damaged by fire, the tenant was still required to pay rent for the term of the lease. In recent years, courts and legislatures in most states have ruled that in situations where the apartment is made unlivable by fire, landlord neglect or some other cause, the tenant cannot be forced to pay the rent. These situations are discussed more fully in the section on landlord-tenant problems. For now, keep in mind that tenants have a duty to pay the rent and that landlords can generally **evict** a tenant who doesn't pay the rent.

Raising the Rent

In the event of increases in real estate taxes, fuel charges, or sewer and water fees, Tenant agrees during the term of the lease to pay a proportionate share of such charges, fees, or increases. (Clause 16)

Generally, landlords cannot raise the rent during the term of a lease. When the term is over, the rent can normally be raised as much as the landlord wants. Some leases, however, include provisions (like Clause 16) that allow for automatic increases during the term of the lease. Many landlords now include such clauses due to the rising cost of fuel and building maintenance. A lease, with a clause of this type, is obviously not as favorable to a tenant as one that keeps the rent the same and requires the landlord to pay increased costs for utilities, taxes, or other charges.

Another factor that can affect whether the landlord may raise the rent is **rent control**. Many communities—especially large cities—have rent control or rent stabilization laws, which put a limit on how much existing rents can be raised. Cities that have enacted rent control laws use various standards to control the rise in rents. Some places limit rent increases to a certain percentage each year. In other places rent raises are tied to the cost of living, the cost of improvements in the building, or are allowed only when a new tenant moves in.

WHERE YOU LIVE

Is rent control permitted in your state? If so, how does it operate and how successful has it been?

The rising cost of rental housing has caused many cities to enact rent control laws.

Rent control laws have been enacted to slow down the rising cost of housing. There are many arguments for and against rent control, and wherever it has been tried, it has been controversial and opposed by many.

PROBLEM 11

Suppose the legislature or city council in your community is considering rent control. Housing costs have been rising steadily and it is proposed that a law be passed limiting rent increases to five percent a year for all rental properties. Read the statements below. Decide which one you agree with and explain why.

Representative of a Tenant Group

There is a severe shortage of apartments and rental homes in the area, and, as a result, landlords have been able to charge just about any rent they want. During the last two years, rents have risen an average of fifteen percent a year. The housing shortage and rent increases have particularly hurt low- and middle-income tenants who are barely able to meet expenses and pay the rent. Only government control can stop the continued and rapid rise in rents. Rent control should be passed by the legislature.

Representative of a Landlord Group

Rent control will result in more rundown housing because area landlords will not have the money to pay for repairs or improvements. In some cases, landlords may be forced to sell or abandon their apartment buildings because it will be uneconomical to operate them without increased rents. In addition, if landlords can't expect reasonable profits, they will not build new apartment buildings. An even greater shortage of rental units will result.

Landlords are only raising rents to meet the increased costs of heating fuel, electricity, taxes, and repairs. Also, landlords are in business to earn a profit and have a right to charge whatever they want. Besides, tenants can always move out and find another apartment if they think the rent is too high. Rent control would be a big mistake.

Quiet Enjoyment

One of a tenant's most important rights is the **right to quiet enjoyment**. This simply means that the tenant has a right to use and enjoy the property without being disturbed by the landlord or other tenants.

Tenants have a right to quiet enjoyment even if it is not stated in the lease, and landlords have a duty to insure that other tenants

---

THE CASE OF THE NOISY NEIGHBOR

Mike and Marcy O'Reilly signed a one-year lease and were pleased when they moved into a beautiful old apartment building in their favorite part of town.

Soon after they moved in, however, they discovered that the building was incredibly noisy and disorderly. During the first week, their next-door neighbor threw several wild parties, keeping them up all night. They also discovered that when their neighbor wasn't having parties, he was receiving visitors at all hours of the day. These visits were almost always accompanied by loud music, shouting, and constant coming and going. The partying often carried out into the halls and the O'Reillys were frequently hassled by some of the visitors.

The O'Reillys complained to the landlord on a dozen occasions, but the late-night parties and noisy visitors went on. Finally, the O'Reillys decided they had had enough and moved out. The landlord then sued the O'Reillys, claiming they owed her for eleven months' rent. Will the O'Reillys have to pay?

---

don't unreasonably disturb the tenants in the building. If the O'Reillys (in the Case of the Noisy Neighbor) complained to the landlord and she did nothing about it, they were probably justified in moving out because of the failure to provide quiet enjoyment. As a practical matter, tenants should complain to the landlord, preferably in writing, if such conditions exist. Unless the landlord knows of the problem, things are unlikely to improve.

Upkeep and Repairs

Landlord shall be under no liability to Tenant for any discontinuance of heat, hot water, or elevator service, and shall not be liable for damage to property of Tenant caused by rodents, rain, snow, defective plumbing, or any other source. (Clause 11)

Traditionally, landlords did not have a duty to maintain the premises or make repairs to a rented house or apartment. In the few places where this is still true, tenants have to make all repairs that are needed to keep the property in its original condition.

Clause 11 from the sample lease states that the tenant must continue to pay the rent whether or not the landlord provides a dwelling fit to live in. Some states have held such provisions to be unenforceable. Today, most states have either passed laws that require the landlord to keep the house or apartment in a condition fit to live in, or the courts have said that a **warranty of habitability** is implied in every lease. This means that the landlord promises to provide a place fit for human habitation. This promise is said

Who is responsible for repair and upkeep in a rented apartment?

**WHERE
YOU
LIVE**

What is your state's law regarding repairs and the warranty of habitability?

to exist whether or not it is written into the lease. Thus, if major repairs are needed—the furnace breaks down, the roof leaks, or the apartment is overrun by insects or rodents—the landlord has a duty to correct the problems.

PROBLEM 12

a. If you were a landlord, what repairs and maintenance would you expect the tenant to perform? Develop a list and explain it.

b. If you were a tenant, what repairs and maintenance would you expect the landlord to perform? Develop a list and explain it.

Besides the warranty of habitability, many communities have enacted **housing codes**. These codes set minimum standards for repairs and living conditions within a rental house or apartment. Landlords are required to meet the standards of the housing code, and they may lose their license to rent, if the standards are not maintained. Housing codes differ from area to area, but in most places tenants have the right to call in a government housing inspector to examine their apartment for code violations.

PROBLEM 13

Which of the housing code provisions reprinted on page 241 do you feel are most important? Are there any housing code requirements not listed that should be included?

While most places now hold landlords responsible for major repairs, remember that the landlord's duty to make repairs differs from place to place and from lease to lease. It is always best to have the responsibility for repairs spelled out in the lease. Also, remember that tenants have a duty to notify the landlord when repairs are needed. If someone is injured as a result of an unsafe or defective condition, the landlord cannot be held liable unless he or she knew or should have known the condition existed.

Use of the Property and Security Deposits

Tenant will use the premises for a dwelling and for no other purpose. (Clause 3)

Tenant will pay a security deposit in the amount of $_____, which will be held by Landlord until expiration of this lease and refunded on the condition that said premises is returned in good condition, normal wear and tear excepted. (Clause 9)

SAMPLE HOUSING CODE

The following are examples of provisions included in a typical housing code:

Maintenance and Repair
- Floors and walls shall be free of holes, cracks, splinters or peeling paint.
- Windows and doors shall be weatherproof, easily operable, free of broken glass, and equipped with workable locks.
- Stairs and walkways shall be in good repair, clean, free of safety hazards or loose railings.
- Roof shall be free of leaks.

Cleanliness and Sanitation
- Each unit shall be generally free of rodents and insects. Common areas shall be free of dirt, litter, trash, water, or other unsanitary matter.

Use and Occupancy
- Each unit shall have a minimum of 120 square feet of livable floor space per occupant.
- Each bedroom shall have a minimum of 50 square feet of floor space per occupant.
- Each unit shall have a private bathroom.
- Common areas shall be accessible without going through another apartment.

Facilities and Utilities
- Sinks, lavatories, and bathing facilities shall be in working order.
- Every room shall have a minimum of 2 electrical outlets and no exposed wiring.
- Water, electricity, gas, heating and sewer services shall be in good operating condition.
- Halls, stairways, and common areas shall be adequately lighted.
- The building shall be free of fire hazards and secure from intruders or uninvited visitors.

WHERE YOU LIVE

Is there a housing code in your community? If so, what does it cover? Who enforces it?

A tenant pays for the right to use a landlord's property. As a general rule, the tenant may only use the property for the purposes stated in the lease. For example, if you rented a house as a residence, you would not be allowed to use it as a restaurant or a dry cleaning business.

If, as a tenant, you are planning to operate any type of home business, you should get the landlord to agree to this in writing or you run the risk of being evicted. Likewise, committing a crime on the property may allow the landlord to end the lease and evict the tenant, regardless of what the lease says.

Housing codes help protect tenants from conditions such as these.

Tenants have a right to use the rental property. But they also have a duty to take care of the property and return it to the landlord in the same general condition in which it was rented. Tenants are generally responsible for the upkeep of the property, including routine cleaning and minor repairs. Major repairs and upkeep of common areas, such as hallways, stairwells, and yards, are normally the responsibility of the landlord, although the landlord and tenant can make different arrangements if they agree to do so.

Tenants are not responsible for damages that result from normal wear and tear or ordinary use of the property. For example, a tenant would not be liable for worn spots in the carpet caused by ordinary foot traffic. On the other hand, damages caused by a tenant's misuse or neglect are considered to be **waste**, and the landlord can force the tenant to pay for such repairs. Moreover, tenants have a duty to let the landlord know when major repairs are needed and to take reasonable steps to prevent unnecessary waste or damage.

In most places, landlords have the right to protect themselves against damage caused by the tenant by asking for a **security deposit**. This deposit is an amount of money—usually a month's rent—that will be kept by the landlord to insure that the tenant takes care of the apartment and abides by the terms of the lease. If the tenant damages the property of the landlord, the security deposit (or a part of it) may be kept to pay for the damage. Also, if the tenant does not pay all the rent, the landlord may also be able to keep the security deposit to cover the portion of the rent still owed.

Some states put a limit on the amount of the security deposit and require the landlord to pay the tenant interest on the money

WHERE YOU LIVE

What is the law in your area regarding security deposits? Is there a limit on the amount that can be required? Does the landlord have to pay interest on the security deposit?

when it is returned at the end of the lease. When a landlord requires a security deposit, the tenant should *always* get a receipt and should keep it until the deposit is returned. The tenant may also ask that the money be placed in an interest-paying bank account.

Whether damages result from normal wear and tear or from tenant neglect depends on all the facts. To protect themselves, tenants should make a list of all defects and damages that exist at the time they move in. The tenant should keep a copy of the list and give another copy to the landlord.

When moving out, a tenant should inspect the apartment again and make a list of any damages. Bringing a friend along as a witness can be helpful in case you have a dispute with the landlord. If there are no damages, the landlord should return your money. If part or all of the money is withheld, the tenant should demand a written statement itemizing the cost of any repairs. If the landlord keeps the security deposit and the tenant disagrees with the landlord's reasons for not returning the deposit, the tenant has a right to sue for the money in small claims court.

Finally, tenants generally have no right to make any changes in the structure or character of the property without the permission of the landlord. Even if the landlord agrees to changes or improvements, the improvement becomes the property of the landlord if it cannot be removed without serious damage to the premises. For example, if a tenant builds new cabinets in the kitchen, they become the property of the landlord and cannot be removed at the end of the lease.

PROBLEM 14

In each of the following situations, the tenant is moving out and the landlord wants to keep part of the tenant's security deposit. Decide who should pay for the damages involved in each case.

a. The tenant moves without cleaning the apartment. The landlord is forced to remove trash, clean the walls and floors, wash the windows, and clean out the oven and refrigerator.

b. The toilet overflows in an upstairs tenant's apartment. The water leaks through the floor, ruining the ceiling and carpet in the apartment below.

c. The tenant's pet stains the carpet. Suppose the lease allowed pets.

d. The stove wears out. Suppose the tenant sells cookware and has had numerous cooking parties in the apartment.

e. The walls are faded and need repainting.

ADVICE CONCERNING SECURITY DEPOSITS

■ Before signing the lease, inspect the apartment and make a list of all defects or damages.

■ Give a copy of the list to the landlord and keep a copy for yourself.

■ Always get a receipt.

■ Ask to be paid interest on your money. In many places you are entitled to this.

■ Before moving out, inspect the apartment and make a list of all damages.

■ Have a friend go through the apartment with you in case you later need a witness.

■ Clean the apartment, repair any damage for which you are responsible, and remove trash so you won't be charged for cleaning.

f. The roof leaks and ruins the hardwood floors. Suppose the tenant never told the landlord about the leak.

g. The tenants paneled the recreation room of their apartment, built kitchen cabinets, and installed drapes and two air conditioning units. When they moved they removed all of their improvements and took them.

Responsibility for Injuries in the Building

Landlord shall not be held liable for any injuries or damages to the Tenant or his guests, regardless of cause. (Clause 15)

Many standard form leases contain clauses stating that the tenant cannot hold the landlord responsible for damages or personal injuries that result from the landlord's carelessness. For example, if a tenant was injured because of a broken guardrail that the

---

THE CASE OF KLINE v. EMBASSY APARTMENTS

Seven years ago, when Sara Kline moved into her apartment, the management locked the building each night at 9:00 p.m. In addition, there was a doorman and a twenty-four hour desk clerk who sat in the lobby. Her written lease, however, said nothing about the landlord providing security measures, and a few years later these services were discontinued. Since that time a number of tenants have been attacked in the building's common areas. One night about 10:00 p.m. Ms. Kline was mugged and seriously injured in a hallway. She sued the landlord for damages.

PROBLEM 15
Assume this case went to trial. Below are two possible decisions of the court. Which one do you agree with and why?

Opinion #1
Landlords are not under a duty to provide police protection in their apartment buildings unless this is specifically promised in the lease. In this case, the lease said nothing about security or safety being provided by the landlord. To hold the landlord responsible now for what is not in the lease would be both unfair and very expensive.

The only duty imposed on landlords is to make repairs and maintain common hallways and entrances. This means that if a tenant is injured as a result of a landlord's failure to repair such items as a broken step or handrail, the landlord can be held responsible. How-

**WHERE
YOU
LIVE**

Can tenants sue land-
lords for injuries or
damage to property in
your state? Will courts
enforce a waiver of tort
liability clause in the
lease?

ever, landlords are not responsible for injuries caused by criminals or others over whom the landlord has no control.

If Ms. Kline was unhappy about the changes in services that oc-curred after she moved in or about the crime in the neighborhood, she was free to move to another apartment with better security. She had a month-to-month lease and could have easily moved out by giving the landlord thirty days' notice.

Opinion #2

Although courts have usually ruled that landlords are under no duty to provide security for tenants, this court believes that implied in every lease is a duty of the landlord to provide protective measures that are within the landlord's reasonable capacity.

Today's urban apartment building is different because there is no way the individual tenant can be protected in all the hallways. Common areas are under the landlord's control, and he has a duty to act reasonably in keeping them safe. In this case, the landlord knew that crimes had been committed in the building and still did nothing.

In addition, the tenant had come to expect a doorman, an employee at the desk in the lobby, and the front door of the building locked at 9:00 p.m. every night. Because these conditions existed when she moved in, the landlord had a duty to maintain the same degree of security all during her lease.

landlord should have repaired, the lease may say that the tenant cannot sue the landlord.

This type of clause is known as a *waiver of tort liability*. Under this provision the tenant agrees to **waive** (give up) the usual right to hold the landlord responsible for personal injuries. Most courts will not uphold such a clause. Therefore, if you or your guest suffers injury as a result of a landlord's carelessness, you can usually recover damages no matter what the lease says. However, you are always better off getting a lease without this type of clause because, if possible, you want to avoid having to go to court. Also, a few courts still enforce this type of clause.

Landlord Access and Inspection

Landlord shall have access to the premises at any time for the purpose of inspection, to make repairs the Landlord considers necessary, or to show the apartment to tenant applicants. (Clause 6)

Most leases provide landlords and their agents with the right to enter the premises to make repairs, collect the rent, or to enforce other provisions of the lease. This provision is called a **right of entry or access** clause. Taken literally, this provision would allow the landlord to enter your apartment at any time, day or night, without your permission.

However, the law in almost every state requires that visits by the landlord be at a reasonable time. Moreover, without your permission, landlords do not have the right to enter your apartment simply to snoop around or check on your housekeeping.

Rules and Regulations

Tenant agrees to observe all such rules and regulations which the Landlord or his agents will make concerning the apartment building. (Clause 18)

Some leases require the tenant to obey all present and future rules that the landlord makes concerning the apartment. In many cases these rules are quite reasonable, but in other cases they aren't. Typical rules include rules against having pets, rules against keeping bicycles or other items in the halls, rules concerning visitors, cooking, storage, children, building security, and hanging pictures on the walls.

It is important to read all the rules and regulations before you move into a building because landlords sometimes use violation of the rules as a reason for trying to evict tenants or for keeping their security deposits. If you are going to sign a lease that requires you to obey all rules—even those made in the future—it is best to have the lease state, "The tenant agrees to follow all reasonable rules and regulations."

PROBLEM 16

a. Suppose you are the owner of a three-bedroom house that you wish to rent. Make a list of all the rules and regulations you would want for your house.

b. Suppose you are a tenant seeking to rent the house in the example above. Which rules would you consider reasonable and which unreasonable?

c. If tenants don't like some of the landlord's rules, what should they do?

Sublease of a House or Apartment

Tenant will not transfer or sublet the premises without the written consent of Landlord. (Clause 5)

The **sublease clause** in most standard form leases requires the tenant to obtain the landlord's permission before subleasing the

These students are renting an apartment for the summer. Do they need a lease?

apartment. A sublease takes place when the tenant allows someone else to live on the premises and pay all or part of the rent.

For example, suppose you signed a one-year lease on a small house. After six months you find a larger house and want to move. If the landlord agrees, a sublease clause would allow you to rent the small house to someone else for the remainder of the lease. In a sublease situation, the original lease remains in effect, so if the new tenant fails to pay the rent, the original tenant can still be held responsible.

To avoid continued responsibility under the lease, a tenant can seek a **release**. If the landlord gives a release, this means the tenant is excused from all duties related to the apartment and the lease.

The landlord does not have to agree to a tenant's request to sublease. Therefore, you are better off if there is a phrase in the lease that says, "The landlord agrees not to withhold consent unreasonably." This way, the tenant would be able to sublease except when the landlord could give a good reason for refusing. Remember, even if your lease or your landlord lets you sublet, you are still responsible for paying the rent to the landlord if the person to whom you sublet does not pay.

PROBLEM 17

a. Why do most leases require the tenant to get the landlord's permission before subleasing an apartment?

b. Assume the lease requires the tenant to get the landlord's permission before subletting. William, the tenant, leaves town and lets his friend Jose take over the lease, but Jose never pays the rent. Does William still owe the landlord the rent?

c. The Bridgewaters rented a four-bedroom house. When Mrs. Bridgewater lost her job, the Bridgewaters decided to take in a boarder to provide extra income. The boarder, a student from a nearby college took good care of his room, but the landlord objected and threatened to evict the Bridgewaters. Assume Clause 5 of the lease on page 232 is in effect. Do you think the landlord can evict the Bridgewaters for taking in a boarder? Explain your answer.

Tenants' Right to Defend Themselves in Court

Tenant confesses judgment and waives any and all rights to file a counterclaim, or a defense to any action filed by the Landlord against the Tenant and further agrees to pay attorney fees and all other costs incurred by the Landlord in an action against the Tenant. (Clause 17)

A **confession of judgment** clause gives the landlord's attorney the power to go to court and admit liability of the tenant in any dispute with the landlord. In addition, the clause obligates tenants to pay the cost of any legal action against the landlord. For example, suppose a landlord wants to evict a tenant. The confession of judgment clause will enable the landlord to start eviction procedures without even having to tell the tenant about it. By signing such a provision, the tenant agrees in advance to let the landlord decide without challenge if a tenant has been at fault in any disagreement. Whether this provision is illegal and unenforceable depends on state law. Even in states where this clause is illegal, some landlords continue to include it to intimidate tenants who don't know their rights.

LANDLORD-TENANT PROBLEMS

Landlords and tenants don't always live up to their responsibilities. Even after a thorough inspection of the apartment and a careful reading of the lease, problems may arise. When either the landlord or the tenant fails to fulfill the conditions of the lease, there is a violation or breach of the lease. Some breaches of a lease are minor and easily corrected. Other breaches of a lease are more serious and may result in an end to the lease, eviction, or other court action.

If the tenant is the cause of the problem, the landlord has certain remedies or actions which can be taken to solve the problem. These include evicting the tenant or bringing a suit to correct the problem. On the other hand, if the landlord is the cause of the problem, tenants also have certain things they can do.

What Tenants Can Do When Things Go Wrong

Some tenants think once they move into an apartment, there is not much they can do if things go wrong. While this was perhaps once the case, in most states this is no longer true and tenants now have many rights.

When problems arise, there are a number of different actions tenants may take:

- Complaints to the landlord
- Complaints to government agencies
- Tenant organizing
- Rent withholding

**WHERE
YOU
LIVE**

Are there any tenant or-
ganizations in your
community? What do
these organizations do?
How effective have they
been?

■ Suing the landlord

■ Moving out

Complaints to the Landlord   If you have a problem in your apartment, the first thing to do is complain to the landlord, the rental agent, or apartment house manager. The landlord may have a duty to make repairs, but the tenant has a duty to notify the landlord when such repairs are needed. Tenants can, of course, speak to the landlord about the problem, but they should also complain in writing and keep a copy of the complaint. By keeping a copy of a written complaint, you'll have a reminder of your request and evidence that can be used in court, should that ever become necessary.

Complaints to Government Agencies   Some city and county governments have established agencies to handle tenant complaints and deal with housing problems. Also, as we learned earlier in the chapter, many communities have housing codes that set minimum standards for repairs, services, and living conditions in an apartment or rental house. Tenants may report unsafe or unsanitary conditions to the agency that enforces the housing code.

When you complain to the government agency that enforces the housing code, request a visit by a housing inspector. Find out when the inspector can come to your apartment and be there for the inspection. Give the inspector a list of the defects in your apartment and point out all of the problems. Get the name of the inspector and ask for a copy of the report. You may be surprised to find out that your apartment has violations you didn't even know about, such as faulty wiring, structural defects, or fire hazards.

The visit by the housing inspector can be an important aid to the tenant. If the inspector finds code violations in the apartment, especially serious ones, the landlord may be ordered to correct the problem. In some places, a landlord who refuses to make the repairs after being ordered to do so can be fined or have his license to rent revoked. Sometimes the housing authorities may even make the repairs themselves and force the owner to pay for them. In extreme cases, the authorities can order the building vacated and have it demolished. In any event, a visit by the housing inspector puts the tenant in a strong position. It establishes a public record of the conditions in the apartment that can be used against the landlord in a court action.

Tenant Organizing   If an individual complaint to the landlord or the housing authorities can improve the position of a tenant, a complaint filed by a group of tenants may have even more force. If conditions in one tenant's apartment are bad, similar conditions may exist in apartments throughout the building. When this is the case, tenants may want to consider forming an organization or

*In many places tenants have organized to improve
conditions in their buildings.*

association. To form a tenant organization, it is often helpful to
contact an already established tenant association for advice and
support. To find a local tenant group, check with the nearest legal
aid office or contact the National Tenants Organization (address
listed in Appendix A). Should the dispute with the landlord reach
the stage where it becomes necessary to withhold rent or go to
court, tenants acting together often achieve better results than
those who act individually.

Rent Withholding   In some of the states that recognize the warranty of habitability, tenants have the legal right to withhold their
rent if the landlord won't make repairs. This means not paying
part or all of the rent until the landlord makes certain repairs or
meets other tenant demands. Obviously, if a group of tenants in a
building have similar problems and withhold rent as a group, this
will have an economic effect on the landlord and is more likely to
bring results.

When rent is not paid by one or more tenants because of
needed repairs, this is sometimes referred to as a rent strike. This is
illegal in some states, so *tenants should always talk to a lawyer or
legal services office before deciding to withhold rent.*

Another type of rent withholding may take place in states
where the law allows tenants to make repairs themselves and then
deduct the bill from the rent. Laws vary on when and how this can

WHERE
YOU
LIVE

Does the law in your community allow a tenant to withhold rent?

be done, but generally it may only be done if the landlord has had adequate notice of the repairs and has not made them. In most cases, tenants cannot withhold rent unless the repairs are of a serious nature, and most places restrict the amount that can be withheld.

Tenants who consider withholding rent should follow certain basic procedures. First, they should have a housing inspector inspect the building for code violations. Second, they should send the landlord a letter by registered mail announcing that they intend to withhold rent unless repairs are made by a certain date. Third, if repairs are not made by the date set, the rent money should be placed in a bank account known as an **escrow** account. In some states establishing a bank account is required and in other states the rent must be paid directly to the court.

If rent is being withheld, the landlord may decide to give in or may try to evict the tenant for not paying the rent. If the landlord tries to evict the tenant, the tenant can go to court and tell the judge about the needed repairs. The housing inspector's report, copies of letters to the landlord, and photographs of the apartment will all help to prove your case. In states that have a warranty of habitability law, courts have held that if repairs are needed and the landlord does nothing about them, the tenant may only have to pay a reduced amount of rent. Once again, remember that rent withholding is illegal in some states, so be sure to check on your state law before taking this action.

PROBLEM 18

The following law is proposed in your state: "Tenants may withhold rent whenever the landlord does not make repairs within two weeks of being notified that such repairs are needed."

a. Take a landlord's point of view and list all of your opinions concerning the law.

b. Take a tenant's point of view and list all your opinions concerning the law.

c. If you were a member of the state legislature, would you vote for or against this law? Why? Would you change the law in any way? If so, how?

Suing the Landlord In most places, if the landlord breaks the lease, the tenant may sue the landlord in court. In this kind of lawsuit, the tenant may ask the court to order that repairs be made or that part of rent previously paid to the landlord be returned to the tenant. If the tenants have made repairs themselves, it also may be possible to ask the court to order the landlord to pay them back. Though this kind of case may be costly in time and money, some places have small claims courts or landlord-tenant commissions, which make the process easier and less expensive.

Moving Out   A final remedy available to tenants is moving out. When a tenant ignores the lease and moves out, this is called an **abandonment**, and the landlord is usually allowed to sue for the remainder of the rent owed under the lease.

There are extreme cases, however, in which tenants may legally break the lease and move without the landlord's permission. Called **constructive eviction**, it occurs when the property is so run-down that it is unlivable, or when the landlord has denied the tenant's right to quiet enjoyment. Most states consider constructive eviction a valid reason for abandonment, but a few don't, so be sure to check your state law and talk to a lawyer before taking this action.

PROBLEM 19

Mr. and Mrs. Walker rented a one-bedroom apartment for $125 a month from Mr. Martinez. It was run down, but they couldn't find anything else for the price. Two weeks after they moved in, the heat went out on a cold night and the Walkers were forced to stay with relatives for several days. The Walkers also discovered that the roof leaked when it rained, that the apartment was overrun by roaches, and that the toilet continually overflowed.

a. If you were the Walkers, what would you do? Which of the possible tenant actions would provide the best solution to their problem? Why?

b. If you were the landlord, what would you do if the Walkers took each of the possible actions listed in this section?

c. Roleplay a telephone call from the Walkers to Mr. Martinez.

d. Assume the Walkers withheld one month's rent and the landlord brought the case to court. If you were the judge, what would you do?

What Landlords Can
Do When Things Go Wrong

While there are many situations in which tenants may have problems with a landlord, there are also times when tenants don't live up to their responsibilities. When a tenant breaks apartment rules or fails to fulfill conditions in the lease, the landlord has a number

of remedies. These include ending the lease, eviction, and court action.

Ending the Lease   Landlords and tenants sometimes come into conflict at the end of a lease. In most places, unless there is a clause that automatically continues the lease, or the landlord has agreed to a new lease, the tenant must move out when the term of the lease is over. If tenants do not move at the end of the lease, the landlord has three choices. First, the landlord can take the tenants to court and ask to have them evicted. That is, the landlord can take legal action to have the tenants forced off the property. Second, the landlord can let the tenants stay in the apartment as **holdover tenants**. In many states, if tenants stay on after the lease is over, the landlord has the right to hold tenants to a new lease identical to the one just ended. Third, a tenant who stays on beyond the end of the lease becomes a tenant at will in some states. This means that either the landlord or the tenant can end the lease with whatever notice the law requires—typically thirty days.

The most important thing for tenants to do when they decide to move is to give the landlord adequate notice. Notice should be given in a letter and a copy should be kept. If there is a month-to-month lease, the landlord should be notified thirty days before the rent is next due. If the lease is for a fixed period, such as one year, the notice should be given at least thirty days before the end of the term.

A common, but more serious, problem arises when a tenant seeks to leave before the end of the lease.

PROBLEM 20

a. Walden signed a two-year lease for $200 a month. After six months, she decided to get married and wants to get out of the lease. What choices does she have?

b. Larkin signed a one-year lease for an apartment near his college. After six months he decided to move back on campus and just packed up and left. Is there anything the landlord can do?

If a tenant has to move out before the end of a lease, it is always best to talk with the landlord and try to get a release. A landlord and tenant can always end a lease by mutual agreement, and, in most cases, this is probably what happens.

Another option for the tenant is to sublet the apartment. While landlords often agree to let the tenants out of a lease or allow a sublease, they don't have to do this. If a tenant moves out or abandons an apartment without the landlord's permission, the landlord has the right to sue the tenant for damages in court. However, in most places the landlord is required to try to rent the apartment to another tenant. The landlord cannot let the apartment sit empty for eighteen months and expect a court to award the full rent. If the landlord rerents the apartment for the remainder of the lease, the original tenant will have to pay only for the period of time during which the apartment was vacant.

Eviction   Eviction is the legal process of having a tenant removed from the property. There are a number of situations that may give a landlord the right to evict a tenant. The most common reason for eviction is a failure by the tenant to pay the rent. However, any serious breach of the lease can give the landlord cause for eviction.

When a tenant fails to pay the rent, the landlord may sue the tenant for the overdue rent and/or start legal action to have the tenant removed. The landlord cannot take the law into his or her own hands and physically throw the tenant out but must always file a case in court. A tenant who does not have the money to pay the rent or who intends to pay the rent late should always contact the landlord and explain the problem. Many landlords are willing to accept overdue rent or partial payments. Even if the landlord has started the eviction process, the tenant can usually stop the legal action by paying the amount owed plus any late fees or court costs.

Landlord-Tenant Court Process   Tenants may not be evicted unless the landlord files a case against them in court. In some places, this court is part of the regular civil court system. In other places, evictions are handled by special courts or landlord-tenant commissions. Landlord-tenant courts are often called summary courts because they attempt to process cases quickly. In many places cases are heard in just a few days or weeks after they are filed.

Eviction procedures vary from state to state. However, the eviction process usually includes the following steps:

1. *Notice*—Before being evicted, the tenant must be given a written **notice** to quit (leave). This notice is a warning that unless the tenant corrects the problem (for example, removes a dog that violates a "no pet" rule), eviction action will be started. Leases often contain clauses through which tenants waive their right to this written notice when they don't pay their rent.

2. *Complaint*—If the tenant does not meet the deadline for correcting the problem, the landlord may file a complaint in court, seeking an order to have the tenant removed from the apartment.

3. *Summons*—After the landlord files the complaint, an officer of the court will serve a summons informing the tenant of the eviction action and setting a date to appear in court. *A tenant should never ignore a summons. Many tenants have defenses to a suit for eviction, but a failure to show up in court automatically results in a judgment in favor of the landlord.* In rare cases, a default judgment

FIGURE 18   Landlord-Tenant Court Process

```
                              Settled
                                |
                                |
                                |
                            Informal
                          Negotiation
                                |
                                |
                                |
   ┌──────────┐   ┌──────────┐
   │ Complaint│   │ Summons  │
   │ Filed by │ → │ Served   │ ────────→  ┌──────────┐
   │ Landlord │   │ on Tenant│            │1st Court │
   └──────────┘   └──────────┘            │Appearance│
                                          └──────────┘
              If Tenant                         If Tenant
              Doesn't                           Shows Up
              Show Up
                │                    │                      │
           ┌────────┐          ┌──────────┐          ┌──────────┐
           │Default │          │Negotiation│         │Sets Trial│
           │Entered │          └──────────┘          │  Date    │
           └────────┘                                └──────────┘
                │                    │                      │
             Evicted              Settled                 Trial
```

may be set aside if the tenant had a good reason for the failure to attend.

4. *Court Appearance*—Tenants should always go to court on the date set in the summons. When tenants appear in court, they are entitled to file an answer to the complaint. This is a written explanation of why the tenant should not be evicted. Another important reason for showing up is that tenants may be able to reach a settlement with the landlord. For example, if the rent is overdue, the landlord might agree to a late payment.

5. *Trial*—If a tenant decides to defend against the eviction action, there will be a trial. Although most cases are decided by a judge, the U.S. Supreme Court has stated that tenants have a right to a jury trial. Possible defenses are that the tenant has paid the rent or has not otherwise broken any provision in the lease. In most states, tenants may also defend by saying that the landlord has failed to make needed major repairs.

6. *Eviction*—If the case is decided in favor of the landlord, the court will issue an order telling the tenant to move out by a certain date. If the tenant does not move out voluntarily, the local sheriff can physically remove tenants and their belongings.

7. *Legal Help*—A tenant who receives a summons or notice to quit should seek legal help immediately. Tenants who cannot afford a private attorney should contact the nearest legal aid or legal services office. If this cannot be done ahead of time, a tenant who shows up in court may be able to have a lawyer appointed by the judge.

PROBLEM 21

Bill Williams has always paid his rent on time, but because of his wife's sudden illness and resulting medical bills he is unable to pay this month's rent.

a. What can Bill do? If the landlord files a suit for eviction, what can Bill do? What can Bill do if he wants a lawyer but can't afford one?

b. For what other reasons might a tenant be unable to pay the rent? If you were a judge in landlord-tenant court, which, if any, of these reasons would you consider valid excuses.

c. Do you think the typical eviction process is fair to both landlord and tenant?

Retaliatory Evictions   Sometimes landlords try to evict tenants because they make complaints or otherwise organize against the landlord. Called **retaliatory eviction**, this action has been ruled illegal in most states.

<table>
<tr><td>

WHERE YOU LIVE

Is there a landlord-tenant court in your community? If so, where is it located and what procedures does it follow? Is there a legal aid or legal services office in your area that represents tenants?

</td></tr>
</table>

For what reasons might a landlord evict a tenant?

WHERE
YOU
LIVE

What is the law in your state regarding retaliatory evictions?

THE CASE OF EDWARDS v. HABIB

Ms. Edwards rented a house from Mr. Habib on a month-to-month basis. Shortly after she moved in, she called the city housing inspector and reported a number of unsanitary conditions. When an inspector came to investigate, he found more than forty housing code violations. The landlord was ordered to correct them.

Instead of making the repairs, Habib gave Ms. Edwards notice that he was ending the lease and that she must move within thirty days. She went to court, claiming that the eviction notice had been given as revenge for her report of the code violations. She said that the First Amendment to the U.S. Constitution gives citizens the right to petition the government and that Mr. Habib was interfering with this right.

Mr. Habib claimed his actions were legal because, according to the law, a month-to-month lease can be ended merely by giving the tenant a proper thirty-day notice without stating any reasons for the action.

PROBLEM 22

a. With whom do you agree, Ms. Edwards or Mr. Habib? Why?

b. List all the arguments in favor of Mr. Habib and in favor of Ms. Edwards. Which is the best argument?

c. If you were a judge, how would you decide this case? Explain your decision.

d. If there were no code violations, could Mr. Habib then evict Ms. Edwards? Should a landlord be able to evict a tenant for any reason?

BUYING A HOME

Many people think the idea of buying a place to live is something that they should not consider. This may be because they are young or because they don't have much money. However, some young people and others, even though they are not wealthy, are able to buy a home through the assistance of government loan programs, personal loans, and other means. In addition, even those who are renting a place should understand the financial, legal, and other important issues involved in owning a place to live. These issues affect their landlords, and, therefore, indirectly affect renters.

Things to Consider Before Buying

Once a person decides to buy a home, there are many things to consider. These include the type of area where the buyer wishes to live and whether the buyer wants to live in a house, an apartment, or some other type of dwelling. When considering purchase of a

home, many people only think of single-family homes, but condominiums, cooperatives, and mobile homes are other alternatives.

A **condominium** is a form of ownership. Any type of building
may be a condominium, but most condominiums are attached
units in apartment buildings or townhouses. Each resident owns
an individual apartment or townhouse. The rest of the property
including hallways, lobbies, elevators, grounds, and parking areas
are owned jointly by all the residents. A person who buys a condominium makes monthly mortgage payments and also pays a
maintenance fee to take care of the jointly owned area.

Condominiums have some of the advantages of both owning
and renting. The condominium owner has the economic advantages of ownership—tax benefits, resale potential, and rise in
value. However, like a renter, the owner of a condominium is also
free of responsibility for maintenance and upkeep of the grounds or
common areas. In addition, like an apartment building many of
the newer condominiums offer extra facilities such as swimming
pools, health clubs, or recreation areas.

Another alternative form of ownership is the **cooperative**. With
cooperative ownership the land and building are owned collec-
tively. Each resident buys shares in a business corporation and is

Mobile homes are an alternative form of housing.

given the right to occupy an individual apartment. A resident of a cooperative does not own his or her apartment but owns a share of the total building. Owners are subject to rules set by the community as a whole and unlike the owner of a condominium the resident of a cooperative may not sell to another person without the approval of the other residents.

Cooperatives are often older buildings in cities where tenants get together, buy the building from the landlord, and restore it. Because cooperatives and condominiums are new forms of ownership, people considering this type of living space should be particularly careful and get good legal and financial advice before buying. Nevertheless, these types of homes may be a good investment and generally cost less. In fact the U.S. Department of Housing and Urban Development (HUD) estimates that over eight million Americans now live in condominiums or cooperatives.

Mobile homes are a low cost alternative to more traditional types of housing. Besides costing less than conventional homes, most mobile homes come furnished, carpeted, and complete with all appliances. Despite what the name implies, most mobile homes don't move around much, rather they are built in a factory and moved to a site where they usually remain.

Like condominiums and cooperatives, mobile homes have become more popular as single-family homes have risen in price. There are, however, certain drawbacks to mobile home ownership. First, mobile homes are financed more like cars than houses. Loans to buy a mobile home are typically for a shorter period than are home mortgages and the buyer is usually charged a higher rate of interest. Second, once you buy a mobile home, you must find someplace to put it. Finally, because some mobile homes are poorly constructed, buyers must be careful to check out the dealer's reputation for service and the warranty that accompanies their mobile home.

After a decision is made about the general area and type of housing desired the buyer should consider the size, quality, and special features they want in a home. Homebuyers should ask themselves the following questions: Are there certain things you must have in a home, such as a modern kitchen, a big yard, an extra bathroom, or a garage? Do you want a new home or an older home? If you buy an older home does it need repairs or modernization? If it needs repairs can you fix it up yourself or will you have to hire someone to do the work?

How much you can afford is an all-important consideration. Homebuyers should consult a banker, real estate agent, or attorney to determine their general price range. Finally, buyers must weigh all the costs associated with buying a home. They should consider the price of the house, but they should also consider the costs of taxes, insurance, maintenance, and travel to and from work.

PROBLEM 23

a. What are some of the factors that should be considered when planning to buy a home?
b. What are the advantages and disadvantages of condominiums, cooperatives, and mobile homes?
c. Read the real estate ads in your local newspaper. What do these ads say about costs and financing? What types of housing are available in your community?

Realtors can help both the buyer and the seller.

Steps to Take in Buying

Real estate agents are representatives of sellers who allow the agents to offer their home. In return, the agents are paid a commission (usually a percentage of the total price, such as six percent) once the house is sold. Buyers should realize that agents wish to sell houses, and, like salespeople in other consumer situations, they may sometimes exaggerate the facts to make a home sound better than it is. At the same time, agents can be very helpful to buyers.

Buying a house sometimes seems very complicated. Agents who do it on a regular basis can be helpful with such matters as finding homes that fit a buyer's special needs or explaining about particular neighborhoods. Agents can also advise about or even help arrange financing and explain local real estate procedures. Ask friends who have used agents and find out which ones they've been satisfied with and would recommend.

Shopping for a Home   As in any consumer purchase, a buyer's chances of obtaining a good buy will probably increase depending on the amount of time spent looking at different homes. Using more than one real estate agent may help in this effort, as well as checking out newspaper listings where real estate companies and other sellers advertise homes. It is sometimes possible to buy a home at a reduced price if you purchase directly from a seller. This is because people who sell their own home do not have to pay a commission to a real estate agent.

An important part of homebuying is determining the present condition of the home. How well is it constructed? Are repairs needed? Is any kind of warranty given? Is it worth the price asked? Once buyers find a home that they like, it is advisable to have an expert inspect the home and determine if there are structural or other problems. These inspectors may also be able to determine how much the house is worth through what is called an **appraisal**. (This differs from the appraisal the bank or other organization does when considering giving the buyer a mortgage.)

Making an Offer If you wish to make an offer on a home, a **sales contract** or *purchase agreement* should be written up and presented to the seller. (Note that some sellers may accept a lower price than the list price.) This offer is sometimes called a **binder** and is usually accompanied by a deposit check, which may go to the seller if the buyer later backs out of the agreement. The sales contract should be reviewed by a lawyer or someone else experienced in buying homes. This is important because all the major terms of sale, including cost, financing arrangements, what comes with the house, and what condition the house will be in when it is turned over, will be determined by this contract. Buyers should always state that their offer is only good if a mortgage can be obtained within a certain period of time. When the seller agrees to and signs the buyer's offer or binder, it becomes a contract that can be enforced in court by either party.

Obtaining a Loan After the contract is signed, the buyer applies to banks, credit unions, insurance companies, or others for approval on a mortgage loan. Comparison shopping is also important here because the interest rate on the loan can vary. A small difference may result in thousands of dollars over the term of the mortgage. Table 4 shows how different interest rates make a big difference in how much buyers pay each month. What can you conclude from this table about shopping for a mortgage loan?

TABLE 4 **Comparing Mortgage Interest Rates**

Cost of House	Down Payment %	Down Payment $	Loan Amount	Years	Monthly Payments at: 11%	13%	14.5%	15%
	10%	$ 6,000	$54,000	30	524.15	597.78	661.50	683.10
$60,000	20	12,000	48,000	30	457.44	531.36	588.00	607.20
	25	15,000	45,000	30	428.85	498.15	551.25	569.25

Buyers usually pay the same amount of money each month for the entire period of the loan. For most buyers it is much easier in the future to make the payments than it is at first. New types of mortgages called **flexible payment mortgages** are sometimes arranged so that buyers pay less in early years, when the buyers' salaries are often lower, and more in future years, when the buyers may be making more money. There are also **variable rate mortgages**, which change the payment when interest rates in an area rise or fall over the years. This can help or hurt buyers, depending on whether interest rates go up or down in future years.

Buyers should explore the possibility of **assuming a mortgage**. A mortgage is assumed when the seller and whoever holds the mortgage (e.g., the bank) allows the buyer to take it over at the old interest rate. Also worth investigating is whether the seller will agree to take back or hold the mortgage for the buyer. In both situations, the buyer will not have to shop around for a mortgage.

In obtaining financing, all the considerations involving credit (discussed in Chapter 3) come into play, including the legal protections against discrimination because of race, color, religion, national origin, sex, marital status, and age (if old enough to enter into a contract).

Buyers trying to finance a home should also consider whether or not they are eligible for a government-insured loan. The most common sources of government assistance are the Veteran's Administration (VA) and the Federal Housing Administration (FHA). Both agencies encourage banks and other lenders to give people loans that otherwise might not be approved. The government does this by telling the lender that it will *insure* the mortgage loan, meaning that if the buyer fails, or is unable, to pay, the government will.

VA loans are available only to veterans of the armed forces, their spouses, or dependents. They require little or no cash down payment and usually have a lower interest rate than the normal mortgage rate. FHA loans assist people who otherwise could not obtain a mortgage due to limited income or insufficient cash for a down payment. The cash down payment required is less than normal (often three to five percent instead of twenty to thirty percent of the total price), and the interest rate may be slightly less than usual.

Another federal agency, the Farmer's Home Administration, loans money directly to buyers in rural areas (having a population of 20,000 or less and being outside a city). This program may also require a smaller down payment and lower interest.

The federal government and some state and local governments are promoting the rehabilitation of older housing by loan programs to help pay for restoration. These programs come through the Department of Housing and Urban Development on the federal level, and state and local housing agencies elsewhere. They often give low-interest loans either to present or new homeowners. One program in some cities is called **homesteading**, whereby older homes in run-down areas are sold to people for low prices (one dollar in some places), if they promise to live in and repair them.

One criticism of government housing programs is the amount of paperwork and the long waiting periods involved. It is not always true that it takes a long time to get loans approved in government programs. However, banks and others who give mortgages generally process loan applications faster than government agencies do.

Another possible problem with VA and FHA mortgages is that the seller is sometimes required to pay **points**, a percentage (e.g., one or two percent) of the entire loan before the loan will be granted. This may reduce the seller's profit and result in some sellers refusing to sell to buyers who wish to get a VA or FHA mortgage.

WHERE YOU LIVE

What federal, state, or local housing agencies exist in your area? Do they have mortgage loan or housing rehabilitation programs? How do they operate?

Title Searches and Insurance   Before the buyer can move into the new home, a lawyer or title company—depending on local practices—must check government land records to make sure the seller has the right to *convey* or give good **title** or ownership regarding this property. The buyers usually will have to pay for this service, called a **title search**. (Buyers should again comparison shop on lawyer fees and all other costs associated with the sale of a home.)

Land records will not necessarily tell the whole story. At some time in the past, there may have been a sale of the home or some other action that gave another person some right to own part or all of the property. If a bank or another organization is giving a mortgage as part of the sale, they will require the buyers to take out and pay for **title insurance** against such a claim ever arising. Buyers should also consider taking out owner's title insurance, which protects their own interest and not just the bank's.

During the period before the house is officially turned over, the buyers should also arrange for homeowner's insurance. This protects them from fire, theft, or other problems that may occur after they move in. Homeowner's insurance also protects the organization giving the mortgage loan, which will probably require that the mortgage loan be paid out of the insurance settlement if there is a fire or other catastrophe.

Closing or Settlement   The **closing** is the final meeting at which the papers are officially signed and the buyer becomes the new owner. It is ordinarily thirty to ninety days after the signing of the sales contract but can be whenever the buyer and seller agree. At this time, buyers, sellers, their spouses, their agents, and lawyers, if any, are present. Any cash owed by the buyer is paid. There are certain charges, called **closing costs,** which must be paid at this time. These costs include title search fees, attorney fees, points, costs of recording deeds and mortgage notes, and insurance. Under a federal law known as the *Real Estate Settlement Procedures Act* (RESPA), the buyer must be given an estimate of these charges before closing. However, if this is done just before closing and after most of the work is completed, it is usually too late to shop around to obtain a better price. Therefore, these estimates should be asked for well in advance of the closing.

Recording Deeds and Mortgage   After the closing, an attorney or some other representative of the seller must record the deed or mortgage in the local courthouse, and a new deed identifying the buyer as the new owner should be mailed to the buyer following the closing.

PROBLEM 24

If you were going to buy, examine the steps in buying a home and make a list of all activities for which you might hire a lawyer. Do you think you could do any of these without a lawyer? Could someone else help you do any of them? If so, who?

Problems Associated with Home Buying

The most common problems the new homeowner is likely to encounter are unexpected repairs. If the furnace breaks down, the roof leaks, or the plumbing system backs up, it is possible that the financial benefits of buying a home will quickly disappear.

What are some advantages and disadvantages of a new house? An older house?

The law does not provide great protection in this area, so the best advice is to inspect the home closely before signing a sales contract. This is done best by hiring a professional housing inspector. Most local governments have inspectors who examine newly constructed homes to see if they meet building and safety standards. Within these standards, builders often have the ability to use materials that vary greatly in quality. In older houses and apartments, buyers must be particularly careful because the government usually does not provide any inspections either before or after a sale. In regard to special types of homes, such as mobile homes, the Department of Housing and Urban Development requires that certain standards be met. Buyers should check to see if a state agency has inspected and approved the particular mobile home they are considering buying.

In recent years, people have begun to try to protect themselves from repair problems. This has resulted in some people asking for warranties from the seller or builder (of a new home) just as one would request a warranty on a stereo or television. In some places a buyer can get Home Owner's Warranty (HOW) on a new house for a small fee. Some companies even inspect homes and then offer a warranty for a fee. Buyers should ask that any warranty or other promise regarding the home be in writing.

For many years the law did not protect purchasers of either new or used homes; the general rule was, "Let the buyer beware." This has changed considerably over the past twenty years, and now most states protect the buyers of new homes through an *implied warranty of habitability*. This means that the law implies that the seller of a new home promises that the house was built with "workmanlike construction" and is fit to live in. Therefore, in most states, if a buyer moves in and then finds a major structural defect, such as a leaking roof, the buyer may file suit against the seller. This rule has usually been held to apply equally to houses that were not completed at the time of sale as well as those that were finished.

Most courts have not been willing to require this implied warranty of habitability in the sale of used housing. This is because courts felt that a builder should not be held responsible for problems that occur years after the house was built or that sellers should not be responsible for problems caused before they bought the home. However, in a few states, when the house had never been occupied before, even though the seller was not the builder or the original owner, the courts have held the warranty to exist. Also, in at least one state court, where it was shown that the basement leaked and the basement walls were cracked, an owner was allowed to sue a builder three years after the house was built, even though the owner hadn't lived in the house all three years. In that case, the owner was required to show that this was the first time the defect had shown up and that the builder caused it.

Warranties on homes may become very important if injuries occur as a result of a problem with the house. In one case, a baby was severely burned by hot water from a bathroom tap. The parents were awarded money damages because they were able to prove that the plumbing system had been installed without a ten-dollar mixing valve, which would have regulated the hot and cold water temperatures and prevented the accident.

PROBLEM 25

John and Martha buy a new home from a builder. Their sales contract doesn't provide them with any warranty or make any promises regarding repairs.

a. If the following things go wrong, should the builder or the homeowner pay for the damages?
—a refrigerator that comes with the house breaks after six months
—the toilet backs up after two months
—after a year a stair, made of a poor quality wood, cracks and Martha breaks a leg
—the electrical system can only handle two operating appliances at once
—whenever it rains, the basement floods
—pipes freeze in the winter and break

b. If the house Martha and John own is twenty years old, would any of your answers to the first question change?

c. What could Martha and John have done before they signed the sales contract to prevent any or all of the problems mentioned in the first part of this question?

Rehabilitation of Older Housing

In recent years, the trend in many American cities and towns has been to restore and redevelop older homes and neighborhoods. Citizens have discovered that older buildings are an important part of a city's special identity and character. Moreover, home-buyers have been attracted by the lower prices and the convenience of inner-city living. As a result of this trend, thousands of townhouses and decayed urban dwellings have been restored in neighborhoods throughout the country.

Most people have applauded rehabilitation because it has preserved historic buildings and neighborhoods, brought in needed tax dollars, and reversed the flow of people moving out of the cities. On the other hand, revitalization has also brought problems. The major problem associated with restoration has been the displacement of lower-income residents. As more well-to-do citizens buy up urban properties, tenants and other lower-income residents have been forced to move out. Housing speculation—buying at a low price and then selling a short time later for a large profit—has become common. Likewise, the conversion of apartment buildings into condominiums has resulted in the eviction or displacement of many tenants.

WHERE YOU LIVE

How has the restoration and historic preservation movement affected your community? In what ways has it helped? Has it caused any problems?

Owning a home takes work as well as money.

**WHERE
YOU
LIVE**

What government housing assistance programs are in operation in your area? Are they working? What can be done to improve them?

How to preserve healthy diverse neighborhoods, which offer housing for lower-income people as well as the middle class, has become one of the biggest issues facing many cities. City officials, neighborhood activists, and government agencies have started a number of programs to help displaced families and to give lower-income residents a share in urban restoration. These programs have included funds for subsidized housing, grants to help low-income residents buy their own homes, repair programs to help moderate-income homeowners keep pace with wealthier neighbors, and relocation assistance for families forced to move.

Housing for Low- and Moderate-Income Persons

People with low and moderate incomes often have difficulty finding decent housing that they can afford. Therefore, federal, state, and local governments have developed programs designed to provide opportunities for such families to rent apartments or buy houses at prices suitable to their incomes. These programs include:

1. Building public housing where rent is charged in accordance with a person's ability to pay (the government pays whatever else it takes to support the project)

2. Paying subsidies to landlords who rent to low- and moderate-income persons

3. Giving interest or tax discounts as encouragement to builders who construct housing for low- and moderate-income persons.

4. Giving cash payments directly to poor persons so that they can afford to find and obtain standard housing on the private housing market

A person interested in a home under one of these programs should go to the local housing, social welfare, or human resources agency. Even if one of these agencies does not administer a housing program, agency personnel should know where to apply. Also, free counseling and advice on housing is provided by local offices of the U.S. Department of Housing and Urban Development (HUD).

Government agencies have detailed rules—based primarily on family income—to determine who is eligible for government-sponsored housing. Even when a person or family satisfies the eligibility standards, housing may not be immediately available. In such cases, the applicant may be placed on a long waiting list. Some cities give preference to the elderly, minorities, persons displaced because of government projects, or families with small children. If a housing agency decides that a person or family does

not meet the income standards, they may be able to appeal. The applicant should ask the agency for a personal interview or hearing to discuss the particular facts of the case.

PROBLEM 26

a. What are the advantages and disadvantages of each type of government housing assistance programs?

b. Assume that you are in charge of housing for poor people in your area and have a three-million-dollar budget for the next year. Decide exactly how you would spend this money, and explain your decision. Who would be eligible for assistance and where in your area would you build any housing projects?

six
INDIVIDUAL
RIGHTS
AND
LIBERTIES

The Constitution of the United States establishes the framework of our federal government with the executive, legislative, and judicial branches. It also guarantees each American citizen certain basic rights. The most important of these rights is found in the first ten amendments of the Constitution, known as the Bill of Rights, and in the Fourteenth Amendment's due process and equal protection clauses.

The original Constitution approved by the states contained only a few provisions guaranteeing the basic rights of individuals. However, citizens in the thirteen states pressured their leaders to add a Bill of Rights. In response, the first ten amendments were approved by the First Congress in 1791 and then quickly ratified by the states. Of these amendments, eight state specific rights which the federal government must grant its individual citizens; two deal more generally with the rights of the people and of the states.

The Fourteenth Amendment was ratified in 1868, just after the Civil War, in an attempt to assure equal rights for former slaves. It required the states to provide "due process of law" and "equal protection of the laws" to all citizens within their jurisdictions.

271

You have already studied some of the individual rights contained in these amendments (e.g., the right to an attorney in a criminal case and the right to be free from unreasonable searches and seizures). Other basic rights, such as freedom of speech and freedom of the press are probably not completely new to you either.

One of the most remarkable features of our Constitution is its endurance. In fact it is the oldest written national constitution in the world. In 1819, Supreme Court Justice John Marshall wrote that the Constitution was "intended to endure for ages to come, and consequently to be adapted to the various crises of human affairs." Therefore, while the language of the Bill of Rights has remained the same, the meanings of the various freedoms have changed to meet new concepts of fairness and justice.

Before studying this area of law, you should keep three basic ideas in mind. First of all, even those rights guaranteed in the Constitution are not, and cannot be, absolute. As we shall see, the totally free exercise of certain rights would, in some instances, restrict the rights of others. For example, suppose someone, as a joke, yells "fire" in a crowded movie theater, creating a danger to persons in the theater. The First Amendment right of freedom of speech would not protect that person against arrest. In deciding such a case, the courts often must balance one right or interest against another. In this case a court would weigh the public danger created against the individual's freedom of speech. Protecting the public from this danger is more important than protecting this individual's right to freedom of speech, so the speaker could be arrested.

Second, in reading the Constitution you will see that the amendments usually restrict "Congress" or "the State" from taking away basic rights. While the Constitution protects citizens from certain actions by the government (federal, state, or local), its protection does not extend to situations that are purely private in nature (i.e., actions by private citizens, businesses, or organizations). For example, the Fourth Amendment protects against unreasonable searches and seizures by the government but not against searches and seizures by private individuals. Therefore, if a

neighbor comes into your house and seizes your television, this *does not* violate your Fourth Amendment rights, though it may constitute the crime of larceny. As you will see later in this chapter, much private discrimination, though not unconstitutional, *does* violate federal civil rights laws passed by Congress.

Third, remember that enforcing certain rights can be time-consuming and expensive. Before deciding whether to try to enforce a right, you should be aware of the time and money involved and weigh these costs against the importance of the right.

This chapter will focus on individual rights issues in the following areas: freedom of speech and expression; freedom of the press; freedom of association; freedom to assemble peacefully and to petition the government; freedom of religion; and the rights to privacy, due process, and equal protection. These freedoms are probably the most important rights we have, for without them all other rights would be meaningless.

FREEDOM OF SPEECH

Congress shall make no law . . . abridging the freedom of speech or of the press or the right of the people peaceably to assemble, and to petition the government for redress of grievances.

—First Amendment

Freedom of speech guarantees the right to communicate information or ideas by speech, writing, art, newspapers, television, radio, and other media. The Constitution protects not only the person *making* the communication but also the one *receiving* it. Therefore, the First Amendment includes a right to hear, see, read, and, in general, to be exposed to different points of view.

As already mentioned, freedom of speech is not absolute and was not intended to be. However, expressing an opinion or point of view will usually be protected under the First Amendment, even if most people disagree with the speaker's message. It is important to remember that the First Amendment was designed to insure that there would be a free marketplace of ideas in which even unpopular views would be represented.

Speech, press, assembly, and petition rights enable and encourage citizens to express and obtain a diversity of thoughts and opinions, to make political decisions, and to communicate these to their government. In short, the First Amendment is the heart of an open, democratic society.

Conflicts involving freedom of expression are among the most difficult ones that courts are asked to resolve. Frequently these cases represent a clash of fundamental values. For example, how should the law respond to a speaker who wishes to make an unpopular statement, even though it may arouse listeners to react violently? Do police stop the speaker or try to control the crowd? Courts must balance the need for peace and public order against the fundamental right to express one's point of view.

PROBLEM 1

a. A famous Supreme Court justice once wrote that the most important value of free expression is "not free thought for those who agree with us, but freedom for the thought we hate." What did the justice mean by this? Do you agree or disagree?

b. Can you think of any public statements or expressions of public opinion that made you angry? How did you feel about protecting the speaker's right to freedom of expression? What is the value of hearing opinions you dislike? What is the danger of suppressing unpopular thought?

Political rallies are a form of free speech.

The language of the First Amendment appears to make its protection absolute (i.e., "Congress shall make *no* law . . ."). However, freedom of speech has at times been limited by government action. To understand these limits you should be familiar with several exceptions to the rule of protecting all expression. These exceptions include: obscenity, defamation, and fighting words.

Obscenity

The portrayal of sex in art, literature, and movies has always been a troublesome topic in our society. Critics say that certain expression is pornographic or obscene and should be barred. Others say that such expression, regardless of its content, should be protected by the First Amendment. Courts have had a difficult time defining obscenity. However, the Supreme Court has permitted expression to be censored as obscene if

1. the average person, applying the standards of his or her community, feels that the work, taken as a whole, appeals to a *prurient* (lewd) interest in sex;

2. the work describes, in an openly offensive way, sexual conduct specifically prohibited by the state's obscenity law; and

3. the work does not, as a whole, have serious literary, artistic, political, or scientific value.

When a state tries to ban pornography it is up to a jury to decide whether or not the expression is obscene according to these standards. The Supreme Court has given juries much *discretion* (free choice) in determining whether the expression is obscene.

Should the government be allowed to ban or censor books, magazines, or movies that are obscene or pornographic? Who should decide if a book or movie is pornographic? How would you define obscenity?

Defamation

The First Amendment does not protect defamatory expression. **Defamation** is expression about a person that is false and damages that person's reputation. When defamation is in spoken form it is called **slander;** when written it is called **libel**. For example, assume a patient said that her doctor's carelessness had caused the death of other patients and others heard this, thus damaging the doctor's reputation. The doctor could sue the patient for slander. If the patient's expression had been in the form of a letter communicated to others, the suit would be for libel. However, if a damaging statement—written or spoken—is proved to be true, the plaintiff cannot win in court.

The Supreme Court has set up special rules that make it more difficult for public officials or public figures to win a defamation suit. Persons communicating about public figures or officials are given broader protection because the Court has recognized the people's right to know about public (as opposed to purely private) affairs. A public official or public figure can win a libel or slander suit *only* if the expression was false, damaging, and made with either malice or *reckless* (an almost intentional) disregard for the truth.

PROBLEM 3

In 1960 a civil rights group took out a full-page ad in the *New York Times* to solicit funds for a right-to-vote campaign in Montgomery, Alabama. The ad contained a list of complaints about the behavior of the Montgomery police force.

The Montgomery chief of police sued the newspaper and the sponsors of the ad. He contended that the complaints about his police force had harmed his reputation. At the trial, it turned out that some of the statements made about the police force were untrue.

a. If the chief can prove harm to his reputation, should he be able to win his libel suit?

b. What effect might his winning the suit have on news coverage? What effect might his losing have on news coverage?

Fighting Words

Finally, the First Amendment does not protect expression when a speaker uses words that are so abusive or threatening as to amount to what the Court has called fighting words. These are words spoken face-to-face that are likely to cause a breach of the peace between the speaker and the person spoken to. Fighting words can be thought of as a verbal slap in the face. Such expression is more like an assault than like information or an opinion whose communication is safeguarded by the Constitution. For example, in 1942, a person was arrested for calling a city official a "goddamned racketeer" and a "damned Fascist." He was convicted because his language had been words "likely to cause an average addressee to fight."

Vagueness

Courts have also ruled that laws imposing restraints on free speech must be clear and specific enough that a reasonable person can understand what expression is prohibited. These laws also need to be clear so that police can enforce them in a nondiscriminatory way. Convictions based on vague, overbroad statutes have been reversed by courts, even if the speaker's expression could have been prohibited under a clearer or more narrowly drafted law. In addition to the rule against vagueness, some actions that may not appear to be speech are sometimes given First Amendment protection. Foremost among these is "symbolic speech."

Symbolic Speech

Conduct that is designed to express an idea is, in some instances, considered to be "symbolic speech" by the courts. While speech is commonly thought of as verbal expression, we have all heard of nonverbal communication. Examples of symbolic speech include sit-ins, demonstrations, and the wearing of armbands or protest buttons. Not all forms of nonverbal communication are protected by the Constitution, particularly if the conduct involves illegal or violent action.

PROBLEM 4

In the two cases below, identify the speakers' interests in expressing their positions and the government's interest in regulating their expression. Then decide whether the action in each case should be protected by the First Amendment as symbolic speech.

a. Bill Spence taped peace symbols to both sides of an American flag. When he hung the flag upside down (a symbol of distress or danger) in the window of his apartment, he was arrested and convicted for violating a state law against improper use of the flag.

b. Raoul Ortega feels that discrimination against Hispanic-Americans is widespread. To protest discrimination he throws a rock through the window of a school. Taped to the rock is the message "End Discrimination Now!"

THE FEINER CASE

In 1951 Irving Feiner made a speech on a street corner in a predominantly black neighborhood of Syracuse, New York. A racially mixed crowd of seventy-five to eighty persons gathered to hear the speech, forcing some pedestrians to walk in the street to pass by. In his speech Feiner called the president a "bum," the American Legion a "Nazi Gestapo," and the mayor a "champagne-sipping bum." He said, "Negroes don't have equal rights; they should rise up and fight for them."

The speech produced angry muttering and pushing from some members of the crowd. One man told the two police officers observing the speech that if they did not "get that S.O.B. off the stand," he would do so himself. Police twice asked Feiner to stop the speech and then, when he refused, arrested him for disorderly conduct. The police claimed the arrest was necessary in order to prevent a fight. Was Feiner denied his First Amendment rights? Why or why not?

Offensive Speakers and Hostile Audiences

Cases such as Feiner's are difficult for courts to decide because the speaker advocates an unpopular position and draws a hostile reaction from some or all of the audience. While the government has an obligation to protect First Amendment rights, they must also protect the general welfare and prevent rioting. At different times the Court has relied upon different legal tests to untangle this thorny dilemma.

One of the oldest tests used is the "clear and present danger" test. Using this test, the court looks at the circumstances under which the expression was used and decides whether, in that situation, there was a clear and present danger of a substantial violation of the law. For example, a speech causing an audience to mutter and mill about in disagreement with a speaker does not present a clear and present danger. But a speech that begins to cause a riot does present such a danger.

Another test is called the "balancing" test. In this test the Court balances the individual's interest in free expression against the interest the government seeks to protect by prohibiting the expression.

Most recently the Court has used what is called the "incitement" test. This means that speech can be prohibited only when it is directed toward inciting or producing imminent (soon to happen) lawlessness and is in fact likely to produce such action. For example, a speaker inciting people to commit **treason** (crimes against the government) could be punished. However, mere support of or teaching about a system of government other than ours is protected under the First Amendment.

THE GREGORY CASE

During a period of racial turmoil in 1969, Dick Gregory and a group of civil rights advocates staged a peaceful and orderly march from City Hall to the home of Chicago's mayor. The purpose of the march was to demand desegregation of Chicago's public schools. As the demonstrators marched through the mayor's neighborhood, several thousand bystanders cursed and threatened the marchers. The police, fearful that they could no longer contain the large crowd, asked the demonstrators to disperse. When the demonstrators refused, they were arrested for disorderly conduct.

PROBLEM 5

a. In what ways are the Feiner and Gregory cases similar? In what ways are they different?
b. As a police officer, how would you have handled each situation? Would you have arrested the speaker or demonstrators, or the hecklers?
c. Assume that Feiner and Gregory are convicted for disorderly conduct. As a judge, how would you rule on their appeals?

FREEDOM OF THE PRESS

If it were left to me to decide whether we should have a government without a free press or a free press without a government, I would prefer the latter.

—Thomas Jefferson

The First Amendment's guarantee of freedom of the press protects against the government's denying citizens information from print media (newspapers, magazines, and books) and electronic media (radio, television, and film). Traditionally, courts have been staunch defenders of freedom of the press. For example, in 1966 the Supreme Court said that "justice cannot survive behind walls of silence" in emphasizing our system's distrust of secret trials. In addition to providing information about news events such as criminal trials, the press subjects all of our political and legal institutions to public scrutiny and criticism.

The framers of the Constitution intended to provide the press with broad freedom. This freedom is considered necessary to the establishment of a strong, independent press that provides a variety of information and opinions so that citizens will be well informed on matters of public importance. However, the exercise of this freedom has sometimes put the press on a collision course with other Bill of Rights protections, such as a defendant's right to fair trial or a citizen's right to privacy.

Among the difficult questions government and the press have confronted are: When can the government prevent the press from publishing certain information? When can the government keep

How does a free press serve our society?

the press from obtaining information? When can the government force the press to disclose information it has? Is freedom of the press limited in special settings, such as schools or prisons?

THE CASE OF THE GAG ORDER

In 1975 six members of a family were found brutally murdered in their home in a small Nebraska town. The man regarded as the prime suspect was arrested the day after the murder. In the next few days publicity about the case was so extensive that lawyers for both sides feared that it would be impossible to provide the defendant with a fair trial. The trial judge issued a "gag order," which prohibited everyone attending pretrial proceedings from releasing "in any form or manner whatsoever any testimony or evidence." Several reporters and broadcast groups went to court to have the gag order declared unconstitutional. Should the gag order be lifted?

Prohibiting Publication

In the Case of the Gag Order, the judge was concerned about protecting the defendant's Sixth Amendment right to a fair trial. The reporters were concerned that the judge had violated their First Amendment right to freedom of the press. This situation presented a conflict between two important Constitutional rights, free press versus fair trial.

This case reached the U.S. Supreme Court in 1976. The Court decided that the gag order was unconstitutional because the trial judge should have taken less drastic steps to lessen the effects of the pretrial publicity. Some of the steps that the Court suggested included: postponing the trial until a later date; moving the trial to another county; asking questions to potential jurors to screen out those with fixed opinions; and carefully instructing the jury to decide the case based only on the evidence introduced at the trial.

The gag order, had it been approved, would have amounted to a **prior restraint** (censorship before publication) on the press. Attempts to censor publications before they go to press are presumed to be unconstitutional by the courts. They can only be approved if (1) publication would cause a certain, serious, and *irreparable* harm; (2) no lesser means would prevent the harm; and (3) the prior restraint would, in fact, work.

In the early 1970s, another example of a government attempt to impose censorship before publication took place when an employee working on a government contract gave several newspapers top secret documents about the Vietnam War. The documents outlined the government's past conduct of the war in Vietnam. The government sued to block publication of the so-called Pentagon Papers, but the Court refused to stop publication, saying that the documents, while perhaps embarrassing, would not cause direct, immediate, and irreparable harm. On the other hand if the documents had, for example, contained a secret plan of attack during a time of war, the Court might have blocked publication.

PROBLEM 6

A state law made it a crime for a newspaper to publish the name of any youth charged as a juvenile offender. A newspaper published an article containing the name of a juvenile charged with the murder of another youth. The newspaper learned the name of the arrested youth by listening to the police radio and by talking to several witnesses to the crime.

a. What is the state's interest in having and enforcing this law?

b. What is the newspaper's interest in publishing the juvenile's name?

c. How should the conflict be resolved?

Denying Access to Information

Another way in which the government tries to control the press is by denying the public access to certain information. Some argue that denying access to information does not violate the rights of the press. Others contend that freedom of the press implies a right to obtain information.

In 1979 the Supreme Court ruled that it was permissible to exclude the press and public from pretrial hearings in criminal cases if done at the request of the prosecution and defendant. This denial of access to information is not considered by the Court to be a violation of the First Amendment. Some trial judges now use this technique, instead of gag orders, to avoid damaging pretrial publicity.

PROBLEM 7

A television station asked permission to inspect and photograph a cellblock in the county jail where a suicide had recently occurred. This section of the jail was also the scene of alleged rapes, beatings, and other serious problems. The county sheriff denied the media's request. The sheriff already allowed a public tour of the jail once a month, although no camera or sound equipment was permitted on such tours. The station went to court, arguing that the sheriff's decision denied their First Amendment rights. How should this

The Federal Communications Commission requires radio and television stations to present both sides of important public issues.

case be decided? Should the press have greater rights to inspect the jail than other citizens?

Requiring the Press to Disclose Information

In addition to preventing publication and denying access, government and the press have argued over the extent to which the First Amendment protects a reporter's sources of information. Reporters contend that requiring them to reveal their sources will make it more difficult to gather and disseminate information, resulting in a press less able to serve the public good. When this problem arises, the freedom of the press comes into conflict with a defendant's right to a fair trial.

THE CASE OF THE SHIELD LAW

In 1976 the New York Times *published a story suggesting that a hospital doctor was guilty of murdering several patients. As a result of the story, New Jersey authorities investigated the case and charged the doctor with murder. Defense attorneys asked the* New York Times *to turn over the names of all the people who had been interviewed during the investigation at the hospital and any other information it had about the case. The defense contended that they could not properly prepare their case without this information. The* New York Times *and the reporter who conducted the investigation refused to turn over any information. They argued that the First Amendment and a New Jersey law which protected a reporter's sources of information allowed them to withhold any unpublished material in their possession. Should the judge allow the reporter to withhold the information sought by the defense attorney? Why or why not?*

FREEDOM OF ASSOCIATION
AND FREEDOM OF ASSEMBLY

The final two rights protected by the First Amendment are freedom of association and the freedom to assemble peacefully and petition the government. Freedom of association means that people have the right to associate with one another and to join or form groups for political, social, economic, or religious purposes. Freedom of association does not appear directly in the Constitution; rather, it grows out of other constitutional rights.

The freedoms of assembly and petition mean that citizens have the right to gather together to demand or request some government action or policy. Citizens exercise these rights in many ways. They write letters to government officials, they lobby in the halls of Congress or their state legislatures, or they hold marches or demonstrations in the streets.

Like other First Amendment freedoms, assembly and petition rights are not absolute. The government may make reasonable rules regarding the time, manner, or place of protests and demonstrations. While government can restrict protests to certain areas or to certain times of day, it cannot prohibit all protests. Nor can government regulate a protest based on what people plan to say.

PROBLEM 8

The American Nazi Party planned a demonstration in the town of Skokie, Illinois. Most of Skokie's residents are Jewish, and many were survivors of Nazi concentration camps during World War II. Many others had lost relatives in the gas chambers. Because of this many residents were strongly opposed to the Nazis demonstrating in their town.

The Constitution protects the right to dissent, but government may regulate the time, manner, and place of public demonstrations.

In order to prevent violence and property damage, the town passed a law that it hoped would keep the Nazis from demonstrating in Skokie. The law required anyone seeking a demonstration permit to first obtain $300,000 in liability insurance, though this requirement could be waived by the town. The law also banned distribution of material promoting racial or religious hatred and prohibited public demonstrations by persons in military-style uniforms. The Nazis challenged the law as a violation of their First Amendment rights.

a. Why would Skokie's Jewish population feel so strongly about this demonstration?

b. Some claimed that the purpose of the demonstration was to incite Skokie's Jews and to inflict emotional harm rather than to communicate ideas. Do you agree or disagree? Should the motive of the speaker affect whether the speech is protected by the Constitution?

c. Does the government have an obligation to protect the rights of the Nazis and other unpopular groups, even if their philosophy would not permit free speech to others? Should Ku Klux Klan or Communist Party rallies have this same protection?

d. How should this case be decided? In what ways, if any, should the town be able to regulate speech and assembly?

EXPRESSION IN SPECIAL PLACES

Schools, military bases, and prisons present special First Amendment problems. When students, military personnel, or inmates express themselves, their rights often come into conflict with the rights of others or interfere with the need to preserve reasonable order. When this happens, courts weigh and balance competing interests based on the facts presented in each case.

THE TINKER CASE

Mary Beth Tinker, her brother John, and three other students wanted to express their opposition to the Vietnam War. They decided to wear black armbands to school as symbols of their objection to the war. Upon learning of this plan, school administrators met and adopted a policy that anyone wearing armbands would be asked to remove them. If they refused, they would be suspended until they returned to school without the armbands. The students wore black armbands to school. Though some students argued over the Vietnam issue in the halls, there was no violence. The five protesting students were suspended from school until they came back without their armbands. Should wearing the armbands be considered a form of free speech protected by the Constitution?

In *Tinker* v. *Des Moines School District* (1969), the U.S. Supreme Court decided that the right to freedom of expression "does not end at the schoolhouse door" and that the wearing of armbands was "symbolic speech" protected by the First Amendment. However, as you have already learned, freedom of speech is not an absolute right. The Court held that the students' right to free speech could be restricted when the school could show that the forbidden conduct would "materially and substantially disrupt" the educational process. For example, a student probably could not insist on giving an antiwar speech in the middle of a biology class. This type of disruption did not occur in reaction to the Tinkers' armbands, nor could it reasonably have been predicted, so their suspensions were unconstitutional.

PROBLEM 9

The following cases involve the rights of student expression. For each case determine (1) whether the precedent established by the *Tinker* decision applies to the case, and (2) how the case should be decided. If you decide the cases differently, explain why.

a. A group of Mexican-American parents were dissatisfied with their school system. They attempted to correct matters through letters and meetings. Students supporting this action wore brown armbands to school. The board immediately passed a rule prohibiting "disruptive, distracting" apparel that would "incite students of other ethnic groups." Several armband-wearing students were suspended. They sued to stop school officials from enforcing this rule.

b. A Cleveland high school had a long-standing rule forbidding the wearing of *all* partisan buttons and badges. Recently, racial tensions had flared in the school as a result of buttons worn by some students. Whenever students wore controversial buttons, school officials required their removal. A junior wore a button encouraging his classmates to attend a "white power" rally. The student refused the principal's request to take off the button and was suspended. He sued to challenge the school's action.

In recent years many cases have raised questions about freedom of the press in schools. As you learned in the *Tinker* case, students carry their constitutional rights with them into school. In some instances, however, freedom of the press may be more limited in school than in the community.

Courts have allowed school administrators to impose prior restraints on student publications if the administrators could reasonably predict that the publication would cause "a material and substantial disruption in the educational process." In addition, administrators can make reasonable rules for the time, manner, and place of distributing publications. However, the courts will examine these rules carefully to insure that they are not unreasonably restrictive or that they do not represent an attempt to suppress unpopular expression.

PROBLEM 10

A student newspaper, supported in part by funds from the county school board, agreed to let the principal review articles before publication. The principal denied permission to print an article entitled "Sexually Active Students Fail to Use Contraceptives" because the school board had banned teaching about birth control from the curriculum. The student editors felt that the First Amendment protected their right to publish this article.

a. Does the First Amendment apply to school publications? Should student publications be treated differently than the daily newspaper in your community? Why or why not?

b. In what ways can school officials regulate a school publication without interfering with First Amendment rights?

c. How would you decide the above case? Give reasons for your decision.

FREEDOM OF RELIGION

Congress shall make no law respecting an establishment of religion, or prohibiting the free exercise thereof . . . .

—First Amendment

The first sixteen words of the First Amendment deal with freedom of religion. The placement of these words at the beginning of the Bill of Rights reflects the deep concern the Founding Fathers had about the relationship between church and state, as well as about individuals' rights to practice their religion freely. Religious freedom is protected by two clauses in the Amendment, the "establishment clause" and the "free exercise clause."

The establishment clause prohibits the government from setting up a state religion. It also prohibits the government from preferring one religion over another or from passing laws that aid or promote religion. The free exercise clause protects the right of individuals to worship or believe as they choose.

Establishment Clause

In discussing the establishment clause, Thomas Jefferson once wrote that there must be a "wall of separation between church and state." However, the wall is not complete. Churches are indirectly aided by government in many ways. For example, church property is exempt from real estate taxes, and churches receive government services such as police and fire protection. In addition, the Supreme Court has permitted states to provide parochial school students with bus transportation and loans of certain textbooks, viewing this as a benefit to the children and their parents, not as a direct benefit to the religious schools.

Much controversy continues to surround the establishment clause. The Court has developed a three-part test to use in deciding whether a law is an unconstitutional violation of the wall of separation.

1. The statute must have a secular (nonreligious) purpose.

2. The primary effect must neither advance nor inhibit (hold back) religion.

3. The operation of the law must not foster excessive involvement of government with religion.

Court cases continue to raise the question of the extent to which government can aid religious schools. In addition to bus transportation and textbook loans, courts have found that providing standardized tests (given and scored by public school employees) and services for students with special needs (at a location other than the private or parochial school) do not violate the three-part test. However, loaning equipment to the schools and providing field trip transportation to destinations chosen by the teachers have both been found to be unconstitutional. The courts felt that these types of aid foster excessive involvement (called *entanglement*) of government with religion. Also, the field trips could have been used for religious activities.

PROBLEM 11

During the Korean War a state board of education decided that a daily prayer should be recited by school children to help them develop the strength to defend the American way of life. The prayer the board developed read: "Almighty God, we acknowledge our dependence upon Thee and we beg Thy blessings upon us, our parents, our teachers, and our country." Several children and their parents challenged the daily prayer as a violation of their freedom of religion.

a. How do you feel about children being required to recite a daily prayer at school? Explain your answer.

b. How would you feel if students could choose a different prayer depending on their religion or could choose not to say any prayer?

c. Does reciting a daily prayer at school constitute an "establishment of religion"?

d. Should the First Amendment forbid all traces of religion in official public life—Christmas carols, the motto "In God We Trust," religious statements by the president?

Free Exercise Clause

When faced with conflicts between an individual's right to free exercise of religion and other important competing interests, the First Amendment claim has not always won. As a rule, religious *belief* is protected, but *actions* based on those beliefs may be restricted if it is in society's interests to do so. For example, the Supreme Court ruled that members of a religion that allowed men to have more than one wife (a violation of the bigamy laws) could not practice this belief in the United States. This decision was based on the Court's opinion that preserving the traditional family is more important than permitting this particular religious practice.

THE AMISH CASE

The state of Wisconsin had a law requiring all children to attend school until age sixteen. However, members of the Amish religion believe that children between the ages of fourteen and sixteen should devote that time to Bible study and training at home in farm work. The Amish believe that high school is "too worldly for their children." State officials prosecuted several Amish parents for not sending their children to school. The parents defended their actions as an exercise of their religion.

Wisconsin v. *Yoder* reached the U.S. Supreme Court in 1972. The Court weighed the rights of the Amish to practice their religion against the state's interest in requiring school attendance. The Court held that, in the case of the Amish, the right to free exercise of one's religion was more important than the two years of required schooling. Among the factors the Court considered was the tendency for Amish children to become employed, law-abiding citizens after completing their religious education.

PROBLEM 12

The following laws restrict, in some way, the free exercise of religion. Balancing the reasons for the law against the individual's interest in religion, which laws would you declare to be unconstitutional?

a. A Tennessee law prohibits "ministers of the Gospel or priests of any denomination whatsoever" from running for the state legislature. A Baptist minister's candidacy is challenged.

b. A state law requires that shops and businesses be closed on Sunday. An Orthodox Jew closes his grocery store on Saturday, the day Jews celebrate their Sabbath, and remains open on Sunday because many of his customers shop then.

c. A city in North Carolina passed an ordinance prohibiting the handling of poisonous reptiles "in such a manner as to endanger public health, safety, and welfare." A religious cult that handled snakes as part of their religion's ceremony refused to obey the law.

d. State law requires that parents provide their children with necessities, including adequate food, clothing, shelter, and medical care. A child is born with a serious illness requiring a blood transfusion in order to live. The child's parents, who are Jehovah's Witnesses, refuse permission for the transfusion because their religion prohibits this medical procedure.

As you may have noticed, the establishment and free exercise clauses relate closely to one another and often come into conflict. Insuring that a law does not establish a religion may cause an interference with free exercise of religion. For example, the controversy over aid to parochial schools has another dimension, namely, does the *failure* to aid parochial schools deprive some persons of the free exercise of their religion? Similarly, laws meant to protect free exercise may appear to establish a religion. For example, Sunday closing laws protect Sunday as a day when individuals can attend church. But to persons whose day of worship is not on Sunday they also appear to be an establishment of religion.

THE RIGHT TO PRIVACY

The makers of our Constitution . . . conferred, against the Government, the right to be let alone—the most comprehensive of rights and the right most valued by civilized men.

　　　　　Olmstead v. *United States*, (1928), dissenting opinion

Today Justice Brandeis's words from the *Olmstead* case continue to have meaning in our daily lives. While the words *right to privacy* or *right to be let alone* cannot be found anywhere in the federal Constitution, most citizens agree that some amount of privacy is a basic right and must be protected.

PROBLEM 13

a. What does privacy mean to you at home? At school? At work? On the phone? In other places?

b. How would you feel if someone listened in on your phone calls, opened your mail before you saw it, or inspected your locker without your permission?

c. In what other ways can your privacy be invaded? How can the law protect the right to privacy?

Since the mid-1960s the Supreme Court has recognized a constitutional right to privacy. The right has been protected both in situations where a citizen has sought to be let alone (as in search and seizure cases), as well as where the citizen wants to make certain kinds of important decisions (such as marriage and family planning) free of government interference.

The Court has said that the Constitution creates "zones of privacy." The zones are derived from guaranties in the Bill of Rights of freedom of speech and association (First Amendment), freedom from unreasonable search and seizure (Fourth Amendment), the right to remain silent (Fifth Amendment), the right to have one's home free of soldiers in peace time (Third Amendment), and the unspecified rights kept by the people (Ninth Amendment).

However, the right to privacy can sometimes come into conflict with other important government interests. For example, the government may need to gather information about individuals in order to solve a crime or to determine eligibility for certain assistance programs. In such cases the government can regulate certain acts or activities, even though an individual's interest in privacy is affected. Deciding whether a constitutional right to privacy exists involves a careful weighing of competing private and government interests.

PROBLEM 14

For each situation below, decide what rights or interests are in conflict and what arguments can be made for each side. Indicate whether you agree or disagree with the law or policy.

a. A public school requires that students obey a dress code and restricts the hair length of boys.

b. The government requires that taxpayers reveal the source of their income, even if it is from illegal activities.

c. A law forbids nude bathing anywhere at a community's beaches.

d. In a prison where there have been several stabbings, inmates are strip-searched every day.

e. A state law requires motorcyclists to wear helmets.

f. The police place a small device in a phone, enabling them to record all numbers dialed on that phone.

g. A state law forbids sexual relations in private between consenting adults of the same sex.

The constitutional right to privacy protects citizens from unreasonable interference by state or federal governments. The privacy rights of citizens are also protected by laws passed by Congress or state legislatures. The Fair Credit Reporting Act (discussed in Chapter 3), for example, gives consumers a right to inspect their credit records and correct any inaccurate information. Do you know of any other laws that protect a person's privacy?

Privacy in the Home

A person's home is, as the saying goes, his or her "castle." Historically, the law has recognized that persons may reasonably expect considerable privacy in their homes. However, in certain instances, such as when police carry out valid search warrants, the privacy of the home may be legally invaded.

THE CASE OF POSSESSING OBSCENE MATERIALS AT HOME

Georgia had a law prohibiting possession of obscene or pornographic films. A man was arrested in his own home for violating this law. He said (and the state prosecutor did not challenge him) that he had the films for his own use and not for sale.

In this case, the Supreme Court recognized a person's right to possess materials, even though they may be "obscene," in one's own home for private use. The Court indicated that individuals have the right to think, observe, and read whatever they please, especially in their own homes.

PROBLEM 15
a. Do you agree or disagree with the Court's opinion?
b. Would you decide the case differently if the man had been showing the obscene films to persons invited into his home? Would your decision be different if he charged people to see the films? Why?
c. Assume a person is arrested for possessing a small amount of illegal marijuana in her home. Could she successfully argue, based on the above case, that the law violates her right to privacy? How are the cases the same? How are they different?

Privacy at School

While the Family Educational Rights and Privacy Act gives students some important rights, courts generally do not extend to students as much of a right to privacy as is given to adults in their homes. For example, many courts have upheld searches of student lockers and desks by reasoning that these items are the property of the school and that students cannot reasonably expect to have privacy in school property.

WHERE YOU LIVE

How do schools in your community notify persons of their privacy rights? What written procedures have been developed to implement this law?

THE CASE OF THE TENTH GRADE DISCIPLINE PROBLEM

Michon, age seventeen, was getting ready to apply to college. Before filling out her college recommendation, the guidance counselor reviewed her school records and found this note from her tenth grade teacher: "Michon has a serious discipline problem. She can't control her talking and will have problems succeeding in school because of this." Her counselor included this remark on the college recommendation form. Is there anything Michon can do about this?

Michon can investigate her files by getting a parent or guardian to ask to see the records. Under the Family Educational Rights and Privacy Act of 1974, parents of students under eighteen and all students eighteen or over or attending post-secondary school have the right to inspect, correct, and control access to most student records. Requests to see school records must be honored within forty-five days. The law also requires that schools develop appropriate written procedures, including notice to parents and students of their rights under this law.

Michon's parents could inspect the records and ask that they be changed if the information was false, misleading, or inappropriate. If their request is denied, they can ask for a hearing. Even if they lose at the hearing, they have a right to put their own explanation of the information in the file.

Federal law prohibits information in school records from being given out without consent of the student or his/her parents.

Privacy on the Job

A number of privacy issues arise when one applies for or holds a job. How much personal information can an employer require from a job applicant or employee? What kind of information can an employer keep in an employee's records? Do future employers have a right to see these records? To what extent can an employer determine an employee's private habits such as dress, grooming, and personal behavior when on the job and during off-duty hours?

> **WHERE YOU LIVE**
>
> Does your state or local government have any laws regarding the use of lie detectors? If so, what are they?

PROBLEM 16

A county police regulation required that a male officer's hair "not touch the ears or the collar except the closely cut hair on the back of the neck." The regulation also limited the length of sideburns and prohibited beards and goatees, although it allowed neatly trimmed mustaches. Patrolman Johnson sued the police department because he felt the regulation was in violation of his rights.

a. What rights or interests are in conflict in this case?

b. What arguments can be made for each side?

c. How would you decide this case? Give your reasons.

d. Should schools require certain dress and grooming standards for students and teachers? Should the military be able to do this for soldiers? Explain.

Except when employers practice discrimination, the law does not do much to regulate the employment practices of *private* business. Some companies, however, have policies that allow open access to personnel records. A few states have passed laws to force business and state government to allow employees to see their records.

In recent years many businesses have used lie detectors, or polygraphs, in an effort to identify dishonest employees. Employers claim this is necessary because employee theft of money and merchandise has risen to $10 billion annually. This cuts into business profits and results in higher prices for consumers. Some employees feel that the use of lie detectors to detect or prevent theft is an unreasonable invasion of their privacy and should be forbidden by law. They claim that the tests are inaccurate and that innocent employees sometimes lose their jobs because of the tests. At least seventeen states have passed laws that limit the use of lie detectors. Other states are considering such laws.

Information Gathering and Privacy

Another privacy problem arises as a direct result of the Computer Age. Computers enable public and private organizations to collect and store detailed information about individuals. Usually individuals are unaware that the information is being collected on them or being given to others.

The federal government's computers contain an astonishing amount of information on individuals. Government figures indicate that there are about 5,000 federal data banks with 3.8 billion entries on identifiable persons. For example, the federal government requires that banks microfilm the front and back of large checks passing through their customer's accounts. In fact, most banks keep copies of *all* checks written or deposited by their customers. While this information can be useful when authorities investigate white-collar crime, it may be unfairly damaging if it falls into the hands of other investigators.

Courts have held that citizens have no right to privacy in their checks or deposit slips, but many people disagree with these decisions. Limited protection is now provided by a federal law passed in 1978. This law requires that a customer receive notice whenever a federal agent seeks a copy of his or her financial records from a bank, savings and loan association, or credit card company. The customer can then ask a federal court to decide whether or not the government's request should be honored. However, the law does *not* protect against requests from state and local governments,

---

THE CASE OF THE FINANCIAL DISCLOSURE LAW

In 1976 Florida voters passed a "Sunshine Law" requiring certain elected officials to make a complete, annual public disclosure of their financial interests. The required disclosure could be either a copy of the person's most recent federal income tax return or a sworn statement identifying each separate source and amount of income over $1,000.

Five state senators sued, arguing that the public's "right to know" was violating their "right to privacy." They also contended that the law placed an unfair burden on political candidates and would deter some people from running for office.

PROBLEM 17
a. Do you think it is important to have disclosure laws for public officials? If so, why?
b. In this case which do you feel is more important, the public's right to know or the individual's right to privacy? Give reasons for your decision.

Data banks are kept by many agencies and organizations such as the Internal Revenue Service, state motor vehicle departments, retail credit companies, the F.B.I., Veterans Administration, state welfare departments, and the armed forces.

private investigators, or credit bureaus to see a person's financial records.

Congressional concern over the collection, use, and dissemination of personal information by federal agencies led to the passage of the Privacy Act of 1974. The act requires, with some exceptions, that federal agencies (1) disclose, on request, what records they have on an individual, (2) allow the individual to correct such records, and (3) not disseminate information without the person's consent, unless it is for a "necessary and lawful purpose." Individuals can sue agencies for violation of their rights under this act.

THE CASE OF THE DAMAGING FILE

Marsha, a member of an organization that opposes the construction of nuclear power plants, believes the FBI has been gathering information on her. She worries that if she applies for a government job, the FBI file may result in her not being hired. Can Marsha find out whether the FBI has a file on her?

In 1977 the act was amended and a Privacy Protection Study Commission was established. The commission's job is to study private and government data collection systems to determine whether additional legislation is needed "to protect the privacy of individuals while meeting the legitimate needs of government and society for information."

DUE PROCESS

No person shall be . . . deprived of life, liberty or property without due process of law . . .

—Fifth Amendment

. . . No state shall . . . deprive any person of life, liberty or property without due process of law . . .

—Fourteenth Amendment

One way in which the Constitution seeks to insure justice is by providing that government follow due process (fair procedures) when dealing with citizens. Due process procedures do not guarantee that the *result* of government action will always be to a citizen's liking. However, these procedures do help prevent arbitrary, unreasonable decisions. The procedures required vary depending on the situation. At a minimum, due process means that a citizen must have some notice of what the government plans to do and be given a chance to comment on the action.

How does due process of law apply to school suspensions?

You are probably familiar with some due process requirements from your knowledge of criminal law. Among the many procedures that the government must follow before sending a defendant to jail (thereby depriving the person of liberty) are: notice of
the charges, an opportunity to be heard at a trial, assistance of a
lawyer, and the right to appeal.

In addition to criminal prosecutions, government takes many
actions that may deprive a person of life, liberty, or property.
Depending on the seriousness of the harm to the citizen, some form
of due process may be required. For example, the state might fire
someone from a government job, revoke a prisoner's parole, or cut
off someone's social security payments. While due process does not
prohibit the government from taking any of these actions, it does
insure that certain procedures will be followed before the action is
taken.

THE CASE OF GOSS v. LOPEZ

*In 1971 widespread student unrest took place in the Columbus, Ohio, public
schools. A number of students who either participated in or were present at
demonstrations held on school grounds were suspended. Many suspensions
were for a period of ten days. Students were not given a hearing before
suspension, though some students and their parents were given informal
conferences with the school principal at a later date. Ohio has a state law
that provides free education to all children between the ages of six and
twenty-one. A number of students, through their parents, sued the board of
education, claiming their right to due process had been violated when they
were suspended without a hearing.*

The Supreme Court decided in the *Goss* case that a student who is
suspended for ten days or less should be offered due process before his
or her suspension. This due process should include: (1) oral or written
notice of the charges; and (2) an explanation (if the student denies the
charges) of the evidence that the school has against him or her, and (3)
an opportunity for the student to present his or her side of the story.

The Court stated that in an emergency situation, the student could be
sent home immediately and a hearing held at a later date. The Court did
not give students a right to a lawyer, a right to cross-examine witnesses,
a right to call witnesses, or a right to a hearing before an impartial person.

In the *Goss* case the Court considered the due process interests of harm,
cost, and risk to arrive at the decision. They ruled that reputations were
harmed and educational opportunities were lost during the suspension;
that the informal hearing would not be overly costly for the schools; and
that while most disciplinary decisions were probably correct, an informal hearing would help reduce the risk of error.

WHERE YOU LIVE

What due process procedures are followed by schools in your area before a student is suspended?

Once it is determined that a person has a right to due process, it must then be determined what process is due. Due process is a flexible concept. The procedures required in a specific situation depend on a balancing of several interests: (1) the seriousness of the harm that might be done to the citizen; (2) the cost to the government, in time and money, of carrying out the procedures; and (3) the risk of making an error without the procedures.

In addition to notice and an opportunity to be heard, due process can include, depending on the situation, a hearing before an impartial person, representation by an attorney, calling witnesses in one's behalf, cross-examination of witnesses, a written decision with reasons based on the evidence introduced, a transcript of the proceeding, and an opportunity to appeal the decision.

If you feel that the government has not followed fair procedures, you may want to consult an attorney. With the attorney's advice and assistance, you could file a complaint directly with the government agency. You may also be able to go to court and seek an order that the government follow due process in dealing with you.

Remember that when the Supreme Court decides a constitutional issue, they set out the *minimum* protection required. No government can offer less. For example, a state could not decide to do away with the "notice" requirement in the *Goss* decision. However schools can (and some do) offer greater due process protections than the Constitution, as interpreted by the Supreme Court, requires.

PROBLEM 18

For each of the following situations, decide whether the citizen should have a constitutional right to due process. If you think there is such a right, what procedures do you think the government should follow?

a. City welfare officials have reasons to believe a person is no longer eligible for welfare. They end payments without a hearing.

b. A defendant, convicted of first degree murder, is sentenced to death. The state supreme court refuses to hear his appeal.

c. A student who is a continual discipline problem is paddled by the teacher. The student is not given a hearing before the paddling.

d. Federal officials plan to build a dam, requiring the flooding of an area where there is now a privately owned farm. The farmer does not want to sell the land or move from her home. No hearing is held, but the farmer is offered the fair market value of her property.

e. A consumer misses two consecutive payments on her car. The finance company takes her car back without any notice or a hearing.

DISCRIMINATION

We hold these Truths to be self-evident, that all Men are created equal, they are endowed by their Creator with certain inalienable rights . . .

—Declaration of Independence

. . . No state shall . . . deny to any person within its jurisdiction the equal protection of the law.

—Fourteenth Amendment

The promise of "equality," as set out in the Declaration of Independence and the Fourteenth Amendment, is one of our nation's most ambitious ideals. But what does equality mean? Is it equal result, equal treatment, equal opportunity, or something else? Citizens claiming they have been denied this promise of equality have flooded the courts and legislatures in recent years. However, the government has found the promise of equality difficult to explain and enforce.

Over time, ideas about equality have changed. For many years the courts held that "equal protection" did not mean that all persons had to have access to the same facilities, such as schools, restaurants, railroad cars, or bus station restrooms. Instead, the law allowed separate facilities for white and blacks so long as the facilities were equal. These old decisions formed the basis of the "separate but equal" doctrine. In the 1954 case of *Brown* v. *Board of Education*, the Supreme Court ruled that separate schools were "inherently unequal" and ordered the public schools integrated "with all deliberate speed." In the years following the *Brown* case, other court decisions and laws required the desegregation of other public facilities as well.

The *Brown* decision started a period of growing national awareness about discrimination. During the twenty-five years following the school desegregation decisions, courts and legislatures were confronted with issues of discrimination based on race, **national origin, alienage**, sex, age, handicap, and income. Unquestionably, the Civil Rights Movement improved the economic and social positions of millions of Americans. However, despite the landmark decisions of the Supreme Court and the civil rights laws passed by Congress, equality remains an elusive goal rather than an accomplished fact. Today society is faced with the problem of how to overcome past discrimination against some (e.g., minorities and women) without causing "reverse discrimination" against others (e.g., whites and males).

The Equal Employment Opportunity Commission works to end discrimination in hiring, promotion, firing, wages, and other conditions of employment.

What is Discrimination?

Many laws discriminate. They do this by classifying people into different groups. Discrimination is an inevitable result of lawmaking. Not all types of discrimination are illegal. So long as classifications are reasonable, they do not violate the equal protection clause.

Everyone is familiar with laws that require a person to be of a certain age in order to obtain a driver's license. These laws discriminate based on age but are not unconstitutional. Persons over a certain age qualify for a license; those under the specified age do not. This classification is considered reasonable. But what if the law required a person to be left-handed in order to get a license? Or what if whites but not blacks, or Polish-Americans but not

Mexican-Americans, could get a license? Would these laws be constitutional? How do they differ from the driver's license law?

PROBLEM 19

Each of the following situations involves some form of discrimination. Decide whether the situation described is reasonable and
should be permitted or unreasonable and should be prohibited. Be
prepared to give your reasons.

a. An airline requires that pilots retire at age fifty.

b. A business refuses to hire a man with good typing skills for a
secretary's position.

c. The owner of a French restaurant wants to hire a head chef. She
only accepts applications from chefs born in France.

d. Persons under eighteen years of age are not allowed into theaters
showing X-rated movies.

e. Women sports reporters are excluded from men's locker rooms
following major league baseball games.

f. A city's bus system is not designed for use by persons in wheel-
chairs.

g. In selecting applicants for a government job, preference is given
to veterans.

h. A girl is not allowed to try out for a position on an all-boy
baseball team.

i. A private club restricts its membership and does not allow whites
to join.

j. Auto insurance rates are higher for young unmarried drivers.

The Fourteenth Amendment provides that no state shall deny
to any person the equal protection of the law. In determining
whether a law or government practice meets this standard of equal
protection, the courts use three different tests, depending upon the
type of discrimination involved.

The Rational Basis Test The standard used to judge most laws
and practices is called the "rational basis" test. Using this test, the
law or practice will be upheld if it is reasonable, that is, if there is
a rational relationship between the classification and the purpose
of the law or practice. For example, not licensing drivers under age
sixteen discriminates against persons under sixteen. This
classification is considered reasonable because there is a rational

relationship between the classification (age) and the purpose of the law (prohibiting immature persons from driving). On the contrary, issuing licenses to left-handers but not right-handers would violate equal protection. The classification has nothing to do with the law's purpose and is, therefore, unreasonable. When courts use the rational basis test, they give wide discretion to the government. In upholding a law or practice judges sometimes say, "This law may not be wise, but it is not irrational or unreasonable. Therefore, it does not violate equal protection."

The Strict Scrutiny Test A law or practice that discriminates based on race, national origin, or alienage is considered to be "inherently suspect." These cases are judged by a more exacting standard called "strict scrutiny." This means that the law or practice will be declared unconstitutional unless the government has a compelling interest requiring the classification. An important reason for this close review is to insure that a person is judged on his or her own merits, not as a member of a group. Also, discrimination based on race, national origin, or alienage typically affects members of minority groups. Because they are of a numerical minority, they are often unable to use the political process to help themselves.

In addition to a compelling interest, the government must have no other less offensive way to achieve the purpose of the law. Issuing driver's licenses to whites but not blacks or to Polish-Americans but not Mexican-Americans would be judged under the strict scrutiny standard. Both of these classifications fail to survive strict scrutiny. While the state may have a compelling interest in highway safety, this is not advanced by a classification based on race or national origin.

Courts also use the strict scrutiny approach to review laws that involve a fundamental right, such as freedom of religion or traveling freely among the states. For example, if a state scheduled an election on a religious holiday, forcing some persons to choose between practicing their religion or voting, courts would use strict scrutiny to resolve the conflict. When this test is used, the person challenging the law or practice is often successful.

The Substantial Relationship Test The Supreme Court uses a third test in reviewing sex discrimination cases. Laws involving sex discrimination must "serve important governmental objectives and must be substantially related to achieving those objectives." In other words, there must be a *close* connection (not merely a *rational* one) between the classification and purpose of the law.

For example, a state law prohibited the sale of beer to males, but not to females, between the ages of eighteen and twenty. The

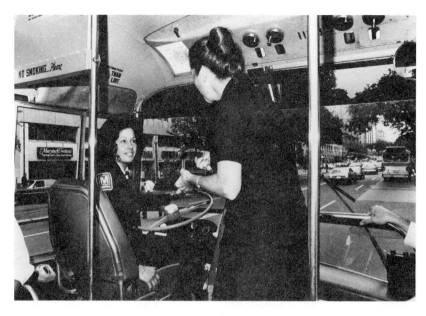

Federal law requires equal pay for equal work, regardless of sex.

reason for the law was that more young males than females had been arrested for drunken driving. However, the law did not prohibit females from buying beer and giving it to males. The Supreme Court found the law to be unconstitutional because there was not a close, substantial relationship between the classification and the law's purpose.

To some extent, the substantial relationship test allows the courts to second-guess the legislature. While the precise meaning of this test is not yet clear, laws and practices that discriminate based on sex will need to be more than reasonable to survive court review.

Equal protection cases are complicated. The courts must first identify the type of discrimination involved and then analyze the problem using the appropriate test. As a general rule, laws and practices are likely to be challenged on equal protection grounds if they discriminate based on race, national origin, alienage, or sex, or if they affect a fundamental right or interest. While many other laws and practices discriminate, few can be successfully challenged under the Fourteenth Amendment.

The Fourteenth Amendment prohibits discrimination by state governments, and the due process clause of the Fifth Amendment prohibits discrimination by the federal government. A *private* act of discrimination is not illegal unless it is prohibited by a specific local, state, or federal law. In the 1960s and 1970s Congress passed some extremely important Civil Rights laws, a number of which are outlined below. These laws were quite far-reaching in prohibiting private discrimination.

Major Federal Civil Rights Laws

Equal Pay Act of 1963

■ Requires equal pay for equal work, regardless of sex

■ Requires that equal work be determined by equal skill, effort, and responsibility under similar working conditions at the same place of employment

■ Requires equal pay when equal work is involved even if different job titles are assigned.

(Enforced by the Wage and Hour Division of the U.S. Department of Labor or by private lawsuit)

Civil Rights Act of 1964 (amended in 1972)

■ Prohibits discrimination based on race, color, religion, or national origin in public accommodations (e.g., hotels, restaurants, movie theaters, sports arenas). Does not apply to private clubs not open to the public.

■ Prohibits discrimination because of race, color, sex, religion, or national origin by businesses with more than fifteen employees or by labor unions. (This section is commonly referred to as Title VII)

■ Prohibits discrimination based on race, color, religion, sex, or national origin by state and local governments and public educational institutions

■ Prohibits discrimination based on race, color, national origin, or sex in any program or activity receiving federal financial assistance, and authorizes termination of federal funding when this ban is violated

■ Permits employment discrimination based on religion, sex, or national origin if it is a necessary qualification of the job

(Enforced by the Equal Employment Opportunity Commission or by private lawsuit)

Voting Rights Act of 1965 (amended in 1970 and 1975)

■ Bans literacy and "good character" tests as requirements of voting

■ Requires bilingual election materials for most voters who don't speak English

■ Reduces residency requirements for voting in federal elections

■ Establishes criminal penalties for harassing voters or interfering with voting rights

(Enforced by the U.S. Civil Rights Commission)

Civil Rights Act of 1968

■ Prohibits discrimination based on race, color, religion, or national origin in the sale or rental of most housing

(Enforced by the Department of Housing and Urban Development or by lawsuit in a federal court)

Age Discrimination in Employment Act of 1967 (amended in 1978)

■ Prohibits arbitrary age discrimination in employment by employers of twenty or more persons, employment agencies, labor organizations with twenty-five or more members, and federal, state, and local governments

■ Protects persons between the ages of forty and seventy

■ Permits discrimination where age is a necessary qualification for the job

(Enforced by the Equal Employment Opportunity Commission or similar state agency)

Title IX of the Education Act Amendments of 1972

■ Prohibits discrimination against students and others on the basis of sex in educational institutions receiving federal funding

■ Prohibits sex discrimination in a number of areas, including student and faculty recruitment, admissions, financial aid, facilities, and employment

■ Requires that school athletic programs effectively accommodate the interests and abilities of members of both sexes. Equal total expenditure on men's and women's sports is not required

■ Does not cover sex-stereotyping in textbooks and other curricular materials

(Enforced by the Department of Education's Office of Civil Rights)

Rehabilitation Act of 1973

■ Prohibits private and government employers from discriminating on the basis of physical handicap

■ Requires companies that do business with the government to undertake affirmative action to provide jobs for the handicapped

■ Prohibits activities and programs receiving federal funds from excluding otherwise qualified handicapped persons from participation or benefits

(Enforced by lawsuit in federal court or, in some cases, state or local human rights or fair employment practices commissions)

Discrimination Because of Race, National Origin, and Alienage

Most Americans accept the notion that discrimination based on a person's race is morally, as well as legally, wrong. Few would now defend the clear discrimination of segregated public facilities or the operation of totally separate public school systems for black and white children. Nevertheless, discrimination is still a problem.

Americans are now trying to come to grips with their history of race discrimination in light of the Constitutions's guarantee of equal protection. In doing this, the government faces the dilemma of responding to the needs of those exposed to racial injustice while avoiding discrimination against others. The following questions focus our attention on the troubling issue of how to use just means to rid society of injustice: Should providing greater opportunities for some who historically have been denied equal protection result in fewer opportunities for others? Should discrimination laws originally passed to protect minorities protect the majority as well? Should the disadvantaged be treated differently in order to treat them equally?

Today, discrimination is likely to be subtle rather than blatant. Moreover, reasonable persons sometimes disagree as to what constitutes discrimination. For example, a town denied a request to rezone land to permit the building of townhouses for low- and medium-income tenants. The town had mostly detached, single family housing, and almost all the town's residents were white. The Supreme Court upheld the denial of the request because they found no *intent* to discriminate. However, when school boards redrew school attendance lines to keep black and white children from attending the same schools, the Court found the boards in violation of the Fourteenth Amendment.

Efforts to rid society of the lingering effects of discrimination have ranged from the court-ordered busing of children to achieve integrated schools to the establishment of **affirmative action** programs to recruit the disadvantaged for jobs and higher education. Controversy and opposition have surrounded implementation of some of these remedies.

When public school segregation was declared to be unconstitutional in the *Brown* case, the schools were opened to students of all races. But in many instances segregation did not end. A number of methods were used to desegregate the schools, including allowing students to attend any school they desired, redrawing neighborhood school boundary lines, transferring teachers, and developing "magnet schools" with special programs to attract a racially mixed student population.

Perhaps the most controversial method of desegregating the schools has been busing. Busing as a means of transporting children to schools has a long history. Even before the 1971 Supreme Court decision that upheld busing as part of a school desegregation plan, almost twenty million children rode buses to and from school.

A school bus arriving under police escort at a big city high school.

**WHERE
YOU
LIVE**

What is the racial
makeup of schools in
your area? How has this
changed over the past
few years? Have there
been court decisions
where you live regard-
ing school desegrega-
tion? Has busing been
ordered? Has it worked?

Supporters of busing claim that requiring some students to change schools can help provide equal educational opportunity and quality education for both black and white children. In addition, they argue that busing, which was once used to support segregation by transporting students to separate black and white schools (dual school systems), is an appropriate remedy. Opponents of busing contend that attending neighborhood schools is better because children will be in school with their neighborhood friends and will be closer to home in case of an emergency. Critics also maintain that the effect of court-ordered busing has been for whites to flee the city's schools, resulting in increased, not decreased, segregation.

PROBLEM 20

a. What are the arguments in favor of busing? Against busing?

b. How do you feel about busing? If you favor it, which antibusing arguments trouble you most? If you oppose it, which probusing arguments trouble you most?

c. Is there a difference between saying that segregation is illegal and requiring that schools have specific percentages of black and white students? Explain.

Besides busing, another remedy for dealing with the effects of discrimination is affirmative action. Concerned that neutral treatment was not enough to make up for years of past discrimination, the federal government started a number of programs designed to provide special training and preferential treatment in education and employment. Those in favor of affirmative action say that preferential admissions and hiring policies are needed to overcome the effects of past discrimination. Those opposed to affirmative action say that the law must be color-blind and that race should never be used as a basis for classification because special treatment for some means discrimination against others.

The issue of affirmative action was squarely presented to the Supreme Court in the case of *Bakke* v. *The University of California* (1978). The medical school of the University of California at Davis had decided that the best way to increase the number of minorities in the student body was to change admission requirements to give certain advantages to minority applicants. Each entering class had 16 of 100 places reserved for minority applicants. Alan Bakke, a thirty-three-year-old white engineer, was twice denied admission to the medical school. He claimed that without the special admissions program he would have been admitted because his grades and test scores were higher than those of the minority students who were admitted. Bakke sued the university, saying that the affirmative action program denied him equal protection of the laws.

In deciding this case the Supreme Court agreed that this special admissions program was unconstitutional and ordered Bakke admitted to the university. However, the decision left many questions unanswered. The court seemed to say that specific racial quotas were illegal, but that race could be considered as one of the factors in the admissions decision, as long as schools seek to obtain a diverse student body. It was not long before the issue of affirmative action was again before the court.

THE WEBER CASE

Brian Weber was a white employee at the Kaiser Aluminum factory in a small Louisiana town. After five years at the plant Weber applied for a position in a training program for skilled workers. He was turned down even though he had more seniority (i.e., more years of experience) than some of those selected.

He was not selected because Kaiser Aluminum had started an affirmative action program designed to increase the number of blacks in skilled positions. To do this Kaiser and the local labor union had agreed to give 50% of the training positions to blacks and 50% to whites. The company felt this was necessary because while nearly 40% of the local work force was black, fewer than 2% of their skilled employees were blacks.

Weber felt that this plan was unfair and that it discriminated against him because of his race. Weber sued the company, relying on Title VII of the Civil Rights Act of 1964 which makes it illegal for employers to discriminate on the basis of race.

PROBLEM 21

a. Consider the *Bakke* case and the *Weber* case. For each of these cases, who is being discriminated against? Who is discriminating? Who is benefiting from the discrimination?

b. Should the discrimination in either case be allowed? Why or why not?

c. What effect would permitting such discrimination have on society? What effect would prohibiting such discrimination have on society?

d. Does statistical underrepresentation of a group in schools or jobs prove discrimination?

What does equality mean to you?

In 1979 Brian Weber lost his case. The Supreme Court found that Title VII had been passed for the purpose of improving employment opportunities for minorities and that it did not prohibit a voluntary affirmative action plan designed to eliminate a racial imbalance. Do you agree or disagree with the decisions in the *Bakke* and *Weber* cases?

PROBLEM 22

Moose Lodge was an exclusive private club. Only members and their guests could eat or drink at the club. One day, a state representative who was a club member brought a black state representative as a guest. The club refused to serve the guest in the dining room or bar.

a. Does this violate either the Fourteenth Amendment or the Civil Rights Act of 1964?

b. Should the law prohibit discrimination in a private club? Why or why not?

Like race, classifications based on national origin and alienage are considered "suspect." The problem with such classifications is that they treat persons as members of a group rather than considering their individual abilities and needs.

In the past, courts have struck down laws that prohibited resident aliens from practicing law or obtaining an engineer's license. State laws excluding aliens from all government jobs are

CASE OF KOREMATSU v. UNITED STATES

In 1942 the United States was at war with Japan. Following the surprise attack on Pearl Harbor, many Americans feared that the Japanese might invade the West Coast. Reacting to public fear, President Roosevelt, with the approval of Congress, ordered military authorities to relocate inland all 112,000 Japanese-Americans then living on the West Coast.

Among the Japanese-Americans ordered to leave their homes was Fred Korematsu. An American citizen, born in the United States, Korematsu refused to go when ordered to appear at a relocation center. Arrested and convicted for violating the relocation order, Korematsu appealed his case to the U.S. Supreme Court. He argued that the president's order and the act of Congress authorizing his removal were unconstitutional because they discriminated against Japanese-Americans solely on the basis of ancestry and without any evidence of disloyalty.

PROBLEM 23
a. Why did President Roosevelt order Japanese-Americans removed from the West Coast? Should the loyalty of Japanese-Americans have been a consideration in this case?
b. America was also at war with Italy and Germany. Why do you think Italian-Americans and German-Americans were not treated in the same manner as Japanese-Americans?
c. Should the government be able to exercise greater power or suspend the Bill of Rights during a time of war? Should the government have greater power even when not at war if acting in the interest of national security? Explain your answer.
d. How would you decide this case? Why?

WHERE
YOU
LIVE

To what extent is discrimination based on race, national origin, and alienage a problem in your community? What steps are being taken, or should be taken, to eliminate such discrimination?

also unconstitutional, although citizenship may be required for high political office.

In distributing government benefits, state laws that deny welfare benefits to all aliens are unconstitutional. However, the power of Congress to exclude some aliens (those living here less than five years) from Medicare has been upheld.

PROBLEM 24

In the early 1970s the San Francisco public schools enrolled several thousand Chinese students who spoke no English. The schools had relatively few Chinese-speaking teachers. Non-English speaking Chinese students sued the school officials, alleging they had been deprived of equal educational opportunity.

a. How should this situation be decided? Does any law guarantee students instruction in their native language?

WHERE
YOU
LIVE

Has the Equal Rights Amendment been ratified by your state? Does your state have its own laws against sex discrimination?

b. A large suburban school district near Washington, D.C., enrolls students speaking more than thirty different languages. Must the schools establish separate programs for each language?

Discrimination Because of Sex

Equality of Rights shall not be denied or abridged by the United States or by any state on account of sex.

—Proposed Twenty-seventh Amendment

Sex discrimination is a relatively new legal topic. However, the movement to secure equal rights for women has a long history. In the 1860s laws were passed in many states, giving married women the right to own property for the first time (see Chapter 4). Then in 1920, the Nineteenth Amendment was passed, guaranteeing women the right to vote. In 1923 a constitutional amendment to guarantee equal rights for women was unsuccessfully introduced in Congress. This amendment was reintroduced every year thereafter, until 1972 when the Equal Rights Amendment was passed by Congress. To become law, the amendment must be ratified by three-fourths of the states (i.e., thirty-eight). The deadline for ratification, already extended once, is 1982. Some states have already passed an equal rights statute or have added such an amendment to their state constitution.

Opponents of the Equal Rights Amendment argue that it would result in a loss of rights for women. For example, state laws that now require a husband to support his wife and minor children

The Equal Rights Amendment will affect both men and women. Can you explain how?

would have to be changed to impose equal responsibilities on both spouses. Opponents contend that this would force women out of the home and into the workplace and that women would also be subject to the military draft, if it were renewed. In addition, some laws now providing special protections for women (primarily labor laws) would become unconstitutional. Finally, opponents claim that in areas where women need equal opportunity— employment, education, and credit, for example—adequate legal protections already exist. To ERA's opponents, women have nothing to gain and much to lose under the amendment.

Supporters of the Equal Rights Amendment argue that governments should treat each person, male or female, on the basis of his or her individual abilities, not on the basis of arbitrary stereotypes. To do less is to deny women the equal protection of the law. They say that opponents have used scare tactics, such as suggesting that the amendment would require unisex toilets. Supporters also reject the notion that the proposed law would force women out of the home. Rather, they say the amendment would allow women to make choices based on the principle of equality of opportunity. With respect to the loss of protective laws, supporters feel that important protections would not be taken from women, but instead be extended to men as well.

PROBLEM 25

a. Do you think the Equal Rights Amendment should become law? Explain.

b. If you favor the Equal Rights Amendment, what arguments against the amendment trouble you the most? If you are against the amendment, what arguments for it trouble you the most?

c. In what ways have society's attitudes changed since the Supreme Court made the following statement in an 1873 case: "The paramount destiny and mission of women is to fulfill the noble and high office of wife and mother." In what ways, if any, do you think these attitudes will continue to change? How might ratification of the Equal Rights Amendment (or failure to ratify it) affect these future changes?

Recent developments in sex-discrimination law date from the mid-1960s. At that time, Congress began to protect the rights of working women with the Equal Pay Act (1963) and the Civil Rights Act (1964), both of which were summarized earlier in this chapter. Not until 1971, however, did the Supreme Court decide a case in which sex discrimination was found to violate the equal protection clause of the Fourteenth Amendment.

As the women's movement challenged both legal and cultural stereotypes in the 1970s, American attitudes toward women and toward sex roles began to change. More people began to believe that the factor of sex alone should not be used to determine legal rights. This changing attitude had an impact not only on laws discriminating against women but also on those discriminating against men.

Congress has taken special steps to end discrimination in federally assisted education programs. In 1972 it passed a law, commonly referred to as Title IX, which prohibits sex discrimination in school activities ranging from faculty hiring to student athletic programs.

Title IX's impact on school athletics has been particularly controversial. The law requires equal opportunity in athletic programs, so the sports offered must effectively accommodate the interests and abilities of members of *both* sexes. For example, assume a school that has a men's basketball team also has enough women interested in the sport to form a team. The law requires that the school establish a women's basketball team or allow women to try out for the men's team. If separate women's teams are established, the school cannot discriminate on the basis of sex in providing supplies or equipment. If only one woman were interested in track (or any other noncontact sport where a men's team existed), the school could not form a team but would have to allow her to try out for the men's team. In contact sports, schools can restrict teams to members of one sex. While athletic opportunities must be equal, the law does not require that total expenditures on men's and women's sports be equal.

When there are violations of Title IX, the government or the person discriminated against can take the issue to court. Title IX also allows the federal government to cut off financial aid to schools that discriminate on the basis of sex.

PROBLEM 26

Title IX states: "No person in the United States shall, on the basis of sex, be excluded from participation in, be denied the benefits of, or be subjected to discrimination under any education program or activity receiving federal financial assistance . . ."

Which, if any, of the following situations do you feel are in violation of Title IX? Assume each school receives federal funds.

a. A college sponsors one glee club, with membership only open to women.

b. A school establishes a women's baseball team, which receives used equipment from the men's team.

Title IX was passed to eliminate sex discrimination in public education, including school athletics.

c. A high school grooming code requires that men's hair length not reach the shirt collar, but women's hair length is not regulated.

d. A U.S. history textbook does not include important contributions made by American women.

e. Female students who want to play football are denied the opportunity to try out for the male team and are not provided a separate team.

f. An eighth grade curriculum offers shop for boys and home economics for girls.

PROBLEM 27

Mrs. Weeks, a telephone company employee, applied for the job of switchman, a position that sometimes requires lifting items weighing about thirty pounds. The company gave the job to a man with less seniority. She was told in her rejection letter that the company had decided not to assign women to the switchman's job.

a. Why did the company decide not to assign women to this job?

b. Was the company's decision fair?

c. Is Mrs. Weeks protected by the law? If so, what law?

d. Are there any jobs women should not have? Are there any jobs men should not have? Explain your answers.

Discrimination Because of Age

The employment problems of older workers pose some serious questions for society. Should persons whose efforts have helped build the economy be displaced in later years by rapidly changing technology? Once displaced from jobs, older workers often have extreme difficulty finding new employment.

In response to this situation Congress passed the Age Discrimination in Employment Act of 1967. This law, amended in 1978, prohibits most employers, employment agencies, and labor unions from discriminating in employment against persons between the ages of forty and seventy. Private employers with fewer than twenty employees, as well as a few specialized occupations, are not covered by the act. The law does not protect a worker where age is an important job qualification necessary to the normal operation of the business. For example, a court has allowed an intercity bus company to refuse to hire inexperienced older drivers because of safety concerns. The U.S. Equal Employment Opportu-

---

THE CASE OF THE FORCED RETIREMENT

A law required that state police officers retire at age fifty. The stated purpose of the law was to make sure that police officers were physically fit. The state police required complete physical examinations every two years until an officer reached forty and then every year until the officer reached fifty, the mandatory retirement age. Officer Murgia passed all examinations and was in excellent physical and mental health when the state police retired him on his fiftieth birthday. Murgia sued the state police, arguing that the operation of the law denied him equal protection. Should the Fourteenth Amendment protect Officer Murgia in this case?

In deciding Officer Murgia's case the Supreme Court said, "the drawing of lines that create distinctions is . . . a legislative task and an unavoidable one. Perfection in making the classification is neither possible or necessary. Such action by a legislature is presumed to be valid." While Officer Murgia happened to be in good health, the Court accepted the fact that physical fitness generally declines with age. Therefore, it was rational to draw a line at some age, and the Court upheld this law.

---

nity Commission handles complaints based on this law (see Appendix A).

Discrimination because of age is not limited to older persons. Many laws and practices discriminate against youth. For example, restrictions on voting, running for public office, making a will, driving, and drinking are generally upheld by the courts.

Although the courts have not used the equal protection clause to protect the rights of youth, some state and local legislatures have passed laws or regulations forbidding discrimination because of age. In addition, the Twenty-sixth Amendment gives eighteen-year-olds the right to vote in federal and state elections.

PROBLEM 28

The following laws and practices discriminate against youth in some way. Should any of them be changed? If so, what changes would you make?

a. Because of a high rate of shoplifting, a store owner will not allow anyone under eighteen into the store unless accompanied by an adult.

b. Youth between the ages of six and sixteen are required to attend school.

c. A state law prohibits a seventeen-year-old from working in a factory and from working on any job for more than forty hours a week.

PERSONS 40-70* YEARS NOTE!
Age Discrimination is Against the Law

The Federal Age Discrimination in Employment Act prohibits arbitrary age discrimination in employment by:

- Private Employers of 20 or more persons

- Federal, State and Local Governments, without regard to the number of employees in the employing unit

* There is no upper age limit for Federal employment.

- Employment Agencies serving such employers

- Labor Organizations with 25 or more members

FILING COMPLAINTS

If you feel you have been discriminated against because of age, contact the nearest office of the Equal Employment Opportunity Commission (EEOC). It is important to contact the EEOC promptly.

FILING SUITS

If you wish to bring court action yourself, you must first file a written charge alleging unlawful discrimination with the EEOC, and in states which have an age discrimination law, with the state agency. This charge should be filed promptly, but in no event later than 180 days after the alleged unlawful practice occurred.

The U.S. Equal Employment Opportunity Commission
2401 E Street, N.W., Washington, D.C. 20506

Discrimination Because of Handicap

No otherwise qualified handicapped individual . . . shall, solely by reason of his handicap, be excluded from participation in, be denied the benefit of, or be subjected to discrimination under any program or activity receiving Federal financial assistance.

—Rehabilitation Act of 1973

The Rehabilitation Act of 1973 was an important step toward legal equality for handicapped persons. As a result of this federal law and of many state and local laws and court decisions, more persons with mental or physical disabilities are moving into the mainstream of American life. *Mainstreaming* is a term used to describe the movement of handicapped persons from special schools and shelters into the community.

Laws to aid the handicapped pose challenges for educators, architects, employers, and community workers. Schools and public buildings are being designed and built "barrier free" to allow easy access for the physically handicapped. In some areas, persons with mental disabilities are moving from large protective institutions into smaller residential facilities in the community.

However, providing equal rights for handicapped persons raises many questions. For example, should public transportation systems be redesigned to accommodate the handicapped? Does the cost to taxpayers of such redesign have an impact on the answer to

THIS FACILITY DOES NOT DISCRIMINATE ON THE BASIS OF HANDICAP REGARDING EMPLOYMENT AND ACCESSIBILITY.

THE CASE OF THE HEARING-IMPAIRED NURSING SCHOOL APPLICANT

Frances Davis, who had a serious hearing disability, applied for a program that would train her as a registered nurse. The program was offered by a state college that received federal funds. With a hearing aid she could hear various sounds, but she could not understand speech unless she was able to see the speaker and lipread.

After applying to the school, she was interviewed by a faculty member. Her hearing difficulty became apparent in the interview and her application was rejected.

The school believed that she could neither participate safely in clinical training nor later care safely for patients. Ms. Davis argued that federal law required the school to modify its program to accommodate a handicapped person otherwise qualified to be admitted. She sued to have the school's decision reversed.

PROBLEM 29
a. Ms. Davis's suit was based on the law quoted at the beginning of this section. Reread it carefully. How should the court decide this case? Explain your decision.
b. Assume a person confined to a wheelchair applied to a law school receiving federal money. Assume further that he was rejected because the faculty believed that he would not be able to complete research assignments because the library was only accessible by stairs. How is his case the same as Ms. Davis's? How is it different? How should his case be decided?

this question? Should all handicapped children of school age be entitled to a free public education that meets their special needs? Should an employer be required to give special proof that a handicapped person is not qualified for a particular job?

Discrimination Because of Income

In some major cases, poor people have been successful in having courts rule that discrimination against them was illegal. However, these decisions have been based on reasons other than equal protection. For example, the Supreme Court has ruled that any person being tried for a criminal offense in which there is a possibility of a jail term has the right to a free lawyer if he or she cannot afford one. This decision was based on the Sixth Amendment's right to assistance of counsel provision.

Federal law requires that public facilities be made accessible to the handicapped.

PROBLEM 30

Many government laws and practices operate to the disadvantage of poor persons. For each statement, decide whether you agree, disagree, or are uncertain as to whether the law or practice should be continued. If you disagree, suggest changes that should be made.

a. To finance the cost of running an election, persons must pay a poll tax in order to vote.

b. Any person unable to pay a traffic fine must spend time in jail to work off the fine.

c. In order to sue for divorce, the parties must pay $75 in court costs and filing fees.

d. Before any housing for low-income persons could be built, the developer must have the local voters' approval.

e. A federal law states that no abortions can be performed with Medicaid funds except to save the life of the mother.

f. To get on the ballot, a political candidate had to pay a filing fee of two percent of the annual salary of the position he or she was seeking.

g. School systems are financed from local property tax revenues (along with funds from the state and federal governments). Schools in poorer neighborhoods have far less money to spend on education than schools in wealthier areas.

State and Local Laws Against Discrimination

When the Supreme Court makes a decision regarding the Constitution, it determines the *minimum* amount of rights that governments must extend to their citizens. Governments may offer greater protection than what the Court says the Constitution requires.

For example, the Civil Rights Act of 1968 prohibits discrimination in the rental or sale of property on the basis of race, color, religion, or national origin. While this law provides important protections, it does not forbid discrimination against homosexuals, single persons, persons with young children, or persons whose income is from alimony or welfare. To protect these and other persons, some state and local governments have passed their own discrimination laws, sometimes called human rights acts, which extend the protections offered by federal law. These laws may cover discrimination based on one or more of the following characteristics:

- age (young or old)
- marital status
- personal appearance
- source of income
- sexual orientation
- family responsibility (having children)
- physical handicap
- matriculation (status of being a student)
- political affiliation

In some places, commissions have been established to receive, investigate, and resolve complaints based on violations of these laws.

WHERE YOU LIVE

Are there state or local laws where you live that extend the protections against discrimination offered by federal law? What state and local agencies are responsible for enforcing these laws?

ADVICE ON ACTIONS TO TAKE WHEN YOUR RIGHTS HAVE BEEN VIOLATED

There is no single procedure to follow for all situations in which your rights have been violated. In handling these problems, you should know that some civil rights are protected by law at both the state and federal level. Sometimes federal law requires that you first try to solve your problem on a state or local level. Also, some civil rights laws have specific time limits for filing a case. Don't delay if you feel that some action should be taken. If you decide to act, some of the options you may wish to consider are listed below.

- Protest in some way, either verbally, by letter, or demonstration.

- Contact an attorney who may be able to negotiate a settlement or file a case for you.

- Contact a private organization with an interest in your type of problem (e.g., the ACLU for First Amendment problems or the NAACP for race discrimination). See Appendix A for a list of others.

- Contact a state or local agency with the legal authority to help (e.g., a state Fair Employment Commission or a local Human Rights Agency).

- Contact a federal agency with the legal authority to help. Although these agencies are based in Washington, D.C., most have regional offices and field offices in larger cities throughout the country. Look in the white pages of the phone directory under "U.S. Government."

- Contact the U.S. Commission on Civil Rights (see Appendix A for address) for general information on where to look for help, or if your complaint goes unanswered.

PROBLEM 31

Review the civil rights laws summarized earlier in this chapter. For each of the following situations, decide which law, if any, could help the person discriminated against? Which agency (or agencies) could be of assistance?

a. A twenty-eight-year-old married man applies for a job as a flight attendant for a major airline. The airline's policy is to hire only single men and women between the ages of nineteen and twenty-six.

b. Dan was a clerk earning $4.20 an hour; Diane earned $3.75 per hour at the same company. Dan spent twenty-five percent of his time typing and the rest of his time filing and running errands. Diane spent sixty percent of her time typing and the rest of her time filing and running errands.

c. A forty-seven-year-old administrative assistant is told by her boss that because of a slowdown in business, she is being let go. When she returns to pick up her final paycheck several weeks later, she discovers that a twenty-year-old woman has been hired to take her place.

d. A college professor from a university in Spain moves to this country. He applies for a job teaching high-school Spanish but is refused because he is not yet a U.S. citizen.

e. A high-school senior with good grades goes to speak with the college counselor at her school. The counselor provides her with information on college programs in nursing, elementary education, and home economics.

f. A women applied to be a correctional officer at the state prison. She is told that state law prohibits the hiring of women prison guards to supervise male inmates at the maximum security prison.

appendix A
ORGANIZATIONS
TO KNOW

I. U.S. GOVERNMENT

Executive Branch

Executive Office of the President
The White House
Washington, D.C.   20500
(202) 456-1414

Office of the Vice President
Executive Office Building
Washington, D.C.   20501
(202) 456-1414

Executive Departments

Department of Agriculture
14th Street & Independence Ave., S.W.
Washington, D.C.   20250
(202) 655-4000
    Responsible for U.S. agricultural policy. Regulates and expands mar-
    kets for agricultural products. Directs food and nutrition services.
    Inspects, grades, and safeguards quality of food products. Involved in
    rural development, forest management, and water and soil conserva-
    tion.

Department of Commerce
14th Street & Constitution Ave., N.W.
Washington, D.C.   20230
(202) 377-2000

> Concerned with economic development and technological advancement. Provides assistance and information to business and industry. Assists development of the U.S. merchant marine and the growth of minority businesses. Provides social, economic, and scientific data to business and government. Conducts the U.S. census. Promotes travel to the United States by foreign tourists, and assists development of economically deprived areas throughout the country.

Department of Defense
The Pentagon
Washington, D.C.   20301
(202) 545-6700

> Develops national security and military defense policies and has overall responsibility for administration of the armed forces and the national defense.

Department of Education
200 Independence Avenue, S.W.
Washington, D.C.   20201
(202) 245-8430

> Administers federal aid programs for all aspects of education, including: preschool through college; adult, vocational, and bilingual education; public libraries; and education for the handicapped.

Department of Energy
1000 Independence Avenue, N.W.
Washington, D.C.   20504
(202) 252-5000

> Has responsibility for energy development and conservation policies. Conducts research on new energy sources and advises the government on energy matters.

Department of Health and Human Services
300 Independence Avenue, S.W.
Washington, D.C.   20201
(202) 245-6296

> Administers federal programs involving all aspects of public health and human services, including: medical research; health care financing; mental health and disease control; alcohol and drug abuse; health services; social security; and public welfare.

Department of Housing and Urban Development
451 7th Street, S.W.
Washington, D.C.   20410
(202) 755-6422

> Has responsibility for programs concerned with housing and community development. Administers programs involving urban planning, mortgage insurance, rent subsidies, home building, and neighborhood rehabilitation and preservation.

Department of Interior
3rd Street & Constitution Ave., N.W.
Washington, D.C.   20210
(202) 523-8271

>Has responsibility for management and conservation of most publicly owned lands and natural resources. Operates and preserves national parks and historical places, protects fish and wildlife, conserves and develops mineral resources, and is responsible for outdoor recreation and Indian and territorial affairs.

Department of Justice
10th Street & Constitution Ave., N.W.
Washington, D.C.   20530
(202) 633-2000

>Has responsibility of enforcing federal laws, representing the government in federal cases, and interpreting laws under which other departments act. Has divisions involved in antitrust, civil law, criminal law, civil rights, natural resources, and tax law. Special bureaus include the FBI, Bureau of Prisons, Immigration and Naturalization Service, U.S. Marshalls, and Law Enforcement Assistance Administration.

Department of Labor
200 Constitution Avenue, N.W.
Washington, D.C.   20210
(202) 523-8271

>Has responsibility for all aspects of labor and employment, including wages, hours, safety and health conditions, job training, pensions and benefits, collective bargaining, and union/management relations.

Department of State
2201 C Street, N.W.
Washington, D.C.   20520
(202) 655-4000

>Has responsibility to supervise and direct U.S. foreign affairs. Responsible for relations with other countries. Speaks for the United States in the United Nations and other international organizations. Represents the United States in negotiations, treaties, and agreements with other nations.

Department of Transportation
400 7th Street, S.W.
Washington, D.C.   20590
(202) 426-4000

>Responsible for U.S. transportation policy. Provides funds for highway planning and construction and urban mass transit. Assists and regulates railroads, airlines, ports, waterways, and highway safety.

Department of Treasury
15th Street & Pennsylvania Ave., N.W.
Washington, D.C.   20220
(202) 566-2000

>Responsible for U.S. tax and money policies. Designs and prints coins, stamps, and currency. Collects federal taxes via the Internal Revenue

Service. Oversees the Secret Service, the Customs Service, and the Bureau of Alcohol, Firearms, and Tobacco.

Legislative Branch

U.S. Senate
The Capitol
Washington, D.C.   20510
(202) 224-3121
 To contact a member of the Senate, write to the address above.

U.S. House of Representatives
The Capitol
Washington, D.C.   20510
(202) 224-3121
 To contact a member of the House of Representatives, write to the address above.

Judicial Branch

Supreme Court of the United States
#1 First Street, N.E.
Washington, D.C.   20543
(202) 252-3000
 Copies of recently decided cases can be obtained by contacting the Clerk of the Court at the address above.

Federal Agencies and Offices

ACTION
806 Connecticut Ave., N.W.
Washington, D.C.   20525
(202) 254-3120
 Administers volunteer programs (including VISTA and the Peace Corps) sponsored by the federal government and provides services to developing nations, minorities, and the disadvantaged.

Civil Aeronautics Board
1825 Connecticut Ave., N.W.
Washington, D.C.   20408
(202) 673-5526
 Regulates air transportation within the United States and between the United States and foreign countries. (The Office of Consumer Advocate receives and attempts to resolve complaints filed by passengers and shippers against airline companies.)

Commission on Civil Rights
1121 Vermont Avenue, N.W.
Washington, D.C.   20425
(202) 655-4000
 Encourages equal opportunity for minority groups and women. Conducts studies and makes recommendations regarding discrimination.

Serves as a clearinghouse for civil rights information. Investigates complaints of denial of voting rights.

Consumer Product Safety Commission
1111 18th Street, N.W.
Washington, D.C. 20207
(800) 638-2666 Consumer Hotline
(800) 492-2937 in Maryland

Establishes and enforces product safety standards, studies causes and prevention of product-related injuries, and conducts surveillance and enforcement programs.

Environmental Protection Agency
401 M Street, S.W.
Washington, D.C. 20460
(202) 655-4000

Responsible for policies and laws that protect the environment, including regulations aimed at land, water, air, and noise pollution, solid waste disposal, pesticides, and other hazardous materials.

Equal Employment Opportunity Commission
2401 E Street, N.W.
Washington, D.C. 20506
(202) 634-7040

Handles complaints regarding job discrimination based on race, color, religion, sex, or national origin. Has power to conduct investigations and bring court actions where necessary.

Federal Communications Commission
1919 M Street, N.W.
Washington, D.C. 20554
(202) 632-6336

Regulates communications media, including radio, television, cable, and satellite. Investigates complaints regarding radio or television broadcasting.

Federal Election Commission
1325 K Street, N.W.
Washington, D.C. 20463
(202) 523-4068

Administers and enforces provisions of the Federal Election Campaign Act. The act requires the disclosure of sources and uses of campaign money for any federal office, limits the amount of individual contributions, and provides for public financing of presidential elections.

Federal Information Center
18th & F Streets, N.W.
Washington, D.C. 20405
(202) 566-1937

Provides assistance to citizens lost in the maze of federal programs and services by directing them to the proper office for help with their problem.

Federal Reserve System
20th Street & Constitution Ave., N.W.
Washington, D.C. 20551
(202) 452-3667
> Serves as the central bank of the United States. Sets banking policies and regulates the availability of money.

Federal Trade Commission
6th Street & Pennsylvania Ave., N.W.
Washington, D.C. 20580
(202) 523-3727
> Responsible for keeping competition among U.S. businesses both free and fair. Will investigate complaints of deceptive or unfair practices involving price-fixing, advertising, packaging, labeling, or credit.

Interstate Commerce Commission
12th Street & Constitution Ave., N.W.
Washington, D.C. 20423
(800) 424-9312 Consumer Hotline during working hours only
> Regulates interstate commerce. The Office of Consumer Affairs, which appears in this listing, handles consumer complaints involving interstate moving companies, buses, trains, and small shipments.

National Labor Relations Board
1717 Pennsylvania Avenue, N.W.
Washington, D.C. 20570
(202) 254-9430
> Prevents and remedies unfair labor practices by employers and labor unions. Conducts elections among workers to determine whether they wish to be represented by a labor union.

National Transportation Safety Board
800 Independence Avenue, S.W.
Washington, D.C. 20591
(202) 472-6066
> Reviews adequacy of federal standards for vehicle safety and highway design and maintenance. Studies and makes recommendations on matters of surface transportation safety and accident prevention.

Nuclear Regulatory Commission
1717 H Street, N.W.
Washington, D.C. 20555
(202) 492-7531
> Regulates commercial uses of nuclear energy. Responsibilities include licensing, inspection, and enforcement.

Occupational Safety and Health Administration
3rd Street & Constitution Ave., N.W.
Washington, D.C. 20210
(202) 523-9362
> Part of the Department of Labor. Sets policy, develops programs, and investigates complaints regarding occupational safety and health hazards.

Office of Consumer Affairs
621 Reporters Building
Washington, D.C. 20201
(202) 755-8875

> Set up by the president to be the consumer's "voice" in Washington. Provides consumer information, advises on consumer policies and programs, conducts consumer education, and will advise citizens where and how to file consumer complaints.

Postal Service
475 L'Enfant Plaza West, S.W.
Washington, D.C. 20260
(202) 245-5023

> Provides mail processing and delivery services to individuals and businesses throughout the United States. (The Consumer Protection Office handles consumer complaints, enforces law to prevent receipt of unwanted mail, and investigates postal fraud and lost mail.)

Small Business Administration
1441 L Street, N.W.
Washington, D.C. 20416
(202) 653-6668

> Provides information and assistance to small businesses on problems of marketing, accounting, product analysis, production methods, and research and development.

Veterans Administration
810 Vermont Avenue, N.W.
Washington, D.C. 20420
(202) 389-3775

> Administers veteran benefit programs, including disability compensation, pensions, education, home loans, insurance, vocational rehabilitation, medical care, and burial benefits.

II. NATIONAL ASSOCIATIONS

American Bar Association
1155 E. 60th Street
Chicago, IL 60637
(312) 947-4000

> Professional organization of lawyers that provides services and information to state and local bar associations. Serves as a resource on most law-related topics.

American Conservative Union
316 Pennsylvania Avenue, S.E.
Suite 400
Washington, D.C. 20008
(202) 546-6555

> A conservative lobbying and educational group that supports a wide range of programs.

Association for Middle-income Housing
103 Park Avenue
New York, NY   10017
(212) 679-1104

> Helps families seeking or living in cooperative housing and citizens interested in promoting middle-income housing.

Chamber of Commerce of the United States
1615 H Street, N.W.
Washington, D.C.   20062
(202) 659-6000

> Federation of individuals, corporations, trade associations, and local chambers of commerce. Represents the business community's views on economic and other national issues.

Foundation for Cooperative Housing
2101 L Street, N.W.
Washington, D.C.   20037
(202) 857-4100

> Interested in improving the quality of housing and urban development, especially for persons of modest income, through the encouragement of cooperative housing.

Institute for Local Self-Reliance
1717 18th Street, N.W.
Washington, D.C.   20009
(202) 232-4105

> Tries to teach people the tools of self-reliance. Provides technical assistance to those concerned with issues of local initiations and independence.

National Abortion Rights Action League
825 15th Street, N.W.
Washington, D.C.   20005
(202) 347-7774

> Initiates and coordinates political, social, and legal action of individuals and groups concerned with maintaining abortion rights. Conducts research and maintains speakers bureau.

National Association of Attorneys General
Iron Workers Pike
Lexington, KY   40578
(606) 252-2291

> Has committees on many legal issues. Publishes a newsletter and a quarterly.

National Center for State Courts
300 Newport Avenue
Williamsburg, VA   23185
(804) 253-2000

> Provides assistance to state courts in improving their structure and administration. Publishes newsletters, journals, pamphlets, and reports.

National Council on Family Relations
1219 University Avenue, S.E.
Minneapolis, MN   55414
(612) 331-2774
> Aimed at providing opportunities for the advancement of marriage and family life.

National Homeowners Association
1225 19th Street, N.W.
Washington, D.C.   20036
(202) 659-3436
> National membership organization that promotes consumer interest in housing, including condominiums. Publishes a homebuyer checklist and a monthly newsletter.

National Right to Life Committee
National Press Building
529 14th Street, N.W.
Washington, D.C.   20045
(202) 638-4396
> Lobbies for constitutional amendments against abortion. Operates as information clearinghouse and speakers bureau.

National Rural Center
1828 L Street, N.W.
Suite 1000
Washington, D.C.   20036
(202) 331-0258
> A nonprofit charitable organization created to develop and advocate rural development policys and to provide information that can help rural people.

III. LEGAL SERVICES

Community Disputes Services
140 W. 51st Street
New York, NY   10020
(212) 977-2998
> Designed to adapt traditional dispute-settling techniques, such as mediation, arbitration, and fact-finding, to meet the needs of different groups and help them develop their own dispute-settlement procedures.

Legal Services Corporation
733 15th Street, N.W.
Washington, D.C.   20005
(202) 376-5100
> Makes grants to local agencies that provide legal services to the poor.

Migrant Legal Action Program
806 15th Street, N.W.
Washington, D.C. 20005
(202) 347-5100
(800) 424-9425

> Provides civil legal representation for migrant and seasonal farmworkers. Farmworker clients must meet federal poverty income levels to be eligible. Staff has both English and Spanish language capabilities.

National Association for Puerto Rican Civil Rights
175 E. 116th Street
New York, NY 10029
(212) 348-3973

> Provides legal services and placement assistance for Puerto Ricans, especially in New York.

National Center for Law and the Deaf
Galludet College
7th & Florida Avenue, N.E.
Washington, D.C. 20002
(202) 447-0445

> Provides legal assistance to deaf and hearing-impaired individuals in various civil matters, including landlord/tenant disputes, public benefits, consumer problems, and wills. Does not handle personal injury, bankruptcy, or domestic relations cases.

National Clients Council
825 15th Street, N.W.
Suite 500
Washington, D.C. 20005
(202) 347-7555

> Provides advocacy of clients' interests and concerns in legal services programs and trains clients to participate in the planning and execution of these programs.

National Legal Aid and Defender Association
2100 M Street, N.W.
Washington, D.C. 20037
(202) 452-0620

> Association of local organizations and individuals that provides legal services to the poor. Publishes a directory of legal aid and defender facilities.

National Resource Center for Consumers of Legal Services
1302 18th Street, N.W.
Washington, D.C. 20036
(202) 659-8514

> Publishes *New Directions*, a review of developments in the field of legal services. Serves as a clearinghouse for information on legal services delivering.

Native American Rights Fund
1506 Broadway
Boulder, CO   80302
(303) 447-8760
> Represents Indian individuals and tribes in legal matters of national significance and publishes a quarterly account of activities.

Pacific Legal Foundation

1990 M Street, N.W.		455 Capitol Mall
Suite 550	or	Sacramento, CA 95814
Washington, D.C. 20036		(916) 444-0154
(202) 466-2686		

> Engages in litigation on a nationwide basis, focusing on environment, land use, energy, international relations, national defense, and welfare reform to protect the free enterprise system.

IV. PUBLIC INTEREST GROUPS

American Civil Liberties Union
22 E. 40th Street
New York, NY   10016
(212) 725-1222
> Nonprofit organization supporting civil liberties through lobbying and test court cases.

Center for Law and Social Policy
1751 N Street, N.W.
Washington, D.C.   20036
(202) 872-0670
> Represents the interests of previously unrepresented citizens before agencies and courts, primarily in the areas of environmental and consumer protection and health problems of the poor.

Children's Defense Fund
1520 New Hampshire Avenue, N.W.
Washington, D.C.   20036
(202) 483-1470
> Concerned with long-range and systematic advocacy on behalf of the nation's children in the areas of education, child health, child welfare, juvenile justice, child care, and family support services.

Children's Rights Incorporated
3443 17th Street, N.W.
Washington, D.C.   20010
(202) 462-7573
> Organization of individuals interested in legislation concerning children's welfare.

Common Cause
2030 M Street, N.W.
Washington, D.C.   20036
(202) 833-1200
> A national citizens lobby devoted to making government at national and state levels more open and accountable to citizens.

Consumers Union
1714 Massachusetts Avenue, N.W.
Washington, D.C. 20036
(202) 785-1906
> Nonprofit organization providing information, education, and counseling about consumer goods and services and the management of a family income. Tests, rates, and reports on competing brands of products, and publishes reports in monthly *Consumer Reports* magazine.

Consumer Federation of America
1012 14th Street, N.W.
Washington, D.C. 20005
(202) 737-3732
> Federation of national, regional, state, and local consumer groups. Helps consumer groups organize and act; lobbies on proposed consumer legislation and publicizes important issues.

Consumer Information Center
Pueblo, CO 81009
(303) 544-5277
> Publishes a catalogue of free federal publications for consumers.

Council for Public Interest Law
1333 Connecticut Avenue, N.W.
Washington, D.C. 20036
(202) 452-1266
> Revises and promotes new mechanisms for the expanded and long-term funding of public interest legal representation.

Environmental Defense Fund
475 Park Avenue South
New York, NY 10016
(212) 688-4191
> Citizens interest group staffed by lawyers and scientists. Takes legal action on environmental issues.

Federal Women's Program
c/o U.S. Civil Rights Commission
Washington, D.C. 20415
(202) 632-6870
> Organized to assure the recruitment and selection of qualified women for employment in the federal government. Works with agencies and community groups, and develops continuing education and training programs.

Institute for Public Interest Representation
600 New Jersey Avenue, N.W.
Washington, D.C. 20001
(202) 624-8390
> Engages in federal administrative practice, encouraging the federal government to consider and be responsive to the views of otherwise unrepresented or underrepresented groups and individuals.

Lawyers Committee for Civil Rights Under Law
733 15th Street, N.W.
Washington, D.C.   20005
(202) 628-6700
> Operates through local committee of private lawyers in ten cities to
> provide legal assistance to poor and minority groups.

League of Women Voters
1730 M Street, N.W.
Washington, D.C.   20036
(202) 296-1770
> Organization promoting citizen participation in the political process.
> Distributes information on candidates, and works for voter registra-
> tion and turnout.

Major Appliance Consumer Action Panel
Complaint Exchange
20 North Wacker Drive
Chicago, IL   60606
(312) 236-3165 (Call collect)
> Helps resolve consumer complaints with major applicances. Several
> manufacturers have tollfree lines for consumers.
>
> | Admiral | (800) 447-1350 |
> |---|---|
> | Westinghouse | (800) 245-0600 |
> | Whirlpool | (800) 253-1301 |

Mexican American Legal Defense and Educational Fund
28 Geary Street
San Francisco, CA   94108
(415) 981-5800
> Concerned with protecting the constitutional rights of Hispanics and
> supporting the education of Mexican-American lawyers.

National Association for the Advancement of Colored People
1790 Broadway
New York, NY   10019
(212) 245-2100
> Citizens interest group seeking elimination of racial segregation and
> discrimination through legal, legislative, citizen action, and educa-
> tional programs.

National Association of Housing and Redevelopment Officials
2600 Virginia Avenue, N.W.
Washington, D.C.   20037
(202) 333-2020
> Engaged in community rebuilding by slum clearance, public housing,
> large-scale private or cooperative housing rehabilitation, and conser-
> vation of existing neighborhood through housing code enforcement
> and voluntary citizen action.

National Center for Youth Law

3701 Lindell Boulevard		693 Mission Street
St. Louis, MO 63108	or	6th Floor
(314) 553-8668		San Francisco, CA 94105
		(415) 543-3307

Litigates youth related issues and publishes a report of activities.

National Foundation for Consumer Credit
1819 H Street, N.W.
Suite 510
Washington, D.C. 20006
(202) 223-2040

Sponsors nationwide free counseling program to consumers in credit difficulty, and provides an educational program for low-income families.

National Housing and Economic Development Law Project
2313 Warring Street
Berkeley, CA 94704
(415) 548-9400

Publishes information on housing.

National Organization for Women
425 13th St., N.W.
Suite 1048
Washington, D.C. 20004
(202) 347-2279

Takes action to bring women into full participation in the mainstream of American society so they can assume all its privileges and responsibilities in full, equal partnership with men.

National Runaway Switchboard
2210 N. Halsted
Chicago, IL 60614
(800) 972-6006—Illinois
(800) 621-4000—National

A 24-hour, tollfree national switchboard for run-aways and their families. Provides information on shelters and counseling services. Offers to relay messages confidentially.

National Trust for Historic Preservation
1785 Massachusetts Avenue, N.W.
Washington, D.C. 20036
(202) 667-6275

Nonprofit organization created to help protect the built environment and our cultural heritage. Offers advice on preservation problems, works with individuals, preservation groups and public agencies to help them plan and carry out preservation programs; sponsors educational programs; issues publications; and owns and operates historical museums.

National Urban League
425 13th Street, N.W.
Washington, D.C. 20004
(202) 393-4332
> Nonprofit charitable and educational social services organization working to secure equal opportunity for black Americans and other minorities. Concerned with all issues that affect their constituency. Publishes information booklets supplying research data on the economic gap between black and white Americans.

Public Citizen Organization
P.O. Box 19367
Washington, D.C. 20036
(202) 659-9053
> Various public interest groups organized by Ralph Nader, including: (1) Congress Watch—lobbying organization that puts out newsletters regarding current issues in Congress; (2) Critical Mass Energy Project—concerned with education regarding nuclear and solar energy and other energy issues; (3) Health Research Group—concerned with research and occupational safety, food, health, and health care delivery, and handles individual complaints; (4) Tax Reform Research Group—puts out newsletter and does research on taxes; (5) Center for Auto Safety—will refer complaints on auto problems and is interested in class action work; (6) Aviation Consumer Action Project—handles individual complaints on airlines, buses, and railroads, and deals with safety issues and lower fares.

Southern Poverty Law Center
1001 S. Hull Street
Montgomery, AL 36101
(205) 264-0286
> Seeks, through legal precedents it helps to establish, to protect and guarantee the legal and civil rights of the poor population in the United States. Publishes bimonthly annual reports.

Women's Legal Defense Fund, Incorporated
1010 Vermont Avenue, N.W.
Washington, D.C. 20005
(202) 638-1123
> Established for the purpose of fighting sex discrimination. Has phone counseling dealing with domestic relations, employment discrimination, credit, and name change.

appendix B
GLOSSARY

Abandonment desertion of people or things.

Abortion a premature end to a pregnancy. Can result from a medical procedure performed in the early stages of pregnancy or from the premature expulsion of the human fetus as in a miscarriage.

Acceleration Clause a provision in a contract that makes the entire debt due if a payment is not made on time or if some other condition is not met.

Acceptance agreeing to an offer and becoming bound to the terms of a contract.

Accessory or Accomplice a person who helps commit a crime. An accessory before the fact is one who encourages, orders, or helps plan a crime. An accessory after the fact is someone who, knowing a crime has been committed, helps conceal the crime or the person who committed the crime.

Administrator a person appointed by the court to supervise the distribution of a person's property after his or her death.

Admissible evidence that can be used or introduced in a trial or other court proceeding.

Adoption legal process of taking a child of other parents as one's own.

Adultery voluntary sexual intercourse between a married person and someone other than his or her spouse.

Advocacy supporting or arguing for a cause.

Advocate a person who speaks for the cause of another or on behalf of someone.

Affidavit a written statement sworn to or made under oath before somone authorized to administer an oath.

Affirmative Action steps taken by an organization to remedy past discrimination in hiring, promotion, education, etc.; for example, by recruiting minorities and women.

Aftercare the equivalent of parole in the juvenile justice system. It involves a juvenile being supervised and assisted by a parole officer or social worker.

Age of Majority the age (usually eighteen or twenty-one) when a person becomes an adult as specified by state law. It gives the individual both the rights and responsibilities of adulthood.

Agency an administrative division of a government set up to carry out certain laws.

Aggravating Factors factors that might raise the seriousness of an offense; the presence of this factor may be considered by the judge and jury.

Alibi a Latin word meaning "elsewhere." An excuse or plea that a person was somewhere else at the time a crime was committed.

Alienage the status of being a person born in a foreign country who has not qualified for citizenship.

Alimony payments ordered by a court that are made by a person to a divorced spouse for personal support.

Allegation an accusation that has not been proved.

Annual Percentage Rate the interest rate paid per year on borrowed money.

Annulment a court order that sets aside a marriage, declaring that it never existed.

Answer a defendant's response to a complaint made in a written statement and filed with the court.

Appeal taking a case to a higher court for a rehearing.

Appeals Court a court in which appeals from trial court decisions are heard.

Appraisal a determination of the value of something, such as a house.

Arbitration a means of settling a dispute by submitting the dispute to a neutral party whose decision is binding.

Arraignment the time at which a defendant enters a plea. For a misdemeanor, this is also the defendant's initial appearance where the judge informs the defendant of the charges and sets the bail.

Arrest taking a person suspected of a crime into custody.

Arson the deliberate and malicious burning of property.

Assault an intentional physical attack, or a threat of attack with the apparent ability to carry out the threat so that the victim feels in danger of physical attack or harm.

Assumption of a Mortgage this occurs when the seller and whoever holds the mortgage on a building allows the buyer to take over the mortgage and make payments at the existing interest rate.

Attachment taking a debtor's property or money to satisfy a debt, by court approval.

Attempt an effort to commit a crime that goes beyond mere preparation but that does not result in the commission of the crime.

Bail money or property put up by the accused or his or her agent to allow release from jail before trial. The purpose of bail is to assure the court that the defendant will return for trial.

Bait and Switch a deceptive sales technique in which customers are "baited" into a store by an ad promising an item at a low price and then "switched" to a more expensive item.

Balloon Payment the last payment of a loan which is much higher than any of the other regular monthly payments, often causing the debtor to default or to refinance the final payment with a new interest charge.

Bar Association an organization of lawyers.

Battery any intentional, unlawful, or unconsented to physical contact by one upon another.

Beyond a Reasonable Doubt the level of proof required to convict a person of a crime. It does not mean "convinced one hundred percent," but does mean there are no reasonable doubts as to guilt.

Bigamy the crime of being married to more than one person at a time.

Bill (1) a draft of a proposed law being considered by a legislature; (2) a written statement of money owed.

Bill Consolidation a form of credit in which the lender combines all of a person's debts into a single debt with one monthly payment. In effect, this is a refinancing of a person's existing debts, often with an additional interest charge.

Binder a buyer's offer to purchase something that is written up and presented to the seller.

Black Market Adoptions a form of adoption, illegal in many states, that bypasses licensed adoption agencies by using a go-between to negotiate between the expectant mother and the adopting parent(s).

Bond a mandatory insurance or obligation. A bail bond is the money a defendant pays to secure release from jail before trial.

Booking the formal process of making a police record of an arrest.

Breach failure to keep a promise or perform a duty. A breach of contract is a failure to carry out the terms of a contract.

Burglary breaking and entering a building with the intention of committing a felony.

Capital Offense an offense which may be punishable by death or life imprisonment.

Capital Punishment the death penalty.

Caveat Emptor Latin phrase meaning "let the buyer beware."

Cease and Desist Order an order given by an administrative agency or a judge to stop some illegal or deceptive activity.

Charge (1) the formal accusation of a crime; (2) a type of credit in which payment is made over a period of time.

Childsnatching the act by a divorced or separated parent of taking his or her child away from the parent with custody and fleeing to another state.

Civil Action a lawsuit brought by one or more individuals against another person, a business, or the government.

Civil Law all areas of law that do not involve criminal matters. Civil law usually deals with private rights of individuals, groups, or businesses.

Class Action a lawsuit brought by one or more persons on behalf of a larger group.

Clause a paragraph, sentence, or phrase in a legal document, such as a contract, lease, or will.

Closing the final meeting for sale of land when property is formally transferred and all payments are made.

Closing Costs closing costs are charges for finishing a real estate deal, and include taxes, mortgage fees, credit reports, and insurance.

Codicil an addition to a will made after the will is drawn up.

Coercion forcing a person to act against his or her free will.

Collateral money or property given to back up a person's promise to pay a debt.

Common Law judge-made law (as opposed to law made by a legislature). Our common law is based on the legal customs and court decisions of England that were followed in the U.S. judicial system when it was established.

Common Law Marriage a marriage created without legal ceremony by a couple living together and publicly presenting themselves as husband and wife.

Community Property property acquired during a marriage that is owned in common by husband and wife, no matter who earned it or paid for it.

Complaint the first legal document filed in a civil lawsuit. It includes a statement of the wrong or harm done to the plaintiff by the defendant and a request for a specific remedy from the court. A complaint in a criminal case is a sworn statement regarding the defendant's actions that constitute the crime charged.

Condominium a building in which residents own individual units or apartments as well as a share of the building's common property, such as elevators, laundry rooms, and garages.

Confession of Judgment a provision in a lease in which the tenant agrees in advance to let the landlord decide without challenge if a tenant has been at fault in any disagreement.

Consent Order a voluntary agreement to stop a practice that is claimed to be illegal.

Consideration something of value offered or received, constituting the main reason for making a contract.

Conspiracy an agreement or plan between two or more persons to commit a crime.

Constructive Eviction a situation in which a tenant may be able to leave before the lease expires without owing rent if a landlord fails to maintain housing in a livable condition.

Consumer anyone who buys or uses a product or service.

Contested Divorce a divorce in which the parties disagree over the ending of the marriage itself or over issues such as custody or the division of property.

Contraband any items that are illegal to possess.

Contraceptives any of a number of devices that reduce the chance of conceiving a baby.

Contract a legally enforceable agreement between two or more people to do a certain thing in exchange for payment in some form.

Convict (1) a person who has been found guilty of a crime and is now in prison; (2) to find a person guilty of a crime or a wrongdoing.

Cooperative a building in which the individual owners buy stock in the building as a whole and each owner has the right to occupy a specific unit.

Corrective Advertising a remedy imposed by the Federal Trade Commission requiring that any false claim in an advertisement be specifically corrected in future ads.

Co-sign an act in which a person, other than one of the original two parties, signs a legal document guaranteeing to pay off the debt or contract if the original signer defaults.

Counterclaim a claim made by a defendant against the plaintiff in a civil lawsuit.

Credit (1) a deduction from what is owed; (2) purchasing goods with delayed payment, as with a credit card; (3) money that is loaned.

Creditor a person who provides credit or who loans money or delivers goods or services before payment is made.

Criminal a person who is judged guilty of commiting a crime.

Cross-examination the questioning during a hearing or trial of witnesses for the opposing side.

Custody the care and keeping of something or someone, such as a child.

Damages (1) the injuries or losses suffered by one person because of the fault of another; (2) money asked for or paid by a court order for the injuries or losses suffered.

Debtor a person who owes money or buys on credit.

Defamation written or spoken expression about a person that is false and damages that person's reputation.

Default failure to fulfill a legal obligation, such as failing to make a loan payment or appear in court on a specified time and date.

Defendant the person against whom a claim is made. In a civil suit the defendant is the person being sued; in a criminal case the defendant is the person charged with committing a crime.

Delinquent a child who has committed an act that, if committed by an adult, would be a crime under federal, state, or local law.

Desertion abandoning one's spouse with no intention of either returning or of reassuming the duties of marriage. Desertion is usually a ground for divorce.

Deterrence a reason for punishment based on the belief that the punishment will discourage the offender from committing another crime in the future and will serve as an example to keep other people from committing crimes.

Direct Examination the questioning of a witness by the side calling the witness to the stand.

Directed Verdict a verdict in criminal cases entered by the judge when the prosecution has not presented enough evidence to show that defendant committed the crime.

Disclaimer a clause or statement that rejects liability for anything not expressly promised.

Discovery the pretrial process of exchanging information between the opposing sides.

Disposition the final settlement or result of a case.

Divorce the ending of a marriage by court order.

Down Payment the cash that must be paid initially when something is bought by installments.

Due Process of Law the idea stated in the Fifth and Fourteenth Amendments that every person involved in a legal dispute is entitled to a fair hearing or trial. The requirements of due process vary from situation to situation but due process basically requires that no law or government procedure be arbitrary or unfair.

Duress unlawful pressure on a person to do something that he or she would not otherwise do. Duress may be a defense to a criminal charge.

Emancipation the voluntary surrender by the parents of care, control, and earnings of a minor. A minor becomes emancipated upon reaching legal adulthood, or before that time if legally married or self-supporting.

Embezzlement the taking of money or property by a person who has been entrusted with it, such as a bank teller or a company accountant.

Entrapment an act by law enforcement officials to induce a person to commit a crime that the person would not have committed otherwise. If proven, entrapment is a valid defense to a criminal charge.

Equal Protection a constitutional requirement of the Fourteenth Amendment which protects against unlawful discrimination by the states.

Error of Law a mistake made by a judge in legal procedures or rulings during a trial that may allow the case to be appealed.

Escrow money or property that a neutral party, such as a bank, holds for someone until that person fulfills some obligation or requirement.

Estate an individual's personal property, including money, stocks, and all belongings.

Euthanasia the act of mercy killing in instances where individuals are terminally sick or injured.

Eviction the action by a landlord of removing a tenant from a rental unit.

Ex Post Facto Laws laws that attempt to make criminal an act that was not a crime at the time the act was committed. These laws are prohibited by the Constitution.

Exclusionary Rule a legal rule which prohibits illegally obtained evidence from being used against a defendant at trial.

Executor, Executrix the person named in a will as responsible for carrying out its terms and paying all debts, taxes, and funeral expenses of the deceased.

Express Warranty a statement of fact or a demonstration concerning the quality or performance of goods offered for sale.

Extortion taking property illegally by force or threats of harm or blackmail.

Family Immunity Laws common law doctrine that prevents husbands and wives or children and parents from suing one another for damages.

Family Responsibility Laws laws that require children to care for their parents in their old age.

Felon a person serving a sentence for a felony.

Felony a serious crime punishable by a prison sentence of a year or more.

Flexible Payment Mortgages mortgages that allow buyers to make smaller payments in the early years of the loan and larger payments in future years.

Foreclosure a proceeding in which a bank or other lender takes a house and sells it if a person fails to make mortgage payments.

Forgery making a fake document or altering a real one with the intent to commit fraud.

Foster Home the residence or home of people who take in a child.

Foster Parents a couple or family who take in and care for a child who is without parents or who has been removed from the custody of his or her parents.

Fraud any deception, lie, or dishonest statement made to cheat someone.

Garnishment the legally authorized means to take a person's money, through payroll deductions or other means in order to pay creditors.

Grand Jury a group of twelve to twenty-three people who hear preliminary evidence to decide if there is sufficient reason to formally charge a person with a crime.

Grounds the basis or foundation for some action; legal reasons for filing a lawsuit.

Guardian Ad Litem a guardian appointed to prosecute or defend a suit on behalf of a minor or other party unable to represent him or herself.

Heirs persons who inherit property and/or money from a person who dies.

Holdover Tenants tenants who are allowed to remain on the property after the lease expires.

Homesteading a program whereby older homes in rundown areas are sold to people for low prices if they promise to live in and repair them.

Homicide the crime of killing a person.

Homosexuality an individual's sexual and emotional preference for a person of the same sex.

Housing Codes the municipal ordinances that regulate standards of safety and upkeep for buildings.

Hung Jury the situation in which a jury cannot reach a unanimous decision.

Immunity free from; protected from some action, such as being sued.

Implied Warranty the unwritten standard of quality required, by law, of a product offered for sale.

Incapacitation a theory of sentencing that stresses keeping a convicted criminal locked up to protect society.

Incest sexual relations between people who are closely related to each other.

Indictment a grand jury's formal charge or accusation of criminal action.

Information a prosecuting attorney's formal accusation of commission of a crime.

Intake the informal process by which court officials or social workers decide if a complaint against a youth should be referred to juvenile court.

Interest money earned for the use of someone's money; the cost of borrowing money. Money put in a savings account earns interest, while borrowing money costs interest.

Intestate dying without a will.

Joint Property property owned by two or more people.

Judgment a court's decision on a case.

Judicial Review the process by which courts decide whether the laws passed by Congress or state legislatures are constitutional.

Jurisprudence the study of law and legal philosophy.

Landlord the owner of property who leases or rents space. The company or person that manages the property for the owner.

Larceny the unlawful taking of someone else's property with the intent to steal it. Grand larceny, a felony, is the theft of anything above a certain value (often $100). Petty larceny, a misdemeanor, is the theft of anything below a certain value (often $100).

Lease a contract between a landlord and a tenant for the use of property for a specified length of time at a specified cost.

Legal Separation or Limited Divorce a situation in which the two spouses are separated but still maintain some marital obligations.

Legislation laws or statutes that have been enacted by a legislature.

Libel a written expression about a person that is false and damages that persons' reputation.

Lien a claim on some property made by a creditor until a debt is paid.

Living Will a document that specifies what a person wants done in the event that he or she is being kept alive by artificial means or has become totally unable to function mentally and physically, with no hope of recovery.

Loan Sharking lending money at high, often illegal, interest rates.

Lobbying influencing or persuading legislators to take action to introduce a bill or vote a certain way on a proposed law.

Mediation the act or process of reconciling a dispute between two or more parties.

Misdemeanor a criminal offense,

less serious than a felony, punishable by a prison sentence of one year or less.

Mitigating Factors factors that may lower the seriousness of an offense; the presence of these factors may be considered by the judge or jury.

Month-to-Month Lease a lease enabling the tenant to leave with 30 day's notice and the landlord to raise the rent or evict the tenant with 30 day's notice.

Mortgage a loan in which land or buildings are put up as security.

Motions requests made by one party to a lawsuit that a judge take some specific action or make a decision.

Mutual Agreement agreement by the parties to the exact terms of a contract, either by signing the contract or by beginning to carry it out.

National Origin country where one was born or from where one's ancestors came.

Necessaries those things which parents have a legal obligation to provide their children and which one spouse has the responsibility to provide the other. These usually include: food, clothing, housing, and medical care.

Necessity a possible defense to a crime if the defendant acts in the reasonable belief that he or she had no choice.

Negligence the failure to exercise a reasonable amount of care in either doing or not doing something, resulting in harm or injury.

Negotiation the process of discussing an issue to reach a settlement or agreement.

No-fault Divorce a divorce in which neither party is charged with any wrongdoing but the marriage is ended on the grounds that there are irreconcilable differences causing the marriage to break down.

Nolo Contendere Latin phrase meaning "no contest." A defendant's plea to criminal charges that does not admit guilt but also does not contest the charges. It is equivalent to a guilty plea, but it cannot be used as evidence in a later civil trial for damages based on the same set of facts.

Notice a written statement intended to inform a person of some proceeding in which his or her interests are involved.

Offer a definite proposal by one person to another to make a deal or contract.

Ordinance a county or city law.

Parens Patriae the doctrine under which the court protects the interests of a juvenile.

Parole release from prison before the full sentence has been served, granted at the discretion of a parole board.

Partial Emancipation the legal doctrine that allows minors to keep and spend their own earnings.

Parties the people concerned with or taking part in any legal matter.

Paternity Suit a lawsuit brought by a woman against a man she claims is the father of her child. If a paternity suit is proved, the man is legally responsible for contributing to the support of the child.

Peace Bond a sum of money deposited with the court to guarantee good behavior for a period of time.

Penal Institution a prison or jail.

Peremptory Challenge part of the pretrial jury selection in which each side is given the right to dismiss a certain number of potential jurors without giving any reason.

Personal Recognizance a release from legal custody based on a defendant's promise to return to court. An alternative to cash bail, this practice is used if the judge decides that the defendant is likely to show up for trial.

Petition (1) file charges in a juvenile justice system; (2) a request to a court or public official.

Physical Incapacity the inability of a spouse to engage in sexual intercourse. This may be grounds for annulment.

Plaintiff the person who brings (starts) a lawsuit against another person.

Plea Bargaining negotiations in a criminal case between a prosecutor and a defendant and his or her attorney in which a guilty plea is exchanged for a lesser charge or a lesser sentence.

Points an initial charge made for lending money.

Precedent court decisions on legal questions that give direction to future cases on similar questions.

Preliminary Hearing pretrial proceeding at which the prosecutor must prove that a crime was committed and establish the probable guilt of the defendant. If the evidence presented does not show probable guilt, the judge may dismiss the case.

Preponderance of Evidence evidence of greater weight or more convincing to prove one party's version of the disputed issue or event; the amount of evidence that overcomes evidence offered in opposition.

Presentence Report a written report by a probation officer that gives the sentencing judge information about the defendant's background and prospects for rehabilitation.

Presentment the initial appearance in felony cases at which time defendants are informed of the charges against them and advised of their rights.

Principal (1) the person who actually commits a crime; (2) the

amount of money borrowed or loaned as opposed to the interest on the money.

Prior Restraint any effort to censor a publication before it goes to press.

Privilege Against Self-incrimination the rule that suspects have a right to remain silent and cannot be forced to testify against themselves.

Probable Cause a reasonable belief, known personally or through reliable sources, that a person has committed a crime.

Probate the process of proving to a court that a will is genuine and then giving out the property according to the terms of the will.

Pro se Latin term meaning "for oneself," "on one's own behalf," typically used to describe a person who represents him or herself in court.

Prosecutor the government's attorney in a criminal case.

Prosecution (1) the process of suing a person in a civil case or of bringing a person to trial on criminal charges; (2) noun—the side bringing a case against another party.

Prostitution the act of performing sexual acts for money.

Protective Order in family law, a court order directing one spouse not to abuse the other spouse or children. The penalty for violating a protective order is jail.

Puffing an exaggerated statement as to the desirability of a product or service.

Receiving Stolen Property receiving or buying property that is known or reasonably believed to be stolen.

Redlining a discriminatory procedure in which certain geographical areas in a community are designated by a bank as ineligible for mortgage loans.

Referenda procedure in which issues are voted on directly by the citizens rather than by their representatives in government.

Regulation a rule made by a government agency.

Rehabilitate the attempt to change or reform a convicted person so that he or she will not commit another criminal act.

Release the giving up of a claim or right by a person. A landlord's act of excusing a tenant from all duties related to the apartment and the lease.

Remedy what is done to compensate for an injury or to enforce some right.

Removal for Cause part of the jury selection process that permits removal of any juror who does not appear capable of rendering a fair and impartial verdict.

Rent Control a law that limits how much existing rents can be raised.

Repossession a lender's act of taking back the property of a debtor who has failed to repay a debt.

Restitution a court order in which convicted persons are required to pay back or otherwise compensate the victim for their crime.

Retaliatory Eviction the illegal action on the part of a landlord of evicting a tenant because the tenant complained about the building or otherwise took action against the landlord.

Retribution punishment given as a kind of revenge to pay back the individual for a wrongdoing.

Revoke to take back or cancel.

Right of Entry or Access the part of a lease that allows a landlord and his or her agents to enter a tenant's premises to make repairs, collect the rent, or enforce other provisions of the lease.

Right to Quiet Enjoyment a tenant's right to use and enjoy the property without being disturbed by the landlord or other tenants.

Robbery the unlawful taking of property from a person's immediate possession by force or threat of force.

Sales Contract a contract that includes all the major terms of a sale and that becomes enforceable when the buyer agrees to and signs the seller's offer.

Secured Credit the act of putting up some kind of property as a protection in the event a debt is not repaid.

Security Deposit money that a landlord requires a tenant to pay before moving in, used to cover any damages, cleaning costs, or unpaid rent, if such fees arise.

Separate Property a system under which property owned by either spouse before the marriage remains that person's property throughout the marriage, and any property acquired during the marriage belongs to the person who acquired it.

Settlement a mutual agreement between two sides in a lawsuit, made before the case goes to trial that settles or ends the dispute.

Slander spoken expression about a person that is false and damages that person's reputation.

Small Claims Court a court that handles civil claims for small amounts of money. People usually represent themselves rather than hire an attorney.

Solicitation the act of requesting or strongly urging someone to do something. If the request is to do something illegal, solicitation is considered a crime.

Speculation the process of buying property at a low price, holding it for a short period of time, and then selling it for a profit.

Status Offenders youths who are

charged with the status of being beyond the control of their legal guardian, habitually disobedient, truant from school, or other acts which would not be a crime if committed by an adult.

Statutes laws enacted by legislatures.

Steering a discriminatory practice on the part of real estate agents that directs buyers or renters to particular areas because of their race or for other reasons.

Stop and Frisk to "pat down" or search someone who the police believe is acting suspiciously.

Sublease the part of most standard leases that requires the tenant to obtain the landlord's permission before allowing someone else to live on the premises and pay all or part of the rent.

Subpoena a court order to appear in court at a specified date and time.

Suicide the deliberate taking of one's own life.

Suit a lawsuit or civil action in court.

Summons a legal notice informing a person of a lawsuit and telling that person when and where to go to court.

Tenant a person renting property.

Tenancy for Years refers to any lease for a fixed period of time. The lease specifies that the tenant may live on the property for a single definite period of time.

Tenancy at Will a situation in which a tenant remains on the rented property beyond the end of the lease. In this situation, either the landlord or the tenant can end the lease with whatever notice the law requires.

Title the legal right of property ownership.

Title Insurance insurance that protects a person's right to his or her property.

Title Search a search of government records to make sure the seller has the right to convey or give valid title of ownership to this property.

Tort a breach of some obligation causing harm or injury to someone. A civil wrong, such as negligence or libel.

Treason the offense whereby a U.S. citizen attempts by overt acts of overthrow or seriously harm the U.S. government.

Trial Courts courts that listen to testimony, consider evidence, and decide the facts in disputed situations.

Uncontested Divorce a divorce in which the parties agree to the grounds and terms of the settlement.

Undertaking putting up bond or stocks as security against theft. An executor of an estate is often named in a will and specifically exempted from putting up bond or undertaking.

Unsecured Credit credit based only on a promise to repay in the future.

Usury charging interest for various types of credit at rates higher than the state's legal limit.

Uttering offering to someone as genuine a document known to be a fake.

Vandalism the deliberate destruction or defacement of property.

Variable Rate Mortgages mortgages in which the monthly payment changes when interest rates in an area rise or fall over the years.

Verdict a jury's decision on a case.

Void   not valid, canceled, not legally binding.

Voir dire   the process in which opposing lawyers question prospective jurors to try to get as favorable or as impartial a jury as possible.

Waive   to give up some right, privilege, or benefit voluntarily.

Warrant   a paper signed by a judge authorizing some action, such as an arrest or a search and seizure.

Warranty   a guarantee or promise made by a seller or manufacturer concerning the quality or performance of goods offered for sale.

Warranty of Habitability   implied or unwritten obligation of landlord to provide a unit that is fit to live in.

Waste   damages caused by a tenant's misuse or neglect of property for which the landlord can force the tenant to make the repairs or can sue for damages.

Will   a legal document that states what a person wants done with his or her belongings after death.

Writ   a judge's order, or authorization, that something be done.

INDEX

PHOTO CREDITS

364

Chapter four

p. 166, *bottom left,* James Carroll; **pp. 166–167,** *top center,* Robert Kingman; **p. 167,** *center,* Dick Swift; *top right,* John Veltri/Photo Researchers, Inc.; **p. 169** Hugh Rogers, Monkmeyer Press Photo Service; **p. 171** J. Berndt, Stock, Boston; **p. 174** Susan Ylvisaker, Jeroboam, Inc.; **p. 175** Chester Higgins, Rapho/Photo Researchers, Inc.; **p. 179** Mimi Forsyth, Monkmeyer Press Photo Service; **p. 180** Thomas Hopker, Woodfin Camp & Associates; **p. 182** Eve Arnold, Magnum; **p. 184,** *top,* UPI Photo; **p. 184,** *bottom,* National Abortion Rights Action League; **p. 185** Bill Owens, Magnum; **p. 187** Bob Sullivan; **p. 189** Ray Lustig; **p. 191** Steve Hansen, Stock, Boston; **p. 194** U.S. Department of Labor; **p. 195** Owen Franken, Stock, Boston; **p. 198** Legal Services Organization of Indiana; **p. 200** Paul Zakoian; **p. 204** U.S. Civil Rights Commission; **p. 205** Ray Lustig; **p. 206** Bob Sullivan; **p. 207** Photo Researchers, Inc.; **p. 209,** *top,* Alice Kandell, Rapho/Photo Researchers, Inc.; **p. 209,** *bottom,* Bob Sullivan; **p. 211** Fredrik D. Bodin; **p. 214** Mark & Dan Jury/Photo Researchers, Inc.

Chapter five

p. 220 Charles Harbutt, Magnum; **p. 221** U.S. Department of Housing and Urban Development; **p. 222** Miriam Harmatz; **p. 224** U.S. Department of Housing and Urban Development; **p. 228** Charles Harbutt, Magnum; **p. 230** Everett C. Johnson, Leo de Wys, Inc.; **p. 234** Paul Zakoian; **p. 237** UPI Photo; **p. 239** Ray Ellis, Rapho/Photo Researchers, Inc.; **p. 242** U.S. Department of Housing and Urban Development; **p. 245** Institute of Life Insurance; **p. 247** UPI Photo; **p. 251** UPI Photo; **p. 254** Bob Sullivan; **p. 257** UPI Photo; **p. 259** Ed McMahon; **p. 260** © Carol Bernson; **p. 261** Fredrik D. Bodin; **p. 265** Ed McMahon; **p. 267** © Carol Bernson; **p. 269** Hube Henry, Hedrich-Blessing

Chapter six

p. 272 Bob Sullivan; **p. 274** Hiroji Kubota, Magnum; **p. 275** UPI Photo; **p. 280** UPI Photo; **p. 283** Leo Choplin, Black Star; **p. 284** Danny Lyon, Magnum; **p. 288** Emilio A. Mercado, Jeroboam, Inc.; **p. 294** Bob Sullivan; **p. 297** U.S. Department of Labor; **p. 298** Bob Sullivan; **p. 302** U.S. Equal Employment Opportunity Commission; **p. 305** U.S. Department of Labor; **p. 307** UPI Photo; **p. 308** U.S. Department of Labor; **p. 309** Alon Reininger, Leo de Wys, Inc.; **p. 312** U.S. Department of Labor; **p. 314** UPI Photo; **p. 316** UPI Photo; **p. 321** U.S. Department of Labor; **p. 322** U.S. Department of Labor

Note: Photos on each chapter-opening spread also appear within the corresponding chapter text (except for the first four photos listed under credits for chapter four). Please refer to text page numbers for credits of photos shown on chapter-opening spreads.

CALIFORNIA STATE SUPPLEMENT TO

STREET LAW

A COURSE IN PRACTICAL LAW

second edition

Thomas A. Nazario, Esq.
Director, Community Legal Education
Adjunct Professor of Law
University of San Francisco
School of Law

West Publishing Company
St. Paul   New York   Los Angeles   San Francisco

NOTICE TO ALL READERS

The information contained in this supplement is not intended to take the place of specific legal advice. Before taking any legal action, one should seriously consider consulting an attorney.

Keep in mind also, that laws in California are constantly changing. As students of law, we should try to keep abreast of these changes since many of them affect our rights and responsibilities as citizens.

CONTENTS

six

INDIVIDUAL RIGHTS AND LIBERTIES · 469

PREFACE AND ACKNOWLEDGMENTS

This supplement has been prepared in order to provide students and teachers with a better understanding of the specific laws in California that are relevant to the legal issues raised in the national *Street Law* text. Although the supplement follows the general outline of the main text, in quite a few instances I have chosen not to address particular units within the given chapters of the main text. The reasons for this are either: (1) that the law in California is very similar to that suggested in the national text or (2) that the text addresses federal or general principles of law applicable in all states, including California. Also, many of the definition of the terms which appear in boldface in this supplement may be found in the glossary of the main text.

I would like to thank Ed O'Brien, Ed McMahon, Lee Arbetman, Jeanne Calderon, and Jodi Lerner for their encouragement and editorial assistance; Jean Mignogna at West Publishing Company for her patience and cooperation; and Julise Johnson, Lon Lazar, Cynthia McLellan, Herb Potter, and Thomas Zaret for their time and commitment to the research and publication of this work.

ONE
INTRODUCTION TO LAW AND THE LEGAL SYSTEM

WHO MAKES LAWS?

In California, laws are made primarily by the state legislature. In some cases, however, state administrative agencies, the state courts, the governor, and the people of California themselves play a substantial role in the making of laws.

The federal government only has the power to pass laws as provided by the United States Constitution. California, on the other hand, has the power to pass any law as long as the legislation is not limited by the state constitution and does not conflict with the United States Constitution. A state's power is, therefore, much more extensive than the power of the federal government, and is normally directed at regulating the activities within its boundaries. This balance allows individual states to pass laws that more accurately reflect local public sentiment and gives the people of California a greater say in their government.

A few examples of activities that the state has the power to regulate are: business activities within the state, conservation, highway and motor vehicle use, marriage, public safety, criminal conduct, and corrections.

State Legislature

The California Constitution vests in our legislature the power to enact law. The California state legislature consists of two houses and is called a bicameral legislature. The state legislature is composed of forty state senators and eighty assembly members. They meet in the state's capital, Sacramento, to introduce and consider approximately 3,000 bills (proposed laws) each year.

State senators serve four-year terms, and assemblymen and assembly women serve two-year terms. They are elected in general (statewide) elections held every even-numbered year during the month of November. Each state senator and assemblyperson represents a senatorial or assembly district that is apportioned or drawn on the basis of its population. Because representation is based on population distribution and not on geographical boundaries, legislative districts change with the population trends. Most changes involve the number of districts in the state and the given district boundaries. Changes are generally made after the federal census has been taken, or about once every ten years. Legislative districts often cross county lines.

FIGURE 1   California Assembly Districts

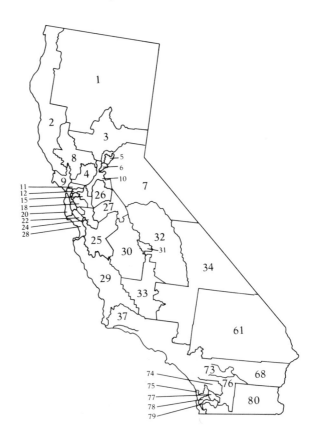

The California Constitution sets out the qualifications necessary to be a member of the state legislature. Essentially, a person must be a United States citizen, at least eighteen years of age, and a resident of California for at least three years. Persons must also have resided in the district they plan to represent for at least one year before the election.

Bills may be introduced either in the senate or the assembly. Most bills require a majority vote of the total house membership to pass, and if passed by one house, the bill may be amended by the other. A majority in the senate is twenty-one votes and an assembly majority is forty-one. If passed, the bill is then sent to the governor. If the governor specifically disapproves (vetoes) a bill, the bill then goes back to the house in which it originated, and the legislature has sixty days to "act" on the veto. The legislature has the power to override the governor's veto by passing the bill again. This time, however, a two-thirds majority is required in each house. It thus takes twenty-seven votes in the senate and fifty-four votes in the assembly to override a governor's veto and enact the proposed law. While this would seem to give the legislature the

FIGURE 2   **California Senate Districts**

final control over a bill, in reality a governor's veto is rarely overturned.

Certain types of bills require a two-thirds majority of both houses in order to become law. These are bills designated as urgency measures (bills that are necessary for the preservation of the public peace, health, or safety), appropriation bills (except appropriations for public school purposes), and constitutional amendments, which also must be ratified by a vote of the people.

Remember finally, that local government entities, such as cities, towns, and villages also have legislative bodies. They may be called councils, boards of supervisors, assemblies, or legislatures. Though the local bodies go by differing names, they work in essentially the same manner and fulfill the same role in local government that our legislature provides at the state level. These local bodies have the power to pass laws affecting their specific locality, and these laws are called **ordinances.**

Voting In California the constitution provides the people with powers to propose, enact, or reject laws by means of the **initiative** or **referendum** process. This process is accomplished by obtaining the required number of signatures on a petition, which then allows either the initiative or referendum to be proposed to the voters. If the initiative is later passed by the voters in the state, it becomes law in California. A referendum, on the other hand, allows voters to approve or disapprove of laws that have been previously enacted by the state legislature. Together, initiative and referendum give the people of California a direct avenue for proposing and in fact making law.

Citizens who wish to vote in California must be at least eighteen years of age as of the date of the election, and must have registered to vote at least twenty-nine days prior to the election. To register to vote, you must fill out a voter registration form and mail it to the elections office in your county. Registration forms are usually available at the county elections office, post offices, libraries, most government offices, and banks. Before an election, registered voters should receive a sample ballot that contains the address of the voter's polling place along with notification of the opening and closing times of the polls. Under California law, a person may arrange with his or her employer to take up to two hours off from work, without loss of pay, in order to vote. The time taken off, however, must be either at the beginning or the end of the person's work shift.

If registered voters are unable to vote at their polling place, they may request an absentee ballot. Applications for absentee ballots may be made either by mail or in person with the county elections office up to seven days before an election.

Remember that an individual citizen's right to vote is one of the most fundamental rights protected by both California and federal law. In California, only those citizens who are imprisoned or on parole, or who have been found legally to be mentally incompetent, may not vote.

Lobbying As mentioned in the national text, when a group, business, or other type of organization desires to influence pending legislation, it may hire someone to try to affect that legislative or administrative action. This person is called a professional lobbyist. These individuals are sometimes employed full-time by an organization, or they may represent the interests of several organizations at once. Lobbyists talk to legislators and administrative personnel and attempt to convince the lawmakers to support their position on a piece of legislation or particular problem. Lobbyists also monitor bills and administrative regulations that might affect the interests of those they represent. They also prepare testimony and presentations for hearings, and in general keep their employers advised of important developments.

In California, as in most states, those who employ lobbyists have a wide range of interests. Lobbyists may represent agricultural associations, private businesses, school districts, governmental agencies, cities and counties, labor organizations, public utilities, and numerous private organizations.

Lobbyists' activities are regulated by the Political Reform Act of 1974. The purpose of this act is to assure the integrity of the governmental decision-making process, while at the same time allowing the people to petition their government and to express freely their opinions on legislation and governmental operations. The act does the following things:

1. It establishes the Fair Political Practices Commission. This commission monitors the activities of lobbyists, investigates possible violations of the act, and imposes fines and/or suspensions for such violations.

2. It requires lobbyists to register with the Secretary of State.

3. It requires lobbyist to file quarterly reports that include a description of the legislative or administrative action that the lobbyist has attempted to influence, the sources and amounts of payments received by the lobbyist, and a list of contributions of $25.00 or more made by the lobbyist in connection with lobbying activity. These reports are audited by the Franchise Tax Board, and potential violations are reported to the Fair Political Practices Commission.

4. It prohibits any kind of deceit or manipulative practices in connection with lobbying activities.

State Agencies

Most of the governmental agencies in California were created by the legislature, but operate within the executive branch of government. Agencies are usually established to help regulate programs, enforce laws, provide services, or evaluate the state's priorities in certain problem areas. Governmental or legislative agencies often go by different names. They may be called boards, departments, offices, or commissions. Sometimes these titles connote the agency's power, size, or relationship to the overall governmental structure. For our purposes, however, it is simply important to realize that state agencies exist and are established primarily to serve the people of California.

Here are a few examples of the many governmental or legislative agencies that exist in California:

Commission on the Status of Women. The Commissionon on the Status of Women works for the maximum participation of women in California society. The commission examines all bills introduced in the legislature that affect women's rights and maintains an information center on the current needs of women.

Department of Consumer Affairs. The primary purpose of the Department of Consumer Affairs is to protect the health, safety, and welfare of California's consumers. The department provides consumers with services and information on their rights and regulates the many licensed services provided to the people of California.

Department of Motor Vehicles. The objectives of the department of Motor Vehicles are: to protect the public interest by identifying vehicle ownership through the process of vehicle registration, to promote safety on the highways by licensing drivers, and to provide a source of compensation to those damaged and/or injured in automobile accidents through the Compulsory Financial Responsibility Law.

Department of the California Highway Patrol. The department of the California Highway Patrol is responsible for assuring the safe, convenient transportation of people and goods on the state highways and on the county road system. Approximately 6,000 uniformed officers are employed primarily for accident control, congestion relief and law enforcement. Other duties include: vehicle inspection, school-crossing guard supervision, enforcement of commercial vehicle weight and safety regulations, and other activities relating to automobile theft and accidents.

Department of Housing and Community Development. The purpose of the department of Housing and Community Development is to promote and maintain adequate housing and a decent environment for all Californians, and to seek solutions to California housing and community development problems.

Department of Parks and Recreation. The department of Parks and Recreation has three basic responsibilities: to preserve choice examples of California's unique landscape, to provide opportunities for recreation, and to preserve and interpret outstanding examples of California's rich cultural history.

Office of Alcoholic Program Management. The office of Alcohol Program Management directs the statewide alcoholism prevention program in California. The principal objectives of the office are to reduce the rate of alcohol misuse and to assist persons impaired by alcoholism in obtaining treatment.

Office of Criminal Justice Planning. The principal objective of the office of Criminal Justice Planning is the reduction of crime and juvenile delinquency. In order to meet that objective, the office provides staff support to the California Council on Criminal Justice, and coordinates comprehensive planning by state and local criminal justice agencies. It also administers grants to state and local agencies in order to encourage research and innovation in the areas of crime prevention.

Public Utilities Commission. The purpose of the Public Utilities commission is to regulate certain privately owned utilities and to assure adequate services at rates reasonable to both the consumers and the utilities. The agency also tries to promote accident reduction by establishing and enforcing safety regulations. The commission has jurisdiction over suppliers of natural gas, electricity, telephone, telegraph and water, and over common passenger and freight rails carriers.

Water Resources Control Board. The objectives and responsibilities of the Water Resources Control Board and of the nine regional water quality control boards are to preserve and enhance the quality of California's water resources and to assure its conservation and efficient use.

Many agencies have local or regional offices throughout the state. The telephone directory in your city or county will usually have the number and address of the offices nearest you. Remember that your local government also has additional agencies that serve people at the local level. In many cases involving local matters, seeking the advice or assistance of the local agency is wise.

Courts in California

The Constitution of the State of California vests the judicial power of the state in the supreme court, courts of appeal, superior courts, municipal courts, and justice courts. The superior, municipal, and justice courts are all trial courts. The supreme court and courts of appeal are the appellate courts and as such, review trial court decisions. The constitution also provides for agencies to deal with judicial administration. The Judicial Council, the Commission of Judicial Appointments, and the Commission on Judicial Performance help in the effective administration of justice, the confirmation of judicial appointments, and the admonishment, censure, removal, or retirement of judges for misconduct or disability.

As of 1980, the California judicial system had a total of 247 courts and 1,246 judges. Excluding traffic and parking violations, about 8 million cases were filed each year. The annual cost of the system is about $425 million, about $55 million of which is paid by the state and the rest by the counties.

Court Systems

The California Supreme Court consists of seven members — a chief justice and six associate justices. It is California's highest court and its decisions are binding on all other courts of the state. The power of review enables the court to pass judgment on important legal questions and to maintain uniformity in the law.

Supreme court justices are appointed by the governor and must be confirmed by the Commission on Judicial Appointments. To qualify for such an appointment, a person must be either an attorney admitted to the practice of law in California or must have served as a judge of a court of record in California for ten years immediately preceding the appointment. After confirmation, the judge serves until the next gubernatorial election when he or she must run unopposed for election. Supreme court justices are elected for twelve-year terms.

Regular sessions are held by the court in San Francisco, Los Angeles, and Sacramento. The court may also hold special sessions elsewhere. Over 3,500 matters are filed with the supreme court each year, of which about 3,000 are petitions for a hearing in cases previously decided by the courts of appeal.

Finally, in addition to its many other responsibilities, the supreme court also reviews the recommendations of the Commission on Judicial Performance and the State Bar of California concerning the disciplining of judges and attorneys.

The Courts of Appeal were established pursuant to a constitutional amendment in 1904, and are California's intermediate courts of review. Some 15,000 appeals and other proceedings are filed with and reviewed in these courts annually.

For purposes of efficiency, California has been divided into five appellate districts, each having a court of appeal composed of one or more divisions. Each division is composed of three or more judges who are appointed by the governor and confirmed by the Commission on Judicial Appointments. Their qualifications, election, and term of office are the same as that of supreme court justices. The legislature has the constitutional authority to create new apellate districts and divisions of the courts of appeal. Currently, the five appellate districts have thirteen divisions and fifty-nine judges. The headquarters for the five appellate districts are: San Francisco (First District), Los Angeles (Second District), Sacramento (Third District), San Diego and San Bernardino (Fourth District), and Fresno (Fifth District).

At the courts of appeal, cases are decided by three-judge panels. Their decisions, or opinions, are published if they (1) establish a new rule of law or modify an existing rule, (2) involve a legal issue of continuing public interest, or (3) criticize existing law. Each year about eighteen percent of the courts' opinions are certified for publication.

The Superior Courts are the state's trial court of general jurisdiction. This means that the superior court has original trial jurisdiction in all cases except those specifically covered by statute. The superior court also sits as a probate court, family court, and juvenile court. In addition, the superior court has jurisdiction of all felony cases and of all civil matters above the jurisdictional monetary limits of the municipal and justice courts.

There is a superior court in each of the fifty-eight counties in California. The number of judges who sit on these courts is set by the legislature and varies from county to county. The less populous counties may have only one judge. Los Angeles County has approximately 200 superior court judges.

Superior court judges serve six-year terms and are elected at general elections by voters of the county in which they will serve. Vacancies are filled by appointment of the governor. A judge of the superior court must be either an attorney admitted to the practice of law in California or must have served as a judge of a court of record in California for at least ten years immediately preceding his or her election or appointment.

The Municipal Court is one of the two types of trial court that exists below the superior court level (the other is the justice court). There are currently eighty-three municipal courts in California. State legislation authorizes the county board of supervisors to divide a county into judicial districts. If the population of a ju-

FIGURE 3   The California Court System

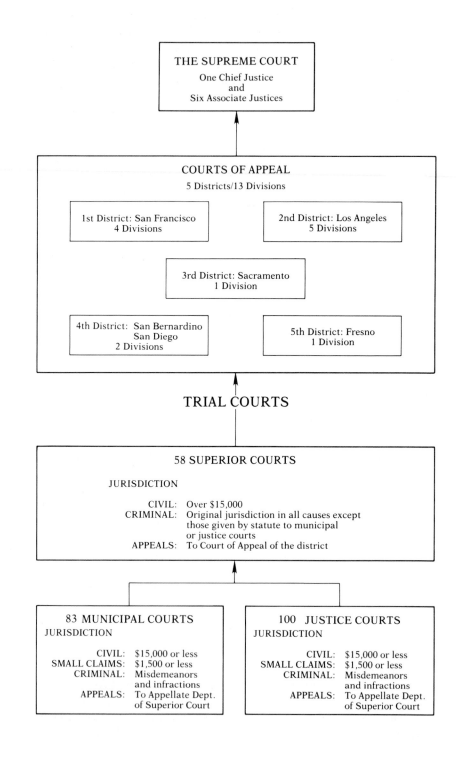

dicial district exceeds 40,000, a municipal court is established in that district.

Municipal courts have trial jurisdiction in criminal misdemeanor and infraction cases, and in all civil cases arising within the municipal court's district in which the amount involved is $15,000 or less. The municipal courts also exercise a simplified small claims jurisdiction in cases not exceeding $1,500. In addition, municipal court judges act as magistrates and conduct preliminary hearings in felony cases to determine whether there is reasonable and probable cause to hold a defendant for further proceedings or trial in superior court.

About 6.7 million cases, or over ninety percent of the state's nonparking violations cases, are handled annually by the municipal courts. In addition, these courts also take care of the estimated 10 million parking-related violations that occur each year.

Municipal court judges are elected for six-year terms on a nonpartisan ballot by voters of the judicial district in which their court is located. Vacancies in the office of municipal court judges are filled by the governor. Municipal court judges are required to be attorneys admitted to the practice of law in California for at least five years immediately preceding election or appointment.

Justice Courts are established in all judicial districts with a population of 40,000 or less. They handle about 600,000 nonparking-related cases and 200,000 parking-related cases each year. Since January 1, 1977, the justice courts have had the same civil and criminal jurisdiction as municipal courts.

Justice court judges are elected for a six-year term, and vacancies are filled by local county boards of supervisors, which also set the number and boundaries of justice court districts in their respective counties. Before 1975, the judges could be either attorneys admitted to the California State Bar or candidates could pass a qualifying examination given by the Judicial Council. Today, however, vacancies must be filled by attorneys only.

The United States Federal Courts located in California are called the United States District Courts and the United States Circuit Courts of Appeal. The United States District Courts are the federal trial courts. These courts handle federal criminal cases, cases in which a United States constitutional question is at issue, and civil cases in which the parties involved are citizens of different states and have more than $10,000 in controversy. Cases involving citizens of different states are known as diversity cases.

There are four United States court districts in California:

1. The Eastern District of California: The court holds sessions in Sacramento and in Fresno.

2. The Northern District of California: The court holds sessions in San Francisco and in San Jose.

3. The Central District of California: The court holds sessions in Los Angeles.

4. The Southern District of California: The court holds sessions in San Diego.

Appeals from U.S. district court decisions are made to the U.S. Circuit Court of Appeals. There are eleven federal judicial circuits. California is in the Ninth Circuit. The U.S. Court of Appeals for the Ninth Circuit meets in San Francisco and in Los Angeles. There are from three to fifteen permanent circuit court judges. Each United States Supreme Court Justice is also a justice for a circuit court. At present, Justice William Rehnquist is the circuit justice for the Ninth Circuit.

FIGURE 4 **The Geographic Jurisdictions of the United States District Courts in California**

FIGURE 5   **Diagram of U.S. Supreme Court and Federal Courts located in California**

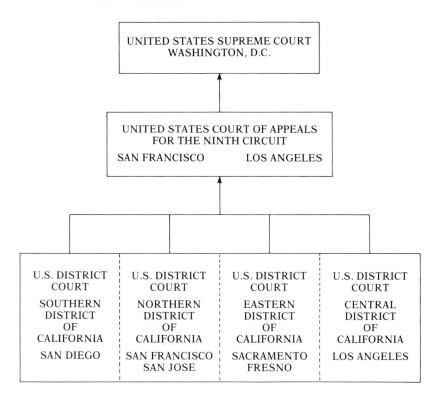

SETTLING DISPUTES OUTSIDE OF COURT

In California, the courts are not the only forums for resolving disputes. Because of the number of legal cases filed with our courts, the costs involved, and the type of case at hand, it may be wiser for parties to seek to resolve problems in other ways. In some instances, the courts require parties to enter into arbitration or mediation in an effort to resolve claims before a hearing in court. In these types of cases, California law makes awards binding on parties who have agreed to the procedure prior to the judicial hearing.

Today, mediation has become common in cases involving property settlements, child custody matters, and minor civil matters. Even in some less serious criminal cases, a prosecutor may refer a matter to a mediation program after a complaint has been filed.

California has many public agencies and private organizations that will mediate actions between the parties involved in a dispute, so they have an opportunity to voluntarily resolve the matter outside of the court system. For example, the Department of Consumer Affairs and the Better Business Bureau, which have branch offices throughout the state, both assist in mediating disputes between consumers and merchants. The American Arbitration Association, a nonprofit organization with offices in San Francisco, Los Angeles, and San Diego, also handles matters involving labor, business, and accident cases, and can refer other types of disputes to appropriate agencies.

A sampling of some other types of dispute resolution programs in California include the following:

Family Law Counseling Services
1600 Shattuck Avenue
Suite 200
Berkeley, Ca. 94709
(415) 548-5551

Housing Alliance of Contra
    Costa County
2480 Pacheco Street
Concord, Ca. 94520
(415) 825-4663

American Association for
    Mediated Divorce
5435 Balboa Blvd.
Suite 208
Encino, Ca. 91318
(213) 986-6953

Christian Conciliation Service,
    San Joaquin Valley
P.O. Box 1348
Fresno, Ca. 93715
(209) 266-5086

District Attorney's Hearing
    Officer Program
1800 Criminal Courts Bldg.
210 West Temple Street
Los Angeles, Ca. 90012
(213) 974-3531

Endispute of Southern
    California, Incorporated
3345 Wilshire Blvd. #407
Los Angeles, Ca. 90010
(213) 387-3515

The New Family Center
210 California Ave.
Suite G
Palo Alto, Ca. 94306
(415) 328-3218

Center for Collaborative
    Problem Solving
2822 Van Ness Avenue
San Francisco, Ca. 94109
(415) 673-0503

Community Board Program
149 Ninth Street
San Francisco, Ca. 94103
(415) 552-1250

Neighborhood Mediation and
    Conciliation Services
70 West Hedding
San Jose, Ca. 95110
(408) 299-2206

Neighborhood Justice Center
1320 Santa Monica Mall
Santa Monica, Ca. 90401
(213) 451-8192

Neighborhood Small Claim
    Night Court
200 West Hedding St.
San Jose, Ca. 95110
(408) 299-4971

San Jose Housing Service
425 Stockton Ave.
San Jose, Ca. 95126
(408) 287-2464

L.A. City Attorney Program
1700 City Hall East
200 North Main Street
Los Angeles, Ca. 90012
(213) 485-5407/5926

Family Court Services of the
  Superior Court
928 Main Street
Martinez, Ca. 94553
(915) 372-2681

Mountain View Rental Housing
  Mediantion Gr.
650 Castro
Mountain View, Ca. 94040
(415) 966-6308

Pastoral Mediation Services
Holy Names College
3500 Mountain Blvd.
Oakland, Ca. 94619
(415) 436-0911

Family Mediation Service
285 Hamilton Ave.
Palo Alto, Ca. 94301
(415) 328-7000

Rental Housing Mediation
  Task Force (RHMTA)
City Hall
250 Hamilton Avenue
Palo Alto, Ca. 94303
(415) 329-2375

Family Mediation Center of
  Marin County
610 D Street
San Rafael, CA 94901
(415) 459-1628

Mediation Services
Administration Bldg.
Civic Center, rm. 243
San Rafael, Ca. 94903
(415) 499-6191

Program for Consumer Affairs
701 Ocean St. rm. 240
Santa Cruz, Ca. 95060
(408) 425-2054

Rental Information and
  Mediation Service
Nelson Community Ctr.
301 Center St. rm. 7
Santa Cruz, Ca. 95060
(408) 425-1001

Divorcing Family Clinic
Center for Legal
Psychiatry
2424 Wilshire Blvd.
Santa Monica, Ca.
90403
(213) 829-9764

Family Court Service
Room 501, Courthouse
222 E. Weber Avenue
Stockton, Ca. 95202
(209) 944-3511

Note that many of these agencies or private organizations are limited in the type of cases they handle. If an agency or organization is not able to help, they can usually refer individuals to an appropriate agency.

THE ADVERSARY SYSTEM

Steps in a Trial

The steps in a trial, as described in the national text are a fairly accurate description of the process in California. In many cases, however, the actual trial process begins with the choosing of a jury (although not all trials involve juries), rather than with the opening statements of plaintiff or prosecutor. In choosing a jury, the attorneys for the parties question the jurors to determine whether there are any reasons why a given juror cannot decide the case in an unbiased manner. If a bias is suspected, a juror may be excused, and another person may take his or her place.

In California, defense counsels may also choose to wait until the plaintiff or prosecuting attorney has presented his or her entire case before making any opening statements.

Judges and Juries

Many of the requirements for becoming a judge in California were described in the section on state courts. The role and duties of a judge in California are essentially the same as those described in the national text.

In California, jury trials may be requested in either civil or criminal matters. In civil matters and in misdemeanor cases, the parties may agree on a jury of less than twelve members but no less than six, and in civil matters only three-fourths of the jury need render a verdict. In criminal felony cases, defendants normally request a jury trial. Here, however, the jury must be made up of twelve persons, and the verdict must be unanimous.

Jurors in California are selected on a random basis from among residents of the county in which the trial will take place. There can be no discrimination on the basis of sex or race. A juror must be a citizen, at least eighteen years of age, and must meet the residency and other requirements of one entitled to vote in the state (see "Voting" this chapter). Jurors must also be able to see, hear, and speak adequately, be of ordinary intelligence, and have sufficient knowledge and understanding of the English language.

In addition to the above requirements, a prospective juror may be disqualified if she or he has been convicted of misconduct while in public office or of a felony or other high crime, or if he or she is serving as a grand juror in any court in the state. In California the court may also excuse a person from jury service upon a finding that the jury service would entail undue hardship for the person or the public. This law replaces a former rule that automatically exempted a number of types of people (e.g., doctors, lawyers, mail carriers, railroad engineers). Peace officers, how-ever, are still exempt. Finally, plaintiffs and defendants have the right to challenge either the entire jury panel or individual jurors. In situations in which the entire panel is being challenged, nor-mally a party to the action believes that the process used to select the panel was illegal.

Challenges made to individual jurors are either "for cause" or "preemptory" (without cause). Jurors are usually removed for cause if something exists in their character or past that might affect their impartiality. Unlike the preemptory challenge, there is no limit to how many jurors may be challenged for cause. In California, each side in a civil case is limited to six preemptory challenges, unless there is more than one party on a side. In the latter instance, the attorneys representing joint parties have eight preemptory challenges. In criminal cases, each party normally has ten preemptory challenges. If, however, the death penalty or life imprisonment is involved, the prosecution and the defense each have twenty-six preemptory challenges.

LAWYERS

There are approximately 85,000 attorneys in the state of Cal-ifornia. Not all, however, are practicing; some teach, are in busi-ness, or work at other professions not necessarily directly related to the practice of law.

As mentioned in the national text, the practice of law varies. For example, a large multinational corporation and an elderly woman living in a public housing project may both require the services of attorneys. Also not only do clients vary, but the kind of law that lawyers practice varies. Today most attorneys specialize in particular areas of law.

How Do You Find A Lawyer?

To help people find an appropriate attorney for their individual needs, most local, county, and city bar associations operate lawyer referral services. Bar associations will generally suggest several lawyers, so the inquirer makes the final selection. In some in-stances, the attorney will charge no fee or a relatively low fee for the first consultation. Look in the yellow pages of your local Cal-ifornia telephone directory under "Attorney Referral Services," "Attorneys," or "Lawyers" for the appropriate phone numbers in your county.

Individuals who do not have the means to hire an attorney may qualify for the services of the Legal Aid Society or Legal Services Foundation. When in doubt concerning the financial qualifications for legal aid or the type of cases handled by a legal assistance office, contact the office directly for information. Check the white pages of your local telephone directory for the number of the agency nearest you.

Finally, governmental agencies and nonprofit public interest groups also provide either free or low-cost legal services when the particular problem is within their area of interest. Such areas include housing discrimination, civil liberties, consumer protection, and social services. Many of these organizations are listed in the yellow pages or may be found through a local referral office. If attempts to find legal help do not bring satisfactory results, call or write:

> The Department of Legal Services
> The State Bar of California
> 555 Franklin Street
> San Francisco, California 94102
> (415) 561-8250

Problems with Your Attorney

The two most frequent disputes between clients and attorneys involve either the attorney's fee or the professional quality of his or her work.

If you believe that an attorney has charged you too much for the services rendered, you should know that in California the Rules of Professional Conduct provide guidelines that every lawyer must follow in establishing fees. These guidelines require lawyers to submit most fee disputes for arbitration if a client files a request with the State Bar of California. To file such a request, contact the bar association office at either of these addresses:

State Bar of California
Office of the State Bar Court
555 Franklin Street
San Francisco, California 94102
(415) 561-8386

State Bar of California
Office of the State Bar Court
1230 West Third Street
Los Angeles, California 90017
(213) 482-8220

If the dispute with your attorney involves more than just the fee, or if the fee is only part of the problem, the Rules of Professional Conduct also cover ethical considerations that all attorneys must follow. A lawyer who violates these rules is subject to suspension or, for severe misconduct, disbarment. Once a complaint regarding a lawyer's conduct is filed with the state bar, the complaint is investigated and hearings are held to decide the matter. The California Supreme Court must review all cases in which either suspension or disbarment is recommended by the state bar.

Some examples of lawyer misconduct are as follows: misusing or stealing a client's money, deceiving a client or the court, abandoning a client's case, taking action on behalf of a client without authority, and violating a client's confidentiality. There are many other rules that lawyers must adhere to, and if a client believes that a lawyer is in violation of the Code of Ethics, a complaint can be filed with either the Los Angeles or San Francisco office of the State Bar of California.

State Bar of California
Office of Trial Counsel
555 Franklin Street
San Francisco, California 94102
(415) 561-8200

State Bar of California
Office of Trial Counsel
1230 West Third Street
Los Angeles, California 90017
(213) 482-8220

Lastly, if a client suffers a financial loss, the deprivation of rights, or a damaged reputation because of an attorney's negligence, the client can take action against the attorney for malpractice. In these circumstances, however, you usually have to seek the assistance of another attorney.

two
CRIMINAL AND JUVENILE JUSTICE

In California, most of the laws that define criminal conduct have been written by the state legislature and may be found in the California Penal Code. Other criminal laws, however, are also included in the Health and Safety Code, Business and Professions Code, Food and Agricultural Code, Corporations Code, Vehicle Code, Fish and Game Code, and the Welfare and Institutions Code.

In addition, persons must also abide by local laws, usually referred to as city or county ordinances. Examples of local ordinances are curfew laws, no smoking laws, and laws requiring smoke detectors or fire escapes in public buildings.

NATURE AND CAUSES OF CRIME

As the national text suggests, sociologists have studied the causes of crime in the United States for some time and will probably continue these studies. A recent three-year California study conducted by the State Commission on Crime Control and Violence Protection identified eleven causes of violence, including poor diet, racism, alcoholism, war, and capital punishment.

This commission noted among other findings the following:

395

■ There is no direct cause-and-effect relationship between any of the negative factors identified, but people subjected to several of them — an abused child, who eats junk food and spends much of his time watching violent TV programs, for example — is much more likely to resort to violent behavior than others.

■ Alcohol is involved in nearly two-thirds of all violent incidents.

■ There is a "strong association" between having been abused as a child and growing up to become a violent adult.

■ The theory that violent TV shows "drain off" violent energy from viewers, thus preventing violence, is not supported by findings.

■ Chemical additives in food and vitamin deficiencies may set off violent behavior.

■ Economic deprivation and frustrated ambitions are "related" to violence.

Among the California commission's more controversial recommendations were laws that would prohibit parents from spanking their children, and new legislation tightening restrictions on the ownership of guns.

In recent years, the California legislature and the people of California have tried to provide additional sevices and financial assistance for the victims of crime. Today, many counties operate victim assistance programs, which offer counseling to help victims overcome the psychological effects associated with being the victim of a crime. These programs also help prepare the victims and their family for the criminal prosecution to come. Finally, if victims suffer a financial loss as a direct result of a violent crime, they may be entitled to compensation from the state for those losses.

Under the California Aid to Victims of Crime Act, a victim must apply to the State Board of Control within one year of the incident for compensation. The application must be verified and include all of the information required by the law (i.e., date, nature, and circumstances of the crime, and financial statement). The board may deny a claim if it finds that the victim participated in the crime, did not cooperate with the police, was not physicially injured or killed, or did not suffer severe financial hardships as a result of the crime.

Upon approval of the application, the board may take any or all of the following actions.:

1. Authorize cash payment, not to exceed $10,000, for medical expenses directly resulting from injury.

2. Authorize cash payment, not to exceed $10,000, equaling loss of wages or support.

TABLE 1 California Crime Rate and Percentage Change

CRIME INDEX OFFENSES	ESTIMATED CRIME 1982		PERCENT CHANGE OVER 1981		PERCENT CHANGE OVER 1980		PERCENT CHANGE OVER 1977	
	Number	Rate per 100,000	Number	Rate per 100,000	Number	Rate per 100,000	Number	Rate per 100,000
Total	1,181,099	4,777	-2.2	-4.3	-1.0	-4.8	28.8	16.4
Violent	201,443	815	-3.2	-5.3	-4.0	-7.7	31.8	19.1
Property	979,666	3,962	-2.0	-4.1	-0.3	-4.2	28.1	15.8
Murder	2,778	11	-11.5	-13.8	-18.4	-21.7	12.0	0.9
Forcible rape	12,529	51	-7.5	-9.5	-8.3	-11.8	16.9	5.8
Robbery	91,988	372	-1.8	-3.8	-1.9	-2.8	47.9	33.7
Aggravated assault	94,138	381	-3.8	-5.8	-8.2	-11.8	21.6	9.9
Burglary	499,468	2,020	-7.5	-9.4	-8.2	-11.7	7.9	-2.4
Larceny-Theft	315,668	1,277	6.2	3.9	19.5	14.9	100.1	80.0
Motor vehicle theft	164,530	666	1.4	-0.8	-5.7	-9.4	14.2	3.3

3. Authorize cash payment, not to exceed $3,000, to or on behalf of a victim for job retraining and rehabilitation.

If a private citizen is injured or killed while attempting to prevent a crime, apprehend a criminal, or rescue a person in immediate danger, that person may similarily seek compensation for financial losses.

GENERAL CONSIDERATION

Classes of Crimes

In California, criminal offenses are divided into three categories: felonies, misdemeanors, and infractions. A felony is the most serious type of crime and is punishable by a fine and/or imprisonment in a state prison or death. A misdemeanor is punishable by a fine and/or imprisonment in a county jail for a period not exceeding one year. An infraction is ordinarily not punishable by imprisonment if the defendant appears in court and/or pays a fine. A person charged with an infraction is not entitled to a jury trial or to an attorney at the state's expense. Most traffic violations are infractions.

Note that many crimes are punishable either as misdemeanors or as felonies. These crimes are called "wobblers," and are considered felonies until such time as a judgment is imposed. Whether a person is convicted of a felony or a misdemeanor can be important for several reasons other than sentencing. For example, felony convictions are weighed more heavily against defendants in future prosecutions, and convicted felons may eventually have more difficulty when trying to vote or seeking employment.

Crimes of Omission

As suggested in the national text, crimes of omission are exceptions to the general rule relating to criminal liability. In California, these exceptions usually arise when a special relationship exists between particular parties such that the state believes a duty of care should be imposed. The failure to fulfill this duty leaves one open to criminal liability. For example, parents are under an affirmative duty to provide for the care of their children. Failure to act or provide support may form the basis of criminal neglect charges. Similarly, doctors and medical assistants have a duty to care for their patients. The failure to provide that care may result in a charge of criminal negligence or manslaughter.

Under California law, doctors, nurses, dentists, teachers, and counselors also have a legal duty to report incidents of suspected child abuse. Again, failure to report could result in criminal charges (see supplement Chapter Four).

PRELIMINARY CRIMES

Solicitation

In California the crime of solicitation applies only to certain offenses. These offenses are bribery, grand theft, robbery, receiving stolen property, burglary, perjury, kidnapping, forgery, arson, extortion, aggravated assault, murder, or rape. One may also be convicted of disorderly conduct if the solicitation is for purposes of prostitution. In crimes other than these enumerated crimes, the solicitor is punishable as the principal only if the target crime is actually committed.

Attempt

In order for a person to be punished for an attempt to commit a crime in California, there must be a specific intent to commit the crime and a direct act in furtherance of its commission. If additional crimes are committed while attempting to commit the target crime, a person can be punished both for the attempt as well as for the additional crimes actually committed. The California Penal Code contains various statutes defining the crimes of attempt to commit specific crimes. These statutes specifically describe acts that constitute the attempted crime. This has been done by the California legislature to help our courts determine at what point "acts in furtherance" constitute the attempt. Attempts in California are usually punishable at about half the severity of the completed crime.

Conspiracy

In California, conspiracy requires a specific intent to do an unlawful act, an agreement between two or more persons, and an overt act in furtherance of that agreement. Conspirators can be held criminally liable for the reasonable and probable consequences of their coconspirators acts, as well as for the crime of conspiracy itself. Abandonment, or renunciation of the conspiracy, will not relieve a person from liability for the conspiracy. If, however, a person withdraws from the conspiracy and communicates that intention to fellow conspirators, the individual will not be criminally liable for any future criminal acts committed by former coconspirators. Note, that a person can be found guilty of both conspiracy and the actual crime, or an attempt.

CRIMES AGAINST THE PERSON

Homicide

In large part, the information included in the national text is applicable in California with a few distinctions.

1. California defines the unlawful killing of a fetus as murder.

2. Felony murder is treated as first-degree murder only if and when the homicide is committed in perpetration or attempted perpetration of certain crimes, namely, rape, robbery, burglary, mayhem, or child molestation. If, on the other hand, the homicide takes place during the commission or attempted commission of any other dangerous felony, the felony murder is treated as a second degree murder.

3. Manslaughter in California is divided into three different categories: voluntary, involuntary (which includes the unlawful killing of a person during the commission of a misdemeanor), and manslaughter in the driving of a vehicle.

The punishment for committing first degree murder is death or confinement in a state prison for a term of twenty-five years to life. If convicted of second degree murder, the punishment is fifteen years to life. Voluntary manslaughter is punishable with a prison term of up to six years, and involuntary manslaughter with a maximum term of four years. Vehicular manslaughter can be punishable as either a felony or a misdemeanor.

Assault and Battery

In order to be found guilty of criminal assault in California, it is necessary to show that the defendant had an actual and present ability to commit a violent injury to another person. Assault is punishable by a fine and/or imprisonment in the county jail. When the assault is against a peace officer, firefighter, or certain other public officials (including a teacher or school administrator) the punishment is greater. When an assault is committed with the intent to commit certain crimes of violence against another person, such as rape, the punishment can be up to six years in prison. An assault with a deadly weapon is punishable by up to four years in prison; if against a peace officer or a firefighter, the penalty may be increased to five years.

A battery is defined as any willful and unlawful use of force or violence on another person. It is punishable by a fine of up to $1000 and/or up to four years in prison.

Rape

Though the information in the national text is generally correct and applicable in most states, California has enacted several laws that dramatically affect our rape laws.

First, forcible rape statutes no longer use the terms "man" or "woman." Instead, the statute applies to "persons," making rape a crime applicable to both men and women. Rape laws also now protect the "spouse" of the perpetrator, and rape is defined as an act of sexual intercourse against the will of the spouse by means of force, fear, or future retaliation. Spousal rape charges must be reported to the police within ninety days and are punishable by up to eight years in prison.

Second; in California statutory rape is called "unlawful sexual intercourse" and is the act of sexual intercourse with a female, not the wife of the perpetrator, who is under the age of eighteen. A violation of this law is punishable either as a misdemeanor or a felony. If the female victim is under the age of fourteen, however, additional charges may be brought, and the perpetrator may be sentenced to up to eight years in prison.

If the accused reasonably and in good faith believed that the minor female was in fact over the age of consent, evidence may be presented to try to reduce the charge.

Although the California Supreme Court recently agreed that this law does discriminate on the basis of sex, since only females can be victims and only males can violate the statute, the court found that a compelling state interest in preventing teenage pregnancies was adequate to legally justify the law.

Third, in California a defense attorney's ability to admit evidence about or to comment on a victim's unchaste character or prior sexual activity has been drastically limited. At the time of trial, the state can also withhold the victim's current address and telephone number from the public record. Finally, in a further effort to reduce the stress on rape victims, California has established rape crisis and assistance centers throughout the state. These centers offer various counseling services aimed at eventually overcoming the trauma associated with the rape.

CRIMES AGAINST PROPERTY

Arson

In California the punishment for arson depends largely on whether the property burned was inhabited or whether it was forest land, real estate, or personal property. Those convicted of arson may be sentenced to up to nine years in prison. It is also a crime to recklessly set fires, and in such circumstances, the state need not prove that the act was willful and malicious. Finally, it is also a crime to burn one's own property with the intent to defraud an insurance carrier.

Vandalism

Vandalism is defined as the malicious defacing, damaging, or destroying of any real or personal property belonging to another, and is punishable by up to six months in jail and/or a fine not exceeding $1,000, if the damage caused is less than $1000. If the damage is $1000 or more, the offense can be treated as a felony. The court may also require the person convicted of vandalism to repair the damage as a condition of probation. In addition, a number of other offenses set forth in the California Penal Code, such as mistreatment of animals, vandalism of a place of worship, damage to a railroad, throwing dangerous substances upon a public highway, and removing or defacing a landmark, constitute separate and distinct acts of vandalism.

Note also that the parents of a child who causes damage to school property may be held liable for up to $5,000 for such damages. If a firearm is used, which the parents have permitted the minor to possess, the parents' liability increases to $15,000 for property damage and $30,000 in the event of bodily injury or death. Parents may also be held liable for up to $500 to reimburse school districts for rewards paid to apprehend their child.

Larceny and Embezzlement

In California, larceny, embezzlement, and obtaining property by false pretenses are all defined as theft, and theft crimes are classified either as grand theft of petty theft. Grand theft is accomplished when the value of the property or services taken is worth over $400 or when a specified item taken is worth over $100. The theft of any firearm, of certain animals, or of property directly from one's person also amounts to grand theft. Petty theft includes all other acts of larceny.

Robbery

All robberies in California are considered felonies and are punishable by up to six years in prison. If the robbery is committed with the use of a firearm, a prison term is mandatory, and additional time may be imposed.

Extortion

In California, extortion applies to unlawfully obtaining an act or service from a public officer, as well as unlawfully obtaining property from a private citizen. The threat used can be to physically injure the victim, accuse the victim of a crime, expose the victim to disgrace, or expose any secret affecting the victim. Extortion may be punished with a prison term of up to four years.

Burglary

A burglary of an inhabited dwelling house or trailer is first degree burglary and is punishable as a felony with up to six years in prison. A house is considered inhabited even if it is temporarily unoccupied at the time of the burglary. All other types of burglaries are second degree burglaries and are punishable either as a felony or a misdemeanor. California does not distinguish between burglaries committed at night or during the day.

Forgery

In addition to forgery, California also has made it a crime to falsify a drivers license or to knowingly write a check against insufficient funds.

Receiving Stolen Property

The crime of receiving stolen property is considered a felony in California unless the value of the property received does not exceed $400, in which case the state may treat the offense as a misdemeanor. Proof that one actually knew that the property was stolen is not required to establish a breach of the law. It is enough that a reasonable person should have known that the property was probably stolen. Innocent parties, who in good faith purchased stolen property and then returned it to the rightful owner, may bring a civil action against the original receiver of the stolen goods, for three times the value of damages, plus attorney's fees and court costs.

Unauthorized Use of a Motor Vehicle

In California, a person may be charged and convicted of one of three distinct crimes relating to auto theft. These are grand theft, theft and unlawful driving, or the taking of a vehicle (joy riding). The crimes vary in severity, and the state may decide which charges to bring depending on the circumstances. The factors that are considered include the age of the suspect, whether there was an intent to permanently deprive the owner of the use or value of the vehicle, whether the suspect has a prior record, and the relationship, if any, between the suspect and the owner of the vehicle.

CONTROVERSIAL CRIMES

Drug Offenses

In 1975, the California Health and Safety Code was amended to define possession of one ounce or less of marijuana as a crime punishable by a fine of up to $100. Possession of amounts over one ounce is punishable by up to six months in a county jail and/or a fine of up to $500. An additional subsection of the California law allows for punishment of up to 10 days in jail and/or up to a $500 fine for possession of any quantity of marijuana on school grounds. Possession of any quantity of marijuana for the purpose of sale, and the cultivation of marijuana are both felonies punishable by a state prison term.

Possession of any one of nearly 135 controlled substances (drugs) deemed to be dangerous is a felony whether or not sale is involved. These drugs include heroin, cocaine, LSD, DMT, STP, amphetamines, PCP, and barbiturates. For a few drugs, such as quadludes, the sanctions are limited to six months in jail and/or a $500 fine. It is also unlawful to possess certain drug paraphernalia or to be in a place where heroine, cociane, mescaline, peyote, or synthetic THC is being used with the knowledge that such activity is occurring.

Sex Offenses

In 1975, the California legislature passed the Consenting Adult Act, which removed the criminal penalties for some sexual acts. As a result, adulterous cohabitation, oral sex, and sodomy are no longer crimes, as long as they involve consenting adults acting in the privacy of their home.

Note that it is still a criminal offense to engage in these activities with persons under the age of eighteen or with individuals incapable of consenting. Bigamy and prostitution are still criminal offenses in California.

Suicide and Euthanasia

Suicide is not a criminal offense in California, therefore an attempted suicide is not a crime. Aiding, advising, or encouraging another to commit suicide is, however, a felony.

Euthanasia is illegal in California and is treated as a homicide. In 1976, however, California became the first state to enact legislation authorizing a terminally ill adult who is of sound mind to request that further medical care be discontinued and that he or she be allowed to die. This statute, entitled the Natural Death Act, is limited and does not allow others, without permission of a court, to take an action that would lead to the death of a particular person (see Chapter Four, "Death and the Law").

DEFENSES

Self-Defense and Defense of Property and Others The information in the national text relating to the defense of self, of other's, and of property applies in California. Note also that California allows individuals to stand their ground and defend themselves. In other words, persons need not attempt to retreat before resorting to the use of reasonable force to protect themselves.

Defendent Committed a Criminal Act but Is Not Criminally Responsible for His or Her Actions

Infancy All children in California under the age of fourteen are presumed incapable of committing a crime. This presumption is, however, rebuttable and the state may present evidence showing that the child had knowledge of the wrongfulness of his or her conduct. The age requirement refers to one's chronological age and not to mental age.

Insanity For a long time, California, like most states, applied the McNaghten test when trying to determine whether a defendant was insane at the time of the commission of a criminal act. As stated in the national text, defendants were relieved of criminal liability if, at the time of the offense, they did not know what they were doing or lacked the ability to distinguish between right and wrong. In 1978, however, the California Supreme Court adopted a new test that allows for the insanity defense if defendants can establish that they lacked the capacity to conform their conduct to the requirements of the law. In response to this seemingly more liberal test, in 1982 the people of California passed Proposition 8. Under this constitutional amendment, defendants are now required to prove that they were incapable of knowing or understanding the nature and quality of their acts and that they could not distinguish right from wrong at the time of the commission of the offense. This differs from the traditional McNaghten Test, which required proof of either of two alternatives, as opposed to proof of both.

THE CRIMINAL JUSTICE PROCESS

ARREST

The information in the national text on arrest is generally applicable to California procedures. Of the 1,700,000 total arrests reported in 1982 in the state, 85% were arrests of adults and 15% of juveniles. Of these arrests, about 75% were for misdemeanors, 23% for felonies, and 2% for other offenses.

It is important to know that resisting arrest in California is a misdemeanor and may constitute a separate offense, even if the primary charge, for which the arrest was made, later proves unfounded. Assaulting a peace officer who is attempting to make an arrest is a felony. The only exception to these rules occurs when a peace officer is using unreasonable force to effectuate an arrest. The person being arrested may then use the minimal amount of force necessary to protect him or herself from bodily injury.

Arrests in California may also be conducted by private citizens. Citizens, however, may only make an arrest if the public offense or misdemeanor is attempted or committed in their presence, or when the citizen reasonably believes that the individual has committed a felony.

SEARCH AND SEIZURE
INTERROGATIONS AND CONFESSIONS

In recent years, California Supreme Court rulings in this area of the law have been more liberal than the rulings of the United States Supreme Court. In other words, the California court has been more inclined to interpret defendants due process rights more broadly. In some cases, rights were given to defendants because the state court believed that although these rights were not required by the U.S. Constitution, they were required by the California constitution. In 1982 with the passage of Proposition 8, the

Victim's Bill of Rights, all this was changed. The people of California, by the initiative and amendment process, required that the state constitution be read in the same way as the federal Constitution, and that strict federal rules be applied in California. Accordingly, the laws applicable in California in the areas of search and seizure and interrogations and confessions are the same as the U.S. Supreme Court rulings delineated in the national text.

FIGURE 6 The Criminal Court Process in California

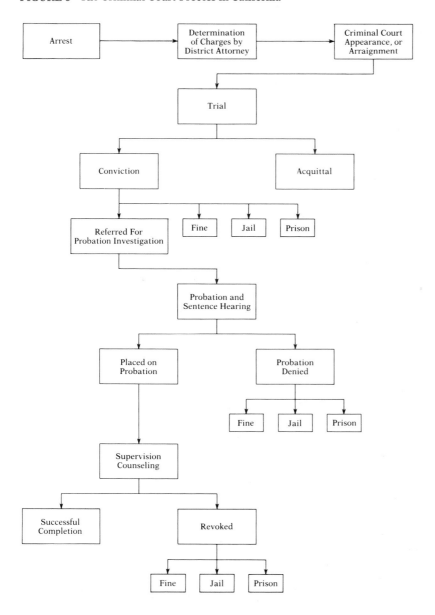

PROCEEDINGS BEFORE TRIAL

Booking and Initial Appearance

Upon arrest in California, a suspect has the right to make three completed phone calls. California law also specifies that a person who has been arrested must be taken before a magistrate without unnecessary delay and, in any event, within two days of his or her arrest (excluding Sundays and holidays).

Bail and Pretrial Release

Until recently, the right to bail in California was governed by a Penal Code section which stated that defendants must be released from custody prior to trial on the posting of bail as a matter of right unless they were charged with an offense punishable by death. Today, the right to bail in noncapital felony cases is limited by the California constitution, which provides for the denial of bail when the court finds a substantial likelihood that the release of the accused would result in great bodily harm to others. The trial court may release other defendants upon the posting of reasonable bail or on their own recognizance, but in doing so the court must consider the person's ties to the community (including employment, the duration and location of residence, family attachments, and property holdings), the person's record of appearance at past court hearings, and the severity of the charge. The financial status of the defendant should not otherwise be considered.

In California the bail bonding services and procedure are similar to those described by the national text except that in California the services of bonding companies are generally used only in felony cases.

Preliminary Hearing

In California the preliminary hearing is used exclusively for felony cases in order to establish whether a crime was committed and if sufficient evidence exists to believe that the defendant committed the crime. Preliminary hearings must be held within ten days of arraignment (initial appearance in court) unless waived by the defendant or unless good cause is shown.

Grand Jury

Grand juries are used in California as an alternative method of bringing those suspected of committing a felony to trial. Information is brought to the grand jury by a county prosecutor, and if, upon examination of the information, the grand jury believes that a particular person may have committed a felony, the jury can issue an indictment for the individual's arrest.

Grand juries are made up of individuals from a given county. In those counties having a population of more than 4 million people, twenty-three people sit on the grand jury. In all other counties, nineteen people serve. If the grand jury has twenty-three members, fourteen must agree before an indictment can be issued. When nineteen members serve, twelve are required to agree for an indictment.

To serve on a grand jury in California, you must be a citizen at least eighteen years of age, a resident of the county for at least one year, be of ordinary intelligence, sound judgment, good character, and possess an adequate understanding of the English language. Jurors serve for a period of one year.

Plea Bargaining

While it is difficult to obtain accurate statistics on the frequency and practice of plea bargaining in California, it is interesting to note that out of a total of 67,411 criminal filings in California Superior Courts in 1982, 53,860 were disposed of before trial. The passing of Proposition 8 in 1982 limited plea bargaining and permits it in serious felony cases only when there is insufficient evidence to prove the case. Because of the relative newness of this law, however it has been difficult to determine what if any real impact the law has had on the practice of plea bargaining in California.

THE TRIAL

Right to Trial by Jury

In California all persons charged with misdemeanors or felonies are entitled to a trial by jury. Persons charged with infractions are not entitled to a jury trial. As mentioned in Chapter One, all juries in felony cases are comprised of twelve jurors. In misdemeanor cases, a jury may be comprised of less than twelve jurors, but no less than six jurors if a reduced number is agreed to by the parties. Verdicts in criminal cases must be unanimous, and jurors are chosen randomly from lists of the county's registered voters as well as from the motor vehicle department's licensee and identification lists.

Right to a Speedy and Public Trial

In addition to the U.S. and state constitutions, the California Penal Code gives a defendant the right to a speedy trial. In fact, under California law, the court must order an action against a defendant dismissed if the defendant has been held for fifteen days without the filing of specific charges or if charges have been filed he or she has not been brought to trial in a superior court within sixty days of the filing of such charges. In misdemeanor cases, defendents must be brought to trial within thirty days of the arraignment if they are in custody, or within forty-five days if not in custody. Again, these time requirements may be waived by defendants if they choose to do so.

As to a public trial, the California constitution and the state law both ensure the defendant's right to a public trial. Courts have held that even in cases involving torture or immorality, the defendant's right to a public trial prevails. In sensitive or volatile proceedings, children and individuals posing a risk to the court may be excluded to protect the court's interest in preserving decorum or to protect the rights of the defendant to a fair trial. A court's total exclusion of the public and the press from a particular proceeding is extremely rare and justifiable only when such exclusion is the only way to protect the defendant's right to a fair trial.

An issue that has received attention recently is the question of whether television cameras may be brought into a courtroom. Traditionally, California has banned the use of photography, recording for broadcasting, and broadcasting in the courtroom while the court was in session. Following the trend in other states, the Judicial Council of California authorized a one-year experiment allowing camera coverage of trials that began on July 1, 1980, and has since been extended. Rules require that a written request be submitted to the judge. The judge may refuse or limit extended media coverage if one of the parties to the trial objects. The rules expressly prohibit the coverage of *voir dire*, off-the-record conferences, and close-up coverage of jurors.

SENTENCING

In California judges may select from various types of sentences noted in the national text. Before doing so, however, they are required by law to have prepared and in fact to have read a presentencing report. This report is furnished by the Probation Department, and the defendant is entitled to a copy. If any errors exist in the report, the defendant may seek to have them corrected either before or at the sentencing hearing. The sentencing hearing must be scheduled within twenty-one days from the conclusion of the trial.

When a defendant is convicted of a felony that requires the imposition of a prison sentence, judges must refer to the state's Uniform Determinate Sentencing Act, which specifically sets out the length of time that individuals must serve in prison upon the conviction of certain crimes. Though somewhat involved, each crime carries three possible terms of imprisonment, for example, two, three, or four years. In the average case, the judge must sentence the convicted criminal to the middle term, here three years. However, if aggravating or mitigating circumstances are involved in the commission of the crime, the judge must either increase the sentence to four years, or reduce it to two years accordingly.

Purposes of the Sentence

Under California law, the primary purpose of sentencing individuals to a term in a state prison is for punishment.

Capital Punishment

Presently in California, the state may impose the death penalty or life imprisonment without the possibility of parole in cases involving felony-murder, treason, and murder in the first degree when, in the judgement of the trier of facts (usually a jury), "special circumstances" have occurred during the commission of the crime. For example if the murder was

- commited for hire;
- preceded by a previous conviction of murder;
- multiple in nature (more than one victim);
- of a witness in a proceding against you;
- committed by explosives;
- committed to avoid a lawful arrest or while escaping from the custody of a peace officer, prosecutor, government official, or firefighter;
- cruel or involved torture; or
- committed by poisoning.

After the defendant is found guilty of a capital offense, then an additional, separate trial is held to determine the penalty. In the penalty trial, if it is concluded that "special circumstances" were applicable to the case, the trier of fact must then decide if the mitigating circumstances outweigh the aggravating circumstances, or vice versa, to determine if the sentence should be death or life imprisonment without the possiblity of parole. Note that in California the death penalty cannot be imposed on any person under the age of eighteen. There are also many appellate and review procedures required before the death penalty can be imposed, and as a result, few offenders have actually been executed in California in recent years.

JUVENILE JUSTICE

Unlike the California adult justice system, the principal purpose of the juvenile justice system is to provide for the care and guidance of minors. Complementary objectives are to protect the public from the criminal acts of minors, to give minors a sense of responsibility, and to preserve and strengthen the family.

For purposes of juvenile court proceedings, minors are generally categorized in three distinct groups; (1) those found to have committed criminal acts (delinquents), (2) those in need of supervision (status offenders or incorrigibles), and (3) those who have been abused or neglected (see supplement Chapter Four).

Who Is a Juvenile?

In California, with certain exceptions, all persons under eighteen years of age who fall in one of the grouping listed above come under the jurisdiction of the juvenile court. Younger children normally come to the juvenile court as either status offenders or children who have been neglected or abused. However the state of California no longer offers children (under the age of seven) a conclusive presumption that they are legally incapable of criminal intent and hence a crime. Instead all minors under fourteen are only rebuttably presumed to be incapable of criminal intent and this presumption can be over come by evidence to the contrary.

In cases involving serious crimes in which the minor is sixteen or seventeen years of age, the prosecutor may seek to have the minor transferred to the adult criminal courts for prosecution as an adult. A determination as to when this action may be appropriate is based on the following:

- Minor's criminal sophistication
- Likelihood of rehabilitation
- Minor's previous record
- Circumstance and gravity of the offense

Finally, minors who have been designated wards of the juvenile court may be kept under the court's jurisdiction until the age of twenty-one if they were less than sixteen when they became wards, or until the age of twenty-five if they were over sixteen when they became wards.

FIGURE 7   The Juvenile Court Process in California

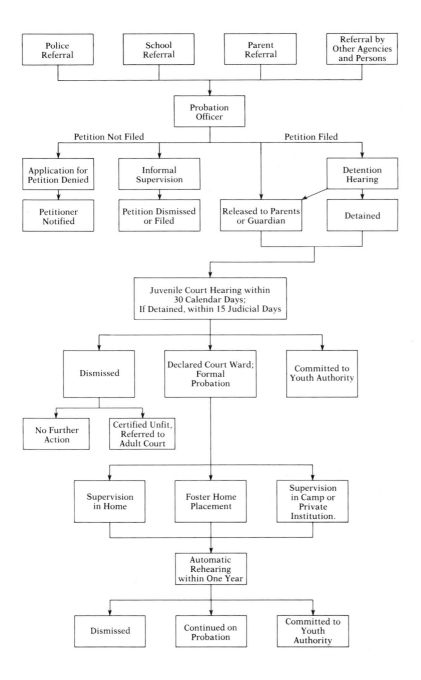

Juvenile Court Today

In addition to the constitutional rights granted by the U.S. Supreme Court, juveniles in California, whether arrested for delinquency or for status offenses, are entitled to a warning similar to the Miranda warnings given to adults. The police or probation officers must also cease questioning if the minor requests either an attorney or the presence of a parent or guardian.

Upon being taken into custody, minors must either be released within 48 hours, or have a petition for wardship filed against them. If the petition is filed, the court must hold an arraignment and detention hearing within the next forty eight hours to determine if the minor should be detained. Finally, detained minors must be given an adjudication hearing (trial) within fifteen days of the date of their arraignment or within thirty days if the minor is not in custody. Minors have the right to counsel, and parents have the right to separate counsel if and when their interests vary from those of the minor. Minors are also accorded most of the procedural due process rights accorded adult defendants. In California, however, some distinctions still exist. For example, juvenile defendants have no right to a jury trial, no right to bail, and the judge may bar the public from juvenile court proceedings.

California law requires that no child under the age of sixteen be placed in any place of confinement (including a courtroom or vehicle) with adults charged or convicted of a crime, except in the presence of a peace officer. The legislature's intent behind this law was to protect minors from possible physical harm and criminal influence. Status offenders must also be segregated from delinquents.

Final judgments or decrees from the juvenile court are appealable, and most juvenile records may be sealed or destroyed upon appropriate petition to the court. Procedures for the expungement of records can be complicated, however, since a person's eligibility often depends on the reasons for the juvenile detention, whether the person was treated as a juvenile or as an adult, and whether the person was convicted of a felony. Nevertheless usually records can be sealed after five years have passed from termination of the juvenile court jurisdiction, or as soon as the juvenile becomes eighteen. Once sealed, the records may only be opened for inspection by a court upon a showing of good cause.

three
CONSUMER
LAW

HOW LAWS
PROTECT THE CONSUMER

Federal Law

Many of the federal government's consumer protection agencies have regional offices in California. For example, the Federal Trade Commission handles complaints from consumers in the areas of deceptive business practices, misleading advertising, credit, and consumer warranties. You may contact them at these locations:

The Federal Trade Commission
450 Golden Gate Avenue,
Room 12470
San Francisco, California 94102
(415) 556-1270

The Federal Trade Commission
11000 Wilshire Boulevard,
Room 13209
Los Angeles, California 90024
(213) 824-7575

State Law

In addition to the federal laws that regulate business activities and protecting consumers in this state, since 1929 California has enacted many specific laws that have broadened the rights and remedies available to consumers. Some of the more important acts passed in recent years include the Consumer Affairs Act, the Consumer Legal Remedies Act, the Consumer Credit Reporting Act, the Song-Beverly Consumer Warranty Act, the Automobile Repair Act, and the Electronic and Appliance Repair Dealer Registration Act. Through these laws, the state has established agencies to help consumers and has given consumers the right to take merchants to court to seek injunctions, restitution, damages, and in some cases triple damages (three times the actual damage), or punitive damages for violations of the law. Finally, many of the consumer protection laws in California specifically provide for a consumer's attorney's fees to be paid in, for example, suits involving unlawful collection practices, credit denials, mobile home sales and leasing, fuel-price discrimination, warranty breaches, motor vehicle sales, and contracts with correspondence schools or dance studios.

Local Law

In addition to federal and state law, many local ordinances typically regulate the licensing and inspection of restaurants and street vendors, the disposal of garbage, and the time at which bars and/or restaurants must close or stop selling alcoholic beverages.

HOW YOU CAN PROTECT YOUR RIGHTS AS A CONSUMER

What To Do Before Buying

In addition to the guides and resources pointed out in the national text, the California Department of Consumer Affairs has its own publication entitled *Consumer Affairs*. This quarterly bulletin discusses proposed changes in state consumer laws, discloses information about products and services, and gives suggestions on alternative purchasing methods. Copies of *Consumer Affairs*, as well as many other publications, can be obtained by contacting the state office of:

The Department of Consumer Affairs
1020 N. Street
Sacramento, California 95814
(916) 445-1254

**Consumer Protection
Agencies and Organizations**

Consumer Groups   California has a host of consumer protection agencies to help resolve the different kinds of disputes that arise between consumers and utilities, banks, charities, schools, funeral homes, health clubs, nursing homes, travel agencies, and merchants concerning particular products and/or services. Agencies may be either privately funded or operated by the state or local government. Check your local telephone directory for a listing of private consumer protection agencies, a radio or television "action line," or a professional association that may be able to help.

Business and Trade Associations   In California the Better Business Bureau, issues reports, handles complaints, monitors advertising methods, distributes publications, and conducts hearings in an effort to facilitate better relations between consumers and the business community. The bureau has offices in many counties throughout the state. Better Business Bureau locations by county are as follows:

ALAMEDA
369 Twenty-second Street
Oakland, California 94612
(415) 839-5900

CONTRA COSTA
1327 N. Main Street
Walnut Creek, California 94596
(415) 933-0310

FRESNO
404-6 T. W. Patterson Building
Fresno, California 93721
(209) 268-6424

KERN
705 Eighteenth Street
Bakersfield, California 93301
(805) 322-2074

LOS ANGELES
417 S. Hill Street
Los Angeles, California 90013
(213) 627-6305
(213) 984-2212
(San Fernando Valley)

130 Pine Street
Long Beach, California 90802
(213) 435-3741

NAPA
2 Florida Street
Vallejo, California 94590
(707) 644-5553

ORANGE
1818 W. Chapman Avenue
Orange, California 92668
(714) 633-9661

RIVERSIDE
1265 N. LaCadena Drive
Colton, California
(714) 825-7280

74273 ½ Highway 111
Palm Desert, California
(714) 346-2014

SACRAMENTO
1410 Twenty-first Street
Sacramento, California
(916) 442-6843

SAN BERNARDINO
502 Inland Center Drive
San Bernardino,
California 92408
(714) 825-7280

SAN DIEGO
4310 Orange Avenue
San Diego, California 92105
(714) 283-3927

SAN FRANCISCO
414 Mason Street, Suite 500
San Francisco, California 94102
(415) 398-4300

Mission Branch Office
3013 Twenty-fourth Street
San Francisco, California
(415) 285-8062

Hunters Point Office
1611 Palou Avenue
San Francisco, California
(415) 647-7746

Chinatown Office
3 Old Chinatown Lane
San Francisco, California
(415) 397-4357

SAN JOAQUIN
343 E. Main Street
Stockton, California 95202
(209) 948-4880

SAN MATEO
20 N. San Mateo Drive
P.O. Box 294
San Mateo, California 94401
(415) 349-1251

SANTA BARBARA
903 State Street
P.O. Box 746
Santa Barbara, California 93101
(805) 963-8657

SANTA CLARA
1153 Lincoln Avenue
P.O. Box 8110
San Jose, California 95125
(408) 298-5880

State and Local Government One of the most active state consumer protection agencies in California is the Department of Consumer Affairs. The agency is devoted primarily to resolving consumer complaints and to licensing firms and individuals seeking to provide services to the consumers of the state. In an average year, the department receives and acts on over 150,000 complaints, many involving consumers' rights in connection with home solicitation, installment sales contracts, and automotive repairs. The department licenses such occupations as accountants, architects, barbers, collection agencies, contracters, cosmetologists, dry cleaners, electronic repairpersons, employment agencies, engineers, funeral directors, hearing aid dispersers, insurance adjusters, marriage counselors, nurses, opticians, pharmacists, physicians, private investigators, psychologists, repossessors, social workers, tax preparers, and veterinarians.

Consumers may contact the California Department of Consumer Affairs at any of these offices:

FRESNO
2550 Mariposa Street
Fresno, California 93721
(209) 488-5011

SACRAMENTO
1021 O. Street
Sacramento, California 95814
(916) 445-0660

LOS ANGELES
107 S. Broadway
Los Angeles, California 90012
(213) 620-4360

SAN DIEGO
1350 Front Street
San Diego, California 92101
(714) 232-4361 Ext. 371

14418 Chase Street
Van Nuys, California 91402
(213) 894-9386

SAN FRANCISCO
455 Golden Gate Avenue
Room 2191
San Francisco, California 94102
(415) 557-2046

ORANGE
730 N. Euclid Avenue
Anaheim, California 92501
(714) 635-1410

SAN JOSE
20 Harold Avenue
San Jose, California 95117
(408) 247-3134

RIVERSIDE
3630 Thirteenth Street
Riverside, California 92501
(714) 635-1410

In addition to the Department of Consumer Affairs, the state also funds the office of the district attorney. District attorneys are elected officials responsible for criminal prosecution and enforcement of state and local laws. Since many violations of consumer rights involve criminal conduct, some of the larger counties in California have a special consumer fraud or consumer affairs division in the district attorney's office. Some of these offices are listed below by county.

ALAMEDA
Investigative Division
1225 Fallon Street
Oakland, California
(415) 874-6536

FRESNO
1100 Van Ness Avenue,
    Rm. 701
Fresno, California
(209) 488-3141

CONTRA COSTA
County Courthouse
Martinez, California
(415) 228-3000

KERN
1415 Truxton Avenue
Bakersfield, California
(805) 861-2421

LOS ANGELES
Consumer Protection
  & Environment
211 W. Temple Street
Los Angeles, California
(213) 974-3971

MARIN
Civic Center
San Rafael, California
(415) 479-1100

MONTEREY
County Courthouse
Salinas, California
(408) 758-4662

ORANGE
700 Civic Center Drive, West
Santa Ana, California
(714) 834-3600

RIVERSIDE
Consumer Fraud
3535 Tenth Street
Riverside, California
(714) 787-6372

SACRAMENTO
Fraud Section
816 H Street
Sacramento, California
(916) 454-2471

SAN BERNARDINO
Consumer Fraud Section
316 N. Mountain View
San Bernardino, California
(714) 383-1134

SAN DIEGO
Fraud Division
220 W. Broadway
San Diego, California
(714) 236-2474

SAN FRANCISCO
850 Bryant Street
San Francisco, California
(415) 553-1752

SAN JOAQUIN
222 E. Weber Avenue
Stockton, California
(209) 944-2411

SAN LUIS OBISPO
Court House Annex
San Luis Obispo, California
(805) 543-3464

SAN MATEO
Hall of Justice and Records
Redwood City, California
(415) 364-5600

SANTA BARBARA
118 E. Figueroa Street
Santa Barbara, California
(805) 963-1441

SANTA CLARA
234 E. Gish Road
San Jose, California
(408) 275-9651

SONOMA
555 Mendecino Avenue
Santa Rosa, California
(707) 527-2311

STANISLAUS
1100 I Street
Modesto, California
(209) 526-6345

VENTURA
501 Poli Avenue
Ventura, California
(805) 648-6131

Taking Your Case to Court

Persons under the age of eighteen are considered minors in California and generally cannot sue in a court of law without the assistance of a parent or guardian.

Consumer complaints are usually filed in a state municipal court or in the superior court if the action involves a large sum of money or a serious personal injury. Many people in California make use of the small claims courts in minor actions involving a dispute of less than $1,500 in value. The small claims court, which is a division of the municipal court, may grant equitable relief in the form of rescission, restitution, reformation, or specific performance, in lieu of or in addition to money damages. Although attorneys are specifically excluded from representing parties in small claims court, California law does provide for small claims court "advisors." These advisors are available free of charge; and are concerned principally with assisting the public in the preparation of claims. In addition, the clerk of the court will usually help consumers with information on filing a suit, contacting a legal advisor, and with the rules that relate to notifying the party you are suing.

In short, your claim must be specific and set out the amount in dispute, and that the defendant in the action has failed or refused to pay. Those parties bringing a suit should understand that they have no right of appeal and that they must pay a nominal filing fee (unless waived by the court). The process normally takes from four to six weeks. Hearings are informal (no regular rules of evidence). Judgments usually direct time of payment, court cost, and/or other forms of appropriate relief. The small claims court is not, however, a collection agency, and will not obtain the money for the plaintiff. At best, the court provides an order and documents to help the plaintiff collect. If the defendant does not appear in court or refuses to pay after judgment is rendered, a demand should be made by letter, telephone, or in person. If unsuccessful, a writ of execution may be obtained from the court clerk. This form directs a law officer to take control of the defendant's assets, such as his or her paycheck, bank account, car, or other personal property in order to pay the judgment (see "Garnishments and Attachments").

DECEPTIVE SALES PRACTICES

Door-to-Door Sales

Under California law, door-to-door salespersons are required to identify themselves, the company they are associated with, and the product they are trying to sell, upon being welcomed at the door. If the salesperson intentionally fails to meet these requirements, a consumer has the right to demand that any contract entered into be terminated and that all payments be returned. Once the payments are returned, the consumer is required to return all goods received under the contract. If the company does not return payment within twenty business days, a consumer may seek relief in court. The court may award twice the amount of the sales price or up to $250, whichever is greater, but in no case will the damages be less than $50.

Consumers in California also have the right to cancel most contracts entered into in their homes for goods or services of $25 or more within three business days after signing the contract. Under this law, the salesperson must give the consumer a copy of the receipt or contract confirming the date of the sale, the salesperson's name and address, a statement informing the consumers of their right to cancel within three business days, and a Notice of Cancellation. If consumers later change their mind about a purchase, they must sign, date, and return the Notice of Cancellation to the seller within three business days. The seller must return any and all money received within ten business days. If the merchandise is not picked up within a reasonable length of time (usually twenty days), the consumer may either use or dispose of the merchandise. Finally, if a consumer was never properly informed of these rights, the three-day period for cancellation begins upon proper notification. These rights do not apply to cases involving emergency repair services.

Referral Sales and Phony Contests

California law requires full disclosure of facts in any contest or game played for gifts or prizes and involving some form of payment on the part of participants. A merchant or advertiser also cannot notify consumers that they have won a prize if, as a condition of winning, the consumer must purchase either goods or services. If someone offers a consumer a prize or gift through the mail, by telephone, or in person, and intends to make a sales pitch while delivering the gift, that consumer must be told of the merchant's intention when the offer is first made.

Advertising and the Consumer

In California it is unlawful to use false or misleading statements in advertising, even if such statements were made without intent to defraud or deceive. This means that even if an advertisement is absolutely true but misleading, it is unlawful. In deciding whether an advertisement is misleading, California courts consider what a reasonable person would assume to be true upon reading the advertisement.

Photographs or illustrations that are included in advertisements and are judged to be misleading are also unlawful. For example, if the item being sold is not the same item shown in the advertisement, the advertisement is misleading. The law also, requires advertisers to prove advertised claims, and merchants cannot advertise used or defective merchandise without stating the condition of the merchandise in the advertisement. When different models of a product are included in the same advertisement, the advertisement must clearly identify which model is being offered at the advertised price. Merchants cannot refuse to sell advertised items to consumers in any quantity that they have available unless the advertisement states a limit on the number of items that will be sold to a single customer. Finally, merchants must have enough of the advertised product on hand to meet a reasonable consumer demand. California law does not, however, require a merchant to give an individual a "rain check". (This allows the consumer to receive the same item at a later date at the advertised, reduced price). Rain checks are however often provided as a matter of individual store policy, but they do not legally excuse the merchant's failure to have enough of the advertised items on hand.

Bait and Switch

California law prohibits the advertising of goods or services with an intent not to sell the item or service advertised. Since the practice of bait and switch involves luring consumers with an advertised item or service with the intent of selling them something other than what was advertised, the practice is unlawful.

Mail Order Sales

In California, all mail order businesses must disclose the name and address of their business on all advertising and promotional materials, including order forms. Upon receipt of payment for a particular product, the company has six weeks (seven weeks if the purchase is by credit) to deliver the goods requested or to take one of the following actions:

- make a full refund;

- advise customer of delay and offer to refund payment within one week; or

- send substituted goods of equivalent or superior quality, and inform the buyer of the opportunity to return the goods and receive a full refund.

If unsolicited goods are sent to a consumer, the goods may be treated as an unconditional gift, and the consumer can keep the item without paying. If the company continues to bill a consumer for the unsolicited goods, the consumer has the right to obtain an injunction requiring the company to stop. "Membership clubs" such as book or record clubs, are also provided for under California law. Members may cancel membership as long as it is done by certified mail and in a manner that does not otherwise breach the terms of the contract they signed with the club. Any goods received by the consumer thirty days or more after the membership club received the notice of cancellation may be considered unconditional gifts by the consumer (former club member).

Repairs and Estimates

In recent years, California as well as other states have taken steps to provide better protection to consumers when dealing with service dealers and repair shops. Today, California law requires the registration of automobile repair shops and that the shops follow strict procedures when providing services to the public. In cases other than minor repairs (e.g., tire change, oil change, or wiper change), the law requires service dealers to provide a customer with the following:

■ a written estimate of the cost of the labor and parts involved in the repair;

■ an itemized invoice describing all labor performed and parts installed; and

■ all old parts that were replaced.

A service repair person cannot proceed with a job without prior authorization from the customer, and if the dealer's estimate is found to be too low once work is begun, the dealer must get written or oral approval for excess charges before proceeding with the additional repairs. If prior authorization is not obtained, the customer does not have to pay any amounts in excess of the original approved estimate.

The California Department of Consumer Affairs Bureau of Automotive Repairs enforces the provision of the California Automotive Repair Act, and if a shop violates the law, the state may suspend or revoke the shop's registration. The bureau has offices located throughout the state;

FRESNO
3374 East Shields, Rm. E-14
Fresno, California 93726
(209) 488-5015

LOS ANGELES
107 South Broadway, Rm. 8019
Los Angeles, California 90012
(213) 620-5347

SACRAMENTO
3116 Brandshaw Rd.
Sacramento, California 95827
(916) 366-5023

SAN JOSE
20 Harold Ave.
San Jose, California 95117
(408) 277-1860

SAN DIEGO
1350 Front Shat, Rm. 3050
San Diego, California 92101
(714) 237-7295

SANTA ANA
28 Civic Center Plaza, Rm. 360
Santa Ana, California 92701
(714) 558-4008

The bureau also operates a toll-free hot-line number for complaints (800-952-5210).

CONTRACTS

Minors and Contracts

In California, the age of majority is eighteen. Upon turning eighteen, persons may still disaffirm many contracts that were entered into before they reached majority, as long as they do so within a reasonable period of time. California law catagorizes contracts entered into with minors into three groups; (1) contracts that are completely void, (2) contracts that are voidable by minors, and (3) contracts that are binding on minors. Void contracts are contracts that are unenforceable by either the minor or the party who contracted with the minor. For example, a contract by or with a minor to purchase real property is unenforceable. Few contracts with minors are, however, completely void. Instead, most are voidable by the minor. Minors may thus enforce a contract when it is to their advantage, or they may disaffirm a contract if it is not to their advantage. Finally, some of the kinds of contracts that are enforceable against minors in California are as follows:

- contracts for "things necessary for his or her support or that of his or her family, entered into . . . when not under the care of a parent or guardian able to provide for such care";
- contracts approved by a competent court for artistic or creative services;
- contracts approved by a competent court for athletic services;
- contracts in which minors relinquish their children to an adoption agency or consent to the adoption of their children; and
- contracts to enter the armed forces of the United States.

Illegal Contracts

A few examples of illegal contracts in California are contracts pertaining to a gambling debt, for the services of a prostitute, for the sale of illegal drugs, or to injure or kill another. Unconscionable contracts for goods, services, or property are also unenforceable.

WARRANTIES

Express Warranties

In California, when a consumer receives a written warranty, the law requires that it be worded in simple language so the average consumer is not misled. If the particular product costs over $15, the information relating to the warranty must be made available to the consumer before the purchase. Requirements to return a warranty card in order to effectuate a warranty are void in California. It is a good idea, however, to return such cards, because the card often records the date of purchase. Finally, a manufacturer who furnishes consumers with a written warranty must maintain service and repair facilities in California reasonably close to the sales area and must provide the consumer with information on the service center. If there is no repair facility in California, the consumer may take the goods to any retailer of like goods in the state. The retailer must, within thirty days, either replace or repair the product or refund the consumer's money.

Implied Warranties

Under California law, virtually all new products that are sold in retail stores come with an *implied warranty of merchantability*. This means that both the manufacturer and the retail seller must furnish goods fit for their ordinary purpose and that these goods must conform to any labels on the container for a reasonable duration. The implied warranty of merchantability does not apply to food, clothing, or personal care or cleaning products.

In addition, if a seller knows of the particular purpose for which the product will be used and if the seller also knows that the buyer is relying on the seller's skill to select suitable goods, an *implied warranty of fitness for a particular purpose* will also be read into the sales contract.

Disclaimers

Under California's Song-Beverly Act, consumers cannot give up any of their warranty rights. Also, a manufacturer or retailer is prohibited from providing a written warranty in order to escape or supersede any implied warranties created by the act. A merchant can, however, disclaim implied warranties in a new product sold without a written warranty, but the disclaimer must be conspicuously attached to the product and must inform the buyer that the product is being sold "as is," "with all faults," or with "risks on buyer and buyer assumes cost of repair." Remember that very few used goods come with warranties.

UNSAFE OR DANGEROUS PRODUCTS

In California the regional offices of the Consumer Product Safety Commission are located at these addresses.

SAN FRANCISCO
555 Battery Street
San Francisco, California 94103
(415) 556-1816

LOS ANGELES
3660 Wilshire Boulevard
Los Angeles, California 90010
(213) 688-7272

CREDIT

Credit Cards and Charge Accounts

The laws and limitations mentioned in the national text on a credit card holder's liability when a credit card is lost or stolen are applicable in California. However, in order to withhold a payment to a merchant over a disputed portion of a credit card bill, the purchase must have been for more than $50, must have been made within the state or within one-hundred miles of the purchaser's home, the card holder must have made a good faith effort to resolve the dispute, and the amount in dispute must not have been paid in a previous bill.

Billing errors, or errors made by the credit card company in computing the amount of money owed on a given transaction, must be corrected within ninety days after receiving a written complaint from the consumer. Failure to correct billing errors within the prescribed period could cause the card issuer to forfeit the amount in dispute or pay triple damages plus reasonable attorney's fees and court costs.

The Cost of Credit

In California, the average allowable rate of interest charged to consumers on the unpaid balance of most credit is eighteen percent annually, or 1.5 percent per month. In many instances, however, financial institutions, such as banks, are exempt from maximum interest rate laws. In addition, many credit card companies and banks charge a fee or service charge for the privilege of owning a particular credit card. The fees usually range from $12 to $40 per year and are normally added to the monthly bill.

Obtaining Credit

The state law in California is similar to the federal requirements noted in the national text. Recently, however, efforts have been made in California to provide additional protection for women. Under the state law, an unmarried woman may not be denied credit if her property or earnings are such that a man possessing the same amount of property or earnings would receive credit, and a married woman may not be denied credit in either her married or maiden name if her property is such that a man possessing the same amount of property or earnings would receive credit. Applicants who suffer damage as a result of the willful violation of these-credit laws may bring an action to recover actual damages, plus specified punitive damages and costs for each violation. They may also ask the court to order the violator to extend credit on such terms, conditions, and standards as normally would be used in granting credit to others.

What to Do if You Are Denied Credit

When applicants are denied credit on the basis of the content of a credit report, California law requires that, upon request, credit applicants may receive, free of charge, a copy of the report. If the information contained in the credit report cannot be verified, it must be deleted promptly by the reporting company. Information disputed by applicants must also be noted, and applicants may, as part of their credit record, enclose a statement (of one-hundred words or less) concerning the contents of the record. Finally, where information has been deleted, or if any notation disputing the accuracy of the information has been inserted in the report, the reporting company must furnish notification of the deletions or additions to any creditor specifically designated by the applicant who has, within six months prior to such deletions or additions, received a report.

DEFAULT AND
COLLECTION PRACTICES

What a Consumer Can Do in Case of Default

In addition to the suggestions listed in the national text, in California the offices of the Consumer Credit Counselors (CCC) provide counseling services to consumers who are trying to resolve debt problems. The CCC is a nonprofit community service organization sponsored by the National Foundation for Consumer Credit, which is supported by creditors in local communities. Though many services are available through the CCC, including financial counseling and referrals, the CCC does not give legal advice. They have offices in the following locations:

OAKLAND
1212 Broadway, Suite 706
Oakland, California 94612
(415) 832-7555

SACRAMENTO
1815 J Street
Sacramento, California 95814
(916) 444-0740

FRESNO
2135 Fresno Street, #213
Fresno, California 93721
(209) 233-6221

SAN DIEGO
P.O. Box 2131
San Diego, California 92112
(714) 234-4118

KERN
P.O. Box 1842
Bakersfield, California 93303
(805) 324-9628

SAN FRANCISCO
625 Market Street, Rm. 1210
San Francisco, California 94105
(415) 421-4586

LOS ANGELES
945 South Western Ave., #203
Los Angeles, California 90006
(213) 737-3130

SANTA CLARA VALLEY
816 North First Street
San Jose, California 95112
(408) 286-8826

MARIN COUNTY
1203 4th Street
San Rafael, California 94901
(415) 457-3532

SANTA ROSA
306 Mendocina Avenue, Rm. 407
Santa Rosa, California 95404
(707) 527-9221

ORANGE COUNTY
1616 East 4th Street
Santa Ana, California 92701
(714) 547-8281

VENTURA COUNTY
P.O. Box 192
Ventura, California 93001
(805) 648-1352

Creditor Collection Practices

The Federal Fair Debt Collection Practice Act and California law prohibit debt collectors from contacting consumers directly if they have an attorney or from contacting consumers at unreasonable hours (after 9 P.M. or before 8 A.M.) or at their employers' place of business when the debt collector is aware that the consumer's employer has rules to the contrary. Debt collectors must also cease their collection efforts if and when requested in writing to do so by consumers, except to advise the consumer that further collection procedures are being terminated or pursued in court.

California specifically prohibits the harrassment of consumers through the use of profane language, repeated or annoying telephone calls, and threats of defamation, criminal actions, or violence. Creditors or collection agencies who violate these rules should be reported either to the local office of the district attorney, to the Federal Trade Commission, or to the

California Bureau of Collection and Investigative Services
1430 Howe Avenue
Sacramento, California 95825
(916) 445-5401

Repossession In California, merchants, banks, or dealers sometimes repossess certain types of property in order to resell the merchandise and recoup money which has not been paid by the original purchaser. Usually the property is either a large appliance, a car, or a trailer home. This procedure is often available to creditors without first obtaining a court order. Persons who have had their property repossessed, are entitled to a fifteen day notice of the intent to resell the property, and may redeem the property prior to sale upon payment in full. Under no circumstances may someone attempting to repossess property, breach the peace, or unlawfully enter another person's home.

Court Action As noted in the national text, creditors may sue consumers who have not paid their bills. If the amount outstanding on the debt is less than $1,500, a business may choose to take the debtor to small claims court. Collection agencies, however, may not sue in small claims court, nor may attorneys represent either party. When claims involve larger sums of money, suits must be filed in the municipal or superior courts. Regardless of the court in which suit is brought, default judgments may be obtained against any parties who have been properly notified of the pending action yet fail to appear.

Garnishment and Attachments In California a writ of execution or an abstract of judgment must be acquired by creditors before they can garnish the debtor's wages or attach property. These documents verify the amount owed and order the sheriff or the county recorder to take appropriate actions. Remember that under the Federal Consumer Credit Protection Act as well as under California law, limits have been placed on the percentage of a person's salary or income, that can lawfully be garnished. California law further protect certain types of property from attachment. The most important of these involves the process of "homesteads." This procedure allows a debtor to safeguard a maximum of $40,000 of equity in his or her home from most creditors, except those who hold the mortgage on the real estate, and creditors who have recorded their abstract of judgment before the debtor has recorded the homestead with the county recorder. Finally, in addition to homestead and wage exemption, California also makes it difficult for creditors to sieze or place liens on such items as clothing, household furniture, and tools of a trade.

CARS AND THE CONSUMER

Buying a Car

The sale of automobiles in California is regulated by the California Department of Motor Vehicles (D.M.V.) The department licenses car dealers and protects consumers against unfair advertising and sales practices. Licensed automobile dealers in California are prohibited from doing the following:

■ distributing false or misleading information about an advertised vehicle;

■ advertising a vehicle that is not actually for sale on the dealer's premises at the time of the advertisement;

■ continuing to advertise a vehicle for forty-eight hours after it has been sold or withdrawn from sale;

■ advertising that a down payment is not needed when it actually is required by the dealer;

■ turning back, resetting, or disconnecting the odometer of any motor vehicle;

■ failing to identify advertised motor vehicles by their serial or license number; and

■ failing to list the total price of the motor vehicle, or refusing to sell it at the advertised price.

In addition, when buying a car from a private individual, it is important to find out if the seller is the legal owner. The best way to check is by visiting or writing to the local office of the DMV registration division. If the legal owner of the vehicle is actually a lending institution, the institution must transfer ownership to you upon sale of the vehicle. The buyer should also be sure that the seller acknowledges the sale, and the buyer should receive the ownership certificate and the current registration card showing that the license fees have been paid. Finally, all automobiles sold in California that are warranted come under the protection of the Song-Berverly Consumer Warranty Act. The manufacturer must thus provide consumers with the specific services offered under the act (see "Repairs and Warranties").

Financing a Car

In California, automobile loans are commonly extended over thirty-six months for new cars, and over twenty-four months for used cars. Recently, however, most lending institutions have increased the time period for repayment of automobile loans from forty-eight to sixty months for new cars with a 20 percent down payment. Cash down payments made to dealers pending financing are refundable. However, a down payment in the form of a trade-in is normally not refundable after five days, unless otherwise specified. If after you finance and purchase a car, it becomes impossible to meet the payments to the lending institution, it might be best to sell the car and pay off the loan, or have the new buyer assume the auto loan from the lender. This avoids the possibility of a returned car being recorded as a default and a repossession appearing on your credit record.

Insuring a Car

In California, the law requires that drivers and owners of motor vehicles maintain proof of financial responsibility. These requirements can be met either by purchasing liability coverage or a surety bond, or by making a deposit with the Department of Motor Vehicles (DMV). The value of surety bonds or the size of the deposit made to the DMV is periodically established by the department in order to ensure that a minimum amount of funds will be available to offset damages that may result from an accident.

The minimum amount of liability insurance that must be purchased in California is 15/30/5. This means that if the insured is responsible for the accident, the insurance company will pay up to $15,000 per person for personal injury, up to $30,000 for more than one person, and up to $5,000 for simple property damage. It is often wise, however, to purchase more insurance, than the required minimum, for example, $150,000 and $300,000 for injury or death. Damages in law suits resulting from automobile accidents can easily reach those figures. With the exception of "no fault" insurance, the other kinds of insurance policies mentioned in the national text are available in California.

Persons involved in an accident who cannot furnish proof of financial responsibility will have their driver's license suspended by the DMV. Licenses are also suspended if a judgment based on an accident has not been satisfied.

What to Do in Case of an Accident

In addition to the suggestions made in the national text, California law requires that accidents involving more than $500 in property damage, or when someone is injured or killed, be reported to the DMV within fifteen days. If the driver cannot make the report, the owner of the vehicle must do so. Failure to report an accident of this nature within sixty days results in the suspension of driving privileges for one year, or until the report is made, or until the person involved in the accident submits proof of financial responsibility.

Also, accidents causing injury, death, or damage to unattended property must, within twenty-four hours, be reported to the local police agency or to the California State Highway Patrol. Finally, failure to stop, or leaving the scene of any accident in which you are involved, is a crime in California. Drivers are required to stop, provide their name and address, and offer reasonable assistance to any person injured. In the event of damage to unattended property, the driver must contact the owner directly or leave a note in a conspicuous place on the damaged property. The penalties for "hit and run" may be severe, particularly when someone has been injured or killed.

four
FAMILY LAW

California family law is different in many ways from the laws of other states and from the material outlined in the national text. There are two principal reasons for these differences. First, California is one of eight "community property" states, and as such abides by many rules that relate to the ownership and distribution of marital property. Second, in 1975 the California legislature passed the Family Law Act, which was an effort to bring state laws more in line with many of the changes that have taken place in the family as a result of the womens' movement. Consequently, statutes were rewritten, and the term "spouse" was used to replace the term "husband" or "wife" and many of the traditional roles that had been associated with the responsibilities of husbands and wives, and that had been written into the law, were discarded. As a result, our current laws give both spouses in a marriage largely equal rights in matters relating to decision making, and the management and control of family affairs and property.

MARRIAGE

Like all states, California has certain legal requirements that couples must meet in order to enter into a valid marriage. The ability of

435

a person to marry is determined by the conditions that exist on the date of the marriage. For example, the parties must, as of the date of the marriage, not be married to anyone else. (Bigamy is a crime in California.) In addition, a person may not marry a close blood relative. The law prohibits marriages to parents, grandparents, brothers, sisters, aunts, uncles, nieces or nephews; and sexual intercourse between such relatives constitutes the crime of incest. California does allow marriages between first cousins or with any other blood relatives who are removed to the third degree or greater. Finally, persons under the age of eighteen are not permitted to marry in California unless they obtain written permission for the marriage from a parent or guardian (only one parent or one guardian's consent is necessary) and a court order granting permission to the minor to marry. When permitting the marriage of a minor, a court often requires the prospective couple to participate in premarital counseling in order to better familiarize themselves with the social, financial, and personal responsibilities associated with marriage.

Annulments in California may be obtained for any of the reasons mentioned in the national text, or upon a showing that one of the parties to the marriage was of unsound mind at the time the marriage was entered into and has since refused to acknowledge the existence of the marriage either by words or conduct. An inability to engage in sexual intercourse is grounds for an annulment in California only to the extent that such incapacity is shown to have become a continuing problem that appears to be incurable.

Formal Marriage

In California, prior to issuing a marriage license, couples must undergo a medical examination (blood tests) to determine if either party has a veneral disease and in some cases whether a woman has been exposed to rubella (German measles). The examination must be performed within thirty days of applying for a marriage license, and the physician's certificate stating that the persons are free of veneral disease must be filed with the clerk of the court. A marriage license is good for a period of ninety days and may be used anywhere within the state. In addition, California requires that a marriage ceremony take place. No specific type of ceremony is called for, but a couple must declare, in the presence of an authorized person, that they take each other as husband and wife. Marriages may be performed by a priest, rabbi, minister, judge, or a court commissioner. The marriage must be witnessed by at least one other person.

Common Law Marriage

California does not have any provisions for establishing a common law marriage within the state. However, the state will recognize a

FIGURE 8 California Marriage License Application

GROOM PERSONAL DATA

1A. NAME OF GROOM—FIRST NAME | 1B. MIDDLE NAME | 1C. LAST NAME | 2. DATE OF BIRTH—MONTH, DAY, YEAR

3. AGE (LAST BIRTHDAY) YEARS | 4. NUMBER OF THIS MARRIAGE | IF PREVIOUSLY MARRIED: 5A. DATE LAST MARRIAGE ENDED | 5B. LAST MARRIAGE ENDED BY (SPECIFY DEATH, DIVORCE OR ANNULMENT) | 6. BIRTHPLACE (STATE OR FOREIGN COUNTRY)

7A. RESIDENCE OF GROOM—STREET ADDRESS (STREET AND NUMBER, RURAL ADDRESS, OR LOCATION) | 7B. CITY OR TOWN | 7C. COUNTY (IF OUTSIDE CALIFORNIA, ENTER STATE)

8A. PRESENT OR LAST OCCUPATION | 8B. KIND OF INDUSTRY OR BUSINESS | 9. HIGHEST SCHOOL GRADE COMPLETED

10A. NAME OF FATHER OF GROOM | 10B. BIRTHPLACE OF FATHER (STATE OR FOREIGN COUNTRY) | 11A. MAIDEN NAME OF MOTHER OF GROOM | 11B. BIRTHPLACE OF MOTHER (STATE OR FOREIGN COUNTRY)

BRIDE PERSONAL DATA

12A. NAME OF BRIDE—FIRST NAME | 12B. MIDDLE NAME | 12C. LAST NAME | 13. DATE OF BIRTH—MONTH, DAY, YEAR

14. AGE (LAST BIRTHDAY) YEARS | 15. NUMBER OF THIS MARRIAGE | IF PREVIOUSLY MARRIED: 16A. DATE LAST MARRIAGE ENDED | 16B. LAST MARRIAGE ENDED BY (SPECIFY DEATH, DIVORCE OR ANNULMENT) | 17. BIRTHPLACE (STATE OR FOREIGN COUNTRY)

18A. RESIDENCE OF BRIDE—STREET ADDRESS (STREET AND NUMBER, RURAL ADDRESS, OR LOCATION) | 18B. CITY OR TOWN | 18C. COUNTY (IF OUTSIDE CALIFORNIA, ENTER STATE)

19A. PRESENT OR LAST OCCUPATION | 19B. KIND OF INDUSTRY OR BUSINESS | 20. HIGHEST SCHOOL GRADE COMPLETED | 21. BIRTH NAME OF BRIDE (IF DIFFERENT THAN 12C)

22A. NAME OF FATHER OF BRIDE | 22B. BIRTHPLACE OF FATHER (STATE OR FOREIGN COUNTRY) | 23A. MAIDEN NAME OF MOTHER OF BRIDE | 23B. BIRTHPLACE OF MOTHER (STATE OR FOREIGN COUNTRY)

AFFIDAVIT OF BRIDE AND GROOM

WE, THE BRIDE AND GROOM NAMED IN THIS CERTIFICATE, EACH FOR HIMSELF, STATE THAT THE FOREGOING INFORMATION IS CORRECT TO THE BEST OF OUR KNOWLEDGE AND BELIEF, THAT NO LEGAL OBJECTION TO THE MARRIAGE NOR TO THE ISSUANCE OF A LICENSE TO AUTHORIZE THE SAME IS KNOWN TO US, AND HEREBY APPLY FOR LICENSE TO MARRY.

24A. BRIDE (SIGNATURE) ▶ | 24B. GROOM (SIGNATURE) ▶

AUTHORIZATION AND LICENSE IS HEREBY GIVEN TO ANY PERSON DULY AUTHORIZED BY THE LAWS OF THE STATE OF CALIFORNIA TO PERFORM A MARRIAGE CEREMONY WITHIN THE STATE OF CALIFORNIA TO SOLEMNIZE THE MARRIAGE OF THE ABOVE NAMED PERSONS. REQUIRED CONSENTS FOR THE ISSUANCE OF THIS LICENSE ARE ON FILE.

25A. SUBSCRIBED AND SWORN TO BEFORE ME ON | 25B. DATE LICENSE ISSUED | 25C. LICENSE NUMBER | 25D. COUNTY CLERK ▶

25E. EXPIRATION DATE | 25E. COUNTY OF ISSUE OF LICENSE | BY ▶ DEPUTY

STATE OF CALIFORNIA, DEPARTMENT OF HEALTH SERVICES, OFFICE OF THE STATE REGISTRAR OF VITAL STATISTICS

VS-117B (8-78)

common law marriage legally established in another state. Thus, if a couple has a valid preexisting common law marriage and moves to California, the state will consider them legally married and will require either a proof of death or a legal dissolution to end the marriage.

HUSBANDS AND WIVES

Financial Responsibilities

In California, husbands and wives are, for the most part, treated as separate individuals who have mutual yet distinct rights and responsibilities. For example, husbands and wives have a mutual obligation to support one another. This obligation extends minimally to providing each other with the necessities of life.

Also as a community property state, California applies particular rules on the division and distribution of property at the time of divorce or the death of a spouse. The laws that govern marital property and its division are complex, and attorneys are often hired to sort out how the family (community) assets are to be divided (see "Child Support, Alimony, and Property Division").

Decision in a Marriage

California does not require that either spouse take the other's name upon marriage, although a spouse may do so if he or she so desires. Husbands and wives may also combine and hyphenate their last names or may simply retain their birth names. These practices are governed by custom, not law. The children from a marriage need not automatically be given the father's or husband's surname. Instead, the law with few exceptions, allows parents to give their child any name they desire.

Spouse Abuse

In California, in addition to civil remedies and protective orders mentioned in the national text, a spouse who has been the victim of physical abuse (usually the wife) may seek the assistance of various types of battered womens' shelters located throughout the state. These shelters generally offer women food, safety, and personal and financial counseling. The police department, your local or community mental health center, or the telephone directory should have the number of a shelter in your community.

California recently enacted a criminal spousal abuse statute that applies not only to husbands and wives but to all persons of the opposite sex who are living together. Depending on the severity of the abuse, a violator can be charged with either a misdemeanor or a felony and can be sentenced to up to four years in prison.

PARENTS AND CHILDREN

Family Planning, Birth Control, and Abortion

In California, minors, whether married or not, have the right to obtain birth control devices without a parent's knowledge or consent. Similarly, the consent of a parent is not legally required before a doctor may perform therapeutic abortion on a minor, as long as the child is capable of giving *informed consent* for the abortion.

The guidelines for abortions in California are similar to those established by the Supreme Court in *Roe* v. *Wade* (see Chapter Four in the national text). Accordingly, an abortion performed in a manner other than those set out by the California State Therapeutic Abortion Act is a crime punishable by imprisonment for not less than two or more than five years.

Married women need not inform or acquire the consent of their husbands before obtaining a therapeutic abortion. Furthermore, in California individuals who cannot afford a therapeutic abortion may not be denied medical care. The California Supreme Court recently decided that the state's medical assistance program (Medi-Cal) must provide medical services to the medically needy on the same basis as those services are provided to persons who are more financially able (see also Chapter Six, "Discrimination Because of Income").

Responsibilities Between Parents and Children

As noted in the national text, parents are legally required to support their children and furnish them with the necessities of life. In California this obligation is shared equally by both parents, and is an absolute and inalienable right enjoyed by the child. The parents' income and overall financial resources are considered in determining if children have been cared for at the level to which they are entitled. Generally, this obligation continues until a child has either reached eighteen years of age or has been emancipated. The responsibility to support a child extends to adopted children as well. A stepparent, however, is not legally responsible for the support of his or her spouses' child (or stepchild). The parents of a minor child are also not liable for the support of a child of their minor child (i.e., their grandchild). Instead, the responsibility rests with the immediate parents, although they are themselves minors. Children who are not adequately supported by their parents may sue their parents for such support.

In the event that the children are illegitimate, paternity suits are sometimes brought to establish parenthood and thus establish the right of the child to receive support. These types of actions are almost always brought against a "putative" or alleged father in order to require him to pay his rightful share of the child's support. In paternity actions, evidence about the mother's relationship with the putative father and with any other man during the time the child was conceived is admissible. An opinion as to whether or not the child resembles the putative father is not, however, admissible evidence. Blood tests may also be ordered by a court, and although the tests cannot establish conclusively that a particular person is the parent, if a party refuses to submit to a court-ordered blood test, the court has the power to resolve the question of paternity against that party.

In California, adults are required to support their parents if their parent are needy and unable to work or maintain themselves. This obligation is limited to situations in which the children have the financial means to provide for their parents.

Furthermore, parents in California are generally entitled to the earnings of their children. However, special provisions do exist to safeguard the property and earnings of children who have professional artistic or atheletic service contracts. In a situation involving a child star or athlete, the court must oversee the child's income and set some income aside to meet his or her future financial needs.

Finally, in addition to the information on emancipation presented in the national text, children in California, are considered emancipated by operation of law (automatically) when they enlist in the armed forces. Also under a new California procedure, a child may petition a court and be declared an emancipated minor if the individual can establish that he or she is at least fourteen years of age, is willing to live separate and apart from his or her parents or guardians, is lawfully managing his or her financial affairs, and has the consent or acquiescence of his or her parents or guardians.

Child Abuse and Neglect

In addition to the types of child abuse noted in the national text, some mention should be made of sexual abuse and incest. In these circumstances, all too often children are abused by stepparents, relatives, or the natural parents. Nevertheless, because of the nature of these offenses, children who report such acts are sometimes neither believed nor defended. Matters may go unresolved, and as a result, the children may suffer long-term psychological effects that require professional counseling.

The California Child Abuse Reporting Statute requires that incidents of suspected child abuse or neglect be referred immediately to the police, the county probation department or county welfare department. Such referrals, must be confirmed in writing within thirty-six hours of the initial report. This duty applies not only to medical professionals, teachers, counselors, and child care providers, but also to film processors who must report any materials that depict children under the age of fourteen engaging in sexual acts.

In California, depending on the severity of the case and the circumstances surrounding the reported incident of child abuse, the state may take any of the following actions:

■ require parents to seek the assistance of social service agencies and/or undergo counseling;

■ temporarily remove the offending parent from the home and require that he or she seek professional assistance and at a later date allow the offending parent supervised visitation with the child and reentry into the home;

■ temporarily remove the child from the home until the parents prove that they have been rehabilitated;

■ seek to permanently remove the child from the home and terminate parental rights to the child; and

■ file criminal charges against parents who wrongfully abuse or neglect a child.

FOSTER CARE AND ADOPTION

California recognizes four types of adoptions: (1) independent adoptions in which the minor is placed with the adopting parents directly by the natural parent, (2) agency adoptions in which the minor is placed in the home of the adopting parents by a licensed adoption agency, (3) stepparent adoptions, in which the stepparent seeks to adopt the step child, and (4) adult adoptions in which an adult seeks to adopt another adult. Upon adoption, persons are legally treated as if they were the natural children of the adoptive parents and may thus inherit through them. Adopted children do not, however, inherit from their natural parents unless they are so provided for in the natural parent's will.

The consent of a child's natural parents is required for an adoption, unless (1) the parent has willfully failed to communicate with and provide support for the child for a period of one year, (2) parent has deserted the child without any provisions for the child's identification, or (3) the child has been relinquished to an adoption agency. A natural parent's consent to the adoption of the child may be withdrawn before the adoption is finalized as long as the withdrawn is approved by the court and found to be in the best interests of the child. Children who are over the age of twelve must consent to their own adoption.

Unless they obtain a court order, persons who are adopted in California generally do not have the right to examine their adoption or birth records to determine the identity of their natural parents. A court will grant such an order only if and when the adoptee can establish a compelling need for the information. For example, courts have provided this information in cases involving adoptees who needed to know their family health history for purposes of medical treatment. California law also provides that if an adult adoptee (eighteen years or older), his or her natural parents, and any living adoptive parent has each filed a waiver of confidentiality form with the state's Department of Social Services or licensed adoption agency, a meeting may be arranged among these persons. Finally, under the new Adoption Information Act of 1983, starting in 1986, the state will begin to disclose the names and addresses of adoptees and natural parents as long as they have reached the age of twenty-one.

ENDING MARRIAGE

Separation

In California informal separations are common. Husbands and wives may, for whatever reason, decide to live separately and apart. When couples do live apart, they often provide for each other by way of a separation agreement. A separation agreement is binding as long as it is entered into freely and is fair to both parties. Sometimes couples who separate temporarily in the hope of a later reconciliation might consider marriage counseling. Most counselors are licensed and often provide troubled couples with sound advice to help them resolve their differences. A public mental health center can usually provide a referral to a marriage counselor.

A legal separation may be obtained only after an appropriate petition has been filed with a court. The purpose of a legal separation is to determine a couples rights and responsibilities. If couples wish to remarry, they must wait until the marriage has been legally terminated. While husbands and wives are living separately and apart, their earnings are presumed to be their individual, separate property, rather than belonging to the marriage, nor community. This is true regardless of whether the separation is informal, temporary in nature, or is a legal separation.

Finally, couples who have separated after living together without the "benefits" of marriage have no obligation of support, nor do they have to equally divide the property that they acquired during their nonmarital relationship unless, as noted in the *Marvin* case, it can be established that there was an express or implied agreement to the contrary. Remember, however, that according to the ruling in the *Marvin* case, this obligation may arise out of a contract that is simply implied from the conduct of the couple while they were living together.

Divorce

In California, a divorce is referred to as the "dissolution of marriage." It may be obtained by court decree only, and, other than death, it is the only means of terminating a valid marriage.

California has a no fault system of divorce. This means that neither spouse has to prove that the other committed a wrongful act, such as adultery or desertion, in order to get the divorce. Instead, there are two simple and very clear grounds for the dissolution of marriage in California. The first and by far the most common ground used is that "irreconcilable differences" exist between the couple that have caused the irremediable breakdown of the marriage. The second ground for the dissolution of a marriage is "incurable insanity." This must be proved by medical or psychiatric testimony which tends to establish that the spouse was insane at the time the petition for dissolution was filed, and will likely remain insane.

Couples seeking a divorce in California have the option of using the counseling services offered by the family conciliation courts located in most counties throughout the state. The purpose of this counseling is not necessarily reconciliation, but is instead to evaluate the problems in the marriage, suggest options, and help the couple plan and cope with the difficulties to come.

The actual process involved in dissolving a marriage in California is fairly simple. Normally an attorney or a spouse begins the process by filing a petition in superior court. This petition must indicate (1) that the spouse petitioning for the divorce has been a resident of California for six months and a resident of the county in which the action is taking place for three months, (2) that irreconcilable differences or incurable insanity exist, and (3) that there is no chance of reconciliation. A hearing is then held to determine whether a restraining order or an order requiring temporary support is needed. If the divorce is not contested, an interlocutory decree (a temporary order providing for the dissolution of the marriage after the completion of a six month statutory waiting period) is normally granted. If a divorce is contested or if the couple cannot come to any agreements regarding property or support, a dissolution trial may be ordered to resolve the dispute.

Under a new law in California, persons may petition the court for a summary or simplified dissolution if they have been married for less than two years, have no children (or present pregnancy), own no real property or not more than $5,000 worth of personal property, are in debt for no more than $2,000 (except for an auto loan), and have not requested alimony. In this type of dissolution, an attorney is not necessary. Petitioners can file the appropriate forms with the clerk of the court and simply wait the required time period for the order granting the dissolution to become final.

Child Custody

In California an award of custody of a child after the parents have separated usually includes both physical and legal custody. The person who gets physical custody has the right to have the child live with him or her. Legal custody means that the parent or guardian has the right to be consulted and make important decisions on behalf of the child. When issues involving child custody or visitation privileges are in dispute, California law requires the parties to submit to mediation before a court hearing can take place. The reasons for this is that often questions envolving child custody are the most emotionally charged and central issues to the parties and parties working cooperatively with a mediator have a better chance of reaching an agreement that will be in the best interests of the child or children involved.

The state's legislative policy regarding child custody is aimed at assuring that, whenever possible, children will have frequent and continued contact with both parents. In awarding custody, the court follows a specific order of preference:

1. An award in joint custody of the child to both parents. This means that the physical and legal custody of a child is shared by both parents, who remain equally responsible for the child's care and upbringing. If it is in the child's best interest to award physical custody to one parent (the custodial parent), the court can not choose that parent on the basis of the sex of the parent. Hence, there is no "Tender Years Presumption" in California. A court may, however, choose the custodial parent on the basis that he or she is more likely to allow the child or children frequent and continuing contact with the noncustodial parent.

2. An award to neither parent, but instead to a person in whose home the child has been living, if that home is a stable, wholesome environment.

3. An award to neither parent, but instead to whoever the court deems suitable to care for the child.

With respect to visitation rights, the law provides that such rights should be awarded to the noncustodial parent "unless it is shown that such visitation would be detrimental to the best interests of the child." Similarly, if a court is considering awarding custody to a nonparent, evidence must be presented to show that the award of custody to a parent would be "detrimental to the child," and that the award to a nonparent is required to serve the best interests of the child.

In California, if a child is mature enough and wishes to state a preference on the issue of custody, the court often takes the child's wishes into consideration when making its decision. The court may also appoint an attorney to represent the child's interests in court. This often occurs when the child is very young or has special needs.

Finally, as mentioned in the national text, parents who are dissatisfied with custody awards sometimes resort to the abduction of the child, or "child snatching." In California, the abduction of a child by a parent who has no right to custody is a criminal offense. Depending on the circumstances, the penalty may be up to four years in state prison, or a $10,000 fine, or both.

Child Support, Alimony, and Property Division

Children in California are entitled to support and education from their parents in an amount suitable to their circumstances. This duty to support the children falls equally on both parents, custodial or noncustodial, whether previously married or not, and is payable until the marriage, emancipation or attainment of majority of the child. A parent who fails to pay child support may be held in contempt of court and sentenced to five days in jail for each violation. A court may also impose a fine of up to $500, place the parent on probation, and/or garnish wages in order to provide for child support. In the event that the state itself must provide for the needs of the child, it will be entitled to reimbursement from the parent.

In California, alimony is called spousal support, and a court may order either spouse to pay any amount that it deems reasonable for the support of the other spouse. Some of the factors that a court considers before awarding spousal support are as follows:

- earning capacity of each spouse and extent to which that capacity was impaired by past domestic obligations;

- age, needs, health, and assets of the parties;

- duration of the marriage;

- time necessary to acquire appropriate education and employment;

- standard of living; and

- ability of the spouse being supported to engage in employment without interfering with the best interests of children in that parent's custody.

Finally upon the termination of a marriage, a court must decide whether and to what extent the property acquired by the parties is either the separate property of one spouse or the community property of both. Normally, property acquired during a marriage is presumed to be community property (unless one spouse can establish otherwise), and as community property, it will be divided equally between the parties at the end of the marriage. Property that was the result of a gift, inheritance, or profits from separate property, or that was acquired either before or after a marriage is presumed separate, and as such will generally remain with the spouse who acquired the property. Note that California applies these rules at the end of a marriage regardless of whether the couple was actually married in California or acquired most of their property in California.

GOVERNMENT SUPPORT FOR NEEDY FAMILIES AND OTHERS

As noted in the national text, many of the programs designed to aid needy families and the poor represent the joint efforts of federal, state, and local governments. Most of the funds distributed by these programs are provided to the states by the federal government, and California, like all other states, must follow certain rules governing allocation. These rules are usually complex and change from time to time.

Social Insurance Programs

Social Security benefits are available to all eligible persons living in California. These programs include medicare, retirement, disability, and survivor's benefits. Specific information on eligibility requirements and entitlements is available at any local office of the Social Security Administration.

In addition, for information on unemployment benefits in California, persons may contact the California Department of Labor:

Unemployment Insurance Service
Department of Labor
450 Golden Gate Ave.
San Francisco, CA 94102
(415) 556-1416

Programs to Aid the Poor

California offers a wide range of programs to aid the poor. Many of these are offered through federal grants and under federal guidelines. Under state law each county is also required to provide aid to indigents, or "general relief" if persons do not qualify for other forms of federal or state cash assistance programs.

Some of the major public assistance programs in California include Aid to Families with Dependent Children, Food Stamps, and the California Medical Assistance Program (Medi-Cal). Also every county in California must make "in home" supportive services available to the aged, blind, and disabled, who might otherwise be institutionalized if they could not get personal care. Other state social services include maternity care, childcare, adoption services, and employment training. Many services are free and are aimed at low-income persons or at certain groups, such as recently arrived refugees.

For additional information on a variety of health and social services programs in California, either visit your county health or welfare department, or contact one of the following state offices:

California Department
of Public Health
744 P Street
Sacramento, California 95814
(916) 445-2725

California Department
of Social Welfare
744 P Street
Sacramento, California 95814
(916) 445-4500

DEATH AND THE LAW

With the adoption of the Natural Death Act, California became the first state to allow adults the right to refuse medical care that would only have the effect of artificially prolonging life. The act, however, is limited. Before a patient's "directive" can take effect, a minimum of two doctors must certify that the person signing the directive is terminally ill and that death is imminent.

Witnesses to directives may not be related through blood or marriage to the party who is terminally ill. The witnesses also cannot be mentioned in the person's will, or have any claim to the estate, or be the individual's doctor, or on the doctor's staff. The directive is valid for a period of five years, at which time a person may sign a new one. The directive is not valid during pregnancy. A directive may be revoked at any time, even in the final stages of a terminal illness, by taking one of the following actions:

■ destroying the directive;

■ signing and dating a written statement revoking it; or

■ informing one's doctor to cancel the directive.

FIGURE 9   California Natural Death Act Directive

DIRECTIVE TO PHYSICIANS

Directive made this _____ day of _____ (month, year).

I _____, being of sound mind, willfully, and voluntarily make known my desire that my life shall not be artificially prolonged under the circumstances set forth below, do hereby declare:

1. If at any time I should have an incurable injury, disease, or illness certified to be a terminal condition by two physicians, and where the application of life-sustaining procedures would serve only to artificially prolong the moment of my death and where my physician determines that my death is imminent whether or not life-sustaining procedures are utilized, I direct that such procedures be withheld or withdrawn, and that I be permitted to die naturally.

2. In the absence of my ability to give directions regarding the use of such life-sustaining procedures, it is my intention that this directive shall be honored by my family and physician(s) as the final expression of my legal right to refuse medical or surgical treatment and accept the consequences from such refusal.

3. If I have been diagnosed as pregnant and that diagnosis is known to my physician, this directive shall have no force or effect during the course of my pregnancy.

4. I have been diagnosed and notified at least 14 days ago as having a terminal condition by _____, M.D., whose address is _____, and whose telephone number is _____. I understand that if I have not filled in the physician's name and address, it shall be presumed that I did not have a terminal condition when I made out this directive.

5. This directive shall have no force or effect five years from the date filled in above.

6. I understand the full import of this directive and I am emotionally and mentally competent to make this directive.

Signed _____

City, County and State of Residence _____

The declarant has been personally known to me and I believe him or her to be of sound mind.

Witness _____

Witness _____

Wills and Inheritance

In California, if a person dies intestate (without leaving a will), all of his or her community property is given to the surviving spouse. If a person dies intestate leaving separate (noncommunity) property, a surviving spouse and one child would each get half of the property. If a spouse and two children survive, then each gets a third of the separate property. If a spouse and more than two children survive, the children must divide their two-thirds share equally, and the surviving spouse receives the other one-third of the separate property. If there is no surviving spouse, then all of the property will be awarded to the children or closest relatives in order of kinship. If there are no relatives, the deceased's estate (property) will go to the state.

If a person has both community and separate property, a will may dispose of only the separate property and half of the community property. The remaining half of the community property belongs to the surviving spouse.

To write a valid will in California, a person must be at least eighteen years of age and be of "sound mine." This means that you must understand the extent and nature of your property and how it will be disposed of under the will.

Technically, California recognizes four types of wills.

1. A nuncupative will, or oral will. These wills are very limited. An oral will may be made only by someone serving in the armed forces, just prior to death, and when the personal property involved is valued at less than $1,000.

2. A holographic will, or a will that has been signed, dated, and written entirely in the handwriting of the person making the will. These wills need not be witnessed. They are strictly examined, and if any type of extraneous information appears on the will, or if information has been crossed out or items have been added, a court will probably invalidate the will.

3. A formal will, or typed will. These wills are the most common, and most attorneys prefer this manner of drafting wills. Requirements for a formal will in California include the following:

- it must be typed or printed;

- it must state in some manner that it is the person's will;

- it must be signed and dated;

- it must be witnessed by at least two witnesses; and

- the party declares to the witnesses at the time that he or she signs the will that it is his or her will.

4. A statutory will. Approved in 1982, California now allows a valid will to be written by simply filling in the blanks on a prescribed form (Figure 10).

These statutory wills, although simple to fill out, are somewhat limited in the options they provide, because the forms cannot be changed or altered. The form was designed principally to aid someone leaving property to a surviving spouse, to children, or to grandchildren. When considering a will, you would do best to consult an attorney.

FIGURE 10   **California Statutory Will Form**

CALIFORNIA STATUTORY WILL OF

_____

(Insert Your Name)

Article 1.   Declaration

This is my will and I revoke any prior wills and codicils.

Article 2.   Disposition of My Property

2.1. PERSONAL AND HOUSEHOLD ITEMS. I give all my furniture, furnishings, household items, personal automobiles and personal items to my spouse, if living; otherwise they shall be divided equally among my children who survive me.

2.2. CASH GIFT TO A PERSON OR CHARITY. I make the following cash gift to the person or charity in the amount stated in words and figures in the box which I have completed and signed. If I fail to sign in the box, no gift is made. If the person mentioned does not survive me, or the charity designated does not accept the gift, then no gift is made. No death tax shall be paid from this gift.

FULL NAME OF PERSON OR CHARITY TO RECEIVE CASH GIFT (Name only one. Please print.).	AMOUNT OF GIFT $ _____ AMOUNT WRITTEN OUT: _____ Dollars
	_____ Signature of Testator

2.3. ALL OTHER ASSETS (MY "RESIDUARY ESTATE"). I adopt only one Property Disposition Clause in this paragraph 2.3 by writing my signature in the box next to the title of the Property Disposition Clause I wish to adopt. I sign in only one box. I write the words "not used" in the remaining boxes. If I sign in more than one box or if I fail to sign in any box, the property will be distributed as if I did not make a will.

PROPERTY DISPOSITION CLAUSES (Select one.)

(a) TO MY SPOUSE IF LIV-
ING; IF NOT LIVING,
THEN TO MY CHILDREN
AND
THE DESCENDANTS OF
ANY DECEASED CHILD.

(b) TO MY CHILDREN AND
THE DESCENDANTS OF
ANY   DECEASED
CHILD. I LEAVE NOTH-
ING TO MY SPOUSE, IF
LIVING. _____

(c) TO BE DISTRIBUTED AS
IF I DID NOT HAVE A
WILL. _____

Article 3.   Nominations of Executor and Guardian

3.1. EXECUTOR (Name at least one.)

I nominate the person or institution named in the first box of this paragraph 3.1 to serve as executor of this will. If that person or institution does not serve, then I nominate the others to serve in the order I list them in the other boxes.

FIRST EXECUTOR. _____

SECOND EXECUTOR. _____

THIRD EXECUTOR. _____

3.2. GUARDIAN (If you have a child under 18 years of age, you should name at least one guardian of the child's person and at least one guardian of the child's property. The guardian of the child's person and the guardian of the child's property may, but need not, be the same. An individual can serve as guardian of either the person or the property, or as guardian of both. An institution can serve only as guardian of the property.)

If a guardian is needed for any child of mine, then I nominate the individual named in the first box of this paragraph 3.2 to serve as guardian of the person of that child, and I nominate the individual or institution named in the second box of this paragraph 3.2 to serve as guardian of the property of that child. If that person or institution does not serve, then I nominate the others to serve in the order I list them in the other boxes.

FIRST GUARDIAN OF THE PERSON. _____

FIRST GUARDIAN OF THE PROPERTY. _____

SECOND GUARDIAN OF THE PERSON. _____

SECOND GUARDIAN OF THE PROPERTY. _____

THIRD GUARDIAN OF THE PERSON. _____

THIRD GUARDIAN OF THE PROPERTY. _____

3.3. BOND. My signature in this box means that a bond is not required for any individual named in this will as executor or guardian. If I do not sign in this box, then a bond is required for each of those persons as set forth in the Probate Code. (The bond provides a fund to pay those who do not receive the share of your estate to which they are entitled, including your creditors, because of improper performance of duties by the executor or guardian. Bond premiums are paid out of your estate.)

```



```

I sign my name to this California Statutory Will

on _____ at _____, _____.
　　　Date　　　　　　City　　　　State

_____
Signature of Testator

STATEMENT OF WITNESSES (You must use two adult witnesses and three would be preferable.)

Each of us declares under penalty of perjury under the laws of California that the testator signed this California statutory will in our presence, all of us being present at the same time, and we now, at the testator's request, in the testator's presence, and in the presence of each other, sign below as witnesses, declaring that the testator appears to be of sound mind and under no duress, fraud, or undue influence.

Signature _____ Residence Address: _____
Print Name
Here: _____ _____

Signature _____ Residence Address: _____
Print Name
Here: _____ _____

Signature _____ Residence Address: _____
Print Name
Here: _____ _____

five

HOUSING

LAW

As of the computation of the 1970 census, California has held the distinction of being the most populated state in the United States. Today, over twenty-five million people live here in homes that range in character from a shack in one of our agricultural valleys to a magnificent mansion above the Beverley Hills.

In part because of the large number of people who live in this state, California has passed a number of laws dealing with the problems of housing. Keep in mind, too, that many California counties have enacted local housing ordinances and/or rent control laws, which must be followed by persons living in those counties.

CHOOSING A PLACE TO LIVE

Cost

The cost associated with your choice of housing is probably no where as great a factor as it is in California. Recent surveys have put the cost of housing in California among the highest in the

455

nation. This is particularly true in the areas of west Los Angeles and San Francisco, where the average cost of buying a home is almost $200,000 or approximately two to three times the national average. These costs also affect the price of renting a home or an apartment, since landlords or owners often pay for the cost of their mortgage with the rent they collect each month. In California it is not unusual to pay over $500 in rent each month for a relatively small housing unit.

Recently, the rising costs of housing have created a need for new financing programs and laws. Buyers now have access to financing programs that require as little as five percent down payment on a new or first home. Although the size of the mortgage will be large, such financing programs make it possible for more people to buy a home.

For renters, many counties have passed, or are considering passing, any one of a number of types of rent control measures placing limits on the rents that may be charged to tenants (see "Raising the Rent").

Discrimination in Housing

In addition to the federal Civil Rights Act of 1964, the Federal Fair Housing Act of 1968, and the Federal Housing and Community Development Act of 1974, the California legislature and our courts have recently decided to provide individuals seeking to purchase or rent housing in this state with additional protections. In short, under the California Fair Employment and Housing Act, as well as other laws, persons in California must be provided with housing on an equal basis regardless of their race, color, religion, sex, marital status, ancestry, or physical disability. These prohibitions on discrimination include attempts to discriminate against unrelated persons living together and attempts to discriminate against blind and/or deaf persons who may be in need of the assistance of a guide or signal dog. The California Fair Housing Act, however, does not prohibit the refusal to rent or lease a portion of an owner-occupied single-family house to a person as a roomer or boarder who would live within the household.

The California Supreme Court recently ruled that "adult only" housing is prohibited (except as it relates to senior citizen housing or mobile home parks). As a result, families with children can no longer be discriminated against in this state.

Although laws prohibiting discrimination against homosexuals have been defeated in the state legislature, several cities and counties, including Berkeley, Los Angeles, and San Francisco, have passed local laws prohibiting discrimination on the basis of sexual orientations and at least one lower count in the state has held that discrimination of this type violates the state's Fair Housing and Civil Rights Act.

In California, the law provides that if you are unlawfully discriminated against, you may bring a suit and collect at least $250 plus actual damages and attorney's fees. You can also defend against an eviction suit, if the basis of the eviction is discriminatory. If the discrimination is accompanied by violence, intimidation, or threat of violence, the person subjected to discrimination may recover not only actual damages but $10,000 in additional compensation. Punitive damages are also available for up to $1,000 for each violation of a blind or physically handicapped person's right to housing.

In California most complaints concerning discrimination in the rental of housing are handled by the California Fair Employment and Housing Commission. The commission has offices throughout the state and may be contracted by writing or calling any of the following locations:

FRESNO
467 No. Van Ness Avenue
Fresno, California 93721
(209) 488-5373

SAN DIEGO
110 West C Street, Suite 1702
San Diego, California 92101
(916) 237-7405

LOS ANGELES
322 West First Street Rm. 2126
Los Angeles, California 90012
(213) 620-2610

SAN FRANCISCO
455 Golden Gate Avenue
P.O. Box 603
San Francisco, California 94102
(415) 557-2005

SACRAMENTO
2222 Sierra Boulevard
Suite 38, Building F
Sacramento, California 95814
(916) 444-9918

SAN JOSE
888 No. First, Rm. 200A
San Jose, California
(408) 277-1264

If and when the alleged discrimination is based on race, ethnicity or religious beliefs, the victim may also file a complaint with the federal Department of Housing and Urban Development (HUD). These complaints, however, may only be filed thirty days after a party has filed a complaint with the California Fair Employment and Housing Commission. In California you may contact HUD at:

The United States Department of Housing
and Urban Development
P.O. Box 36003
450 Golden Gate Avenue
San Francisco, California 94102
(415) 566-3840

RENTING A HOME

The Lease

California recognizes three types of rental agreements.

1. Oral agreements. In many circumstances, landlords are allowed to rent their home or apartment simply on the basis of an oral agreement, which includes the amount of rent to be paid and when the rent is due. In these instances, the period of time between when the tenant's rental payments are due (e.g., week-to-week or month-to-month) determines the length of notice that landlords are required to give tenants before raising the rent or asking them to leave. An oral agreement to lease a home or apartment is not enforceable if made for more than one year.

2. Written agreements. These are the most common type of rental agreement. Normally a standard form is used and can be purchased by the landlord at a stationary store or from a real estate association. These agreements usually contain many restrictions on the use of the property, and require that rent be paid in advance on a month-to-month basis.

FIGURE 11   **Typical California Rental Agreement.**

RENTAL AGREEMENT
(Month to Month)

THIS AGREEMENT entered into this _____ day of _____, 198____,

by and between _____, "Owner" (Landlord)

and _____, "Resident" (Tenant),

IN CONSIDERATION OF THEIR MUTUAL PROMISES AGREE AS FOLLOWS:
1. Owner rents to the Resident and the Resident rents from the Owner for residential use only, the premises known as:

_____, CA.

2. Rent is due in advance on the _____ day of each every month, at $_____ per month, beginning on the

_____ day of _____, 198___

3. Except as prohibited by law, this agreement may be terminated by either party after service upon the other a written 30-day notice of termination of tenancy. Any holding over thereafter shall result in Resident being liable to Owner for "rental damages" at the fair rental value of $_____ per day.

4. Premises shall be occupied only by the following named persons:

_____   _____

_____   _____

5. Without Owner's prior written permission, no bird or animal, no water beds or liquid filled furniture, or

_____ shall be kept or allowed in or about said premises.

6. Resident shall not violate any Governmental law in the use of the premises, commit waste or nuisance, annoy, molest or interfere with any other Resident or neighbor.

7. Except as provided by law, no repairs, decorating or alterations shall be done by Resident, without Owner's prior written consent. Resident shall notify Owner in writing of any repairs or alterations contemplated. Decorations include, but are not limited to, painting, wallpapering, hanging of murals or posters. Resident shall hold Owner harmless as to any mechanics lien recordation or proceeding caused by Resident.

8. Resident has inspected the premises, furnishings and equipment, and has found them to be satisfactory. All plumbing, heating and electrical systems are operative and deemed satisfactory.

9. Except as prohibited by law, Resident shall keep the premises and furniture, furnishings and appliances, if any, and fixtures which are rented for Residents exclusive use in good order and condition. Resident shall pay Owner for costs to repair, replace or rebuild any portion of the premises damaged by the Resident, Resident's guests or invitees. Resident's personal property is not insured by Owner.

10. Resident shall pay for all utilities, services and charges, if any, made payable by or predicated upon occupancy or Resident, except:

_____

11. The undersigned Resident(s), whether or not in actual possession of the premises, are jointly and severally liable for all obligations under this rental agreement, and shall indemnify owner for liability arising prior to the termination of the rental agreement for personal injuries or property damage caused or permitted by Resident(s), their guests and invitees. This does not waive "Owner's" duty of care to prevent personal injury or property damage where that duty is imposed by law.

12. Resident shall deposit with Owner, as a security deposit, the sum of $ _____ ,

payable _____ . Owner may claim (withhold) of the security deposit only such amounts as are reasonably necessary to remedy tenant defaults as follows:
    (a) in the payment of rent, or
    (b) to repair damages to the premises caused by Resident, exclusive of ordinary wear and tear, or
    (c) to clean such premises, if necessary, upon termination of the tenancy.
  No later than two weeks (14 days) after the Resident has vacated the premises, the Owner shall furnish the Resident with an itemized written statement of the basis for, and the amount of, any security received and the disposition of such security and shall return any remaining portion of such security to the Residents.

13. If any legal action or proceeding be brought by either party to enforce any part of this Agreement, the prevailing party shall recover, in addition to all other relief, reasonable attorney's fees and costs.

14. Notice upon Owner may be served upon: _____

at: _____ , CA.
Said person is authorized to accept legal service on behalf of Owner.

15. No portion of said premises shall be sublet nor this Agreement assigned. Any attempted subletting or assignment by the Resident, at the election of Owner, shall be an irremedial breach of this Agreement.

IF APPLICABLE:

A. House Rules: By initialing as provided, Resident acknowledges receipt of a copy of house rules, and has read them, a copy of which is attached hereto, marked as page _____, and are incorporated herein by reference as though fully set forth at length. Said
    Initial_____ house rules shall be deemed covenants of this agreement.

B. Inventory: By initialing as hereinafter provided, Resident acknowledges the subject premises are furnished in accordance with the attached inventory and a copy thereof is attached hereto, marked page _____, and is incorporated herein as
    Initial_____ though fully set forth at length.

C. Addendum: By initialing as provided, Resident acknowledges that additional terms and provisions have been agreed upon which are designated as an Addendum, a copy of which is attached hereto, marked page _____, and is incorporated herein as
    Initial_____ though fully set forth at length.

The undersigned Resident acknowledges having read and understood the foregoing, and receipt of a duplicate original.

_____   _____
        OWNER   RESIDENT

_____   _____
  BY AUTHORIZED AGENT   RESIDENT

                             _____
                                  RESIDENT

California Apartment Association

3. A lease. A lease is different from other forms of agreement because it sets out the terms of the tenancy for a specific period of time, and assure that tenants can stay at the residence without an increase in rent for as long as they abide by the terms of the lease. Leases for a period of more than one year must be in writing. In general, leases are more often used in commercial property or homes then in apartments.

Landlord-Tenant Negotiation

In California, the law requires that when a landlord and a Spanish-speaking tenant have arrived at the terms of a rental agreement that calls for a tenancy of more than one month, the landlord, upon request of the prospective tenant, must provide the tenant with a copy of the agreement or lease in Spanish before he or she signs it.

RIGHTS AND DUTIES OF LANDLORDS AND TENANTS

Paying the Rent

In California, tenants who fail to pay their rent on time may be asked to pay a reasonable late charge and/or be served with "three-day notice to pay or quit" (pay or get out!). If tenants are served with this notice and do not comply, the landlord may sue in court and request an eviction order. (Note that if the due date for the rent falls on a Saturday, Sunday, or legal holiday, California law allows a tenant to pay the rent on the next business day.)

Raising the Rent

When a tenant has a lease, the rent cannot be raised unless the terms of the lease specifically allow for an increase. The rent can generally be increased under a written or oral rental agreement as long as adequate written notice is given to the tenant. For example, when rent is paid monthly, a written rent increase notice must be given at least thirty days prior to the increase. Under California law, notice of rent increases must be served on tenants in one of the following methods:

1. By personal service (having someone actually hand the notice to the tenant);

2. If the tenant is not available, by leaving the notice with a "person of suitable age and discretion" at home or work and mailing a copy to the tenant; or

3. When neither of the first two methods is available, the landlord may serve notice by posting the notice in a conspicuous place on the property, leaving a copy with someone residing in the rented premises, (if some can be found) and mailing a copy to the tenant.

California law allows landlords who rent their premises under an oral or written agreement to raise the rent as much as they desire, as long as the rent increase is not in retaliation against tenants who are exercising their legal rights (see "Retalitory Evictions"). Also, and in part because of the relatively high rent previously mentioned, many counties in California have recently enacted rent control ordinances. These ordinances vary to some degree, but most limit the percentage that a person's rent can be increased during a given year to about 4–10 percent. These increases may be used by landlords to offset the costs of maintaining the property and at the same time help to protect tenants from skyrocketing housing costs.

Note that most rent control ordinances only protect tenants who have been living in a particular residence for over a year. The ordinances do not protect new tenants. As a result, many rent control laws have been criticized because they allow landlords who want to raise rents over the legal limits, to simply evict an old tenant and then charge a new tenant a much higher rent. If your county has passed a rent control ordinance and if a dispute arises over the amount of a specific increase, contact your county's local rent board.

Upkeep and Repairs

In 1974, the California Supreme Court ruled that every housing rental agreement in California has an "implied warranty of habitability." This implied warranty requires that landlords maintain their rental units in a condition fit for human occupancy, as defined by local and state housing codes. A landlord may not relinquish this obligation, and landlords who allow their rental units to fall below required standards may be subject to an inspection by the local health, fire, or building department. Landlords found to be in violation of housing codes may be fined up to $500 for each violation and/or imprisoned for up to six months. In addition, a tenant may be able to enforce the codes by suing the landlord, using rent money to make repairs, or withholding the rent entirely.

Use of the Property and Security Deposits

As noted in the national text, a security deposit may be used by landlords to cover unpaid rent or the cost of cleaning or repairing damage to the rental property that was caused by something other than ordinary wear and tear. In California, a landlord may require a security deposit equal to, but no more than two months rent, if the house or apartment is unfurnished. When the rental unit is furnished, the security deposit can be no more than three months rent. California does not require interest to be paid to tenants on funds left as security deposits, but requires only that the deposits be returned within two weeks after a tenant has vacated the landlord's property. When less than the original security deposit is being returned, receipts indicating the costs of legitimate deductions or repairs must be given to the former tenant. If a landlord withholds these funds in bad faith for a period longer than two weeks, a tenant may be entitled to $200 in punitive damages against the landlord. Note that under California law, security deposits and/or cleaning fees are refundable even when the rental agreement or lease states otherwise.

Responsibility for Injuries in the Building

In California, *exculpatory clauses*, or *waiver of tort liability* clauses, are invalid, and thus do not affect the general responsibility of a landlord for injuries sustained by tenants and/or their guests. In short, landlords have a duty to exercise ordinary care in the management of their premises in order to avoid exposing anyone to an unreasonable risk of harm. Failure to fulfill this duty may amount to negligence and, in turn, liability on the part of the landlord. Some examples of cases in California in which landlords have been held liable are as follows:

- a fall that resulted from a loose handrail on a stairway;

- a fire that resulted from a defective heater or wiring; and

- a rape that resulted from lax security.

Landlord Access and Inspection

In California, clauses in rental agreements that give a landlord the right to inspect are limited to reasonable times (9 A.M. to 5 P.M.) and reasonable notice (normally 24 hours). A landlord has the legal right to enter a rental unit without a tenant's consent in the following situations:

- an emergency;

- to make necessary or agreed upon repairs, alterations or improvements, to supply necessary services, or to show the place to prospective or actual purchasers, mortgagors, tenants, workers, or contractors;

- after the tenant has moved out; or

- pursuant to a court order.

Sublease of a House or Apartment

In California, unless there is a clause to the contrary, tenants have the right to sublet their rental house or apartment. Most rental agreements, however, include clauses that require a tenant to get the landlords, concent before subletting. When this is the case, the landlord's consent may not be withheld unreasonably.

Tenants' Right to
Defend Themselves in Court

A confession of judgment clause is invalid and thus unenforceable in California.

LANDLORD-TENANT PROBLEMS

What Tenants Can Do
When Things Go Wrong

Complaints to Government Agencies   In addition to the general authority that local governmental agencies have, California law also provides that if a landlord refuses to repair substandard housing for a period of six months, the state may, upon notification by county officials, deny the owner the benefits of all state income tax deductions for such property.

Tenant Organizing   There are a number of local tenant organizations in California that give advice to tenants on their rights and organizing. Here are but a few.

Chain — Los Angeles
2936 West 8th Street
Los Angeles, California 90005
(213) 381-5139

Housing Action
Committee
110 Pine Place #1
Santa Cruz, California 95060
(408) 426-1091

Housing Action Project
Arcata
Barlow House, #109
Humbolt State University
Arcata, California 95521
(707) 826-3825

Housing Action Project
P.O. Box 2166
Santa Barbara, California 93120
(805) 962-3660

Oakland Tenants' Union
2647 E. 14th Street
Oakland, California 94601
(415) 653-4613

Westside Fair Housing
Council
10835 Santa Monica
  Boulevard #203
Los Angeles, California 90025

San Francisco Tenants' Union
558 Capp Street
San Francisco, California 94110
(415) 282-6622

Rent Withholding In California a tenant or a group of tenants, unless they have agreed to maintain the premises in exchange for rent, have the right to withhold rent if a landlord does not fulfill his or her obligations under the implied warranty of habitability and refuses to make necessary repairs. The landlord, however, must be given notice of the items in need of repair and given a reasonable time in which to repair them. Also, the defects must not have been caused by the tenants themselves or their guests.

After withholding rent, if the landord then makes the repairs, tenants must resume regular rent payments. In some circumstances, a court may decide that the tenant does not have to pay the full amount of rent withheld, but only the reasonable value for the premises over the period of disrepair. California law also gives tenants the right to make repairs themselves or to hire someone to do repairs and then deduct the cost from the next month's rent. The repair and deduct statute can only be used under certain circumstances. For example, it cannot be used to repair items that were broken as a result of the negligence of the tenants or their guests. Furthermore, the statute cannot be used more than twice in a twelve-month period, and finally, the cost to the landlord cannot be more than one month's rent per repair in each instance.

Moving Out California recognizes the doctrine of **constructive eviction**. Under the law, if landlords fail to fulfill their duty, and do not provide a dwelling fit for human habitation, or "substantially" interfere with a tenant's ability to enjoy the premises, then the tenants may move out without notifying the landlord and without incurring liability under the rental agreement. Note, however, that if tenants cannot prove that the dwelling was "not fit for human habitation," they may still have to pay rent. It is wise to consult an attorney before you resort to this action.

What Landlords Can Do When Things Go Wrong

Ending the Lease In California, tenants who have had a lease and elect to remain in the house or apartment after expiration of the lease are considered **holdover tenants.** Such tenants normally assume a month-to-month tenancy, or a tenancy at will, unless specified in eight-point type to the contrary on the face of the lease.

It is always wise and often required for tenants to give a written notice thirty days in advance of their intention to leave a rental premises. Unless so specified in the lease, California does not require notice of tenant's intent to leave at the end of the lease.

Tenants who leave before the end of their lease may be excused from their obligations under the lease if the move was necessitated by an emergency such as change of employment or illness. Remember that tenants are usually allowed to sublet the premises, or they may try to get the landlord to release them from the provisions of the lease. Written notice of a tenant's intention to move should be given as soon as possible. If tenants must leave the premise vacant, California law requires that the landlord try to find a new tenant as soon as possible in order to reduce the extent of the former tenant's liability.

Eviction   Unless tenants have a lease, they may be asked to leave their rental premises for no reason upon proper service of a thirty-day notice from the landlord. A landlord may also go to court immediately to evict tenants who have still not paid their rent after a "three-day notice to quit" has expired. If, however, the tenant refuses to leave, landlords may not take it upon themselves to lock tenants out or to cut off tenants' utilities. In such circumstances, California courts have awarded punitive damages against landlords, and by statute, tenants may recover actual damages plus $100 a day plus attorney's fees and court costs when their utilities have been are maliciously cut off.

Landord-Tenant Court Process   In California an unlawful detainer proceeding is the only manner in which landlords may seek to evict tenants who refuse to leave after they have received proper notice of such a request. The unlawful detainer complaint and summons must be served in accordance with the law, and as the national text suggests, it is very important for tenants to answer and to appear in court. Landlords can bring these actions in either municipal or small claims court. It is normally advisable to have an attorney.

Retaliatory Eviction   In California the Civil Code gives tenants a broad range of protection against retaliatory evictions, and prohibits conduct on the part of the landlord that is motivated by feelings of retaliation against a tenant. In short, when a tenant has complained to a governmental agency about the habitability of a dwelling, or when a tenant has exercised his or her rights under the repair and deduct statute, the law provides that a landlord may not, for a period of sixty days thereafter, attempt to terminate the tenancy, increase the rent, or reduce any services previously furnished.

BUYING A HOME

Things to Consider Before Buying

In recent years, condominiums and mobile homes have become very popular in California. One problem which has been associated with condominiums is that many landlords have converted housing, which was previously available as rental units, to condominiums, and as a result those tenants who could not afford to purchase the condominiums were forced to move and try to find new and affordable housing. Because of the impact of condominium conversions on low-, moderate-, and fixed-income individuals, California has passed legislation on this matter.

Under California law, conversion plans must now be approved at a public hearing before a local planning commission. (Commission decisions may be appealed to the city council or the county board of supervisors.) Tenants are entitled to a 180-day notice of the conversion plans and receive a 90-day option to purchase the unit in which they are living after the owner has obtained final approval for the conversion.

Mobile homes, although purchased by the resident, are usually moved and placed in a mobile home park where the land is owned by someone else. For these reasons, both consumer protection laws and landlord-tenant laws apply to mobile home owners. For example, when you buy a new mobile home, the dealer must give the purchaser a written warranty. The warranty must state that the dealer, or manufacturer, or both will repair "substantial defects" in the mobile home's materials or workmanship within one year of the date the mobile home is delivered to the purchaser. If appliances are installed in the mobile home by the dealer or manufacturer, they also are warranted. Mobile homes sold in California must meet minimum fire and safety standards and be approved by the California Department of Housing and Community Development.

The owners of mobile home parks must abide by special rules that protect tenants on their property. Briefly, these laws provide for written rental agreements, limits on fees that may be levied, extended notice and eviction requirements, and allowances for the tenants' sale of their mobile homes.

Steps to Take in Buying

Obtaining a Loan   In part because of the relatively high cost of buying a home in California, many banks and lending institutions are beginning to offer longer term mortgages in addition to the flexibile-payment and variable-rate mortgages noted in the national text. In some cases these mortgages allow for forty-year payment plans, rather than the twenty- and thirty-year plans traditionally offered. This helps reduce the average monthly mortgage payment, and thus makes housing more affordable.

Problems Associated with Home Buying

Under California law, purchasers of new homes are given the benefits of an implied warranty. These warranties are read into purchase contracts and cover the quality and habitability of the house. Purchasers are protected against major structural defects and may sue sellers or builders of homes if defects results in damage or injury to the purchasers or their guests.

Housing for Low-and Moderate-Income Persons

In California, subsidized housing is available to low-income and elderly persons through government-owned public housing projects or through rent-subsidized, privately owned housing. Eligibility for such programs is limited to individuals who are handicapped, disabled, displaced, or at least sixty-two years of age, and to families of two or more related persons. Income requirements vary, depending on the family size and county of residence.

The types of programs administered in California by the county local housing authorities include the following:

■ **Conventional public housing**, is owned and operated by the local housing authority;

■ **Section 23 leased housing**, are privately owned dwellings leased by the local housing authority and then sublet at reduced cost to low-income households; and

■ **Section 8 housing**, provides rent subsidies paid directly to landlords of privately owned rental units on behalf of the low-income tenants.

The rent paid by tenants in all three programs is based on family income, number and age of members, and on other characteristics that might effect the family's ability to pay rent. Generally, however, amounts charged to tenants for rent and utilities can be no more than twenty-five percent of the monthly family income.

six
INDIVIDUAL
RIGHTS
AND
LIBERTIES

As noted in the national text, the United States Constitution, primarily through the Bill of Rights, guarantees certain basic rights and liberties to all citizens of our country. These rights and liberties are not, however, absolute. The U.S. Supreme Court determines the extent of our individual rights and sets minimal guidelines that all states must follow in order to protect the rights of persons living in this country.

California has its own state constitution that also provides persons living in our state with basic rights and liberties. In many instances, the language and provisions found in the California constitution are similar to the specific provisions or amendments of the U.S. Constitution. Nevertheless, since both documents apply to the state and are of independent force, the California Supreme Court must often consider the provisions of both constitutions before ruling on matters involving our individual rights and liberties.

One should keep in mind three points when considering California law. First, because the federal and state constitutions are so similar, the federal courts have played the major role in the development of individual rights law in our state. Second, since the

469

primary role of the California Supreme Court is to interpret California law, the court has on occasion held, that state law requires greater constitutional protection than federal law. The California Supreme Court may thus expand on the minimal protections afforded under the U.S. Constitution. Third, the California constitution is much easier to amend and is much longer than the Federal Constitution. As a result, it contains many additional provisions, which account for some of the distinctions that exist between California and federal law.

FREEDOM OF SPEECH

Every person may freely speak, write and publish his or her sentiments on all subjects, being responsible for the abuse of this right. A law may not restrain or abridge liberty of speech or press.

—Article I § 2 (a) of the California Constitution

The California freedom of speech provision is similar to the First Amendment. The California Supreme Court, however, has on occasion read the California provision more broadly than the U.S. Supreme Court has interpreted the First Amendment. This has afforded individuals greater protection to express their beliefs in this state. For example, in a recent case, the California Supreme Court held that under the California constitution students could solicit signatures opposing the White House position on a United Nations resolution, even though the students were on a privately owned shopping center and their petition was not related to the operation of that shopping center. This decision differs from U.S. Supreme Court decisions that have held that such conduct could be restricted.

Obscenity

In California, the definition of "obscene" or "harmful" matter is essentially the same as that adopted by the U.S. Supreme Court and discussed in the national text. There are, however, some important distinctions. For example, under the U.S. Supreme Court definition of obscenity, one must find that "the work does not, as a whole, have serious literary, artistic, political, or scientific value." Under California's Law, it is more difficult to find a work obscene, because the material must be "utterly without redeeming social importance."

FREEDOM OF THE PRESS

Prohibiting Publication

As noted in the national text, the problem with the evolution of "gag orders" has been based on the conflict that exists between the First Amendment right to free speech and a free press, and the Sixth Amendment right to a speedy and public trial by an impartial jury. Today, by agreement of the California Judicial Council, gag orders are rarely issued because they constitute a prior restraint on the press, and the courts require that very restrictive standards be met in order to justify this type of restraint.

Denying Access to Information

In California most juvenile court proceedings are closed to the press or general public. Judges at their discretion may allow the press into juvenile court, as long as the judge believes that the press has a direct and legitimate interest in the particular case, and the judge is satisfied that the press will not identify the juvenile either by name or photograph.

Regarding trials involving adults, it has been held that a newsreporter's rights are no greater than those of the general public. In California members of the press may thus be excluded from a courtroom if and when their First Amendment rights are outweighed by the defendant's right to a fair trial. A defendant also has the right to specifically request that a courtroom be closed to the press and to the general public during pretrial proceedings.

Requiring the Press to Disclose Information:

Article I § 2 (b) of the California constitution provides the press with one of the broadest shield laws in the nation. The provision, as amended in 1980, prohibits persons employed by or connected with specified news media from being adjudged in contempt for refusing the disclose the source of any information procured while so connected or employed.

FREEDOM OF ASSOCIATION AND FREEDOM OF ASSEMBLY

In California the freedom of association is not expressly written into the state constitution, just as this right is not expressly found in the federal Constitution. Instead, the right is gleaned from the in-alienable rights section of the California constitution, (Article I §1) and from the freedom of assembly section, (Article I § 3). As noted in the national text, the freedom of association protects only peaceful and lawful association activities.

The freedom of assembly section on the other hand has been expressly written into the California constitution and reads as follows:

The people have the right to instruct their representatives, petition government for redress of grievances, and assemble freely to consult for the common good.

EXPRESSION IN SPECIAL PLACES

In California, the right of students to free speech in schools is protected by statute and by the constitution. In fact, several provisions of the California Education Code specifically provide for

■ wearing of buttons, badges, and other insigna;

■ refusal to salute the flag;

■ distribution of literature;

■ preparation and distribution of student newspapers and publications; and

■ the right of students to peacefully publicize their grievances on school grounds.

Nevertheless, school authorities may establish reasonable rules regulating the time, place, and manner of students' expression in order to safeguard the orderly operation of the school.

FREEDOM OF RELIGION

Free exercise and enjoyment of religion without discrimination or preference are guaranteed . . . The legislature shall make no law respecting an establishment of religion. . .

—Article I § 4 of the California Constitution

Establishment Clause

In California, although our tax laws provide property tax exemptions for religious institutions, and although counties provide churches with fire and police protection, Article XVI § 5 of the California constitution specifically prohibits the use of public funds to aid religious purposes or institutions. Prayers or Bible reading are also prohibited in public schools, even if done without comment and even if students have the options of being excused from the exercise. Bibles may be kept in school libraries, however, and used as instructional materials for historical or poetic reference, as long as they are not used in the teaching, either directly or indirectly, of sectarian or denominational doctrines. Finally, the Education Code provides that pupils, with the written consent of parents or guardians, may be excused from school to participate in religious exercises or to receive moral and religious instruction at their respective places of worship.

Free Exercise Clause

This provision of the state constitution has been interpreted in much the same manner as the free exercise clauses of the United States Constitution. Not all infringements of religious beliefs are constitutionally impermissible. For example, the state may require that immunizations or blood transfusions be given to children, even when these actions would be in opposition to some religious belief. The state can also prohibit polygamy (the practice of having more than one spouse) and may require observance of child labor laws. Finally, although the California Penal Code once prohibited the operation of certain businesses on Sunday, the legislature has since repealed those laws.

THE RIGHT TO PRIVACY

Unlike the U.S. Constitution, the right to privacy has been expressly written into the California constitution.

All people are by nature free and independent and are inalienable rights. Among these are enjoying and defending life and liberty, acquiring, possessing, and protecting property, and pursuing and obtaining safety, happiness and privacy.

—Article I § 1 of the California constitution

Privacy in the Home

An interesting case recently decided by the California Supreme Court shed some light on the extent of one's reasonable expectation of privacy in the home. The case involved the search by a police officer of a locked tool box belonging to a seventeen-year-old boy which he kept in the bedroom of his home. In short, although the minor himself refused to consent to the search, his father gave the police officer permission to proceed. The search revealed nine bags of marijuana, and the boy was arrested. The supreme court, however, held that minors are entitled to protection against unreasonable searches and seizures. This right was inferred from a recognition of the minor's right to privacy in his home, as well as from the protection against unreasonable searches and seizures afforded all persons under Article I § 13 of the California constitution.

Also worthy of mention is the fact that California has an Invasion of Privacy Act. This statute prohibits the use of wiretapping devices and techniques for the purpose of eavesdropping on private communications. In a recent California case, however, a state court held that the recording of telephone conversations with the consent of one participant did not violate the other person's right to privacy under the state constitution or the state's privacy act.

Privacy at School

In California, unless teachers and school administrators are acting under the direction of a peace officer, they need not have probable cause to search either a student or a student's locker and seize weapons, drugs, or any other prohibited materials. This does not mean that these searches may be conducted at random. The search must be reasonable and related to the school official's duty.

To better understand this rule, consider one case in which school officials obtained information from an unreliable source that a student has been selling dangerous drugs on campus that morning. The student was interviewed by the administrators, who noticed his bulging pockets. After the student refused to answer questions about the contents of his pockets, he was forcibly searched. Dangerous drugs and marijuana were found in his possession.

This search was held to be proper and lawful. The court noted that school authorities have a special duty to protect the students under their care from drug peddlers, and the search was related to those duties. The court also stated that administrators have the right to use moderate force in carrying out these duties.

Again, the same standards apply in the search of students' lockers. Also, confessions made by students to school officials concerning illegal activities may be reported to the police, and school officials are not required to give the student "Miranda"-like warnings.

Finally, as to matters contained in a student's record. Requirements in California are similar to those delineated in the national text. Under California law, parents may seek to correct or remove information from their child's file if that information is

■ inaccurate;

■ unsubstantiated personal conclusions;

■ conclusions or inferences outside the observer's area of competence; or

■ not based on the personal observation of a named person indicating the time and place of the observation.

School districts are also required to notify parents in writing of their rights under California law upon the date of their child's initial enrollment. Insofar as practical, this notice should be in the native language of the student.

Privacy on the Job

The California Fair Employment and Housing Act prohibits any nonjob-related inquiry, made either verbally or in the application process, that directly or indirectly limits a person's employment opportunities because of race, color, religion, national origin, ancestry, medical condition (if cancer-related), physical handicap, marital status, sex, or age (if over forty). In addition, employers in California cannot require any employees or applicants to submit to a lie detector test, nor can an employer request employees or applicants to voluntarily submit to such a test without notifying such persons of their legal rights. Public employers are prohibited from gathering information on the prior arrest records of applicants, unless such arrests led to a conviction.

Information Gathering and Privacy

As noted in the national text, the disclosure requirements of the Federal Privacy Act of 1974 apply only to federal agencies and the information they have gathered on persons in this country. This legislation, however, motivated California to pass the Information Practices Act. Modeled on the federal law, the purpose of the state legislation is to restrict the use of information gathered by state agencies, to make the agencies accountable for their information gathering practices, and to increase individuals' awareness of the state informational practices.

State law requires that the Office of Information Practices assist individuals in identifying records that may contain information about them and help individuals in securing access to such records. For further information contact:

California State Office of Information Practice
801 Capital Mall
Sacramento, California 95814
(800) 952-5562

The California Right to Financial Privacy Act also requires financial institutions to maintain records of all examinations and disclosures that have been made regarding a particular customer's file and requires that these records be made available to customers upon request.

DUE PROCESS

A person may not be deprived of life, liberty, or property without due process of law. . .

—Article I § 7 of the California Constitution

Regarding due process rights in schools, California law provides specific grounds for the suspension or expulsion of students. These grounds include damaging or stealing school or private property; causing or threatening to cause physical injury to another; possessing, selling, or furnishing dangerous weapons, drugs, alcohol, or other controlled substances; using or possessing tobacco; committing an obscene act; partaking in habitual profanity; and disrupting school activities. The law also provides that suspension, like expulsion, be used only when other means of discipline have failed to bring about proper conduct. Some of the due process safeguards provided to parents and students under state law require that a notice of the suspension be given to the parent or guardian within one school day of the beginning of the suspension. This notice must contain a statement of the facts leading to the suspension, the date and time when the student is allowed to return to school, a statement of the right to a conference, a statement of the right to have access to the pupil's records, and a request that the parent or guardian attend the conference. The conference must be scheduled within twenty-four hours of the suspension, and the appropriate school official must also attempt to contact the parents or guardians by telephone in order to explain the information contained in the written notice.

Finally, reasonable corporal punishment may be administered by teachers, principals, and other certified personnel to pupils provided that two conditions are met: (1) the school district in which the child attends has adopted rules and regulations authorizing such punishment, and (2) the pupil's parent or guardian has submitted prior written approval for the administration of such punishment. Written approval is only valid for the school year in which it is submitted and may be withdrawn by the parent or guardian at any time.

If the punishment is found to be unjustified or excessive, the person inflicting the corporal punishment may be found guilty of a crime, and may be sued civilly for injuries or damages incurred by student by his or her parents or guardians.

DISCRIMINATION

A person may not be . . . denied the equal protection of the law.

—Article 1 § 7 (a) of the California Constitution

This section of the California constitution provides the people of this state with the broadest protection against unlawful discrimination. Article I § 8 more specifically prohibits unlawful discrimination in employment. These constitutional guarantees have been judicially interpreted to mean that no person or class of persons shall be denied the same protection of the law enjoyed by other persons similarly situated.

What Is Discrimination?

The principal purpose of both the federal and the state constitutions has always been to restrict or limit the powers of congress or the state legislative branch of government. The constitutions therefore only guard against discrimination that has been either directly or indirectly approved by the state. Strictly private conduct on the part of individuals or institutions that is discriminatory in nature may or may not be illegal, depending on whether the federal government or the state of California have passed any specific laws prohibiting such conduct. California has passed such legislation, and in many cases California has sought to provide persons in this state with similar or greater protections than those offered under the federal law.

Discrimination Because of
Race, National Origin, and Alienage

California laws that prohibit discrimination on the basis of one's race, national origin, or alienage in the areas of bussing, affirmative action, education, and employment basically follow the same guidelines noted in the national text. Under Article I § 20 of the California Constitution, however, aliens (noncitizens) are specifically given the same rights to own property as citizens. Also under a new statute in California, private clubs that are licensed or certified to provide services (usually a state liquor license) may not discriminate against persons because of race, color, sex, religion, ancestry, physical handicap, marital status, or national origin with regard to the delivery of such services.

Discrimination Because of Sex

California does not have a general clause in its consitution similar to the proposed Equal Rights Amendment. However, in 1971 the California Supreme Court did use Article I § 8 of the Constitution, which prohibits discrimination in employment on the basis of sex, to help reach a decision that held that discrimination based on sex is "suspect," and that laws providing for such discrimination will require examination or justification under the strict scrutiny test or standard. This case was extremely important, because the U.S. Supreme Court has never required the strict scrutiny test under the federal Constitution. Indeed, when the courts apply this test, they almost always find that the discriminatory law or practice is unconstitutional.

Finally, California has a number of specific laws that grant many of the same rights provided under Federal statutes, as well as some additional rights in the areas of education, athletic programs, and employment. An example of one such law is found in the California Government Code. It provides that employers may not discriminate against women because of pregnancy. Prohibited acts include the refusal to allow reasonable pregnancy leave, customary benefits, or, when reasonable, the transfer to a less strenuous or less hazardous position.

Discrimination Because of Age

In California, unlike federal law which protects those between the ages of forty and seventy, it is unlawful to suspend, discharge, or refuse to hire or promote any individual over the age of forty because of his or her age, unless the individual fails to meet the bona fide job requirements. Also, under a recent change in the law, most employers can no longer require compulsory retirement, as long as employees can show that they are still capable of performing their duties.

Many laws, on the other hand, have been upheld by our courts, even though they discriminate against the young. Remember, in California you must be eighteen years old to vote, to run for office, to make a will, to enter into most binding contracts, or to marry without consent of a parent or guardian. You must be twenty-one years old to purchase alcoholic beverages.

Discrimination Because of Handicap

California, like many other states, has recently tried to recognize the special difficulties of handicapped people and has taken some steps to help the disabled reach their full potential as members of society. It is now unlawful for employers to refuse to hire persons because of a disability, or to discharge or otherwise discriminate against them in wages or conditions of employment. In short, unless it can be demonstrated that an individual's disability would prevent that person from performing a particular job, persons with a handicap may not be denied equal opportunity to obtain or advance in a position solely because they are disabled. Also, as mentioned in Chapter Five, the disabled are also protected against discrimination in the purchasing or renting of housing.

California law specifically states that the blind or otherwise physically disabled person shall not be denied admittance to or equal use of any public facility solely because of their handicap. Newly constructed or rehabilitated public buildings are required to provide access for the physically handicapped. In addition, the state assists school districts in providing special educational programs and related services essential in helping handicapped children realize their full potential.

Discrimination Because of Income

In order to better understand this type of discrimination, you should realize that one's income often determines one's ability to purchase certain goods and services in life. Legal problems arise, however, when one's income begins to affect one's ability to exercise certain basic rights or to receive services that should be provided to all persons regardless of income. In determining whether a constitutional violation has occurred, the courts examine the relative importance of the right or service being denied someone because of their income level or relative wealth.

In California, this issue has been addressed on several occasions by the supreme court. One case dealt with a law limiting state funding for abortion. The Court held that the law was invalid under the privacy and equal protection guarantees of the California constitution. The court further stated that the purpose of the Medi-Cal program was to alleviate hardship and suffering incurred by those who cannot afford needed medical care, and that the restrictions limiting funding for abortions subjected low-income women to significant health hazards and interfered with their constitutional right to procreative choice.

California also does not allow discrimination based on income in emergency medical care. Accordingly, a hospital with an emergency room cannot refuse to provide available medical treatment if somone is in danger of loss of life or has a serious injury or illness, simply because the person does not have money, insurance, or credit.

Finally, in *Serrano v. Priest*, a well-known California case dealing with the area of education, the supreme court held that the state's public school financing system, which relied heavily on local property taxes and thus caused substantial funding differences among individual school districts in amounts of revenue available per pupil, did indeed unlawfully discriminate against the poor and violated their fundamental right to education.

State and Local Laws
Against Discrimination

In California, many local counties and cities have passed additional ordinances with the intent to either protect specific groups or to guard against specific types of actions aimed at discrimination. Often, this legislation is directly related to how many and how politcally organized certain groups are within a given locale. For example, San Francisco has a specific ordinance that prohibits discrimination based on sexual orientation. Berkeley has passed many local ordinances that assist the handicapped and students. San Diego has laws that assist the elderly and retired individuals. Consequently, if you believe that your rights may have been violated, it is important to check with your local government, as well as with state and federal officials to see if a particular type of discrimination is against the law.

†